SEX IN THE WESTERN WORLD

SEX IN THE WESTERN WORLD

The Development of Attitudes and Behaviour

by

Jean-Louis Flandrin

Ecole des Hautes Etudes en Sciences Sociales, Paris

Translated from the French by

Sue Collins

Services for Export and Language, University of Salford, Salford

**ho
ap** harwood academic publishers
chur • reading • paris • philadelphia • tokyo • melbourne

Harwood Academic Publishers

Post Office Box 90
Reading, Berkshire RG1 8JL
United Kingdom

3-14-9, Okubo
Shinjuku-ku, Tokyo 169
Japan

58, rue Lhomond
75005 Paris
France

Private Bag 8
Camberwell, Victoria 3124
Australia

5301 Tacony Street, Drawer 330
Philadelphia, Pennsylvania 19137
United States of America

Originally published in French in 1981 as *Le sexe et l'occident: Evolution des attitudes et des comportements* by Editions du Seuil, Paris
© 1981 by Editions du Seuil, Paris
Front cover photograph of *Le Déjeuner sur l'Herbe* by Edouard Manet.
Reproduced with permission of the Courtauld Institute Galleries, London

Library of Congress Cataloging-in-Publication Data

Flandrin, Jean Louis.
    [Sexe et l'Occident. English]
    Sex in the Western World : the development of attitudes and
    behavior / Jean-Louis Flandrin : translated from the French by Su
    Collins.
        p. cm.
    Translation of: Sexe et l'Occident.
    Includes bibliographical references (p.) and index.
    ISBN 3-7186-5201-3
    1. Sexual ethics—Europe—History. 2. Sex customs—Europe--History. 3. e. I. Title.
    HQ31.F65413 1991
    306.7'094—dc20

Contents

Chapter 1
Why Study the History of Sexuality? 1

I. LOVE

Chapter 2
Civilisation and Feelings 13

Chapter 3
Love and Love Affairs in the Sixteenth Century . . 37

Chapter 4
The *Créantailles* Rite in Troyes between the
Fifteenth and Seventeenth Centuries 49

Chapter 5
Love and Marriage in the Eighteenth Century . . . 73

II. SEXUAL MORALITY AND MARITAL RELATIONS

Chapter 6
The Christian Doctrine of Marriage 89

Chapter 7
Contraception, Marriage, and Sexual Relations
in the Christian West 99

Chapter 8
Man and Wife in the Marriage Bed 117

III. THE CHILD AND PROCREATION

Chapter 9
Childhood and Society 129

Chapter 10
Attitudes towards Young Children and Sexual
Behaviour 139

Chapter 11
Ancient and Modern Adages Concerning the
Child within the Family 203

Chapter 12
The Young Woman in Ancient French Proverbs . 231

IV. THE SEX LIVES OF SINGLE PEOPLE

Chapter 13
Late Marriages and Sex Lives 239

Chapter 14
Repression and Change in the Sex Lives of
Young People 267

Chapter 15
Family Life and Illicit Love in England 291

Notes and References 311
Index 353

Chapter 1

Why Study the History of Sexuality?

As twentieth century Europeans, we are conscious of our long history and, like the noblemen of old, we are quite proud of it. Their history was for them proof of their nobility; ours has for a long time made us feel that we were "civilised", as opposed to those people supposedly without a history, and whom we referred to as "primitive" or "savage". How could such pride be justified? The ways of thinking, feeling and acting which formerly marked the nobility were not acquired in one generation; nor were those of the modern Western world. Yet we ourselves have for a long time asked only that history soothe our vanity, like those gentlemen who gloried in the heroic deeds of their ancestors but cast a modest veil over their family's slow passage from the commonest of the common ranks to the nobility. We have not troubled ourselves to determine how we became what we are, how much our present and our future depend on the past, and to what extent those who do not have the same history as we do can be or become similar to us.

Let us carry this comparison a little further. In the seventeenth and eighteenth centuries, those noblemen who complained so often about the adversities of the time never tried to find out whether the dying out of so many illustrious families was not, in part, the result of patterns of behaviour peculiar to the nobility — such as economic or demographic behaviour — which, along with the ideals of nobility, they had inherited from their ancestors. Have we not similarly inherited from the past those difficulties which confront us in our daily lives?

1

It is widely believed today among Western peoples that we have specific difficulties relating to sex, and that they are attributable to our fundamentally Christian moral traditions. But will we overcome our difficulties by ruthlessly renouncing our forefathers' morality and by attempting to adopt that of the Nambikwara or other peoples reputed to be close to nature? In reality, we are not free to deny our heritage: it is an integral part of us. The more we try to ignore it, the more we are its prisoners.

Furthermore, it surprises me that in a century when psychoanalysis excites so much enthusiasm, there is so little consciousness of the power which the past exercises. There is something illogical in scrutinising so attentively the past experiences of individuals undergoing psychoanalysis, and yet paying so little attention to their collective past, or at least to that of it which survives in our culture.

No man behaves naturally, in the sense that all human behaviour has been moulded by a culture. All cultures have evolved progressively and have been profoundly marked by past organisations and traumas. From birth, we have been surreptitiously pervaded by the past, through literature, morality, law, language, sciences even, technology and the arts, all that which makes up our culture. May I be forgiven for going into such detail about that which is self-evident. But when I hear sociologists, psychologists, psychoanalysts, sexologists, journalists...and many historians speaking of sexuality, I get the impression that they forget these obvious facts. By not paying the past the attention it deserves, they prevent us from liberating ourselves from it.

I do not accept just any analysis of the past. Too often, it seems to me, history functions like a faulty memory, which only retains that which hurts us — ancient hatreds, distrust of previous generations, misplaced loyalties — and increases the tendency to see the present as a simple repetition of the past. On the other hand, when the past permeates through ways other than history — through language, literature, morality, law, etc. — as is the case with sexuality, among other things, then history could have a therapeutic function. By acknowledging what we have repressed of past events, by showing the relationships which existed between a given ancient attitude towards sexuality and other aspects of Western culture, whether or not still in existence today, history should allow us to reassess our value system, and thus to overcome present difficulties.

It is not the responsibility of the historian alone to take charge of these reassessments. Even less should he be expected to surround his contemporaries with insurmountable dilemmas, allegedly confirmed by history. Thus, he will not conclude from the obvious relationship in Western societies between the increase in marrying for love and the upsurge of divorce, that we must either return to the "marriage of convenience", or ignore what is unacceptable in so many contemporary divorces. It is enough that he knows how to find suitable material from the past to sustain reflection on present problems, and how to go deeper into the field to loosen the ties which are strangling us. The various chapters of this book will, I hope, be able to contribute by modifying our visions of love, of marriage and marital relations, of the parent-child relationship and of the sex lives of single people in a culture forgetful of history.

Love has for centuries been the favourite subject of poets and novelists, hence probably of their public. There is nothing new, in this respect, between for example the sixteenth and the twentieth century. But is it really the same sentiment which has been called "love" throughout this period of five hundred years? Have the reasons for loving and the objects of love remained the same? Has amorous behaviour changed? In order to answer these questions fully, more in-depth studies than those found in the first section of this book would be necessary. They do, however, bring to light unmistakable differences in how love is represented, in society's attitudes towards it, and even more obvious changes in its role in the choice of partner and in sexual relations between partners.

On the whole, the status of love in the sixteenth century was more complex than nowadays. There were those who extolled the virtues of platonic love and those who favoured the most carnal love. Ecclesiastic or secular moralists, on the other hand, tended to condemn amorous passion in all its forms, without troubling themselves to distinguish — as has often been done in the twentieth century — "real love" from simple desire.

As far as secular culture — as shown by proverbs and laws — was concerned, it was particularly a question of limiting love's role in the formation of marriages. The purpose of marriage was to establish alliances between families and to ensure the handing down of inheritances, so therefore those who married for love alone in fact risked undermining the social order. If young people could not be prevented from falling in love, they could at least be made to understand that their love affairs were only tolerable outside of any matrimonial intent.

For its part, the Church condemned all profane love as incompatible with sacred love. It particularly stressed the dangers of love between man and wife, no doubt considering that too many of the faithful were unaware of them: "That husband is a sinner who, transported by excessive love, made love to his wife so ardently in order to satisfy his desire, that, were she not his wife, he would wish to be involved with her" wrote a sixteenth century preacher. Throughout the Middle Ages, theologians had repeated that ancient axiom, handed down by St Jerome: "Adulterous is also the man who loves his wife too ardently". It is only recently that the Catholic Church has praised marital love, following the Protestant example. "Conjugal relations are immoral when there is no longer any love", write today's theologians, because they are an "expression of love". And a high-ranking prelate asserts: "God's first requirement of lovemaking is that it be based on love". This goes against traditional attitudes, which no religion does willingly.

According to ancient Christian morality, sexuality was given to us only for procreation and it is a perversion of God's work to use it for other reasons. This doctrine, which implies continence during all periods when conception is impossible or untimely — during pregnancy, menstruation, the period of "impurity" after childbirth, the years of breast-feeding — and which advises total continence to couples once they have children,[1] is rational and consistent but too austere to have been well followed: St Augustine recognises this unequivocally. Therefore, as far back as the theological renaissance of the twelfth and thirteenth centuries, theologians feared that this excessive austerity took from marriage its role as remedy for those weak people incapable of living in continence. Gradually, they recognised married couples' right to "administer the remedy of marriage" at any time, even when conception was impossible or untimely, i.e. dangerous for the woman or the child. This liberalisation undoubtedly had beneficial effects upon faithfulness and the stability of marriage, but it introduced elements of inconsistency into the doctrine. The period from the fourteenth to the nineteenth century sees increasing conflict between the sexual rights of married couples and their duties towards their children, and this process seems to me to have encouraged the use of contraception in marital relations.

Patriarchs rejoiced at an increase in number of either their children or their flocks. Both were felt to be a benediction, an obvious increase in power, rather than an encumbrance. Whether our contemporaries have many children or none at all, they tend to consider them more as a burden, something which restricts their freedom and wealth, and certainly does not increase their power. Granted, there are still good reasons for having a limited number of children, yet in the minds of our contemporaries, the reasons for not having any often seem to predominate. I note that Moheau himself, in the eighteenth century, found such reasons predominant, and that as early as the seventeenth century Colbert thought it necessary to tempt married couples with money in order to encourage large families. Today however, the ancient attitude remains among most Third World peoples, irrespective of their religion.

Could the fertility of marriages in a society be explained simply by the absence of effective contraceptive techniques? I am not questioning the importance of knowledge of the techniques in this field any more than in others, and I have shown elsewhere[2] how learning about more effective contraceptive techniques could upset traditional customs and fertility. I doubt, however, that this explanation of technical ignorance alone is sufficient: a society which really wants to curb its fertility finds a way; and conversely the failure of birth control programmes in the Third World proves that making effective contraceptive techniques available to couples is not in itself enough to change their fertility rate. Is the key not a changing of the parent-child relationship?

In fact, the sense of responsibility towards the child seems to have increased from the end of the Middle Ages until the present day: this can be surmised from numerous indicators discussed in the third section of this book. In it I do not state — as some writers have done recently[3] — that paternal or maternal love was unknown before the mid-eighteenth century: there is unequivocal proof of its existence at much earlier periods. Seventeenth century parents, for example, were often reproached for excessive love of their children: Mme de Sévigné is a well-known example.[4]

However, the question I am dealing with here is the status of the child *vis-à-vis* his parents, not the existence in a specific person of strong paternal, maternal or filial emotions. Let us examine again the Holy Scriptures: Abraham's sacrifice is only a great ordeal because he is passionately attached to his son. But what distinguishes this patriarch from a father today is that he does not feel he owes his son anything. It is to God, the creator of all beings and particularly of Isaac,[5] that he owes everything. Whereas today we feel a special sense of duty towards those who owe their existence to us and who are dependent upon us, ancient culture, until recently, spoke only of man's duties towards his creator.

Paradoxically, Christianity, which has made such use of this principle, is perhaps also the originator of the converse principle. God, it says, is the true creator of children; he only entrusts them to us, and we owe it to Him to look after them with care and love. This idea was expressed as far back as in St Paul. But it is not until centuries later that the parent-child relationship is truly changed by it, perhaps not until the seventeenth and eighteenth centuries. Indeed, it is not until this period that catechisms and sermons really develop this theme.[6] The next step seems to me of less significance: once the sense of responsibility was well instilled and new parental patterns of behaviour moulded, it was of little importance whether one felt accountable to God or directly to the child. The fact is that the child could henceforth be considered a burden too heavy to carry and married couples thus had reasons for avoiding procreation within marriage.

This is even more true since attitudes towards death changed during the eighteenth century: recent studies[7] show that, without in principle ceasing to believe in God and in eternal life, people appear to have no longer accepted the deaths of loved ones with as much resignation. Although these studies do not tell us a great deal about reactions to the deaths of infants, it seems to me that they confirm the hypothesis that people were not as resigned as formerly. A century earlier, the idea of the child's innocence was a reason for accepting its departure for the beyond; henceforth it is a reason for no longer accepting it. It became fashionable for young mothers of the socio-cultural elite to nurse their babies themselves and, during breast-feeding, to refuse their husbands anything which could lead to premature conception, considered to be dangerous for the infant. According to eighteenth century confessors, it was one of the main reasons for couples practising *coitus interruptus*. This evidence would need to be corroborated, but such a task is not impossible.

If the fertility of marital relations in ancient culture was due only to the absence of effective contraceptive techniques, then extramarital relations ought to have been equally fertile. Most historians and demographers appear to have adopted this vision of things, and they have based discussions on sexual activity outside marriage on the illegitimate birth rate. If, on the other hand, the fertility rate is thought to be related to people's intentions, then the hypothesis of lower fertility for illicit sexual activity must be considered, since the purpose of the latter was traditionally "pleasure alone", whereas the purpose of marital relations — according to ecclesiastic and secular moralists — was procreation. Equally, a discussion of single people's sex lives cannot be based on the illegitimate birth rate alone. This is what I wrote in 1969, in *Contraception, Marriage and Sexual Relations in the Christian West*, which is reprinted in the second section of this book. In this section I also questioned the idea put forward by J. T. Noonan that the classification of contraception and masturbation among the "sins against nature", considered as the most serious of the sexual sins, discouraged not only married couples, but also fornicators and adulterers.

This chapter was intended only to revive research, as I clearly stated in the first and last pages. Moreover, having at that time no clear idea as to what the sex lives of single people might have been like, I was incapable of putting forward new theories to contrast with those I was criticising. Therefore it is difficult for me to comprehend, even today, why from 1972 onwards, several historians[8] considered it worthwhile attacking my alleged theories. It is true that, since they themselves devised these theories and expressed them to their own liking, it was then easy for them to ridicule them. Under such duress, I was forced to throw myself into the debate concerning the sex lives of single people which forms the fourth section of this book. I do not know if I should in the end rejoice that I was thus given the chance to write, or regret the controversial journey taken by my contribution to this research and the relinquishing of that which I was doing at the time on marital relations.

By way of a summary of the main conclusions, I will first stress again the limits and dangers of a purely quantitative approach. Everyone has a sex life. The question is to find out what it consists of, i.e. what forms libido takes beneath the double influences of repression and eroticism which exist, more or less openly, in all cultures; how sexual desire is structured, to what extent it reaches its goals, and the result for the subject and for the objects of his or her desire.

I will then repeat that the interval between sexual maturity and marriage lengthened — in France, and undoubtedly in several other Western European countries — from the early Middle Ages to the end of the eighteenth century,[9] particularly for young women. Lastly, from the last centuries of the Middle Ages to the nineteenth century, the sexual behaviour of single people seems to have changed dramatically beneath the effect of increased repression.

Towards the end of the Middle Ages, young men from the towns frequented prostitutes freely — they were, in fact, plentiful and cheap whereas "honest" young women could not practise any but "solitary pleasures" without great danger to their honour. In the country, there was a different pattern; relations with prostitutes were unquestionably less common; but young men and women of a marriageable age were free to go around together and to engage in quite serious flirtations, in some regions at least. Everything dealing with this question remains however hypothetical: for the time being we only have information on these activities for a small number of provinces, generally peripheral to the kingdom of France, and the evidence about young people's sexual practices is debatable.

Better information is available, however, on repression: the closing of municipal brothels as early as the sixteenth century and the marginalising of prostitutes; the suppression — at very different times depending on the region — of the ancient liberties of courtship, the strict banning of pre-marital cohabitation and concubinage, all under pain of excommunication, or indeed fines and imprisonment; the locking away of noble and bourgeois adolescents in colleges where, it was thought, it would be easier to watch over their morals. However this repression, which can be considered an important aspect of the Catholic Reformation in France, began before the Council of Trent and continued into the nineteenth and twentieth centuries: in Savoy, at the beginning of the nineteenth century, the decree of excommunication was revived against young people who still practised *"l'albergement"*;* and at the beginning of the twentieth century the gendarmes were dispatched against the *"maraîchineurs vendéens"*.[†]

What is the result of this long effort for the purification of morals? The sublimation of sexual urges? Suppression and neurosis? Erotic dreams which may almost become obsessions and solitary masturbation? I do not see why we must choose between these equally probable effects of repression. I expect that they coexisted, in a proportion which it is not easy to determine. It seems to me particularly difficult to assess the importance of sublimation — short of following Freud who deems it exceptional or to measure the progress and the retreat of suppression and neurosis, which are also ideas too modern to have retained the attention of contemporaries. I doubt that these phenomena ever concerned the majority of single people; and I absolutely do

---

*   a custom in Savoy in which young women allowed one suitor into their bed for
       the night.
†   a tradition in the Vendée allowing young men and women of a marriageable
       age to openly "French kiss" and, less openly, to engage in mutual masturbation.

not see what allows people to believe that they were more widespread in the seventeenth century than in the eighteenth and nineteenth centuries. Conversely, there are numerous indications that masturbation increased between the thirteenth and the twentieth century, and its increase can be noted in all social classes. It seems to me to be psychologically linked to the increase in solitary dreaming and in introspection, which has strongly marked our modern contemporary culture.

Finally, at no time do statistics on illegitimate pregnancies and pre-marital conception appear to me to tell us the most important things about the sex lives of single people. Like statistics concerning foundlings, they tell us in particular about society's attitudes towards illegitimacy, concubinage and unwed mothers, which are important subjects of social history rather than of the history of sexuality.

I. LOVE

The first two chapters in this section were both written in 1964. Both are the work of a beginner and are prospective in nature. I wanted to identify changes in how love was represented as objectively as possible. I then intended to study these changes in depth in handwritten and printed sources. "Civilisation and Feelings" appeared in Annales ESC, in September/October 1965. "Love and Love Affairs" is previously unpublished.

"The Créantailles Rite in Troyes" is an article written in 1977 based on a collection of two hundred and twenty-five court cases which Béatrix Le Witta had just studied for her master's degree. As it was intended for the review Ethnologie française (in which it appeared in the fourth quarter of 1978), I was particularly interested in the question of rituals. However, the article also shows us the concrete part that love could play in the shaping of a couple, and interesting developments with regard to this between the first half of the sixteenth, and the second half of the seventeenth century. I was first struck by the developments which favoured love (cf. les Amours paysannes, pp. 53–57, and Families, pp. 171–2), whereas Béatrix Le Witta had been especially aware of the contradictory developments. In fact, both are worthy of our attention. Nothing is easy.

This feeling of complexity is evident in the last chapter in this section, "Love and Marriage in the Eighteenth Century", which was first presented to the French Historical Studies Society Congress at Berkeley, at the beginning of April 1977, and then published in the French journal XVIIIe siècle (no. 12, 1980). Whereas the first three chapters were analyses of a limited corpus, the final one is more a synthesis of my conclusions on the subject in 1977.

Chapter 2

Civilisation and Feelings:
A Survey of Book Titles

Are feelings an unchanging fact of life? Can we easily understand the feelings of men from the past simply because we are human and have within us all human nature? That is what the classicists have always said and what the majority of historians still seem to believe. But myself, I start from a conflicting view: no understanding of what another feels is possible unless one understands his awareness of his feelings. Visible manifestations of behaviour can be described in today's terms; obvious relationships between stimuli and behaviour can be established statistically, which is unquestionably useful; but the psychological reality of human behaviour can only be approached via the subject's inner awareness of the same.

A subject's private thoughts are not irremediably inaccessible to scientific study. Although in the final analysis all individual behaviour is unquestionably original, that is not to say that it is not greatly influenced by the culture within which it develops. The outward manifestations of our drives can only be shaped by the conventions of a specific culture; our feelings only become apparent to us when expressed in the words and images which this culture offers us. A historical explanation of the psychological reality can be derived only from these conventions.

With this in mind, I intend to present here an initial inventory of the ideas relating to love and to sexuality in sixteenth century French society, and to demonstrate that, considered individually or as a whole, they are not compatible with those which are current in our culture.

Where do we begin an inventory of the ways in which the mental outlook of a given society is constructed? With which records? For it is accepted that not all of the conventions into which awareness is locked appear in any one context. Social taboos weigh heavily upon certain of these conventions, especially in the field which we have chosen; and these taboos are restricting to a greater or a lesser degree depending on how they are expressed. Some things can be thought but not said; others can be said but not written; and certain things can be written which one would hesitate to publish. Thoughts, words, private letters and printed texts represent different levels of communication, each of which would deserve an individual inventory. But it is at yet another level, that of book titles, that I undertook this initial inventory. I would like to indicate the characteristics of these book titles.

At the level of titles, the ideas mentioned in them are there for all to see. While it can be assumed that taboos will play a greater role in the choice of words in a title, the most valued ideas of the civilisation in question will certainly be found there. Since the title, by means of a very limited number of words, must both convey information about the book's contents and attract the reader — these two requirements existing in both the sixteenth and twentieth centuries, despite profound changes in titling techniques — the titles testify to the popularity of ideas among those ideas which make up the fabric of the mental outlook of the society in question. I will therefore propose the following hypothesis: the frequency with which a word appears in titles is a sign of the legally and socially accepted influence of the idea which it expresses. Its rarity or its absence may signify its non-existence in the language of the time, its limited value, or the existence of a taboo. In order to decide between these three possibilities, it is generally necessary to study other levels of language. But it seems probable to me that the frequency with which a word appears in titles is a surer sign of its value and power than the frequency of the word at other levels.

In this way, book titles give us the value of words accepted in a chronologically and geographically defined society and thus constitute a useful level for a synchronic study of language. Book titles are even more useful for diachronic research, the study of changes, which is so dear to the historian's heart. For if the frequency of a word testifies to the strength of the corresponding idea, variations in its frequency will be signs of changes in the language and in mental outlook. My purpose here is, of course, not only to point out such changes in titles, but also to be conscious of them and to trace their chronology.

In terms of level of public expression, however, this relatively homogeneous chronological series has undergone specific modifications which must be taken into account.

First and foremost, the technique of titling has changed: the "table of contents-type title" has become the shorter "punchy" title. In the sixteenth century, titles are long because they attempt to reveal the book's contents. Many study books, written in Latin, give a long table of contents, from which only the author's name, more or less abridged and typographically buried, can be picked out as a means of identifying the whole work. A number of literary works, written in French, may have similar but scarcely more readable titles. As the century goes on, the clearer the distinction becomes between the name or title of the book in the true sense of the word, and an explanatory subtitle. It is not, however, until the seventeenth and eighteenth centuries that subtitles are typographically distinguished from, and subordinated to, the title. Finally, today subtitles have generally disappeared. Our titles are therefore shorter and more carefully thought out. Even if they are increasingly unfaithful to the book's content, the words which they use are still more carefully chosen than they were in the sixteenth century.

Moreover, the annual number of titles has increased considerably, which makes comparing frequency difficult. Finally, what makes this exercise even more difficult is that, while almost all contemporary titles are catalogued, it is unknown exactly what proportion of titles from the sixteenth century have come down to us. The haphazard way in which book titles have disappeared may have changed the orientation of the lexical whole in the inventory. Fortunately we have an idea of the type of books missing: they are mainly minor, mediocre and popular works. Whilst undoubtedly the majority of the books printed in the sixteenth century, they now only represent a minority among the books which have survived.

Under these circumstances, it is often appropriate to substitute a qualitative study for a quantitative one, which means looking for the contexts where a word is used rather than its absolute frequency. By doing this we will often see changes emerging by the appearance of a word in new contexts, or by its being given a new meaning in the same context. Finally, whilst variations in frequency are valid in a chronological framework where flaws of homogeneity are negligible, they cannot constitute a reliable basis for comparing the results of two surveys concerning different periods.

In spite of this, it is useful for future research to compare the results of inventories made from the viewpoint of very dissimilar periods such as the sixteenth and twentieth centuries. In this way, our attention can be drawn to issues which would not otherwise have been suspected, and hopefully it will be possible to pick out which of those changes revealed by continuous study over a period of fifty or a hundred years are long-term.

For the present period, I studied the twenty-two thousand titles in the catalogue *les Livres de l'année 1961.* For the sixteenth century, I used Baudrier's and A. Cartier's catalogues, which describe approximately thirteen thousand books published in Lyons out of the fifteen thousand for which records still remain. These books from Lyons represent slightly more than one quarter of the French books surviving from the sixteenth century.

Twenty-two thousand short titles from 1961 and thirteen thousand long titles from the sixteenth century represent two sets of words which are numerically very similar. In each of these two sets, I picked out approximately two hundred and fifty words which figure in my field of study. In this article I will only discuss those which refer to feelings, actions or social institutions: about sixty words in all.

Bearing in mind that this distinction might appear anachronistic, let us begin with those words which refer to concrete social phenomena, like actions or social institutions. For they pose few "translation" problems and our knowledge of social changes will enable us to assess the differences in the two sets of words in this field.

Some of these differences can be explained by changes in our institutions and our customs with which we are already familiar. This explanation alone, however, is rarely enough.

This will always be our explanation when there is unquestionably a new phenomenon behind a new word in the language, like "*le strip-tease*" for example. Indeed, whatever part visual stimulus played in sixteenth century erotic games, it is quite inconceivable that the strip-tease as we know it existed, with its rituals, its traditions, and, in short, its institutional character.

When the word is old, it is more difficult to make a connection between the appearance or non-appearance of the word and the existence or non-existence of the phenomenon to which it refers. The idea of divorce, for example, was known in the sixteenth century; theologians discussed it and some princes practised it. It is therefore possible that it is only by chance that the word did not appear in the titles of the Lyons books and that it might one day be found in book titles from Paris or Geneva. But it is much less likely that it would not be found in titles from 1960 or 1962, also by chance. The fact that "divorce" occurs in 5 titles in 1961 makes this almost certain and is explained by its position as an institution and common practice in contemporary society.

There is less danger of chance playing a part in the occurrence of the ideas of abduction (in French "*rapt*" or "*ravissement*") and clandestine marriage in the titles; but at the same time the realistic explanation must be strongly qualified.

As far as the titles are concerned, we find the words "*raptus*", "*ravissement*" and "*mariage clandestin*" in eight of the titles from Lyons, whereas neither "*rapt*" nor "*mariage clandestin*" appear in 1961. However, not only do these words still exist in our language, but to a certain extent these phenomena still exist in our society: young women leave the family home to run away with their lovers, and a certain number of marriages are hastily performed in towns where the engaged couple is not known. Nonetheless, if we are justified in saying that the reality of abduction or clandestine marriage no longer exists, this must be either because the phenomenon is considered differently or because it no longer holds the place in our lives that it once did.

As far as abduction is concerned, our laws, and the collective consciousness behind them, only retain two elements which are uncharacteristic of the old perception of abduction: violence and the victim's legal minority. The ideas of rape and the corruption of a minor, both of which go beyond the idea of abduction, have been widely substituted for it.

The idea of clandestine marriage has not disappeared, but has altered slightly and has lost some of its importance. It still exists in law and indeed is legal grounds for annulling a marriage. But clandestine marriages are, in reality, no longer an agonising problem in our society. They are no longer a matter for the attention of the State's highest organs, as they were in the sixteenth century. The decrease in importance of clandestine marriage can be explained by profound changes in social structure and in the institution of marriage. However the important point here was only to show how this is plainly revealed in the titles.

The disappearance of the idea of adultery from the 1961 titles must have a similar significance. It is obvious that adultery itself has not disappeared from our society; but it no longer holds the same place as in the sixteenth century. In the titles from Lyons, "*adultère*" and "*adulterium*" are only present in legal contexts, whereas in legal practice today, divorce proceedings have replaced trials for adultery. Legally, adultery is no longer any more than grounds for divorce. Comparing the titles of law books shows us how the key idea of divorce has been substituted for the key idea of adultery. It is fully understood that this transformation must have some kind of repercussion on the meaning of these two ideas in our daily use. I see the beginning of proof for this in the presence of the word "*adultère*" in a sixteenth century work of marginal literary standing[1] and the presence of the word "*divorce*" in the title of a play from 1961.[2]

The titles may reveal that certain other phenomena have changed their status in the structure of our society, which may be equivalent to a change in nature. Such changes may be shown by differences other than the presence or absence in titles of certain words. This is true of marriage, rape and sexual sin.

Marriage is a fundamental institution, both in sixteenth century society and in ours. Words referring to it (including "*épouser*", to marry and "*noce*", wedding) abound in the titles from the sixteenth century and from 1961, whereas its opposite, celibacy, rarely appears.[3] The abundance of words is, however, disproportionate: three times as many words relating to marriage are found in the sixteenth century titles as in the modern ones,[4] and the occurrence of these words is also in the ratio of three to one.[5] Although the total numbers of titles we are working with are too dissimilar to be able to draw any conclusions from such a numeric ratio, this ratio probably reflects the decreasing importance of marriage in our society. However, the most important point is the shifting of this phenomenon, shown by the fact that the idea is found in different contexts and in association with different ideas.

The first striking feature is that, in the sixteenth century, there is a wealth of polemic literature concerning marriage, which calls the institution into question or ridicules married couples.[6] In the 1961 titles, this comic streak does not appear, nor is marriage called into question: peace has been established.

The second feature is the presence of marriage in the titles of tales of chivalry, in combination with "*l'alliance*" and especially "*les amours".*[7] We must particularly notice this use of the plural form in French; it appears that, in noble society, marriage — "*le beau mariage*" — was an important value in a life of adventure.

Lastly, in the sixteenth century, weddings hold an important place in occasional literature.[8] Not only does this show that the Court poet was doing his duty, but it indicates the status of ceremony and festival in the idea of marriage.

None of this remains today. After literary texts, the idea of marriage is found most often in religious and legal contexts both in 1961 and in the sixteenth century. The words with which it is associated are different however. Legal works in the sixteenth century dealt with questions on the form of marriage;[9] today, only questions of substance appear. In the religious context, the word "*mariage*" becomes associated with "*amour*" — this time in the singular in French.[10] It is found in new contexts — philosophical and medical ones — associated with "*bonheur*" [happiness], "*sexualité*" and "*fidélité*".[11] Finally, it must be noted that, in literature, it often occurs in new editions of classic works or works which are already quite old.

Even more subtle contrasts are found with the ideas of sexual sin and rape. The words may be emphasised by the titles, and the tone may be favourable, unfavourable or ambiguous.

Judging by the richness of the vocabulary and its frequency of occurrence in titles, rape ("*viol*") would seem to hold a greater place in sixteenth century titles than in those of today.[12] Yet obviously a ratio of two to one cannot be considered when the actual figures are four and two, since chance could easily play a part. We must therefore return to the titles and see whether the idea is presented in a similar manner. In the sixteenth century titles, which are particularly long in this case, rape is of secondary importance,[13] whereas, in contrast, the 1961 titles highlight it, by their very conciseness.[14] At the same time, it is noticeable that the titles from Lyons refer to actual rapes, whereas in the 1961 titles, rape is only an image or a symbol. In the final analysis, the impression given is that the reality of rape was more familiar to people in the sixteenth century, but that today the idea of rape has acquired a more symbolic meaning.

Studying the idea of sexual sin ("*péché sexuel*") leads to similar observations. Although it appears less frequently in the sixteenth

---

*   Translator's note: The French word "*amour*" can be used in the singular or the plural, but with slightly different meanings. In the singular, it means "love", the emotion, whereas in the plural it means "love affairs".

century titles than in the modern ones, it does so in association with a richer and more precise vocabulary[15] and is almost as well highlighted, despite the length of the titles.[16] The vital difference is to be found elsewhere: in the idea's clarity in the sixteenth century and its mystery today. In the Lyons titles, the idea of sexual sin is unmistakable, even when the idea appears only by a slip on the part of the typographer.[17] In the 1961 titles, it is only hinted at, more or less justifiably.[18] In particular, and this can be said of more than just the titling technique, there is more simplicity and seriousness in the sixteenth century expressions, as well as a certain amount of humour, than there is an attempt to make an effect, in the 1961 titles. The word seems to have gained in prestige and in mystery; and it is not even certain that the unknown phenomenon to which it refers is expected to cause repugnance.

Let us now look for trends for these social phenomena in our two sets of words. The sixteenth century set of words gives the impression of a more highly prized world, whereas the set of words from 1961 reveals two different trends: an effort to see the world more objectively, through words without emotional value, and words whose emotional value is ambiguous.

An initial example of the trend towards an objective understanding of the phenomenon is found in the links between adultery and divorce: the sixteenth century titles focus on adultery and anathematise it; today's titles, no longer so concerned with that focal point, deal instead with the new institution, divorce, with no apparent emotion. This trend towards objectivity and away from emotions is shown even more clearly with the idea of cohabitation or concubinage. In the Lyons titles, the idea appeared in the word "*concubinarii*",[19] a word weighted with violent condemnation, whereas today it is understood directly and objectively in the title *Evolution contemporaine du concubinage*.

These two examples are drawn from the legal context, passing only from canon law, which condemns, to civil law, which observes. It is not yet possible to speak of society's overall attitude, but we can see the same trend in other contexts in connection with an idea which seems to have been divided up: sodomy.

Excluding colloquial or even coarse words, such as "*bougre*" [bugger] — which does not appear in book titles — homosexuality seems to have been scarcely expressed, in the sixteenth century, except through the idea of sodomy, which goes beyond homosexual relations and does not include all their complexities. The ideas of sodomy and homosexuality are therefore different, but are more closely related than adultery and divorce are.

Looking in the titles for words relating to this field, we find the title of a popular work, recounting *l'Histoire véritable du P. Henry Mangot, jésuite, bruslé à Anvers le 12 avril 1601, estant convaincu d'estre sodomiste...* The idea appears only in the form of the adjective "*sodomiste*" against which the title carries violent condemnation. No further mention of it is made in the titles from Lyons. On the contrary, in 1961 the idea of homosexuality appears in two medical titles, without any sign of condemnation.[20] I am not trying to claim that today society as a whole accepts homosexuality, but that, through medical research, it now appears more objectively, whereas formerly references to it were always disapproving.

This trend towards more objectivity could lead to the belief that nowadays social taboos are lesser, or even non-existent. On the contrary, a certain number of taboos have become greater, for example the one concerning sexual relations.

We have already seen that the idea of rape has become less familiar. In the Lyons titles, the image of the physical act is, granted, obscured by the image of reprehensible violence,[21] but it is not entirely sublimated and symbolised, as it is in the 1961 titles. A similar trend can be observed when mentioning intercourse by its biological results, i.e. reproduction.

Undoubtedly there is a richer selection of words relating to reproduction (including "*engendrer*", to beget and "*fécondation*", impregnation or insemination) in the 1961 titles than in the titles from Lyons: the idea is present twelve times as against four, in the use of six words as against three.[22] But, of these twelve occurrences, six pertain to animals, three to the Virgin Mary's immaculate conception, and only one overtly refers to procreation in man: *Un contresens de la maternité: la fécondation artificielle.* There too the image is well hidden!

The taboo seems to weigh somewhat less heavily among the titles from Lyons. Of two medical books dealing with procreation in man, one at least is very explicit.[23] It is even more interesting that the image appears very naturally in a literary work intended for great public notice, Amadis de Gaule's ninth book. It is worth quoting the entire phrase: *...de deux autres fils et filles engendrez insciemment par iceluy Amadis en l'excellente Royne Zahara de Caucase...;* obviously today it would be expressed differently. Sixteenth century literature rarely looks for inspiration in procreation,[24] but when it does find it, no attempt is made to hide the facts.

If one looks for direct mention of intercourse without the intervention — or screen — of its biological results, no examples are found in the contemporary titles, but five in the titles from Lyons. However these five must be qualified.

Of the three words used to refer to the actual act, "*coïtus*" is the clearest and the bluntest, and is also the one found three times. Yet it is worth noting that it is a Latin word, confined to books with limited circulation. It is then worth commenting that, in these three titles, the word is not found where it would attract the most attention. The first example is one of these interminable table of contents-titles common at the time: *Haec sunt opera Arnaldi Villa Nova, que in hoc volumine continentur...* In the midst of a jumble of various subjects one can detect: *De coïtu*. Nowadays, this title would be: *Arnauld de Villeneuve, The Complete Works*, and for purely technical reasons, the word "*coïtus*" would be moved to the table of contents.

The word appears again in the titles of two monographs by Marzio Galeotti, published in a collection in 1552: Galeotus Martius Narniensis, *De doctrina promiscua*. The titles of these monographs could very well have been placed on the title page, as with Arnauld de Villeneuve's works, but the changes in titling techniques between 1504 and 1552 caused them to be removed from it. To return to the two monographs, their author, Marzio Galeotti, was a Florentine humanist doctor and astrologer, who died at the beginning of the sixteenth century. One of his monographs is entitled: *De mulieribus in viros conversis et maris aut foeminae in coitu sit major voluptas*. However surprising it may appear today, this subject was studied by the majority of doctors in antiquity and the Renaissance. The other monograph, more original in subject, is important in that it touches on the taboo with which we are concerned: *De coitu et eius vocabulo supresso ab antiquis*. Unfortunately, I am not yet able to say whether this book is an attempt to restore an ancient taboo to a society in which it no longer existed, or to highlight an ancient secret.[25]

In addition to the Latin word, the act of intercourse is portrayed by two verbs: "*habiter*" [in its ancient meaning, to have intercourse] and "*prendre une fille*" [literally, to "take" a woman]. These words, being French, can reach a wider audience than the Latin term. However it must be noted that they have other meanings which have nothing to do with sexuality; as though a taboo prevented a word relating only to the sexual act from circulating at such a high level of publicity. Neither, however, is really a euphemism or a metaphor.

Like *"coïtus"*, the verb *"habiter"* is used with a specific meaning in the medical language of the time. Moreover, neither word appears where it would attract a great deal of attention.[26] As for *"prendre une fille"*, this expression is found in the title of a morality play, i.e. in a context with a wide audience, hence, with a moderate amount of publicity.[27] But the image is immediately concealed by one of reprehensible and refined violence.

Finally, the taboo may be explicitly stated. One 1584 title, which states its intentions in the clearest manner, and can thus be compared with Marzio Galeotti's allusion, is: *Val. Martialis epigramata, ab omni rerum obscenitate verborumque turpitudine vindicata. Opera et industria Andrea Frusij societatis Jesu Theologi.* This work was republished in Lyons in 1593.

The two expressions *"obscenitas rerum"* [the indecency of the matters] and *"turpitudo verborum"* [the disgrace of the words] do not tell us of a taboo in titles, but in the texts themselves. It would be useful to clarify the forms, dates and extent of the purging of ancient texts. This title alone tells us that the taboo applies to words as much as to things. Providing that other similar expressions have not escaped us, it also allows us to put a date on this concern for modesty (*"pudeur"*). In any case, the year 1584 corresponds quite well to what is known of Tridentine attitudes and the Jesuits' educational work.

If words such as *"turpitudo"* and *"obscenitas"* are not now found in book titles, it is not so much due to a loosening of the taboo on titles, as that they themselves have become victims of taboos concerning titles. As early as the seventeenth century, it was preferable to indicate concern for purging by the expression *"ad usum Delphini"* [for the use of the Dauphin]. Today the word *"expurgé"* is more than enough.

This comparison of titles from the sixteenth century and from 1961 gives the impression of a reinforcing of the taboo on the image of the physical act and on the words which allude to it too realistically. I interpret the series of words relating to those acts as of secondary importance and a diversion of attention from the "climax" of sexual relations. Let us not talk of love, which includes a totality of relations — both physical and sentimental to varying degrees and let us retain only those words designating one part of this phenomenon. The titles from Lyons only contain one such word, *"mignardises"* [affectation], generally in association with *"récréations"* and *"devis"* [speech or discourse]. In these examples, it seems to evoke sweet words exchanged between lovers or read together.

The 1961 titles are verbose in a different way. As far as actual words are concerned, they titles may contain the word "*confidences*", although the contexts in which it appears are difficult to define. In any case, it is sensuous pleasures which in particular are conjured up by the use of words such as "*baisers*" [kisses], "*embrasser*" [to kiss, to embrace], "*caresses*", "*flirt*", and to which "*strip-tease*" can possibly be added.[28] The very brevity of modern titles highlights these words and makes them the stuff of dreams. Thus, one can say that titles are much more "sexualized" in 1961 than in the sixteenth century; in point of fact, it is actually an incomplete sexuality, of secondary importance, the main elements being literally considered obscene.

However, although consciousness of the obscene has been exaggerated, taboo elements are tackled today by two different means. Firstly, by the use of traditionally condemned words, such as "*péché*" and "*viol*", which we have discussed. By highlighting these words, away from their usual contexts, they are made inexplicable and ambiguous. In any case, titles are not the only area where taboos are avoided in this way.

But these taboos are avoided particularly by the use of words which appear objective, under cover of scientific obligations. We have already demonstrated that, in the shift from "*sodomiste*" to "*homosexuel*" and particularly to "*homosexualité*", there is a decrease or decline in the traditional taboo. In the 1961 titles we find numerous ideas which did not exist in the titles and language of the sixteenth century: debauchery (in French "*libertinage*"), eroticism, nymphomania, erotomania, masochism, sadism, homosexuality and especially sexuality. These ideas, save that of debauchery, are more modern.[29]

Thus it could be said that our society will accept any phenomenon, providing that the author first distances himself by using a term which appears scientific. This convention is perhaps related to the one whereby formerly taboo phenomena were cloaked in a mythological mantel. However, I have not found obvious examples of that convention in the titles from Lyons. Moreover, there seems to be more than one example of hypocrisy in the words used today: there is a real trend towards distancing, which may be applied to acts as well as to words. Writers such as D.H. Lawrence seem to have been painfully aware of this.

The idea of sexuality seems to be representative of this trend. No doubt it stems from necessities within one particular science, i.e.

biology. The Larousse dictionary defines the word as meaning: "*caractères spéciaux déterminés par le sexe*" [special characteristics determined by one's sex]. Yet today the idea extends beyond the biological context. Of the four times the word is used in 1961, only once does it really correspond to this definition.[30] Of the three other occurrences, one is found in a work of popularised medicine,[31] the second in a historical essay,[32] and the third in a philosophical essay.[33] This word, originally a very scientific and objective one, is taking on a new and increasingly complex meaning. But although it is a catchall for formerly taboo ideas, it is possible that the use of the word increases to the detriment of those ideas accepted by the greater part of the society.

A similar case is the word "*liaison*", which is used to designate a relatively stable sexual relationship outside of marriage. It does not seem to have existed in the sixteenth century. How might they have perceived such relationships? No doubt in terms of the derogatory ideas of adultery and concubinage; but also in terms of the concept of love.

In theory, our second group is made up of much less tangible phenomena, perceived in words which are less straightforward to define. That will make comparison difficult, but show us other means of differentiating.

If one confines oneself to the frequency of words, one is immediately struck by a similarity, which could for that matter have been predicted, i.e. the numerical preponderance of the word "*amour*" (See translator's note p. 19) in our two sets of words. Among the titles from Lyons, one hundred and five uses of the singular form and one hundred and nine of the plural form are found, and in 1961, one hundred and five uses of the singular and sixteen uses of the plural. This is more than the total of all the other words in this category put together.[34]

It could be concluded from this that love holds a similar place in both collections of titles. This is particularly true since, when the contexts in which the word appears are examined, a certain number of similarities are found: in both periods, the word is found in religious, philosophical and moral contexts, and particularly in what today's bibliographers still call "*belles-lettres*". In 1961, however, it appears in two new contexts: history and medicine.

Its appearance in the historical context is the less significant of the two. It is not that the word "*amour*" can be likened to the word *"moeurs"* [morals] which could be found in sixteenth century history books; one feels that the two words have neither the same meaning nor the same value. However, those present-day history books which deal with love have a similar position in our society to that held by tales of chivalry in the sixteenth century.[35] Serious historians today can accept only the word *"sexualité"*, which we have already discussed.

In contrast, the presence of the word in a medical context is worthy of our attention. One would be inclined to attribute it to the simple extending of medical materialism to the field of psychology, whereas the situation is certainly less straightforward. In the sixteenth century, medicine was, to a certain extent, more imperialist than today: medical procedures of the time were unfailingly concerned with acting on the psyche by very physical methods. Whereas today we consider melancholy, choler and phlegm as specifically psychical phenomena, doctors in the sixteenth century considered that these "humours" were purely physical phenomena. The fact that these words are now part of everyday language shows that a distinction cannot be made between medical ideas and ideas in everyday use. As early as the sixteenth century, and without separating their physical side from their psychical side, these ideas existed in the everyday language of the society in question.[36] Their presence in many books written in French and aimed at a large audience, contributes towards proving this.

Thus, the appearance of the word *"amour"* in titles of medical books involves more than just a widening of doctors' concerns for the psyche. We must recognise that a science which formerly wanted to ignore love and was able to deny it implicitly, began to consider it an emotional reality. Beyond the inertia of graeco-roman problematics, which was largely linked to the use of Latin, it does seem that the issues concerning love as a feeling, the only ones to be considered by other groups within society, were not strong enough to have replaced the largely out of date issues concerning sensual pleasure in medical thinking. From its appearance in modern medical texts, following a noticeable decrease in the mention of sensual pleasure, it must be concluded that not only was there a change in medical thought, but also a clear affirmation of love as an emotional reality.[37]

If one examines the titles more closely, one is struck by the fact that love was the subject of so much debate in the sixteenth century. Seven of the book titles from Lyons, representing in total seventeen editions, criticise profane love in general or one of its more specific aspects;[38]

and seventeen titles are found, representing twenty-four editions, which make an effort to present an image of "*l'amour honneste*", in short, acceptable love.[39] In contrast, of the 1961 titles, only three attack love, and only two attempt to impose a way of loving.[40]

Part of sixteenth century civilisation rejects love as an insane pattern of behaviour in God's eyes. This idea is given by the adjectives "*fausses*" [false] and "*folles*" [crazy], which are found particularly in titles from the end of the fifteenth and the beginning of the sixteenth century. After 1503, the response to the adjective "*faux*" is the adjective "*vrai*" [true]: the "falseness" of certain love affairs is not denied, but there is one true love. During the first half of the century, it is a way of loving, an ideal love within love affairs, which is gradually defined. This love is honourable — "*honneste*" — because it does not go against sexual taboos, being "*chaste*" and "*pudique*" [modest]. Finally, in the second half of the century, the prestige of amorous exploits is intensified — the need for them is therefore felt — by the adjective "*pudique*", or by new epithets: "*loyales*", "*merveilleuses*", "*insignes*" [distinguished].

In 1961, on the other hand, love is accepted unconditionally. In order to reinforce the positive value of the word, adjectives expressing quantities ("*grand*", long), an excess ("*fou*", crazy), a force ("*l'amour plus fort que la mort*", a love stronger than death), or an absolute ("*d'un seul amour rêvant*", dreaming of one single love) are used. The full meaning of the idea is therefore clearly established. The words no longer need to be qualified in order to be favourably received; the controversial phenomena — desire, sensual pleasure, eroticism — arise outside of love and are open to either favourable or unfavourable opinions. Does this change of attitude really concern the same phenomenon? Without trying to define the word's meaning, let us note that in the sixteenth century tales of individuals' love affairs are often told, as in "*les amours de X*" or "*les amours de X et de Y*".[41] In order to deal with generalities, in titles like *la Fontaine d'amours*, where neither the subject nor the object of love are specified, there is often recourse to a collection of individual love affairs.[42]

If we consider the sixteenth century as a whole[43], which is this article's intention, we find references to the existential reality of love almost as often as references to its essential reality.[44] In 1961, on the other hand, "love" as a universal phenomenon is mentioned much more frequently than individual love affairs. Even when dealing with one particular individual, reference is made to love universally. Instead of speaking of Nicole's love for Jean-Pierre, for example, or of

Nicole's love affairs, as would have been done in the sixteenth century, one book is called *Nicole et l'Amour*.

No doubt this is an abstraction which perhaps did not exist in the sixteenth century. Indeed, aside from the essence of love, the allegory of love which existed then was rather coloured by ancient mythology. And as though the abstraction was not immediately understandable, most of the titles enjoy an ambiguity of meaning when they use the singular form without an article, which is the most frequent case.[45] Even a book which is as orientated towards the essence of love as Mario Equicola's[46] begins with a description of the allegory.

In 1961, no trace of the ancient or medieval allegory appears in titles. And yet love, today, is not a pure essence. In general, it has acquired an existence, a presence, which is no longer visible to the eye, but to the heart.[47] Love is now, on the whole, an absolute value of our civilisation and if, from this fact, its invisibility and the heart's or the soul's sensitivity to its existence can be brought together, one may ask whether there is not a new divinity, whose relation to the allegory of years ago is similar to that of the God of the Scriptures with the divinities of the classical pantheon. It has a divine power in which one has faith (*L'amour plus fort que la mort, L'amour brisa le sortilège*), it is the object of eternal expectation (*L'amour viendra peut-être*), of anguished expectation (*L'amour vint et s'en fut, Amour peux-tu revenir*) of worried and painful mysticism (*L'amour s'en va, Amour réponds-moi, Amour sombre tourment*), of theology (*l'Amour et la Mort, l'Amour et le Divin*), it is the basis of a moral code (*le Chemin de l'amour, la Condition de l'amour, Amour, Mariage et Bonheur*). What does it lack which prevents it from being God? When one looks at the way in which certain passages in the holy Scripture are highlighted ("*Dieu est amour*"), one sometimes wonders whether love does not justify God instead of being justified by him. But let us go no further than the 1961 titles: by chance, perhaps, they did not say that.

Moreover, this divine being which is love only appears in some of the titles. I highlighted it only because it appears to me to be the biggest comparative change with the sixteenth century. At the beginning of the sixteenth century, love was the positive relationship which united lovers; at the end of the century, it was more an abstract framework within which relationships existed;[48] after having jumped over an unknown number of hurdles — internalisation is assumed to be one of them — we discover that in the 1961 titles one of the lovers has totally disappeared, and that, often, the other remains alone before a transcendent reality upon which he seems to call.

If the authors' names are to be believed, women have played an important role in the formation of this religion of love.[49] But they are not the only ones involved, either as authors or as audience.

There is another example of the shifting of attention from the object to the action in the increased use of the verb *"aimer"* [to love]. In the titles from Lyons, the word appeared only six times, whereas in 1961, it appears twenty-eight times. It used to appear only in the contexts of religion and profane love,[50] whereas in 1961 it appears four times in the religious context, fourteen times in the context of profane love[51] — often it is difficult to distinguish the former from the latter by the title alone — and ten times in various other contexts.[52]

No doubt this increase in the use of the verb *"aimer"* indicates a new importance of the psychological phenomena, but there is something else as well. In the sixteenth century, its use in the context of profane love was only given by two different titles, whereas the verb *"jouir"* [meaning both to enjoy and to climax] appeared five times in four different titles, all dealing with profane love.[53] In 1961, on the other hand, the verb *"jouir"* never appears. In other words, in the sixteenth century, the desire to enjoy one's love affairs was exhibited, whereas today only the desire to love is still exhibited. Undoubtedly, this is both the reinforcing of a taboo and the changing of an idea.

In actual fact, in a sexual context, the verb *"jouir"* had a less precise meaning then than today: it included the actual orgasm, but not only that. It is another characteristic of our language to make a more marked distinction between feelings and sensuality.

Indeed, in our sexual context, *"amour"*, *"affection"* and *"tendresse"* [tenderness] are emotional phenomena, involving the heart (*"le coeur"*), whereas pleasure and sensual pleasure (*"volupté"* or *"jouissance"*) affect only the senses. The nouns used in the sexual context in the sixteenth century do not allow this distinction.

Not only does the idea of feeling (*"le sentiment"*) not appear in the titles from Lyons, but it seems unknown in the sixteenth century. Several dictionaries attest to the existence of the word *"sentement"*, but it designates an idea of the senses rather than of the heart.[54] Moreover, the heart, as the centre of feelings, appears only in the titles of two religious works,[55] one novel,[56] and one single essay in Italian,[57] i.e. in a total of six books, whereas in 1961 this idea is found in fifty-one titles, only eleven of which refer to religious books.[58] Lastly, *"tendresse"* appears neither in titles nor in dictionaries. And the adjective *"tendre"* or the noun "*tendreté*" indicate a sensual quality, not an emotional phenomenon.

As for the purely sensual phenomena, they are only perceived through Latin nouns, "*libido*", "*Venus*", "*voluptas*" or through a French word which comes from the Latin, such as "*volupté*".[59] These words appear only in ancient books,[60] medical books,[61] or, with a pejorative sense, in religious books.[62] They are never found in a sexual context. When the French word "*Vénus*" is found in this context, it is to designate a mythological character and adventures and is not an allegory of sexual pleasure. Of the seven French titles, representing sixteen editions, in which the word "*Vénus*" is found, only one suggests the allegory of love: *La nouvelle Vénus, par laquelle est entendu pudique amour*. In the absence of any adjective, it cannot then be said that "*Vénus*", in the context of sexual literature, represents a phenomenon more sensual than love itself. As for the adjective "*vénérien*" [sexual or, in medical texts, venereal], which, interestingly enough, I did not find in the titles from Lyons, it seems to be more used in a literary sense than the adjective "*amoureux*" [amorous], without being any more concerned with the sensual side of love, nor, of course, having the horror value which various diseases have given it for us.

It is possible that, in the sixteenth century, the sentimental side is seeking to be expressed, but that the language prevents it from being expressed directly and clearly. "*Amour pudique*" is not contrasted with other types of love in the same way as feeling is contrasted with sensual phenomena, but rather on the same plane of behaviour as that on which acceptable behaviour is contrasted with unacceptable behaviour. It is perhaps tempting to restrict it to two alternatives: "If it is not sensual, it must be sentimental." But nothing in the titles shows awareness of such an alternative.

By seeing the interesting changes in meaning and usage of the words "*amitié*" [friendship], "*affection*" and "*passions*", one gets a clear impression that a new phenomenon is seeking definition.

The word "*amitié*" only appears in the titles after 1559 and always in the context of profane love.[63] To a certain extent it seems to take over from "*honneste et pudique amour*", which disappears from the titles around this time.[64] But this word "*amitié*" might just as easily refer to normal relations between people of the same sex as between people of different sexes.[65] Thus, it does not succeed very well in characterising the specific feeling of the lover.

The idea of "*affection*" gradually becomes closer to the idea of "*amitié*". The word, as we understand it from the titles[66] and in dictionaries,[67] seems firstly to designate passionate desire, the instinct which pushes the lover towards the loved one. As such, it is liable to as many derogatory meanings as favourable, but at the beginning of the seventeenth century in novels like *l'Astrée*, one no longer finds any but favourable meanings. It appears to be the doublet of "*amitié*". It is a phenomenon which one can "*témoigner*" [show] or "*cacher*" [hide] and which may "*plaire*" [please] or "*déplaire*" [displease] the person to whom it is "*assuré*" [assured].[68] But it is always the object who receives the proof of this affection, never the subject.

The concept of love in modern society, expressed through the words "*sentiment*" and "*tendresse*", is egocentric. It is a contemplation of self. The sixteenth century concept, on the other hand, using "*amitié*" and "*affection*", is objective.

The words which draw attention to the lover, on the contrary, do not allow a distinction to be made between the sentimental or the sensual plane where perception is situated. Only its agreeable or disagreeable nature is distinguished: "*jouir*", "*plaire*" and "*plaisir*" indicating agreeable perceptions; "*déplaire*", "*angoisses*" and "*passions*", disagreeable perceptions. In any case, neither the truth, the depth nor the honesty of these perceptions are discussed in the titles. They are merely described complacently,[69] or deplored and a search for a remedy takes place.[70] No doubt the change in meaning of the word "*passions*" must be noted, from the sense of "torment" to the sense of "irrepressible desire", with which meaning it replaces the word "*affection*" in the seventeenth century. But the objects of this desire, or those responsible for the distress, may be high or low, spiritual or physical.

In fact, in the sixteenth century, there were different ways of perceiving these psychological phenomena. In the fields of medicine and religion, they are perceived as sensual phenomena. Through amorous casuistry, one perceives behaviour as acceptable or unacceptable from the outside, but within the subject, one can only distinguish the pleasant from the unpleasant. Judging by the 1961 titles, we seem to hardly be concerned with this distinction nowadays.

Thus, simply comparing the words which appear in book titles shows us that, beneath differing attitudes towards them, human phenomena, even those which are as apparently natural as sexual phenomena, may be globally different. Yet it is difficult to define this difference in general terms.

On the one hand, we have observed the increasing distinction between psychological phenomenon and social phenomenon and, within improved psychological phenomena, the creation of a new distinction between feelings and sensuality. As for objective phenomena, objects of science, in titles, they are seen to rid themselves of their traditional values, these values taking refuge in psychological phenomena which are less easily studied.

New ideas appear however, which characterise acts as much as feelings, for example, sadism and masochism. Their novelty is caused by syncretism rather than differences. Finally, other ideas, such as those of rape or sin, seem to gain in value — but in ambiguous value — what they lose in familiarity. I believe therefore that attempting to define them globally would be to betray the richness and the diversity of these changes. Nonetheless, we have only considered here some elements for assessment.

For as we have said, titles indicate only those ideas which a civilisation dares to display. In order to truly understand the significance of this display, it is necessary to know how it is related to what is not openly displayed in that same time period. In other words, an inventory must be made of what appears in printed texts and private correspondence, and an attempt must be made to indirectly gain access to the levels of oral expression, of the conscious and the unconscious. In order to truly know what human life is like in a given society, one must first truly know the conventions within each of these different levels. In order to describe a society's attitude towards this reality one must establish how these conventions are divided between the different levels of public expression.

In order to reconstruct our civilisation's history, it is necessary to follow the changes in language at these different levels from one day to the next. For the time being, it seems to me desirable to undertake this according to two research directions: a study of the changes at a given level, that of titles for example, which seems the most readily accessible; and a survey across the different levels at a given time, and in a specific linguistic field, in order to gain an idea of the relationships between the levels.

In conclusion, I would like to specify the social content of this kind of historical study. It is important to be conscious of the fact that it does not involve the whole of society. For the historian, there are unfortunately social classes which remain silent: those which think, speak and act but do not write and read little. It is not possible to approach the history of their attitudes by the direct methods proposed here. But it must be mentioned that these classes elude us to the extent that they do not participate in the history of our civilisation. Our perspective is to understand, through the forms of expression, the life of all those who we can consider to be our spiritual forefathers. In other words, we must also specify their place in society and draw conclusions as to the sociological significance of their forms of existence. But the life of the others, of our biological ancestors, does not interest us in the same way. That constitutes, as it were, another story.

Appendix I

Sixteenth Century		*1961*	
Coelibatus (1)	1	Célibat	2
Connubium, connubialis (3)	11		
Connubiales (1)	3		
Matrimonium, matrimonialis (7)	14	Matrimonial	10
Mariage (34)	66	Mariage	31
Se marier, marié(e) (15)	19	Marié	4
Epouser (6)	12	Epouser	2
Epousailles (2)	2		
Prendre femme (1)	1		
Noces, nuptial (10)	10	Noces	2
Nuptiae, nuptialis (4)	9		
Fiançailles (1)	1	Fiancé(e)	5
Sponsus (1)	1		
Sponsalia (1)	4		
Ménage (2)	2	Ménage	1
		Couple	1
		Divorce	5
Adultère (2)	2		
Adulterium (2)	6		
Concubinarij (1)	1	Concubinage	1
		Liaison	1
		Aventure (amoureuse)	1
		Flirt	1
Amours	77	Amour(s)	26
Amores (2)	4		
		Confidences	0
Mignardises (3)	3		
		Caresses	1
		Baisers	2
		Embrasser	1
		(Flirt)	(1)
		Strip-tease	2
Engendrer (1)	2		
Generatio (1)	1	Génération	1
Procreatio (1)	1		
		Fécondation	2

		Conception, conceptio	3
		Reproduction	3
		Insémination artificielle	3
Coitus (3)	3		
Habiter (1)	1		
Prendre une fille à force (1)	1		
Violer (1)	1	Viol	1
Violement (1)	1	Violée	1
Violée (1)	1		
Raptus (2)	2		
Ravissement (2)	3		
Mariages clandestins (4)	6		
Péché (1)	1	Péché	5
Pécher (1)	1		
Stuprum (1)	1		
Turpitudo verborum (1)	2		
Obscenitate rerum (1)	2		
Porneographie terentiane (1)	1	Pornografia	1
		Libertinage	1
Erotasmes, antérotiques (2)	2	Erotisme, érotique	6
		Erotomanie	1
		Nymphomanie	1
		Masochisme	1
		Sadisme	1
Sodomiste (1)	1		
		Homosexualité, homosexuel	3
		Sexualité	4
		Sexologie	1

The numbers in brackets indicate the number of different titles in which these words occur. The other figures indicate the total number of occurrences found in the thirteen thousand sixteenth century titles and the twenty-two thousand titles from 1961.

Appendix II

Sixteenth Century		*1961*	
Amour	105	Amour	105
Amor	27		
		Eros	1
		Agapé	1
Amours	89	Amours	16
Amores	4		
Aimer	6	Aimer	28
Amitié	5	(Amitié)	(7)
Affection(s)	1		
Passions	4		
Angoisses	2		
		Tourment	1
		Sentiment, sentimental	3

	Tendresse, tendre 2
(Pudique) . . . . (13)	Pudeur 4
	Haine 2
	Désir 6
	Démon charnel 1
	Démon de midi 1
Libido 1	
Vénus 1	
Voluptas 1	Volupté 3
Volupté 1	
	Plaisir(s) 4
(Heur, Bonheur) . . . . (5)	Bonheur 6

Only those occurrences of these words in association with love have been indicated. The words in brackets are those sixteenth century words similar to the words which today express feelings in this context.

Chapter 3

Love and Love Affairs in the Sixteenth Century

In French, the word *"amour"* can be used in the singular or the plural.* In actual fact it is found much more often in the singular: in the twenty-two thousand titles of books published in 1961, the singular is used one hundred and five times and the plural sixteen times. Today, the plural form is nothing but a literary relic. Conversely, in the sixteenth century the plural form was found as often as the singular: in the thirteen thousand titles from Lyons catalogued by Baudrier,[1] the singular form is used one hundred and nine times and the plural eighty-nine times. Thus we must try to discover what both the singular and the plural forms meant at that time.

My first observation is that in the religious context, the singular form is always used in speaking of the love between man and God. It is only in the context of profane love that both singular and plural may be used.

My second observation is that during the sixteenth century, there is a gradual change in how the singular and plural forms are used. In order to show this change clearly, we must distinguish between the different uses of the word *"amour"*.

---

* Translator's note: Nowadays, *"amour"* is usually used to mean "love" and *"amours"* to mean "love affairs".

"AMOUR" DEFINED BY THE LOVER OR THE LOVED ONE

Defined by the Lover Alone

The singular form is only used once, compared to twenty times for the plural. This one occurrence of the singular concerns the love of Jesus Christ (for the sinner); all the occurrences of the plural pertain to profane love, e.g. "La plaisante et délectable histoire de Gerileon d'Angleterre...avec *les amours d'iceluy*..."

Defined by the Loved One Alone

There are eight indisputable examples of this category. In each case, the singular form is used, e.g. *...et ceux d'Agesilan de Colchos, au long pourchas de l'amour de Diane, la plus belle princesse du monde*. It is worth noting that only four of these titles relate to divine love. Divine love, grammatically speaking, is a love whose lover is defined.

There are six titles for which it is difficult to determine whether love is defined by its lover or its loved one. Four of these refer to the love of God — God's love for man or man's for God? — and one to the love of the king — the king's love for his subjects or his subjects' for him? In these five titles, the singular form is used. From this we can conclude that either God and the king are the loved ones or that, in these cases, it is of little significance whether they are lovers or loved ones and that the singular form is used in order to distinguish this kind of love from sexual love.

In the sixth title, *les Amours d'Ismenius*, the plural form is used. If our proposed rule holds true, Ismenius must be the lover — the one who loves.

Defined by Both Participants

Approximately twenty titles indicate both the lover and the loved one. Four follow the pattern: *l'Amour de X pour Y*, and fourteen the pattern: *les Amours de X et de Y*. Thus, there is uncertainty as to the correct use within the century as a whole, but gradual change over the century is very clear: all such titles which use the singular form were published between 1528 and 1560. After 1560, the use of the plural form becomes the rule.

It is possible that at that time, when so much thought was given to language and spelling, a rational course of action was decided upon:

the plural form should be used to indicate reciprocity. And in point of fact, there are two loves in such cases, X's love for Y and Y's for X. Yet there are problems with this explanation.

In some examples, we cannot be certain that there is reciprocity, e.g. *Des extrêmes amours d'un chevalier de Séville dit Luzman à l'endroit d'une belle demoiselle appelée Arbolea* (1580); or *De l'amour d'un serviteur envers sa maîtresse* (1571). In each of these two examples there is only one lover and one loved one, and yet the singular form is used in one case and the plural in the other. Hence our logical explanation alone is not enough.

A third example will strengthen this conviction: *Les Merveilleuses Amours du Prince Darinel de Grèce et celles de la belle Richarde de Paris* (1583 and 1597). For the most part, the plural form seems to be associated with adventure novels, the majority of which are translated from Spanish. It is worth pointing out that the plural form is used in the Spanish titles as well. It is possible that, in the period 1570–90, in which such adventure novels increase in number, "*les amours de...*" is used to mean "episodes in the amorous adventures of..."

Examples in Which Neither Lover Nor Loved One is Specified

In those titles in which neither the lover nor the loved one is specified, there is no obvious rule for choosing between the singular and the plural form. In such cases, a chronological study is interesting. We shall examine the different forms of this usage separately.

"En Amour(s)"

If we exclude "*en l'amour de Dieu*", in which the lover or the loved one is specified, there are seven titles which contain this expression:

1536: *...en amours maints maux a supporté...*

1547: *...La Fortune de l'Innocent en amours*

(1555–1597): *...pour se bien gouverner en amour*

1577: *...pour bien et honnestement se gouverner en amour*

(1580–1590): *...les plus beaux traits dont on peut user en amour*

1583: *...pour bien et honnestement se gouverner en amour*

1592: *...Les demandes que les amoureux font en amour*

By examining these admittedly few examples, we see a distinct shift from the use of the plural to the singular over the century, and more specifically between 1547 and 1555.

"D'amour(s)"

This expression is found in the titles of seventy-seven books from Lyons. Since several of these cannot be accurately dated, we must be slightly arbitrary in distinguishing between what was in current use before and after 1540. Before 1540, we find six or seven singular forms as compared to between twenty-two and twenty-five plural (i.e. more than 75% are plurals). Between 1540 and 1600, there are between thirty-six and forty-four singulars (depending on whether or not one counts some examples found elsewhere than on the title page) and thirteen or fourteen plurals (i.e. approximately 75% are singulars): the proportion has been reversed.

Nonetheless, if we consider different editions of the same book, the shift from the use of the plural to the singular is not clear-cut. There are of course examples of a marked and incontrovertible shift: *la Prison Damours* (Paris, 1526) becomes *la Prison Damour* in the editions published in Lyons in 1528 and 1583. Yet sometimes publishers remain faithful to either the singular or the plural form from the beginning to the end of the century. At other times, they seem to vacillate between the plural and the singular right up to the last decade of the century:

La Fontaine damours   (J. de Channey, 1513–1533)

La Fontaine d'amour   (J. de Tournes, 1545)

La Fontaine damours   (B. Rigaud, 1570)

La Fontaine damour   (B. Rigaud, 1572)

La Fontaine d'amours   (B. Rigaud, 1588).

When does this vacillation begin? The singular is first used in 1503, but this remains the only example until 1527, while there are between ten and sixteen titles containing the plural form in the period 1490–1527. Between 1527 and 1540, the plural is used between nine and fifteen times compared to the singular being used five or six times. After 1545, this trend is reversed. Between 1560 and 1590 there was a return to the plural form, furthered by the increase in book titles referring to "*Devises*" [mottoes] and particularly "*Aventures d'armes et d'amours*", usually translated from Spanish. In spite of this, the singular form is on the whole more common in this fifty-year period. Between 1590 and 1600, there is no longer one single occurrence of the plural form in twelve book titles.

We would need to continue our research beyond 1600 in order to determine whether the predominance of the singular form became definitive. But on the whole the trend is clear and is similarly revealed if we consider only the first edition of each book. This gives the following figures:

1490–1539	6 singulars	16 plurals
1540–1559	9–13 singulars	5 plurals
1560–1589	2 singulars	6 plurals
1590–1600	6 singulars	0 plurals

By dividing the century into four periods in this way, we also see clearly how the period 1560–1589 deviated from the pattern of the rest of the century. But, from 1490 to 1539, there were six singulars as compared to sixteen plurals, whereas from 1540 to 1600, there are between seventeen and twenty-one uses of the singular as compared to eleven of the plural.

One might wonder whether this reappearance of the plural form is of any conceptual significance. Indeed, this was the period of religious wars which was perhaps more characterised by brief affairs and rapid sensual pleasures, rather than by sentimentality and the worship of Platonic love. At the same time, moreover, the history of the book trade shows the convincing return of "theological" literature and a decline in humanist books, i.e. the opposite shift to the one which took place in the first half of the century.

Be that as it may, studying the expressions "*en amour(s)*" and "*d'amour(s)*" shows that at the end of the fifteenth century and during the first years of the sixteenth, the plural form was the rule in the titles of books concerning profane love. Indeed, the "s" does not appear to be the unimportant relic of a grammatical case used in medieval times. On the one hand, this is because the Latin titles show clearly that the "s" in the French is an inflexion indicating a plural: *les Arrests d'amours*, by Martial d'Auvergne, for example, is rendered in Latin by *Arresta amorum*. On the other hand, this is because at the same time period "*amour*" is written without an "s" in references to sacred love.

After 1527 — as far as the books from Lyons are concerned — something happened which caused people to vacillate between the plural and the singular form. For these two expressions in which love is defined neither by the lover nor by the loved one, the plural form was able to serve as a kind of determiner preventing any confusion between sexual love and sacred love. Then, after approximately 1527, this determiner gradually fell into disuse, as though people hesitated to follow an outdated tradition. This was perhaps because, in circumstances and for reasons which we should perhaps enumerate, profane love claimed the same status as sacred love. In other words, profane love came to be regarded as sacred.

"L'amour"

Let us consider again the titles in which "*amour(s)*" is defined neither by the lover nor by the loved one, and study again the chronological division of the singular and plural forms.

1490–1520	1 singular	10 plurals
1520–1529	7 singulars	8 plurals
1530–1539	7 singulars	2–6 plurals
1540–1549	7 singulars	2 plurals
1550–1559	15 singulars	3 plurals
1560–1569	0 singulars	1 plural

(The latter period marks the beginning of the religious wars: love is no longer topical, either in the titles from Lyons or in the list of titles from Paris compiled by Renouard. When the word does appear, it refers, albeit with some exceptions, to the love of the prince and the love of God. Love of women is no longer found anywhere except in books published in Italian.)

1570–1579	11 singulars	4 plurals
1580–1589	11 singulars	5 plurals

(The years 1570–89 represent the period famous for novels about soldiering and love affairs translated into French from Spanish.)

1590–1599	16 singulars	0 plurals

It is hardly surprising that this chronological division confirms what we had already concluded after studying the expressions "*en amour(s)*" and "*d'amour(s)*", for all we have done is add to them "*l'amour*" and the allegory "*Amour*", which have no plural form.

It is more interesting to note that the first use of the singular form is qualified, i.e. to a certain extent, defined. In order to try to distinguish those cases in which the singular is used to refer to abstract reality and not to the allegory, albeit with no formal criteria, we shall enumerate those cases where "*l'amour*" is qualified and those where it is not.

1500–1509 1 qualified 0 not qualified

1510–1519 0 qualified 0 not qualified

1520–1529 3 qualified 1 not qualified

1530–1539 1 qualified 2 (2 editions of the same book)

1540–1549 3 qualified (1) not qualified

1550–1559 3 qualified 1 not qualified

1560–1569 0 qualified 0 not qualified

1570–1579 2 qualified 2 not qualified

1580–1589 4 qualified 5 not qualified

1590–1599 0 qualified 3 not qualified

The figures given are low and thus may only by chance indicate such changes; but they do point up a contrast between the period 1500–1560 and the period 1560–1600. In the first, there are eleven occurrences where "*amour*" is qualified as compared to five where it is not, whereas in the second, there are six occurrences which are qualified as compared to ten which are not. Thus we could propose the following hypothesis: the singular form was necessary because "*amour*" was qualified, i.e. defined, in book titles during the period 1500–60. True, this hypothesis is fragile. Quite apart from the fact that the numbers considered are low, there is another serious problem: in 1529 there is an example of the singular form preceded by the definite article and not qualified. Nevertheless, let us continue with this analysis: which qualifiers are used with the singular and the plural forms?

QUALIFIERS OF THE SINGULAR AND THE PLURAL

Positive Qualifiers

We shall begin by excluding three adjectives: "*céleste*", "*divin(e)*" and "*humain*". These are determiners and, as such, can only be used with the singular form. Eight positive qualifiers remain:

vray [true]:   1503; 1544; 1546 and 1574

honneste: 1520, 28, 29, 33; 1554; 1581; 1581; 1582

pudique(s) [modest]:   1520, 28, 29, 33; 1544,46; 1547; 1559, 75, 79, 89; 1582 *chaste*:   1556; 1581 (1599)

sincère: 1544; 1546

loyalles: 1559, 75, 79, 89; 1576; 1577

merveilleuses: 1579, 83, 87, 88, 97

insignes [distinguished]:   1589

(*délectables*):   1599

The first noteworthy fact is that, until 1556, all the positive adjectives referring to love are used with the singular form. Some, such as "*vraye*", "*honneste*" and "*sincère*" will continue to be used with the singular form alone right up to the end of the century.

Adjectives such as "*loyalles*", "*merveilleuses*" and "*insignes*", on the other hand, appear only in the second half of the century and are always used with the plural form. This dividing up of the qualifiers between the singular and plural forms allows us to better discern their meanings: "*vray*", "*honneste*" and "*sincère*" define a kind of love; whereas "*loyalles*", "*merveilleuses*" and "*insignes*", used with plural forms, serve only to embellish amorous exploits.

Before 1559, "*pudique*" used to be always found with the singular form; after this date is it always used with the plural form. This was the most fashionable adjective before 1559. It is significant that after 1559 "*pudique*" becomes used with the plural form. "*Honneste*", which had been associated with "*pudique*" from the very beginning, is associated with "*chaste*" after this date.

Negative Qualifiers

There are four of these:

faulse [false]:   1497; (1496–1515); 1506, 12, 29, 38

folles [mad]:   1538

impudique [immodest]:   1556

mal commencé [badly begun]:   1555, 74, 82

Is it merely by chance that the negative qualifiers first appeared with the plural form, whereas the positive ones were used with the singular form in the first half of the sixteenth century? "*Fol amour*" is found on page 187 of a book from 1556, in the title of a short poem: therefore the singular form existed at that time, although we have not found it in a book title. Yet for the time being we have no proof of its existence before the mid-1500's. It is in 1556 also that "*impudique*" is first found as the opposite of "*chaste*".

Clearly, profane love was considered — at least in one part of society at the end of the Middle Ages — as insane behaviour in comparison with celestial love. The use of the plural form perhaps underlined how unstable and ephemeral love of man is, for, whereas human beings are many, there is only one Creator. Divine love gathers people together, whereas profane love affairs cause division. And yet, in our collection of book titles from Lyons, a kind of profane love tries to become accepted as "*vrai amour*" after 1503, because it claims to be "*honneste*" and "*pudique*". Such love, which is probably Platonic love,[2] gradually acquires this honourable nature and becomes accepted as that which we call "*l'amour*", i.e. profane love in general. This seems to be established around the mid-1500's: at that time, the positive qualifiers are seen to be used with the plural form as well, whereas the negative ones are sometimes used to qualify a singular. A period of ambiguity begins, which is still in existence today. It is worth noting, moreover, that no negative adjective qualifies love after 1560, at least not in those books which appear from their titles to be profane.

Appendix

Chronology of those titles in which neither the lover nor the loved one is specified

Singular	Plural
	c. 1490 *L'hospital damours*
	1497 *Le Grand Blason de faulses amours*
	pre-1500 *...en l'observance d'amours*
	1492-1515 *Les demandes d'amours avec les réponses*
1503 *Le livre de vraye amour*	c. 1500 *La conqueste du chasteau damours*
	1506 *Le Grand Blason des faulses Amours*
	1512 *Le Grand Blason des faulses Amours*
	1513-1538 (Avignon) *La Fontaine d'Amours*
	1515-1533 *Le Sophologue damours*
	1516-1527 *Lalant et le venant du chasteau damours*
1520 *Le Peregrin traictant de l'honneste et pudique amour*	
1527 *Le jugement d'amour*	1527 *Les 51 arrests donnés au grand conseil damours*
	1527 *Le petit messagier damours*

1528 *Le peregrin...l'honneste et pudique
    amour*
1528 *La prison d'amour*
1529 *Le peregrin...l'honneste et pudique
    amour*
1529 *...préceptes et documents sur l'amour*

1517-1567 *A Cupido le Dieu d'Amour*

1530-1531 *...preceptes et documents contre
    l'amour*
1532 *Le jugement damour*
1533 *Le LIIe arret d'amour*
1533 *Le Peregrin...l'honneste et pudique
    amour*
1533 *Le LIIe arrest d'amour*

1536 *...preceptes et documents contre lamour.*
1537 *Le pourquoy d'amour*
1544 *Colloque du vray, pudic et sincere
    amour, concilié entre deux
    amans...plusieurs autorités et spirituels
    propos*
1545 *La Fontaine d'Amour*
1546 *Colloque du vray pudic et sincere
    amour*
1547 *La Nouvelle Venus par laquelle est
    entendue pudique Amour*
1547 *Le Tuteur d'amour.* . . . .
1547 *Opuscules d'amour*
1548 *...conformeté de l'amour au navigaige*
1549 *...de quels boys se chauffe Amour*

1551 *Leon Hebreu de l'amour, t. I,
    Dialogues d'amour*
1551 *Philosophie d'Amour de Leon Hebreux*
1552 *momerie de 5 postes d'amour*
1552 *Les Azolains de Mgr Bembo, de la
    Nature d'Amour*
1553 *Amour immortelle*
1554 *1er églogue de F. Baptiste de
    l'honneste amour*
1555 *...d'éviter l'amour mal commencée*
1555 *L'amant ressuscité de la mort d'amour*
1555 *Les Affections d'Amour de Parthenius
    Les Narrations d'Amour de Plutarche*
1555 *...aux soudars d'amour et aux bacheliers
    et apprentis d'amour.* . . . .
1555 *Debat de folie et d'amour*
1556 *...profit du chaste amour... domage de
    l'impudique*
1558 *L'amant resuscité de la mort d'amour*

1528 *Lalant et le venant du chasteau
    damours*

1529 *Le Grand Blason des faulses amours*

1529 *Les deux soeurs disputant d'amours*
1528-1536 *...toutes les regles damours*
1517-1567 *Le siege damours*
1517-1567 *...faulcete de ceux qui suivent le
    train d'amours*

c. 1535 *...des dames suivant le train
    damours*
en amours maint maux ha supporté
1538 *Grand blason des faulses Amours*
1544 *...qui dit si proprement d'Armes
    d'Amours et de sespassions*

la fortune de l'Innocent en amours

1550 *Les Angoisses et remedes d'amours du
    Traverseur*

Epître d'un nouvel relevé du mal d'amours
1555 *L'Amour des Amours*

1558 *Questions d'Amour*
1559 *Philosophie d'Amour de Leon Hebreu*
1559 *Lamentation et complainte d'un*
   prince...à l'encontre de sa Dame

1559 *...devis joyeux surla police d'amours*

1561 *Devises d'Armes et d'Amours*
1570 *Complainte que fait un amant contre*
   amour et sa Dame
1570 *La Fontaine d'Amours*
1570 *Questions d'amour*
1572 *Le Jardin d'Amour*
   La Fontaine d'amour

1572 *Les Amours d'Olivier de Magny*
1573 *Instruction pour les jeunes dames sur*
   l'amour, le mariage
1574 *...punition de ceux qui contemnent et*
   mesprisent le vray amour
1574 *...d'éviter l'amour mal commencé*
1576 *...en forme d'un discours de la nature*
   d'amour

1576 *Les aventures estranges d'armes et*
   d'amours de...
1577 *...honnestement se gouverner en amour*
1577 *...tant de l'amour que de la guerre*

1577 *Aventures estranges d'Armes et*
   d'Amours de...
1578 *Chant Anterotique sur une vision*
   d'Amour et Prudence
1580 *...tant de l'amour que de la guerre*
1581 *...étranges effets d'un amour chaste et*
   honneste
1581 *...traittans partie de l'amour, partie de*
   la guerre

1581 *...hauts et chevalereux faits d'amours*
   du prince Méladius
1581 *Dialogue de l'amour honneste*
1581 *Les déclamations, procédures et arrets*
   d'amours
1582 *...d'éviter l'amour mal commencée*
1582 *...les variables et etranges effets de*
   l'honneste Amour
1583 *...bien et honnestement se gouverner*
   en amour
1583 *...questions d'amour*
1583 *La prison d'Amour*

1583 *...mignardises et devis d'amours*
1586 *...partie de l'amour et partie de la*
   guerre
1588 *...tant de l'amour que de la guerre*

1588 *Jardins d'amours La Fontaine*
   d'amours
1591 *Le premier livre de la Flamme d'amour*
1592 *Les effets de l'amour*
1592 *Demandes et responses que les*
   amoureux font en l'amour
1592 *...les divers effets d'Amour*
1592 *Le premier livre de la Flamme d'Amour*
1593 *...les miseres de la guerre et de la force*
   de l'Amour
1595 *Lettres douces pleines de désirs et*
   imaginations d'Amour
1595 *Philosophie d'amour de M. Leon*
   Hebreu
1595 *Le repentir d'amour de Dieromène*

1596 *...la complainte que fait un amant
   contre Amour et sa Dame*
1596 *Questions d'amour*
1597 *...Equicola...De la nature d'Amour
   tant humain que divin*
1598 *...Equicola...De la nature d'Amour
   tant humain que divin*
1598 *...la vengeance d'Amour envers ceux
   qui médisent de l'honneur des Dames*
1599 *Lettres douces, pleines de désirs et
   imaginations d'Amour*
1599 *Les chastes et delectables jardins
   d'Amour*

Chapter 4

The "Créantailles" Rite in Troyes Between the Fifteenth and Seventeenth Centuries

Even those historians who are interested in popular culture and peasant customs have long neglected the data provided by folklore; perhaps this is because they felt incapable of judging its value by means of "historical criticism". Despite their interest in the past, folklorists, for their part, have frequently considered folklore to lie outside the study of history. Though historians and European ethnologists have been conversing and working together for several years now, the problem of the relationship between folklore and the prevailing culture remains difficult to resolve and is rarely studied.

It is appropriate to situate this article within the context of thoughts concerning this problem. The "*créantailles*", subject of this article, was a popular rite fundamental in the formation of couples in Champagne, although up until now folklorists have paid little attention to it.[1] This article will be based on information from a series of documents familiar to historians: the trials for broken promises of marriage preserved in the archives of the *officialité* of Troyes.[2] After first describing the rite itself as depicted in fifteenth and sixteenth century trials, we will look at why it disappeared from such trials in the second half of the seventeenth century.

CREANTAILLES IN THE FIFTEENTH AND SIXTEENTH CENTURIES

The French verb *"créanter"* (or *"cranter"*), a term of feudal jurisprudence, seems to have existed only in Champagne with the meaning referred to here. According to the *Dictionnaire de Trévoux*, "the people of Champagne say...*créanter* a young woman" meaning "to promise her, to give her in marriage". As we shall see, the meaning of the word, as shown in the fifteenth and sixteenth century trials, is not exactly the same. For us, the most important part of this eighteenth century evidence is the claim that it is a regional word: this is the first indication of the localised, and hence popular, nature of the *créantailles* rite. Moreover, the fact that fifteenth and sixteenth century judges in Troyes Latinised the word *"créantailles"* so readily was no doubt because the Church's Latin contained no word which corresponded exactly to this practice among the faithful.

Granted, out of eighty-nine trials in this period, only twenty-eight use the term: the others refer only to *fiançailles*, to various promises, to "marriage contracted" or to be solemnised,[3] etc. Thus, it is important to first analyse the terminology of the time.

Promises of marriage could be exchanged in various ways, with varying degrees of solemnity and ritual. For example there is the case of Jean Guillot, a fuller by trade *(27^A)*: when his wife was ill, he "promised [his servant] Jeannette several times that he would marry her if his wife died". Once his wife was dead, "he renewed his promises". After that, he "deflowered" Jeannette and had sexual intercourse with her several times, the result being that she gave birth to a child which he provided for. What does Jeannette ask for? A dowry of twenty *livres tournois*. Neither she nor the *promoteur*,[4] and even less the judges, consider such promises followed by intercourse to be a marriage.

Yet numerous other cases, which, at first glance, seem similar, are considered to be marriages which are *"accompli"* or at least started. For example, Didière Beloce testifies that, over the previous two years, while she was living at the home of Jeannin Benoît's father, Jeannin asked her several times to "give herself to him". Before she would give in to his demands, he "promised to take her as his wife. *Didière, for her part, promised to take him as her husband.* They had intercourse for the first time in the accused's father's barn." At the time of the trial, Didière, whom Jeannin had "deflowered", was pregnant with his child. The *promoteur* concluded that "the accused and Didière are sentenced to have *the marriage which they contracted and even consummated* by their physical relations, solemnised by the Church" *(19^A)*. Whereas Jean Guillot had merely promised marriage to his servant, Jeannin Benoît and Didière Beloce exchanged promises of marriage, which is very different. It was the reciprocity of promises which made the marriage. There is every reason to suppose that such promises were given in a solemn way, using established phrases, similar to those used by Pierre Pellart, also known as Mordienne, when he promised marriage to Jean Jacomart's widow: "I promise you, Marguerite," he said, "that I will never have another wife than you until I die", and Marguerite replied: "Pierre, I promise you upon my faith that I will never have another husband than you until I die"; and while saying that they held hands *(76^A)*. Such "words which make a marriage" — as they were called by those accused who denied having spoken them *(3^A, 7^A)* — were ritual, even if they are slightly different from one trial to another and from one deposition to the next within the same trial.

Nevertheless, even though theologians, canonists and judges of the time considered a man and woman to be permanently united by this simple exchange of words, the faithful often required more. Such is the case for Jeanne, daughter of the late Thévenin Dame, who, giving in to Jean Duchasne's entreaties, opened her door to him one night. After they "spoke of marriage", he "promised to marry her before the feast of St Martin". She replied "that it meant nothing to speak of it if he did not give her anything in the name of marriage". Therefore he gave her "one *grand blanc** which she received in the name of marriage" *(18^A)*. This ritual of a gift given in the name of marriage, which was necessary to overcome Jeanne's distrust, was very common in the diocese of Troyes in the fifteenth and sixteenth centuries. It even seems to have been an essential part of the *créantailles* rite, since we are told that Henri Thibault promised his daughter named Marguerite *"ex uno pomo seu piro"* [with a fruit tree or pear tree] *(44^A)*. Since the Church did not deem this necessary in order to contract a marriage, it was apparently of popular origin.

To judge by the thirty or so trials which describe these ritual gifts, exactly what was given was of little significance: in three cases the gift was one or several coins; in two cases it was a traditional woollen belt called a *"chanjon"*, a length of ribbon, a pin, a plain ring, a ring set with stones or silver canes; in one case a picture of Notre-Dame in silver, a

---

* the *grand blanc* was a form of currency, equal to 13 *deniers*.

pewter goblet, woollen braid, a red *hoqueton*,[5] a spray of gladioli, a blackthorn branch, two bunches of grapes, a pear, a piece of cake, soup and even a tune on a flute. In three cases, the young people gave each other a drink — wine or water; in three cases, their hands were joined and, in a fourth, they "touched each other's hand"; and lastly, in three cases, the young man kissed the young woman in the name of their marriage, the kiss usually occurring after another gift or an exchanging of words and marking the end of the ceremony. It is worth mentioning that two men stretched the ritual's tolerance to the limit: Pierre Pellart, after promising marriage to Jean Jacomart's widow, said to her as he took her in his arms on his bed: "Look, Marguerite, so that you are not afraid that I might abuse you, I will put my tongue in your mouth in the name of marriage"(76[A]). The other, Pierre Charles, "deflowered" Guillemette Cornivault in the name of marriage. Guillemette, "when asked whether he gave her something in the name of marriage, said no, but that, when they had intercourse, he told her that he was doing the act in the name of marriage, and that that was enough" (46[A]).

Of the approximately thirty trials which describe the ritual associating of a gift and words of marriage, two thirds call the ritual "*créantailles*". We have every reason to believe that the ritual was identical in the eight other *créantailles* trials, in which the ritual is not described; and that, in the ten cases in which a similar ritual is simply called "*mariage clandestin*", "*promesses de mariage*", etc., that it is still the *créantailles* rite.

Such reasoning gives us a total of about forty such *créantailles*, which must be contrasted with about forty cases of "*fiançailles*" in the fifteenth to sixteenth centuries. In most cases neither word is used lightly: according to the *promoteur*, Barbe Georget acknowledged before several people "that she had *créanté* [become pledged to]" François Guillaumat by accepting two bunches of grapes from him, "in the name of marriage", and "despite this she became *fiancée* to another in Church" (62[A]); Marguerite Malot "contracted marriage with two men: Jean Poulain de Magicourt, her *fiancé*, and Colinet Bruley de Pougy, her *créanté*" (23[A]); Robert Couvert and Perrette Durand "became *crantés* a long time ago, not in Church but clandestinely, and despite that, the defendant has since become *fiancé* in Church to another woman" (17[A]). Unlike the "*fiançailles* in Church" — or the notarised contract of marriage which first appear in the trials in the seventeenth century — the *créantailles* ritual did not involve representatives of the authorities, such as a priest or a notary, being present. It is this fact in particular which makes it a popular custom, and which is its most interesting aspect for us here.

No matter what the origin of *fiançailles* may be, in the fifteenth and sixteenth centuries, they were controlled by the Church, at least in the diocese of Troyes: "In order to get married there must always be a *fiansailles* including promises of marriage, saying in the following way: you promise by your faith that you will take such a woman as your wife, if the Holy Church will consent. And then the woman must make the same promise, using similar words".[6]

It is true that in this series of trials, there are some young people who were *fiancés* by laymen. But it is significant that, in two of the four cases, not just any laymen were used: in one case it is the sexton from the priory of Saint-Phal who is said to have pretended as a prank to *fiancer* Antoine Robin, also known as Carteron, with the naïve Denise Basin one Sunday during Lent (42[A]); in the other it is the schoolmaster from Moussey, chosen because of his occupation (71[A]). Barbe Montaigne had just accepted Jean Gratien's proposal of marriage: "Very well, I declare you *fiancés* then", said one of the people present. "You don't even know your ABC, you will not declare us *fiancés*," replied the defendant. Seeing the schoolmaster from Moussey coming towards them, he added: "Here comes the schoolmaster who will declare us *fiancés*"; and asked him to do so.

The Church wanted to be in control of these *fiançailles* and punished those who took the place of the priest. For example, there is the case of Gautier Lebourrelier and Marie, Jean Petit's widow: after living together for a year, they eventually decided to "contract a clandestine marriage by promising marriage at the home of an innkeeper, who, *playing the priest's role, declared them fiancés*". The innkeeper was condemned to paying a fine of two pounds of wax (2[A]). Is it not in order to avoid a similar fate that the schoolmaster from Moussey, when asked to betroth Jean Gratien to Barbe, replied "that it would be better if they promised each other to become *créantés*"? And is this not also why in the presence of judges he remembers only that "the defendant kissed Barbe in the name of marriage", whereas numerous other witnesses saw him leading the so-called *créantailles* as a priest would a *fiançailles* in Church, himself saying the established words in the presence of the engaged couple who were happy merely to reply "yes" or to nod their heads?

Having said this, we must admit to a certain amount of ambiguity in the use made at the time of the terms *créantailles* and *fiançailles*. For example there is the case of Geoffroy Babeau and Marguerite Hugot

(34^A): when they were young adolescents, the boy gave a gladiolus to the girl — perhaps as a game — while saying to her: "Here, Margarete, I give you this in the name of marriage". Those who were present then took their bread and "like little children", broke it and cut it "over their aprons" and said: "They are *fiancés*, let us celebrate the *fiansailles*; they are *créantez*". Can we attribute the confusion between the two terms here to childish ignorance or to the playful atmosphere of the scene? In any case, the two engaged couples were declared *fiancés* by the official on 18 May 1504 — proof that previously they were not considered engaged in the eyes of the Church.

There is ambiguity in the opposite sense in the case of Jean Mercier and Jeannette Brodey who "contracted a marriage *de futuro* in the presence of their parents and who became "*créantés per manum sacerdotis*" [by the hand of the priest] (40^A). This is, however, the only case of its kind.

In general, no priest was present for the *créantailles*, whereas the priest presided over the *fiançailles*. In addition, the structure of the two ceremonies was different. In the *fiançailles* — as we can conclude from the Troyes trials, from the synodal statutes of 1374 and from a ritual traditional in Troyes[7] — only the priest spoke, the couple contenting themselves with agreeing, making the required gestures and repeating his words. The priest united their hands as a symbolic gesture. The words used reinforced the couple's semi-passivity, because they said they "had been *fiancés* by the priest" more often than "having *fiancé* their intended". In the *créantailles* rite, on the other hand, the young people were ordinarily more active; and the verb "*créanter*" was more often used in the active form: the young man would *créanter* the young woman, the young woman would *créanter* the young man or they would *créanter* "each other" or "mutually". When the ceremony took place with the families present, at the father's instigation, he never said that he had *créanté* his daughter as was said in other regions or other times that a father had "promised her" or "given her" to such and such a person.

Does this mean that young people always became *créantés* on their own initiative and freely? Obviously not: some cases show that they could do so under pressure from their parents, guardians or masters. There was pressure from the master, for example, in the *créantailles* of Robert Couvert and Perrette Durant (17^A). Four months earlier, his mistress had spoken to him of "marrying said Perrette, and finally, after speaking to him of it several times, she said to him: 'You must become engaged to her. Give her something in the name of marriage'.

He immediately gave her a length of ribbon and said: 'I give you this length of ribbon in the name of marriage, if God and the Holy Church are in agreement', according to what Perrette said, or without saying anything, if one believes the defendant".

There was pressure from guardians in the case of Marguerite Cadenelle and Gabriel Songis (*63^A*). According to the *promoteur*, "the defendants became *créantés* clandestinely in the following manner: the defendant gave Marguerite a ribbon in the name of marriage and she accepted it as such". As for Marguerite, she says "that she was forced by her guardians" to contract the intended marriage and that she has not reached a marriageable age, given that she is only ten or eleven years old.

Lastly, parental pressure is particularly obvious in the *créantailles* of Jeanne Runjat and Jean Maillart (*80^A*). "The day after the feast of St Christopher, the defendant was called several times by her father to contract her *crantailles* with the plaintiff. At first she refused to come, but in the end, for fear of her father, whom — according to the witness' testimony — she feared like fire, she came: 'Come here', her father said to her immediately, 'here is Jehan Maillart, to whom I want to give you in marriage. Will you marry him?' — 'Whatever you want, father', she replied. Then a cousin of the plaintiff said: 'Come, Jehan, give her something to drink in the name of marriage'. However the witness does not know whether Jean Maillart became *créanté* to his sister — in fact she claims to have only pretended to drink the wine offered in the name of marriage — but he does know that shortly afterwards she threw herself on the bed and remained there all that day and the next, crying and lamenting."

True, in the vast majority of trials studied, the young people became *créantés* of their own initiative, without their parents being present. But such *créantailles* were more likely to come to trial because they were more clandestine, less well thought out and often contrary to the parents' wishes. Thus, it is entirely possible, probable even, that those *créantailles* carried out with the families present and with the parents' consent, which are in the minority in the trials we have studied, were the majority in real life.

We have commented on the diversity of objects given in the name of marriage and their often unorthodox nature. Is it possible that, in the choice of such objects, a form of humour was being expressed, which was equally part of the *créantailles* tradition. One example might be the case of Nicolas Estrapel (*8^A*) for example, who was reported to have said to several witnesses: "You don't know this, but

I became *créanté* to Jehanne and gave her bread in the name of marriage". Yet before we pay too much attention to this idea, it is worth noting that such unorthodox gifts are not seen in those ceremonies carried out within the family. When their parents were present, the couple gave each other a glass of wine $(5^A, 80^A)$, a length of ribbon $(17^A, 63^A)$, a kiss (5^A), a ring (53^A), silver canes (84^A), all of which appear to be ritualistic. This suggests that the unorthodox nature of objects given in the name of marriage was not part of the *créantailles* tradition: no doubt it results merely from the lack of preparation for clandestine *créantailles*. One of the partners took advantage of an opportunity to become betrothed to the other who, often caught unawares, went along with it. In fifteenth and sixteenth century society such rites were so binding that anyone who was caught unawares would find himself well and truly betrothed.

The trial brought by Nicole Loyseau against Claude Nonnette in 1499 (22^A) is proof of this. According to the plaintiff, Claude gave her a cup of water a month before, saying: "Here, drink this in the name of marriage". Nicole claimed to have taken the cup, saying: "I take it", and to have drunk in the name of marriage. Afterwards, the defendant is said to have boasted several times of having become *créanté* to Nicole. The *promoteur* rules that Nicole and Claude be condemned to solemnise the marriage in Church. However, according to witnesses' testimony, it seems that Claude Nonette was in the home of his master, who works in the oil trade, with several young women, one of whom, who was not Nicole, said to him: "My darling love, give me something to drink". Claude, taking some water in the cup, replied: "Take this, drink it in the name of marriage." It was Nicole who took the cup in her hand and drank, but without saying anything. One of the witnesses afterwards heard her say to the defendant: "Is giving someone a drink in the name of marriage becoming *créanté?*" Ruling on his intentions at the moment of the gift, the judges dismissed the charges against the defendant. However, it is significant that Nicole believed that she could force the young man to marry her because she had by chance taken a glass of water intended for another; and that Claude, without even attempting to debate his intentions, was afraid that he might indeed be forced to marry her.

We have not yet discovered what role the *créantailles* rite played in the process of the forming of the couple and what its function was in the fifteenth and sixteenth centuries.

The following story is almost unique in the series of trials we have examined, but might in actual fact have been common, if not normal

(5^A). The defendant, Jean Biret, had asked Henriette, Baudonnet Le-
gouge's widow, to become his wife several times since Christmas. She
replied that she consented. The evening before the Purification, the
defendant, being at Henriette's father's house, said that if her father
agreed he would very much like to have Henriette as his wife. Her
father said that he agreed since his daughter agreed. Henriette then
said to her father: "Because you agree, I agree as well". So the father
told his daughter to sit at the table beside Jean Biret, then he poured
some wine into a glass and told Jean Biret to give his daughter a drink
in the name of marriage. Jean Biret obeyed without saying anything.
Henriette drank without saying anything either. After that, Henriette's uncle said to her: "Give Jean something to drink in the name
of marriage as he gave you something to drink". Henriette gave the
defendant something to drink. He drank from her hand, then said: "I
want you to accept a kiss from me in the name of marriage", and he
kissed her. Then those who were there said to them: "You are *crantez*
to each other; I remember the wine". The defendant replied: "That is
correct". Thus, this was a prudent *créantailles*, following as it did the
young man's proposal, the young woman's acceptance, and the agreement of her family. One might assume that the next step was the
marriage being solemnised in Church.

In fact there was a trial because Jean Biret no longer wanted to get
married. He denied the whole story. Because her only witnesses were
her own relatives, the authenticity of Henriette's story could not be
established. That was believed to justify the *promoteur's* decision that
the *créantailles* had been carried out clandestinely, a surprising decision at first glance. He concluded that the agreement should be purged
of its clandestine nature and Henriette requested the same ruling in
other words: that Jean Biret "be sentenced to solemnise their *fiançailles*
in Church".

Various facts suggest that there was conflict between the secular
créantailles rite and the religious *fiançailles* rite: the 1734 synodal statutes which rule that the rite of *fiançailles* is necessary; the legal proceedings against laymen who usurped the priest's place in the
ceremony, and particularly the *promoteurs'* insistence on condemning
the clandestine nature of *créantailles*, sometimes even when the ceremony took place with the family present. Moreover, it seems that
some couples got married immediately after becoming *créantés*, i.e.
without becoming *fiancés*, whereas others became *fiancés* in Church
without ever being *créantés*: twenty trials would seem to indicate the
former course of action[8] and fifteen the latter.[9]

Yet the trials only indicate this by remaining silent — either on the subject of the *fiançailles* or the *créantailles* — which, strictly speaking, does not prove anything. In addition, nine other trials show young people who, after becoming *créantés* and before actually getting married, became *fiancés* in Church, either of their own initiative,[10] or on the order of an official.[11] Included among these are several prudent couples who had become *créantés* with their families present. Of eleven *créantailles* which were regarded as being clandestine, ten took place without parents present, often in order to thwart their matrimonial plans, and many were followed by sexual relations, which changed the *de futuro* marriage into a consummated marriage. Given the current state of research, the most probable hypothesis is that the *créantailles* and the *fiançailles* in Church were usually two consecutive stages in the process of the formation of the couple, at least until the end of the sixteenth century. There is the example of Nicolas Dare who "was *créanté* to Marguerite Dautruy...on Saturday 23rd of May 1587. They became *fiancés* the following Saturday, the 30th of the same month and married the following Monday, the first of June 1587".[12]

Even in those cases in which the trials make no reference to *fiançailles*, it seems that *fiançailles* in Church were necessary: in sixteenth century parish registers, before the Council of Trent, no marriages are found which were not preceded by *fiançailles* and by the publishing of the bans. When the tribunal sentenced couples who were *créantés* to solemnising their marriages, it is therefore understood that this solemnisation began with the *fiançailles* and the publishing of the banns, culminated with the wedding ceremony and no doubt lasted until the benediction of the marriage bed.

As for the *créantailles*, we never find mention of them following after the *fiançailles*: they always preceded them. On the other hand, in the few fifteenth and sixteenth century trials which report some kind of financial agreement between the partners — or between their parents such an agreement, takes place before the *créantailles*. It was "after his parents and the plaintiff's parents had between them agreed a *covenant relating to his marriage* to the said Jeanne" that Jean Maillart "became *créanté* to her" and that they drank one after the other in the name of marriage *(80^A)*. Similarly, in the proceedings begun against Catherine Gent *(84^A)*, "the plaintiffs state that *after an agreement between the parents of the two parties*, François gave the defendant two silver canes in the name and the loyalty of marriage and she accepted them in the name of such, and afterwards they were *fiancés* in Church". Such agreements might also occur in marriages arranged directly by the two young people, without their families' intervention. Thus Guillemette, daughter of the late Jean Martin, said that, "when agreeing their covenant of marriage, Jean Charbonnat had told her that he owed only 10 or 12 *livres tournois* in debts"; and it is not until after these covenants that he gave her "a silver picture of Notre-Dame in the name of marriage and that she accepted it as such" *(82^A)*. In all these cases, the secular *créantailles* ceremony was to solemnise the financial agreement between the young people or their families, like the notarised contracts which appear later in our series of trials.

It goes almost without saying that in the fifteenth and sixteenth centuries neither the *fiançailles* in Church nor the *créantailles* rite were as sacrosanct as the sacrament of marriage: couples who were *créantés* or *fiancés* could, through mutual consent, have their union dissolved by an official. Three trials show this *(1^A, 78^A, 87^A)*. Nonetheless, the legal strength of the *créantailles* at this time must be stressed: "When any man has given a promise of marriage to any woman, the priest must in no way marry him to another woman...if there were not an obvious and clear reason whey they could not or should not marry each other", stipulated the 1374 synodal statutes (loc. XXI). In the same way, the trials we have studied show that when a woman had become *créantée* to one man then *fiancée* to another in Church, the tribunal chose to break off the *fiançailles* *(16^A, 17^A)*. Moreover, the passage of time in no way weakened the legal effectiveness of the rite: Geoffroy Babeau and Marguerite Hugot, for example, were brought before the tribunal eight years after becoming *créantés*. And, even though they had perhaps only done it as a game, in their earliest adolescence, the tribunal sentenced them to solemnising their marriage. Thus it must be accepted that, far from trying to cause the secular *créantailles* rite to disappear and to replace it with the ecclesiastical *fiançailles* rite, the Church in the Middle Ages accepted and supported the *créantailles* with all its powers. Admittedly it added the religious rites of *fiançailles* and marriage in Church, but it did recognise the *créantailles* as being the first of the rites in the formation of the couple.

One could even wonder whether this rite, in the form and with the effectiveness which we know it to have had in the fifteenth and sixteenth centuries, the popular and secular nature of which we have constantly stressed, might not, however, have been largely dependent on the rites and doctrine of the medieval Church. Indeed, the words spoken by the couple were similar to those which they exchanged in the presence of the priest, at a *fiançailles* ceremony or marriage, and they were very respectful of the Church's will. Moreover, there is nothing which proves that before Christianity in Champagne — or before the triumph of the Lombard doctrine of Christian marriage — young people were able to contract marriages against their parents' will so easily and so effectively, through such *créantailles*; and, on the other hand, it is obvious that this popular practice is in perfect agreement with the doctrines of medieval theologians and canonists. We shall now see that the issuing of new marriage regulations caused all trace of the *créantailles* to disappear from trials for broken promises of marriage and caused other rites to appear. It is very likely that these other rites already existed in the Middle Ages, in this region as well as in others, and that the *créantailles* did not disappear from popular practice in the seventeenth century. But obviously the *créantailles* had been recognised by legislation in the Middle Ages and this was no longer so in the seventeenth century. As a result their legal ineffectiveness made their eventual disappearance inevitable.

THE DISAPPEARANCE OF THE *CREANTAILLES* RITE IN THE SEVENTEENTH CENTURY

Not only does the word "*créantailles*" no longer appear in any trials for broken promises of marriage in the period 1665–1700,[13] but it seems that the very phenomenon of the *créantailles* also disappeared, i.e. the association of ritual words and symbolic gifts which bound the couple together irrevocably.

Admittedly promises of marriage still exist in the seventeenth century, and to be valid, they must still be reciprocated: thus one can assume that some type of formal procedure remained. The fact that they were often exchanged with the couple's relatives present is an additional indicator of formality. For example, Jean Ganichon and Claude Prestat promised to marry each other "at a gathering of their relatives" *(39^B)*; as for Elizabeth Bernard, she exchanged her promises with Jean Grosos "in the presence of her mother, grandmother, uncle, aunt, family and friends" *(8^B)*. But, whereas so many trials in the fifteenth and sixteenth centuries reported the words spoken by each of the partners, none of those from the seventeenth century seem to trouble themselves to do so. This might suggest that the words spoken have become less ritualistic.

As far as other rites for promising marriage are concerned, six trials stress the existence[14] or absence[15] of written promises and seven refer to notarised[16] or to uncertified[17] marriage contracts, whereas none of the above were ever mentioned in fifteenth and sixteenth century trials.[18] The increasing importance of the written form seems to take the place of oral promises, which decline in ritual value. Moreover, the royal declaration dated 26 November 1639 makes the new rites compulsory in the kingdom: article 7 forbade "all judges, even those of the Church, to receive proof by witnesses of promises of marriage, or in any way other than in writing, which must be carried in the presence of four close relatives of both parties, even if they are of lowly station".[19] We must note however that the transition from the oral to the written was slow — which indicates that it was only done as the result of a decree — and that it was far from being accomplished by the end of the seventeenth century: of one hundred and fourteen trials for broken promises of marriage, one hundred and six seem to have involved oral promises only. Admittedly, the 1639 declaration was complied with in that no witnesses were ever called in order to establish whether such promises had been made. Yet, in these one hundred and six trials, the judges based their decisions on the oath taken by those involved to have promised or not to have promised marriage, rather than on the examination of any written documents.

A third factor which indicates the disappearance of the *créantailles* rite is that no trials in the period 1665–1700 refer to gifts given in the name of marriage which, in the fifteenth and sixteenth centuries, were a way of symbolically reinforcing the sacred nature of the words exchanged. On the other hand, twenty-five of them refer to "*arrhes*" [literally, a "deposit", in the sense of "payment as a pledge for fulfilment of contract"] being given or received "in the name of said promises" and it is important to know whether such *arrhes* were not just another name for the the gifts in the name of marriage found in the traditional *créantailles* ceremony.

Obviously the *arrhes* mentioned here are not one of the rituals in the wedding ceremony:[20] they were made before the wedding as were the gifts in the name of marriage before them. Like the latter, the former seem to have been intended to reinforce — or ratify — the promises of marriage. Indeed promises and *arrhes* are often linked in the accounts of trials: either the defendant admits to having made the one and received the other $(51^B, 79^B)$ or she claims to have promised nothing and to have received nothing by way of *arrhes* $(46^B, 69^B, 92^B, 11^B)$; she either uses expressions such as "having received twelve *livres* and a muff by way of *arrhes* for these [promises]" (51^B), or "in the name of said promises" $(7^B, 65^B)$ or "in the name of said marriage" (128^B). Moreover, the paying of the *arrhes* apparently took place in a ceremony at least as solemn as the one in which the promises were made: for example Marie Huot, who exchanged promises of marriage with Jean Besançon, refers to "*arrhes* received in the presence of his father" (79ᴮ), whereas she does not feel it necessary to specify how or in whose presence the promises were exchanged.

Lastly, it is clear that in the seventeenth century the paying of a deposit did not constitute a new ritual: on the contrary it was an ancient rite, clearly documented in the wedding ceremonies in pagan Rome and which the Church introduced into northern Europe during the Middle Ages.[21] However, the Troyes trials did not mention it in the fifteenth and sixteenth centuries[22] — and said almost nothing of contracts of marriage, which the deposit was long intended to ratify. Thus we may wonder whether the gifts in the name of marriage given during the *créantailles* in Champagne might not have been a mutation of the *arrhes* given formerly; and whether the reappearance of the *arrhes* — and of contracts of marriage — in seventeenth century trials might not be explained by the romanising of the judges' vision — of which there are many examples, as much among judges of the Church as among lay judges — rather than by a change in the rituals involved in the formation of the couple.

Even if the gifts in the name of marriage in the fifteenth and sixteenth centuries, and the *arrhes* in the seventeenth were one and the same thing, the change in name is still significant: perhaps it reflects the judges' desire to get rid of the concept of the *créantailles*. In fact, there are many differences between such *arrhes* and gifts in the name of marriage.

The first of these is that *arrhes* appear to have been paid after the promises of marriage and not at the same time: Joachim Simon speaks of the marriage begun between himself and Savine Dieu, "followed by the contract and the writ", and Savine acknowledges that there were "promises of marriage, a contract agreed and a writ given in favour of said promises" (7ᴮ). In the same way, Elisabeth Bernard acknowledges that between herself and Jean Grosos "there was a contract of marriage agreed between the two parties, *after which* a *fiançailles* took place and four gold rings were given to her by said Groos" (8ᴮ). The majority of the other trials provide no indication as to when the deposit was paid, but none of them imply that it was given and received at the same time as the promises.

Secondly, such deposits were usually of greater value than the gifts formerly given in the name of marriage. Unorthodox objects such as a pear, soup, a blackthorn branch, or a tune for a flute are no longer found, but rather rings $(7^B, 8^B, 16^B, 24^B, 53^B, 57^B, 127^B)$, crosses of gold and silver $(16^B, 57^B)$, gold monograms (57^B), silver and gold Madonnas (53^B), a purse embroidered in silver and gold (16^B), other pieces of silverware $(3^B, 69^B)$ or even a sum of money $(16^B, 51^B, 53^B)$, or presents which were utilitarian or flattering to the woman (53^B). We have every reason to believe that these *arrhes* given to the young woman by the young man after the promises, after the notarised contract, or even after the *fiançailles*, were no longer regarded as a symbol, as they were in the fifteenth and sixteenth centuries, but rather as a guarantee of these promises. Indeed legal manuals define the word *"arrhes"* as follows: "Usually the *fiancé* gives presents to the *fiancée*, which she retains, in case the *fiancé* refuses to fulfil the promise of marriage."[23]

Lastly, it must be pointed out that there was inequality between the sexes insofar as the paying of a deposit is concerned. In the fifteenth and sixteenth centuries, it might be that the young woman gave her loved one an object in the name of marriage first $(6^A, 12^A, 41^A)$, or that she gave him a gift after he gave her one, which re-established the balance $(1^A, 6^A, 68^A)$. In the seventeenth century, on the other hand, it was always the young man who paid the deposit — in the Troyes trials at least — the young woman merely receiving it without giving anything identical or similar in return. In order to explain this imbalance, it must be understood that a young woman's honour suffered more than the young man's should there be a broken engagement: thus the *arrhes* might have been intended as a means of dissuading the young man from breaking off his promise and of compensating the damage done to the young woman's honour if indeed he did break it off.

Thus, the *arrhes* referred to in the seventeenth century Troyes trials are definitely very different from the gifts in the name of marriage in the fifteenth and sixteenth centuries. Any relationship which might have existed between the *arrhes* and the gifts would indicate the impact of judicial practice on the rituals of the formation of the couple in popular practice, rather than on its unchanging nature.

No matter what form they took, it is indubitable that in the seventeenth century promises of marriage lost the sacred nature which they had in the fifteenth and sixteenth centuries; and this obviously had a more drastic effect on the *créantailles* rite than had all the changes in form.

Promises of marriage obviously remained somewhat binding, if not sacred, because the Bishop's tribunal continued to be the only means of dissolving them. However, whereas in the fifteenth and sixteenth centuries they were usually only dissolved for serious and canonical reasons, in the second half of the seventeenth century the reasons for dissolution were much more numerous, sometimes trivial or even unstated. The reasons given by the young man who wants to break his promises and those upon which the tribunal bases its decision are of little importance: with few exceptions,[24] the result of the trial is always the same, the promises are cancelled. Thus, even if the ritual of the *créantailles* had survived despite not being mentioned in the records, it is obvious that it had lost most of its effectiveness.

We shall now look at the causes and consequences of these changes. The main reason for such promises' loss of significance is to be found in the new definition of marriage given by the Council of Trent. The *Tametsi* decree, admittedly, repeated that "clandestine marriages made freely by the consent of the parties, are real and accomplished marriages, as long as the Church has not annulled them". Yet it removed their legal effectiveness by stipulating that "the holy Synod declares it utterly impossible for anyone to try to contract a marriage other than in the presence of the *curé* — or of a priest having a licence from the *curé* himself or from the Ordinary — and of two or three witnesses, and declares null and void — by virtue of this decree which invalidates and annuls them — any marriages contracted in this way".[25]

According to the royal declaration of 1639, that would mean that this form of marriage in front of witnesses and with the services of a priest were "not only necessary because of the precept" — i.e. compulsory on pain of mortal sin — "but also required for the sacrament".[26] Thus, ecclesiastical tribunals were henceforth able to "un-unite" those who got married clandestinely without being affected by the Scriptures' "What therefore God has joined together, let no man put asunder".[27] Not only were they able to do so, but, in a situation in which one of the betrothed no longer wanted to get married, tribunals had to do so in order to guarantee the contracting parties complete freedom of consent at the decisive moment of the marriage in Church.

The royal jurists' interpretation of the *Tametsi* decree was not however indisputable to all theologians. If clandestine marriages had been real marriages in God's eyes for centuries, was it possible that all of a sudden, solely because of an ambiguous and controversial decree, this was not longer so? Had not the fathers of the council, in the same decree, stressed the value of such marriages and condemned "with anathema those who deny that such marriages are real and accomplished"? In 1581, the provincial council of Rouen apparently continued to consider such marriages to have a certain amount of sacramental value since it considered anyone who, having clandestinely married another, went on to marry a third person in Church, to be an adulterer. As for the Church's judges, no matter what their understanding of the decree might have been, it is certain that well into the seventeenth century they continued to force some betrothed couples to "solemnise their marriages". Moreover, medieval theologians had always made the distinction between a "marriage by words in the present" and a "marriage of the future": usually the trials for breaking of marriage promises concerned the latter, and the Council of Trent having decreed nothing new concerning them, theologians were thus able to continue to consider promises of marriage as binding as they had in the past.

The Church's judges only ceased judging these cases in this way after it was forbidden by Parliament. "An official abuses his powers when he forces people to make and execute promises of marriage by ecclesiastical censure" declared a ruling on 1st June 1638.[28] Already on the 9 June 1637, after having an appeal referred to it as being an abuse against the Troyes official, Parliament quashed his sentence. During the trial, the counsel for the prosecution had claimed that "until such time as the marriage has been made and solemnised, it is acceptable for the parties to retract and they are perfectly free to do so, all kinds of promises notwithstanding...; if one of the parties refuses to consent to the marriage being celebrated, the official cannot make any other decision."[29]

Although the King's men were giving lessons in liberalism to the Church's judges on this point, we must not forget their intention in doing so. In fact they had been defending parents' powers over the marriage of their children rather than the freedom of the contracting parties for almost a century: the edict of February 1556–1557 concerning children's marriages had allowed parents to disinherit those children who married without their consent; the Blois edict in 1579, followed by the one of January 1629, had invented and strengthened the idea of abduction and seduction which allowed men or women to be put to death for marrying a young man or woman under the age of twenty-five without his or her parents' permission; lastly the royal declaration of 1639 reorganised and completed the system for defending parental authority, by tackling oral promises of marriage and in particular those which were exchanged without any family present. It may be that the ease with which marriage promises could be dissolved, imposed by Parliament, helped young people to escape from marriages which their parents wanted to force them into, as we shall see; but for Parliament the important point seems to have been to allow parents to break off any promises made without their consent.

It remains to be seen to what extent these laws were successful in this aim. Without giving us a definite answer to this question, the records of trials provide several interesting points.

Promises of marriage had been a formidable weapon in the hands of young people who had other ideas for marriage than did their parents: it was enough for them to promise marriage to their loved one before their parents made them contract another engagement; then to make the fact known to the *promoteur* who had the second promise annulled and *sentenced* the lovers to "solemnise the marriage begun between them". In the fifteenth and sixteenth centuries, parents were powerless before such a strategy, unless the unwanted *créantée* was a young woman who had lost her reputation and a member of the young man's family confessed to the tribunal to having had sexual relations with her and several witnesses were found to add weight to his confession. However, the trials from Troyes show only one such plot (69[A]). On the other hand, they suggest that, among the young women who claimed to have become *créantée* to their lover before their fathers made them contract another engagement, there were perhaps those who purely and simply invented such clandestine *créantailles*, or antedated them, and attained their objective with the help of willing witnesses (80[A]). Article 7 of the 1639 declaration is probably based on the desire to prevent such fraudulent manoeuvres on the part of young people.

The new regulations not only dramatically changed judges' attitudes: it also upset the strategy used by young people and by their parents.

Twenty-seven seventeenth century trials tell of parents or guardians of one of the betrothed opposing the marriage which the young people promised to contract. In those cases in which the betrothed is of age, he must still undertake difficult administrative and judicial processes in order to overcome his parents' opposition. Faced with this prospect, no doubt many young people backed down. In the sixteen cases in which the betrothed was a minor — or at least in the fourteen in which we are sure of the sentence — the promises were broken. Thus the royal jurists did not struggle in vain for a century in favour of parental authority.

However, for their part, young people were able to take advantage of the ease with which marriage promises could be dissolved in order to escape from those which their parents had forced them to make. In the fifteenth and sixteenth centuries, promises were only broken for lack of consent in cases of serious violence on the part of the parents or death threats. In the seventeenth century, "violence" or "constraint" are only mentioned in three trials (2^B, 3^B, 109^B), and the judges show little interest in the exact nature or degree of such violence. In seven other cases, one of the betrothed is able to get his promise dissolved because he made it "against his will" (2^B, 32^B), "on his parents' prompting" (32^B, 109^B), "out of respect" (2^B, 3^B, 8^B, 32^B) or "deference" (3^B) for them, in order to "please" them (4^B, 16^B, 114^B), "obey" them (7^B, 32^B) or to "satisfy their wishes" (11^B, 16^B). Although henceforth parents are able to prevent their children from following up promises of marriage made without their agreement, it is however more difficult for them than previously to force them to marry the partner of their choice: docile on the day of the engagement, the child has until the celebration of the marriage to rebel.

Moreover, whereas in the fifteenth and sixteenth centuries couples who did not love each other were still sentenced to solemnise their marriage, in the seventeenth century, judges agree that it is impossible to marry without love. Jeanne Pluot is released from the promise she made to Nicolas Lasnier because she "has never loved and still does not love said Lasnier and would choose death rather than marry him" (2^B); Odart Courtois is released from his promise to Marie Bertrant "for whom he cannot feel friendship" (11^B); Hubert Collot is released from the promise which he exchanged with Marguerite Rosdin, because the scars on her face "make him feel horror and aversion for said Rosdin" (13^B). Such references to feelings, almost absent from fifteenth and sixteenth century trials, are found in the seventeenth century among nobles and the bourgeoisie as well as among the working classes; hence "demoiselle Françoise Mansard" has broken off the promise which she made to François de Courcy, "an equerry, formerly a captain in the company of the light cavalry of Sommièvre, and lord of Louvrigny and Dogny", "given the cooling of said defendant for said plaintiff, and in order to avoid the bad effects which could result from a marriage made against her wishes" (26^B).

Does this prove that marrying for love is becoming normal practice in the second half of the seventeenth century?[30] Nothing is less certain, since the ease with which promises of marriage could be dissolved makes any comparison invalid. Clearly seventeenth century lovers can no longer resort to clandestine marriage, as those in the fifteenth and sixteenth century could. Moreover, those cases, frequent around the middle of the century, in which reference is made to the betrothed couple's feelings, seem to have subsequently become increasingly rare: nine out of twenty between 1665 and 1669, four out of nineteen between 1670 and 1679, five out of fifty-four between 1680 and 1689, and two out of thirty-seven between 1690 and 1699, i.e. approximately 45%, 21%, 7% and 5% respectively. Providing that this is not due to inattention on the part of the archivist, upon who we are dependent, such a change must attract our attention. Yet does this mean that the couples' feelings were considered less and less often — and in particular young men's feelings, six of whom pleaded lack of affection in the first period, then only four in the following decade, then one, then none? Or, on the contrary, does it mean that engagements without love were increasingly rare, particularly among young men? The evidence is all in agreement, but its meaning is ambiguous: of ten cases in which parental constraint is mentioned, seven are from the first five years, and only three from the following thirty years. As for the five trials in which young people complained of having been *fiancés* at too early an age, they all took place during the first ten years.

On the other hand, it is clear that at this time neither public opinion nor even the judges any longer accept the canonical ages for *fiançailles* (seven) nor for marriage (twelve for girls, fourteen for boys). Marguerite Cadenelle's trial *(63^A)*, 1527–1528, reflected earlier attitudes: whether she was as she claimed between ten and eleven years of age, or between thirteen and fourteen as her betrothed alleged, she was barely of a marriageable age when the tribunal "judged her to be *in sponsam de futuro seu creantatam*" [a future wife or *créantée*] to Gabriel Songis. In 1669, on the other hand, Barbe Guénard is released from her promise to Claude Billote, "given the young age of only fourteen which the defendant had reached at the time of said promises...and the fact that she has said that at said time she was not able to decide on her inclinations and affections, which she now recognises that she cannot attach to said plaintiff in order to marry him" *(16^B)*. Two other young women, in 1666 and in 1674, succeeded in having promises they had made dissolved, because of being fourteen at the time. The second said, "in order to end it, that she was only aged fourteen when the promises were made, at which time she could not discern what was good for her, even if three years was taken before the carrying out of said promises in order to decide whether she could feel friendship for said plaintiff" *(35^B)*. Again in 1674, a young man makes it known that he became *fiancé* "at the age of only 17, without under-standing what he was doing" (32^B). Thus clearly there was a gradual change in the ideas as to the youngest age at which young women and men could contract marriage. This change, which had no obvious legal basis, suggests a change in the attitudes towards young people's feelings.

Moreover, this hypothesis was made from the close relationship between the late age at marriage — well established in western Europe as early as the seventeenth century — and the *mariage d'inclination*. It is not impossible that the rise in the average age at marriage between the sixteenth and eighteenth centuries is in part due to the ideological changes which we have just mentioned. However, it could also be explained, conversely, by the legal reinforcement of parental powers. Martin Hurion, prevented by his father from marrying Anne Amiot, proclaims in front of the judges that, "having given his word and his faith to said Amiot, he would like to marry her if it pleases justice to command him thus, protesting, in case of impediment by his father to said marriage, that the only difference he would make in the carrying out of his promise would be to marry her at another time in order to repair the honour of said Amiot, or never to marry" (5^B). Obviously it must be understood that he waited until the age of majority — thirty years of age for young men — before disregarding paternal opposition. In the same way we can suspect that there was a clash between Jeanne Arson's matrimonial intentions and her mother's for her, when Jeanne announces her intention not to "marry before reaching the age of twenty-five" (54^B) — the age of majority for women.

Lastly, the rise in the average age at marriage is no less an ambigu-ous indicator of the increase in *mariages d'inclination* than the former indicators: not only is it probably due to a great extent to economic and social causes,[31] but it could be explained by the reinforcing of parents' authority as much as by greater concern for young people's feelings. In other words, at a time when tribunals accepted the invio-lability of the *créantailles* rite, parents and children were looking to impose their wills by making the first move; in the seventeenth century, however, the strategy of the *fait accompli* is no longer useful, both sides being able to arrange to have engagements with which they are not happy broken off. Thus, henceforth, common wisdom com-mands that parents and children take the time to come to an agree-ment; and when agreement is impossible, children must wait until they reach the age of majority before imposing their choice.

Let us then sum up our findings:

1. In Champagne, in the fifteenth and sixteenth centuries, the series of religious rites of the marriage ceremony were preceded by a secular ceremony, the key part of which was a gift given in the name of marriage. Except for canonical impediment or separation by mutual agreement, this ceremony was considered to link the future married couple irrevocably.

2. Although the *créantailles* rite in Champagne was a popular one, it seem to have been too well adapted to the medieval theologians and canonists' doctrines of marriage not to be related to them in any way. Thus, it remains to be established whether this doctrine created or supported similar secular rites elsewhere.

3. The disappearance of any mention of the *créantailles* in trials from Troyes in the second half of the seventeenth century does not prove that they disappeared from popular practice, particularly since the words "*créanter*" and "*créantailles*" were still being used in Champagne in the eighteenth century.[32] However, they do seem to have been dropped from usage in the nineteenth and twentieth centuries;[33] and, as early as the eighteenth century, from information given in the *Dictionnaire de Trévoux*, it was the father who *créantait* his daughter — as he promised or gave her in marriage in other regions at the same time — whereas in the fifteenth and sixteenth centuries young people used to *créanter* each other. This linguistic change is surely connected in some way with the legal changes which took place in the second half of the sixteenth century and in the seventeenth: for example, with the 1639 declaration which made any promises exchanged without parents' consent or without their presence invalid. At the same time, oral promises, reduced in legal value in favour of written promises and notarised contracts, undoubtedly lost their strong ritualistic element; gifts in the name of marriage seem to have disappeared, or to have changed their nature and significance as well as their name; and the fact that it became easier to get out of promises of marriage in any case caused the *créantailles* to lose their former importance. No doubt seventeenth and eighteenth century peasants were too attached to rituals to have maintained unchanged a ritual which henceforth was of little legal value.

4. It is due to the *créantailles* ritual that many lovers in the fifteenth and sixteenth centuries were able to get married against their parents' wishes; but it is also by means of the *créantailles*, without

the presence of a priest, that parents were able to pledge their children irrevocably — particularly their daughters — into love-less marriages. The number of such forced *créantailles* was no doubt much higher than is suggested by the trials. Thus the decrease in value of the old secular ritual — a decrease in value which was aimed at reinforcing parents' authority and was in fact successful in this — nonetheless allowed many young people to release themselves from engagements contracted against their wishes, under pressure from their parents. In fact, it is difficult to know whether the new matrimonial regulations had the result of increasing or decreasing the *mariage d'inclination;* but it is clear that by upsetting parents' and young people's strategies it contributed — to an extent which it is impossible to specify — to raising the age at marriage, which was a great regulator of the birth rate in the ancient demographic system.

Chapter 5

Love and Marriage in the Eighteenth Century

Love is constantly discussed in Western literature and has been since at least the twelfth century. But this love, with a few notable exceptions, was never marital love and rarely even pre-marital. In the social circles dealt with in writings concerning love, families were preoccupied with their heirs' legitimacy, and love was only tolerated as long as it yielded no children. That does not necessarily mean that only Platonic love was tolerated. In any case, the Church and devout people generally condemned such "profane love" because, in contrast to sacred love, they considered it "insane", "sensual", or "carnal".[1]

On the other hand, the purpose of marriage in all levels of society (not only for Kings and Princes), was to unite two families and to allow them to reproduce, rather than to gratify two young people's love. Even in peasant marriages, material considerations and social prestige were fundamental in the choice of a partner. Consequently there was little moral concern as to whether the couple loved each other: only that they carried out their conjugal duties scrupulously. When the moral code took an interest in their love, it tended to be condemning excesses.[2]

It is clear that this situation has changed. Today, nobody — least of all the Catholic Church — appears to doubt the sanctity of love, at least when it is "real" love, which involves mind, heart and sexuality at the same time. Our society no longer accepts the idea that one can marry — or even remain married — without desire and without love. And, conversely, marriage seems to us so much the necessary out-

come of love that, more and more often, adulterous love affairs lead
to divorce and remarriage.

Love and marriage seemed to come together somewhat more in the
eighteenth century, at least among the social elite. Here, I would just
like to present several indications of this coming together from the
prevailing ideology. Given the current state of research, however, it
is difficult to conclude that the behaviour of the elite really changed
in the eighteenth century. As for the behaviour of the masses, it is not
impossible that it evolved in the opposite direction. This question will
be dealt with in the second half of this chapter.

LOVE AND MARRIAGE IN THE PREVAILING CULTURE

Evidence from Book Titles

We will consider, to start with, the titles of those books — approximately forty-five thousand in number — for which a privilege or tacit
permission was requested from the *Librairie* administration between
1723 and 1789. These titles have been analysed by computer,[3] and
thus, without a great deal of effort, we can see the frequency of, and
the associations between, all the words contained in them. This first
step leads me to make three observations.

Firstly, love and marriage are frequently alluded to:

"*Amour*"	is found in 367	titles
"*Amoureux(se)*" [lover]	38	
"*Aimer*", "*Aimable*" [to love, lovable]	39	
"*Amant(s)*" [lover(s)]	35	
"*Affection*", "*Affectueux*" [affection, affectionate]	35	
"*Coeur(s)*" [heart(s)]	208	
"*Désir(s)*"	15	
"*Passion(s)*"	18	
"*Plaisir(s)*"	69	
"*Sentiment(s)*"	179	
"*Sentimental*"	17	

Having already studied the words in sixteenth and twentieth century titles[4], I come to the conclusion that the frequency of the word

"*amour*" remains constant over five centuries. On the other hand, since the sixteenth century, there has been a considerable increase in the occurrence of "*coeur*" and a significant increase in the idea of "*sentiment*", which did not yet exist at the end of the sixteenth century.[5] It is not until 1785, towards the end of the period in question, that the word "*sentimental*" appears in the series of book titles — at first, it is true, in conjunction with the word "*voyage*", because of the success of *le Voyage sentimental de Mr Yorick*.

As for words relating to marriage, they are also well-represented in the eighteenth century titles. But at first glance, they seem to be neither more or less well-represented than in the sixteenth and twentieth centuries:

"*Mariage*"	is found in 143	titles
"*Mari(s)*" [husband(s)]	21	
"*Marié(e)(s)*" [bride and/or groom]	12	
"*Epoux(se)*", "*Epouser*" [spouse, to marry]	26	
"*Conjoints*", "*Conjugal*" [couple, marital]	13	

Secondly, it is rare to find words relating to love and marriage together. In fact, no allusion is found to marriage nor to marital relations in the thirty-eight titles containing the word "*amoureux*"; in the thirty-nine containing "*aimer*" or "*aimable*"; in the thirty-five containing "*amant(s)*"; in the thirty-five containing "*affection(s)*" or "*affectueux*"; in the two hundred and eight containing "*coeur(s)*"; in the fifteen containing "*désir(s)*"; in the eighteen containing "*passion(s)*"; nor in the sixty-nine containing "*sentiments*".

If some words relating to marriage and to feelings are found together, it is never in more than a small proportion of the titles. Out of three hundred and sixty-seven titles containing the word "*amour*", only thirteen, i.e. 3.8%, allude to marriage; out of seventeen titles containing "*sentimental*", only one, i.e. 5.9%, applies it to marriage. In the same way, and with few exceptions, only a small proportion of the titles containing a word relating to marriage are found to also allude to feelings. Of the one hundred and forty-three titles in which "*mariage*" appears, only four, i.e. 2.8%, allude to feelings; of the twenty-one titles where "*mari(s)*" appears, only two, i.e. 9.5%, allude to feelings. The example of the word "*conjugal*" is therefore an exception since, of the ten titles containing it, six, i.e. 60%, associate it with "*amour*".

Thirdly, the number of titles containing words relating to both love and marriage increased over the century, as the following table shows:

	1723–1749	1750–1769	1770–1789
References to marriage / titles containing "amour"	$\dfrac{1}{29} = 1.1\%$	$\dfrac{3}{123} = 2.4\%$	$\dfrac{9}{152} = 6\%$
References to feelings / titles containing "mariage"	$\dfrac{0}{40} = 0\%$	$\dfrac{1}{34} = 2.9\%$	$\dfrac{4}{69} = 5.7\%$

A similar conclusion can be drawn from the history of the expression *"amour conjugal"* in these titles. During the forty-seven year period ending in 1770, it appears in only one title. Even then it is in the title of a medical book — *"la Génération de l'homme ou le Tableau de l'amour conjugal"* (1731) — which does not appear to refer to the emotional side of marital love, but solely to its physical side. On the other hand, over a twenty-year period after 1770, the expression appears in the titles of five literary works which seem to be concerned with the emotional side of marital love:

1772: *Sophie ou l'Amour conjugal, drame en cinq actes imité de l'anglois*

1775: *Arsace ou De l'amour conjugal, roman oriental*

1780: *L'amour conjugal*

1785: *Anecdotes intéressantes de l'amour conjugal*

1786: *L'Amour conjugal aux abois, anecdote revue et exposée avec précision, par Maître Poulain.*

One should note the indication of anglomania in the first title and the fashion for Oriental tales in the second. No doubt the references to England and to the Orient were necessary in order to gain acceptance for a product which the French public was not yet used to. Moreover, I have the impression that the English had long practised real marital love or been interested in it — many English works and French travellers bear witness to this — and it is not inconceivable that the popularity of marital love in France at the end of the eighteenth century was one of the effects of anglomania.

Comments on Marital Love

Obviously, the idea of marital love is not an eighteenth century invention. It is found as far back as 1694, in the first edition of the

Dictionnaire de l'Académie française — under the headings *AMOUR* and *CONJUGAL*. Even before that time, Thomas Corneille had used the expression; and since the Middle Ages, theologians have spoken of it, mostly, it is true, in Latin. From its appearance in book titles after 1770, I conclude only, that among the elite of the time, there was a passing fad for marital love. This fad was popular enough for several publishers to take the risk of devoting entire books to this subject, which, with one exception, they do not appear to have dared previously.

It must be stressed that, up until the 1770's, Catholic moralists were themselves little interested in marital love, even when dealing with marriage or love. Of eighteen catechisms published between the Council of Trent and the end of the eighteenth century, I found only one which stipulated that couples should love each other: the catechism of the diocese of Blois, published in 1778.[6] Undoubtedly, it is no mere coincidence that it too is dated after 1770. It seems to me it was then a new idea to require of couples something other than external signs of kindness or respect and the scrupulous observation of the duties which marriage entailed. Even if the Catholic Church was involved in this new trend, it was only indirectly, through the search for bad feelings and the examination of conscience demanded of the faithful in the seventeenth and eighteenth centuries.[7] In any case, between 1770 and 1789, it was not the Church which proclaimed this requirement most clearly: not one of the books whose titles mention marital love is a book of Catholic morality.

Moreover, in the series of catechisms, the only one which preached marital love vigorously was not Catholic. The *Catéchisme de la morale...à l'usage de la jeunesse*, published in Brussels in 1785, uses the language of philosophers and takes most of its ideas from them. The whole first chapter is about love, a term which "in general means all affection which is natural; and which leads, so to speak, in spite of itself, towards the loved one". Several kinds of love are distinguished: paternal love, maternal love, filial love, marital love, all of which must confirm this general definition. Marital love is the first of all: "That which has above all and must maintain the most absolute influence on the heart".

However, it is not certain that by the end of the eighteenth century, enlightened opinion had the same idea of marital love which we have today. We in fact imagine that couples are motivated by love. The author of the 1975 *Catéchisme de la morale* did not intend to write about this passion. "We will say nothing", he says, "of the penchant nature gives one sex for the other; that gentle and terrible emotion which makes one wonder whether the Supreme Being gave it to man in His favour or in His anger, which makes all beings happy and man unhappy...which, if it sometimes soothes the savage soul, even more surely damages weak souls; the most seductive pleasure of all, but which, by its very nature, seems to try to separate us by the pitfalls with which it is surrounded, and which the wise man renounces in order to avoid the countless evils which follow." At that time, therefore, one could be in favour of marital love and yet more than hesitant towards love itself. Marital love was envisaged as a tamed passion, a tender and reasonable emotion, it was sometimes even called "a duty", as in the theologians': "The sacred bonds of wedlock make it the couple's strict duty to love one another....Give this love substance by basing it on virtue. If it had no reason other than beauty, charms and youth...it would soon pass, as they do; but if it is tied to qualities of the heart and soul, it will stand the test of time." If marital love could be considered anything but a duty, it must have been possible to marry for love.

Marrying for Love

The author of the 1785 *Catéchisme* expressed it clearly: "The life of an estranged couple is hell! If you wish to live happily beneath that yoke which is marriage, do not commit yourself if you are not loved." And further on: "A marriage contracted without affection is a kind of abduction; a person following his natural instinct belongs only to the one that possesses his heart. Hymen's gifts should only be received from the hands of Love: to acquire them in any other way is literally to usurp them."

Of course, there is no proof that this anonymous *Catéchisme* expresses the unanimous opinion of the elite at that time. Even if there were many texts in the same vein, there were also those opposed to marrying for love. The titles studied show us at least one, perhaps two, in the second half of the eighteenth century: in 1754, *les Engagements rompus par l'amour ou Aventures du sieur de Cormandières* [Promises Broken by Love or the Adventures of Monsieur de Cormandières], and particularly in 1787, *les Dangers d'un amour illicite ou le Mariage mal assorti, tiré de la vie du Cte de C., histoire véritable* [The Dangers of Illicit Love or the Badly-Matched Married Couple, a true story based on the life of the Count of C.]. It is obvious that writers were against marrying for love until the end of the eighteenth century and well into the nineteenth. But it is also obvious to me that something in the attitude of the elite towards marrying for love changed during the eighteenth century: to my knowledge, no sixteenth or seventeenth century author had defended it, whereas in the second half of the eighteenth century, many sang its praises.

While we know that marrying for love has prevailed in the twentieth century, even if there have sometimes been reactionary periods, it appears that the process begun in the eighteenth century on the whole continued into the nineteenth. This hypothesis is confirmed by successive editions of the *Dictionnaire de l'Académie française*. It is only from 1798 onwards that the expression "*mariage d'inclination*" appears under the headword *MARIAGE*, an expression which it had until then been judged unnecessary to include. It is undoubtedly more significant that in 1835 "*mariage de convenance*", "*mariage de raison*" and "*mariage d'intérêt*" [money or social match] are found after "*mariage d'inclination*", and are thus pointed out as it were. In the 1876 supplement, the *Académie* feels it necessary to define these three expressions and to conclude that they "are used in contrast with *mariage d'inclination*", the latter therefore becoming a point of reference which it was felt there was no need to define. It is probable that at the beginning of the Third Republic the "*mariage d'inclination*" was becoming widespread in middle-class ideology, and even in practice.

On the eve of the Revolution, public opinion had not yet reached that point. Even those authors who militated in favour of marrying for love used new arguments to defend the old edicts forbidding young people to marry without their parents' consent. One final quotation from the 1785 *Catéchisme*: "It is however just that boys and girls, who cannot discriminate, are not free to bind themselves with an indissoluble knot without their parents' permission. It would be an act of appalling inhumanity on the latter's part to abandon their children to the lack of consideration and the foolhardiness which are only too common at their age, when it is a matter of deciding their marriage and hence their future happiness or unhappiness. Guardians may prevent their children from pledging themselves, or postpone their pledge, if they judge it unworthy or precipitate of them, and the children will have no right to complain. They must of course assist when the marriage appears appropriate." Here, it is no longer a matter of knowing if the young man's love is based on the young girl's virtues or only on her sex-appeal: the word "appropriate" refers back to social conventions. The laws of the sixteenth and seventeenth centuries prohibited marrying for love to the extent to which it risked upsetting the social order. Eighteenth century writers sing its praises, on condition that, with the recklessness of youth, one did not become infatuated with a person of lower rank. It was not possible for them to go further, because each individual's rank in society depended on the goods which he inherited from his parents and those which his marriage brought him. Marrying for love can only be accepted unhesitatingly when the bulk of the inheritance is cultural. It is still rare today in France for couples not to have the same social origins, as a recent study showed.[8] And yet, marrying for love is standard practice. It is not only that one has a greater chance of meeting people from one's own social background, but also that one is more likely to love them, because the similarity of cultural background encourages affinity of thought. Today it is education, in its widest sense, which is a similar factor in determining an individual's place in the social hierarchy, and which fashions his tendency to love a certain type of person. Conversely, in the eighteenth century, contradictions were great — perhaps greater than at any other time — between the tendency to be loved that education gave and the social status which basically remained dependent upon birth and fortune. It is therefore not impossible that the century which made marital love fashionable was also that in which the greatest number of noble and middle-class women found love only in the arms of their lovers.

LOVE AND MARRIAGE IN POPULAR PRACTICE

Traditional Characteristics

In peasant society, the idea of love existed well before the eighteenth century. But it remained active, whereas during the seventeenth century, love became perceived as increasingly passive in the prevailing culture. In the nineteenth century, peasant proverbs and songs still speak of loving as something which is done rather than something which is felt. Thus, in an old song still sung in the nineteenth century, in the town of Montbéliard, a peasant says to the suitor who has asked for his daughter's hand:

> Ma fille est encore trop jeunette,
> Encore trop jeunette d'un an
> Faites l'amour en attendant.

> [My daughter is still too young,
> Still a year too young,
> Make love to her while you wait.]

"Make love to her" meant "court her". The meaning is not in any doubt, but there are many reasons for thinking that this courting did not content itself with courtesy visits and did not remain on a purely spiritual plane: young men and women showed their attraction through physical means, such as thumping, slapping, pinching, twisting arms, squeezing hands — described by nineteenth century folklorists with surprise and irony — but also, undoubtedly, by kissing and hugging, which gave them considerable pleasure, if the detailed descriptions from the beginning of the twentieth century of the most lively of the ancient courting customs, the "*maraîchinage vendéen*"[9] are to be believed.

It is interesting that today the expression "to make love" refers basically to the physical act. Intercourse seems to have been the only sexual pleasure which — in both peasant and courtly tradition — belonged to marriage and not to courtship. To conclude from this that seventeenth and eighteenth century peasants — or the highborn ladies of the Middle Ages — made love in an entirely Platonic manner, would be a large and somewhat reckless leap.

The great difference between peasant love and courtly love is the fact that the latter was bestowed upon married women — noble morality demanding essentially that they not present their husbands with illegitimate children — whereas peasants only made love to young women they were to marry, while waiting to marry them, or at least to marry one of them. Thus there was a closer link between love and marriage in the peasant tradition that in the courtly tradition.

And yet the distance between the old peasant marriage and our marrying for love is great. Freer to choose their partners than were young nobles and middle-class men, peasants were however, more tied in this matter to their parents' authority than we are. And if, more than young people from the social elite, they were able to follow their inclination, they also had to take into account all kinds of economic and social constraints. Nineteenth century folklorists have described in great detail the haggling between heads of family — for example in Auvergne or in Brittany — which of necessity preceded a marriage agreement; and eighteenth century records on parental permission also reveal the material constraints which weighed on peasant marriages, even in a region as liberal and supportive of marrying for love as Normandy.[10]

One final trait, probably linked to the latter point: the time for loving, for peasants, ended with marriage. All the observers at the beginning of the nineteenth century were surprised by the roughness of rural folk towards their wives, as much as by the freedom young women were allowed before marriage. I do not mean to say that no peasant was ever in love with his wife: there are numerous stories — *Rétif de la Bretonne* for example — which prove that they could be, particularly in the early years of marriage. But, whereas during courtship the woman was queen, at least free to bestow or refuse kisses and hugs, once married, she became her husband's slave and he had the right to demand pleasure — among many other things — from her by force and blows rather than "through love". The great contrast between love and marriage had existed in the courtly tradition but was gradually disappearing from the elite's behaviour. Yet it was maintained in peasant culture and behaviour throughout the eighteenth and nineteenth centuries.

Developments

It may be relatively easy to characterise peasant behaviour in comparison to ours and to that of the elite of that time, but it is much more difficult to study its development, particularly during the eighteenth century alone. Certain indicators suggest that peasant practices of love and marriage evolved in the same direction as those of the elite, albeit undoubtedly more slowly; others that it evolved in the opposite direction.

In the trials for broken promises of marriage brought before the Troyes *officialité* during the second half of the seventeenth century, lack of inclination or the cooling of "friendship" was almost always cited in order to break off engagements which had become unwelcome. This argument was always accepted by the court. On the contrary, at the beginning of the sixteenth century, the court was completely unmoved by this argument and litigants rarely used it. Are we to conclude from this that, in the seventeenth century, neither peasants nor judges any longer accepted loveless marriages — a concept which appeared quite valid at the beginning of the sixteenth century? Yet in another respect, young people in the Middle Ages and at the beginning of the sixteenth century had the option, if not the right, to get married secretly against their parents' wishes. In that way they could — even at the last minute — cause their parents' marriage plans to fail, break off the most formal engagement, and succeed in being married in Church to the person to whom they had been secretly promised. After the Council of Trent, and particularly in the second half of the seventeenth century, such secret engagements were no longer valid, and young people could no longer marry the one they loved against their parents' wishes — at least not before the age of twenty-five or thirty. All in all, it is not possible to say whether there was more or less marrying for love in the seventeenth and eighteenth centuries than in the Middle Ages and at the beginning of the sixteenth century.[11]

From studying the cases on file at the Parliament in Toulouse, Yves Castan draws the conclusion that the young people of the Languedoc behaved much more freely in the eighteenth century than in the seventeenth, and that in particular they showed much more initiative in their choice of partner.[12] However, we do know that in the Pyrenees, in Savoy, in Champagne and without doubt in many other regions, Catholic reformers declared war mercilessly against the traditional courting customs and finally made them disappear. In Champagne in the eighteenth century, the right to court young women in *"escraignes"*,* abolished by the Bishop of Troyes in 1680 under threat of excommunication does not seem to have reappeared.[13] The Savoyard custom of *"albergement"* — which allowed young women to admit one of the suitors who had come to spend the evening into their bed to spend the night there — was forbidden after 1609 under threat of excommunication and disappeared gradually between this date and 1820.[14] In the town of Montbéliard, where a similar custom existed, it is known that the civil authorities found it unacceptable in 1772. But the peasants of this region fought to retain the old freedoms of pre-marital courting and they survived until the end of the nineteenth century.[15]

Studying the numbers of pregnancies and pre-marital conceptions results in contradictory observations from one region to another, and the facts noted are open to several interpretations. In Nantes, the proportion of young women who became pregnant after exchanging a promise of marriage, which was 63% in 1726–1736, rose to 73% in 1757–1766 and to 89% in 1780–1787. This trend is corroborated by the proportion of marriages between social equals, which rises similarly in Nantes, Aix-en-Provence,[16] etc. But that is not found everywhere: in Carcassonne, a recent study reveals that a decreasing proportion of women had been seduced by a man of their social milieu and that promises of marriage were stated less and less by the women.[17] Apparently, in the Carcassonne region the gulf between love and

---

*   igloo-shaped huts made of lumps of earth or sod in which young people from Burgundy and Champagne spent their winter evenings

marriage became greater, as opposed to what was happening in Nantes or Aix. But this could also mean that, when they had been seduced by a man of their social milieu and he had promised to marry them, these promises were more often kept, so that an increasing proportion of young women who got pregnant out of wedlock, because they were able to marry their seducer before the child's birth, no longer had to declare their pregnancy and thus escaped registration.

In fact, an increase in pre-marital conception can be noted almost everywhere in France. The increase in its occurrence during the nine months preceding the wedding implies that this increase does not indicate a greater impatience to enjoy the rights of marriage on the part of the engaged couple but rather that a greater proportion of marriages were decided after the young women became pregnant and probably because of her pregnancy. In other words, one could say that this proves the increase in marrying for love.[18]

However, it must not be forgotten that this rapid increase in pre-marital conception is noticeable as far back as the seventeenth century,[19] i.e. after the Kings of France decreed a whole series of laws preventing children from marrying against their parents' wishes. What, if any, is the connection between these facts? Does the increase in pre-marital conception only prove the existence of the danger that the royal laws were trying to contain, i.e. the growing disobedience of young people? Or was it rather young people's reaction to their parents' growing tyranny? It is in fact known that some young women deliberately allowed their lovers to get them pregnant in order to force their parents to allow them to marry. It is also known that up until the seventeenth century they could marry their lover by simply exchanging promises of marriage before witnesses, an avenue of escape which was taken away from them by the Council of Trent and the royal laws. The increase in pre- marital conception could therefore only indicate the resistance of marrying for love against marriage arranged by the parents, just as the increase in popular revolts in the seventeenth century indicate a fruitless resistance against the rise of the absolute monarchy.

This hypothesis, although still unconfirmed and perhaps statistically unconfirmable, is even more probable since, from the mid-seventeenth century in towns and from the mid-eighteenth century in the country, the illegitimacy rate began to rise, and to become significant in the mid-nineteenth century. This clearly indicates that a steadily increasing number of ordinary young women could not marry the young man whom they had "loved" — if I may be allowed to use the more physical meaning of the verb "to love".

The widening of the gap between love and marriage in popular practice, could be explained by a demographic and economic development increasingly unfavourable to marriage. Some demographers seem to accept this hypothesis, which however, remains difficult to prove, since the average age at marriage and the celibacy rate did not rise at the same time as the illegitimacy rate in all places. The rise of the latter is definitely caused to some extent by the development of laws and judiciary practice. From the beginning of the sixteenth century to the Napoleonic Code, unmarried mothers were increasingly helpless against their seducers.[20] There is no doubt of this. The only difficulty is to measure the impact of this legal revolution on illegitimacy.

Finally, the increase in the illegitimacy rate could be the result of the breaking down of traditional behaviour. More and more young women from the country went to the towns looking for work, where they did not find the same protection from the lust and loutishness of men as in their villages: those who "made love" to them with more or less explicit promises of marriage were not forced to keep them as most often happened in the villages.[21] Moreover, even in their own villages, as the old way of "making love" had become more persecuted by the Church or the State, young women had more and more to practise it in secret; and they were therefore less able to count on their companions or the other young men of the village to prevent their lover from going too far. It is surely no coincidence that the region of France where the old freedoms were retained the longest — the Vendée — was also the French *département* with the lowest illegitimacy rate in the nineteenth century, because there young women gave themselves to their lovers almost only in public.

It is true that, in other regions, the old customs had allowed lovers to go off alone together, for example in Savoy or in the town of Montbéliard. But then they forced the young man to promise to respect the young woman's virginity and in spite of a few lapses which the Catholic or Protestant reformers pointed out, it is probable that he generally kept his promise. However, when all the pleasures of love were forbidden to young people, those who did not resign themselves to chastity adopted behaviour which broke the rules and which no longer spared their girl-friend's virginity.[22]

No matter what the value of these explanations, the facts remain that the increase in pre-marital conception is not indisputable proof of the increase of marrying for love and that the increase in the illegitimacy rate shows unquestionably that the gap between love and marriage grew. Given the present state of research, I therefore have strong reasons for doubting that popular behaviour in the eighteenth century was able to develop in the same direction as bourgeois ideals.

II. SEXUAL MORALITY AND MARITAL RELATIONS

The first chapter in this second section, entitled "The Christian Doctrine of Marriage", is a fairly free review of John T. Noonan's tome Contraception, a History of its Treatment by the Catholic Theologians and Canonists (Cambridge, Massachusetts, 1966). In fact, this book, by allowing me to position my knowledge in the context of the last two thousand years, helped me make great progress in my own work. This review was originally published in the journal Critique, in May 1969.

The second chapter, "Contraception, Marriage and Sexual Relations in the Christian West" goes back to, and develops, a discussion begun in Emmanuel Le Roy Ladurie's seminar in 1967. It was published in a special issue of the journal Annales ESC (Histoire biologique et Société, November/December 1969), then, in English, in Biology of Man in History, edited by R. Forster and O. Ranum (Baltimore, Johns Hopkins University Press, 1975). The last two comments included in this edition appeared for the first time in the English version.

"Man and Wife in the Marriage Bed", an extract from a lecture on the history of women given at the University of Paris VII in 1975, was published in abridged form by the journal Autrement, number 24 (Couples), April 1980.

Chapter 6

The Christian Doctrine of Marriage
Based on a Book by John T. Noonan[*]

Do we know how much the Church's attitude towards marital relations has changed, and our Western civilisation with it? Can we trace
assess the path taken since the beginning? In order to clarify the
current debates on contraception, John T. Noonan finds it necessary
to point out the stages meticulously. Too meticulously perhaps, since
only two stages seem to me to be essential from the point of view of
doctrine: the forming of the traditional doctrine during the first centuries A.D. and its radical transformation in the twentieth century.
Between these two periods lie seventeen or eighteen centuries of
stability. Not, of course, immobilism, since the Fathers of the Church
and medieval theologians developed the doctrine, improved and
justified it and sometimes did not hesitate even to question some of
its very foundations. But St Thomas Aquinas' structures in the thirteenth century, and indeed St Augustine's in the fifth century, though
essential to the history of theology, in no way change the attitudes
adopted from the second century onwards. And, from the fifteenth to
the eighteenth century, new arguments do not gain enough support
to bring about revolution: neither do those of Martin Le Maître whose
audience scarcely reaches beyond the Sorbonne, nor those of Thomas

---

[*]   Contraception, a History of its Treatment by the Catholic Theologians and Canonists,
       Cambridge, Massachusetts, 1966, translated into French as Contraception et
       Mariage, Paris, Éd. du Cerf, 1969, 722 pp.

Sanchez, the great marriage theologian, from the powerful *Compagnie de Jésus*.

Thus, from the second to the twentieth century, the pursuit of sexual pleasure is vigorously condemned, and that which we call love remains virtually foreign to the Christian debate concerning marriage. Marriage itself, however, is accepted, ritualised, strongly defended against those who see it as nothing but fornication. The fact is that the two are radically different, not only because marriage is an indissoluble bond, but because of their aims: fornication is the pursuit of pleasure, marriage is the duty of procreation. And any pursuit of pleasure within marriage makes sexual intercourse adulterous.

Must we agree with the theologians in their justification of this attitude? St Augustine bases Christian hostility to physical pleasure on his theory of concupiscence. Rooted in man's very being since the Fall, this intrinsically bad force cannot be driven out by baptism. It is this force which causes our reason to lose control of our genital organs. Also, during sexual intercourse the moment inevitably arrives when concupiscence overpowers the mind. Therefore sexual intercourse is only legitimate if its purpose is good, i.e. procreation, which balances the evil.

But the condemnation of pleasure and the rehabilitation of marriage through the concept that procreation is good existed before Augustine's theory construction. As far back as the second century, St Justin writes: "We Christians, either we marry solely in order to produce children or, if we refuse to marry, we are completely continent." And Athenagoras, in 177, instructed Christian couples to avoid sexual intercourse during pregnancy "as the labourer, casting his seed upon the ground, awaits the harvest to sow again."

Where did this doctrine come from? Certainly not from the Old Testament, which sings the praises of physical love, and in no way condemns pleasure as such and even allows some extramarital relationships for men. The absence of specific instructions against contraception, when compared with the condemnation of sodomy, bestiality and various other perversions, appears to signify tolerance in a people who did after all know about *coitus interruptus*.

Neither can the New Testament account for the attitude of Christians in the second century. When St Paul condemns practices "against nature", it is no more than another wording of the Jewish condemnation of homosexuality. And no text makes procreation the justification for marriage. The apostle defines it as a remedy for concupiscence, like a contract giving the woman's body to the man and the man's to the woman; and when he glorifies the physical union of married couples, it is as a symbol of the relationship of Christ with His Church. The only positive value in marriage, if there is one, is therefore love.

Moreover, the first Christian texts particularly cherished chastity and virginity, and it is thus that they are clearly distinguished from the ancient law. Christ, upon whom the Christian tries to model his behaviour, was not married. Moreover, in Matthew 19: 12, He glorifies voluntary eunuchs. The marriage of Joseph and Mary, which will long be the ideal of Christian marriage, is a marriage without physical relations. And, from the very beginning, Mary's virginity is emphasised. Paradoxically then, virginity becomes the Christian way to fertility, just as the cross is the way to life. It is the word, not the flesh, which is fertile, and which causes the Church to increase.

The situation changes from the second century onwards, when the pressure of Gnosticism becomes dangerous. It is generally said of this little known religious movement, with its many sects, that it rejected reproduction and all acts of the flesh. In the Gospel, Gnostics highlight the passage concerning voluntary eunuchs in Matthew 19: 12, and some sects actually look to castration as the definitive remedy for concupiscence. Gnostics look also at Matthew 24: 19 and Luke 21: 23: "And alas for those who are with child and for those who give suck in those days". Regarding these words as sacred, they disregard the context. From the gospel according to the Egyptians, which the Church had not yet declared to be apocryphal, they accept that death will reign "as long as you, women, bear children"; and from the gospel of Thomas: "blessed is the womb that has not conceived and those breasts which have not given suck". Generally, they reproach Christians for following the physical way of the Old Testament rather than the paradoxical ways of the New Testament.

In short, are these Gnostics not the true Christians? The most faithful interpreters of the Gospel? The only ones who still, a century after the death of Christ, live in the expectation of the Kingdom? Orthodox Christians, on the other hand, allow themselves to be won over by the secular world.

This idea is even better corroborated by the fact that several of the men denounced by Clement of Alexandria as being the leaders of the Gnostic sects — Carpocrates, Valentinus, Marcion of Pontus, Basilides, Tatian — are members of the Church or have just been driven away from it. And as for the marriage doctrine which he sets against their doctrine, he based it, often verbatim, on the writings of the hellenized Jew, Philo of Alexandria, as found in Pythagorean treatises and, above all, in Stoic morality. In the face of these uncompromising interpretations of the Gospel, is not Christian orthodoxy a sort of dishonest compromise with Greek thought, indeed with pagan society?

This is no doubt true to a certain extent: Christian orthodoxy defends an institution which possesses nothing fundamentally Christian against the Gnostics, and for the simple reason that many Christians have always lived in marriage as have the Jews and pagans around them. The key to choice in orthodoxy is that it is defensive and conservative.

But nothing allows the assertion that the Gnostic attack is more specifically Christian. This is true firstly because these sects — perhaps incorrectly grouped by their opponents under the Gnostic label — preached interpretations contrary to the word of Christ. If it was necessary to defend the right to physical relations within marriage against Tatian's and Jules Cassien's Encratites, it was necessary to remind the antinomian sects that a chaste life was necessary in order to reach the kingdom of heaven.

It is possible that Noonan's presentation of it from the outset wrongly accentuates their differences as regards sex. Because Clement accuses Prodicus' disciples of secretly committing adultery, should they all be called antinomians? To what extent must we accept that Basilides' disciples "do not live purely, whether they claim the ability even to commit sin thanks to their perfection, or whether they believe they will be saved by nature, even if they sin in this life, because they possess innate choice"? Perhaps they simply worry less about deeds than Clement and worry more about divine choice. If Valentinus' disciples, according to Iranaeus, "fornicated and committed adultery, often seduced the women they were teaching and, living together as brothers and sisters, often made their sisters pregnant", is it not a case of accidents being blown up out of all proportion by an opponent?

However, without being entirely convincing, certain accusations go further and cannot be ignored. "There are those", writes Clement, "who call Aphrodite Pandemos — i.e. physical love — a mystic communion...They have committed the sacrilege of giving the name communion to any sexual relationship...These thrice wicked men treat physical and sexual relations like sacred myths and believe that they will lead to the kingdom of heaven". The latter appear to commend themselves to Valentinus. As for Carpocrates' disciples, they are said to have preached the community of women, using the example of Nicolas who, having brought his very beautiful wife before the apostles, had declared that anybody could have sexual intercourse with her in order to put into practice the words: "The flesh must be mortified". Clement tells us that they used the Eucharist improperly, since, after their banquet, "they have intercourse wherever and with whomever they want".

Finally, it is not impossible that, in the religious luxuriance characteristic of the Roman world in the second century, certain sects regarded all kinds of sexual experiences as sacred and that that was squared with an attitude hostile to procreation. It is possible that some sects based this belief on Paul's words to the Ephesians (5: 25–33): "Husbands, love your wives, as Christ loved the church and gave Himself up for her, that He might sanctify her, having cleansed her by the washing of water with the word...". If the pressure of these antinomian sects was really dangerous, it is understandable that the champions of orthodoxy looked elsewhere other than to love for the justification of marriage and that they did not take up Paul's argument.

Upon what could they base their reply to the Gnostic attack? The New Testament allowed the antinomians' unbridled sexuality to be condemned but no positive justification of marriage could be found to set against the ascetics' arguments. The Old Testament might have been able to provide it, but it carried no weight with the Gnostics. Basilides maintained: "Christ came to destroy the Jews' God"; and, Christians having already abandoned many Jewish rules, the Old Testament was not an unquestionable authority for them either. It is doubtless for lack of arguments that Clement had to resort to the "law of nature", the concept sanctioned by Paul in Romans 2: 15, developed by the Stoics and referred to by Philo. In the same way, Iranaeus taught that the liberation effected by Christ did not abrogate this law and that all the natural precepts were common to Jews and Christians.

This concept was to allow Christianity not only to clarify its relations with Judaism as it wished but to open itself widely to Greek philosophy and to make it bear fruit for centuries. Was this only due to the anti-gnostic polemic on marriage? That has not been proven. In any case it is sure that it served particularly as regards sexuality and that, despite the drastic changes undergone by the sciences of nature since antiquity, theologians and rationalist moralists still use it: *Humanae vitae* is the proof of that.

And yet the Church has recently given up the Stoic-Christian doctrine of marriage. The important aspect of this change is not the re-examination of the multisecular condemnation of contraception to which Noonan devotes the largest part of his research, but the fact of going beyond the duty/pleasure and pleasure/procreation conflicts.

For eighteen centuries, the Church refused to accept human love other than emasculated and transformed into charity. As such, it no longer had anything to do with sexual appeal and appeared only rarely in debates about marriage. In the Middle Ages, love was never a legitimate purpose of marriage. Fulfilling one's conjugal debt and wanting to have children were the only two valid reasons for sexual intercourse. The concern for "avoiding sexual incontinence" is added belatedly, and, aside from these three reasons, there can only be the pursuit of pleasure, that is to say adultery. This then has been the "Christian" question of marital relations for centuries.

Not only is sexual urge considered as the effect of concupiscence, but that which is irrational in amorous attraction is condemned. From William of Auxerre in the twelfth century onwards, theologians advise confessors to ask the question: "Would the husband want relations with his wife even if she were not his wife?" If yes, he is guilty of loving too ardently, automatically suspected of practices which do not conform to the "natural" model of sexual intercourse — with a view to seeking "excessive pleasure" — and must, in any case, be accused of mortal sin.

During the twentieth century, on the contrary, love has become the basis for the sacrament of marriage and for the Christian model of married life. In 1925, Dietrich von Hildebrand writes that the marital act "does not have procreation alone as its goal", but that it "also has a meaning for the man as a human being — to be the expression and the fulfilment of married love and of life in a community — and that, in addition, it is in some way part of the idea of the sacrament of marriage". Since then, this personalist doctrine of marriage has continued to gain support. In 1956, Cardinal Suenens writes: "God's first requirement regarding lovemaking, is that it be based on love", and, in 1964, the Second Vatican Council bases marriage as much on love as on procreation.

How did this revolution take place? Noonan fails to ask the question, and elements of the answer he provides are scattered throughout the book.

In fact, the roots of the new doctrine go back a long way. We shall leave out St John Chrysostom, quickly forgotten by Western theologians. But as far back as the twelfth and thirteenth centuries, love, while not being accepted as sufficient reason for marriage nor as a legitimate reason for sexual intercourse, does enter into theologians' ideas of married life. For the twelfth century, several passages from Peter Lombard's *Sentences* could have been cited. In the thirteenth century, St Thomas Aquinas observes that copulation "even in animals creates a gentle society" and that between human beings "a man loves his wife mainly because of the physical relationship". He accepts that, in the order of love, love for one's wife, based on the union of the flesh, is rightfully more intense than love for one's father or mother. St Bonaventure observes too that in marriage "there is a certain uniqueness in love, in which a third party has no share", for, he says, "there is something miraculous for a man to find in a woman satisfaction which he can find in no other woman". But such statements are rare, ambiguous and apparently still not echoed by the Church.

In the fifteenth century, Denys le Chartreux declared that man and wife should love each other with a love which was "multi-faceted, special and warm": spiritual love which makes them want the security of their partner, natural love born of human companionship, "social" love because their are involved in each other's lives, it is also a physical love based on "sensual delights" and "worldly comfort". Because the marital act is good when it is for the right reason, man and wife "are said to love each other rightfully with a physical love". Denys le Chartreux is thus the first to say that in marriage spiritual love and physical love may be brought together.

Several writers will echo him a century later, Thomas Sanchez in particular. Sanchez goes beyond the questions of legitimate reasons for sexual intercourse by maintaining that the marital act is always legitimate when carried out by Christian couples in a state of grace. One never makes love "for pleasure alone", he specifies, as long as one does nothing to prevent procreation. By saying that, he frees couples' spontaneity from Stoic-Christian restraints. Going further, he permits "the hugs, kisses and caresses usual among couples to show and reinforce their love for each other" and that even if there is a risk of involuntarily spilling sperm. By defending these caresses outside their role in foreplay, he recognises love as one of the main values in marriage.

Sanchez did not dare to make marital intercourse a legitimate expression of love. He had already gone too far for people to follow him. Even in the eighteenth century, very few theologians accept his conclusions. Among this small number, however, was Alfonso de

Liguori whose doctrine was imposed in the nineteenth century by Roman absolutism. His doctrine, without a doubt, furthered the doctrinal transformation of the following century and, for the moment, as far as behaviour was concerned, furthered the progress of contraception within marriage.

But the driving force of the transformation lay elsewhere: away from theological speculations, in the real world. Indeed, the Church could not permanently ignore the twentieth century's new scientific discoveries, beginning with the psychoanalytical study of human behaviour. Moreover — and Noonan appears to be less conscious of this — sooner or later the Church had to adapt to a society which was no longer pagan; to accept love as it had accepted procreation, since love had been accepted as a value among the Western elites.

The birth of what was called Western love remains obscure. What does it owe to Christianity, to Cathar heresy, to Islam? The discussion is not finished. But, it is certain that the rules of courtly love are the antithesis of those of medieval marriage. The bond between the servant and his lady is freely chosen and not imposed by the families' interest; and, if it includes more physical liberties than has been said, its purpose is never procreation. For centuries, in order to be accepted, love had to proclaim itself chaste, as a sign that it remained restricted to being outside marriage; and, for centuries, Christian moralists saw in it only physical disorders, bawdiness and adultery.

When was the association between marriage and loving behaviour made? In the seventeenth century, those who marry for love alone are still severely judged. Is it then during the sensitive eighteenth century that marriage becomes based on emotions and, at the same time, the traditional duty of procreation begins to be forgotten? Is it during the nineteenth century, when so many couples are described as being passionless because they are starting to be a problem? The precise research which would provide answers to these questions has not yet been carried out.

Noonan, despite commendable efforts to move away from purely theological sources,* hardly provides any information on this mental revolution. Although he clearly sees the original paradox of Christian marriage, he does not really appear conscious of the second: for more than a thousand years, the Church wanted to impose a doctrine

---

*   As for the question of contraception, the central topic in Noonan's book, fascinating chapters are devoted to the relationships, in each period, between the doctrine and the scientific and technical state of the society and between the doctrine and behaviour within marriage.

derived from pagan morality on a Christian society, and it was only outside of the institution of marriage that it was possible to glorify love without being guilty of heresy. What is taken as a sign of de-Christianisation — ignoring the duty of procreation — is connected to the triumph of a model, almost certainly secular in origin, but slowly constituted within a Christian civilisation. It is for theologians to tell us whether it corresponds more closely to the original texts than the former does.

Chapter 7

Contraception, Marriage, and Sexual Relations in the Christian West

An understanding of demographic behaviour implies a knowledge of the behaviour patterns of the populations being studied. From this statement one proceeds immediately — too immediately — to the idea that in a Christian society, such as that of the medieval or modern West, the prescriptions of the religious law are decisive. True, one cannot neglect them; but they are not everything. Church doctrine has never been passively accepted by an entire population; it does not build upon virgin consciences. Each social milieu adapts doctrine to its own needs, its customs, its traditional beliefs.

I suspect that no one questions this on the level of generalities; but when making a detailed study, it is often easier to proceed as if unaware. Thus the inquiry into behaviour must focus on the diffusion of church doctrine, on the one hand, and on the dilemma of the "good Christian or the sinner," on the other. Of course, it is extremely difficult to know what each social group does with that doctrine, to what degree it accepts it, refuses it, or transforms it. To stimulate new research, we must at least stress our ignorance and not conceal it.

With regard to contraception, which is my concern here, I will not attempt to study the examples provided by one specific group, as this introduction seems to imply. The thesis presented here may be too general, considering the limited sociological scope of my documentation and its chronological dispersion. Indeed, this study does not result from painstaking research; I am simply trying to show the inadequacy of the ideas which have until now been accepted and to stimulate new research.

Let us recall briefly the generally accepted ideas. The most radical thesis was that of "unthinkableness" so brilliantly defended by Philippe Ariès[1] which asserted that, until a recent date, contraception was unthinkable in the Christian West and that love, sexual intercourse, and procreation formed an integral whole. Because this notion was largely grounded upon in silence of medieval theologians, it was rapidly proved invalid. Father Riquet soon found fault with it on the basis of the vices denounced in the penitentials of the early Middle Ages.[2] Most recently, an American scholar, John Noonan, has shown the importance of medieval condemnations against contraception in its many forms.[3] It is henceforth difficult to maintain that no one thought of separating sexual intercourse and procreation, and that all those theological debates, all the work of the preachers and confessors, were concerned with a problem which did not exist in the practices of the day. Noonan believes that this sin was committed by married couples as well as extramaritally. But were these contraceptive measures used on a scale appreciable at the statistical level on which demographers function?

Demographers have long accepted the existence of efficacious contraceptive techniques in medieval society. However, they have considered them as limited to the milieu of prostitution, and for the rest of the society they have held fast to the idea of a "natural fecundity". This is a misleading concept, and people have begun to question it. If the majority of demographic historians have kept a cautious and ambiguous silence concerning the fertility of extramarital sexual relations,[4] others have not hesitated to determine the frequency of such relationships on the basis of the number of illegitimate births.[5] I shall discuss this rash position in the second part of this article.

First, however, I will concentrate on denouncing the immediacy of the relationship between the behaviour of medieval Christians regarding contraception and the doctrine of the Church as formulated by the theologians of the period. Indeed, it is clear that may Christians acquainted with this doctrine not only did not follow it but did not accept it. That is, on this point they conformed to a moral ideal which was not that of the Church of their day.

How else can we interpret the well-known testimony of Monseigneur Bouvier, bishop of Le Mans, concerning the Catholic couples in his diocese in 1842?

> Almost all young couples do not wish to have a large family and nevertheless are morally incapable of abstaining from the marriage act. Questioned by their confessors on the way in which they exercised their marital rights, *they generally appear to be extremely shocked* and, once warned, do not abstain from the conjugal act, nor can they be won over to an indefinite multiplication of the species ...

> All willingly agree that infidelity toward one's spouse and willful abortion are very grave sins. And only with great difficulty can some of them be persuaded that they are obliged, under pain of mortal sin, either to observe perfect chastity in their marriage or else to run the risk of engendering a numerous posterity.[6]

Must the discrepancy between the behaviour which these young Catholic couples considered appropriate and that which the Church was trying to impose upon them be attributed to the influence of openly anti-Christian models in a society which no longer had any religion but the religion of the State? Perhaps in part. But there seems to be more to it than that. To support this, interesting evidence can be found from the eighteenth century, that is, before the Revolution had freed conjugal morality from ecclesiastical surveillance. Father Féline wrote in his *Catéchisme des gens mariés* (1782):

> The majority of husbands imagine that everything is permitted them and do not think of seeking advice. They cannot be persuaded that a confessor has the right to enter into the discussion of these sorts of questions. They appear scandalized if one happens to bring up the subject in the confessional.

> Women, through bashfulness, modesty, shame, dare not declare their anxiety. They wait for the confessor to speak to them about it first. It is not rare to find [women] who, after several years of marriage and an infinite number of transgressions, reply coldly to a confessor who has the charity to question them concerning conjugal chastity, that they never confessed the sins for which they are being reproached because their previous confessors had never asked about them.[7]

Admittedly, this evidence is less explicit than the preceding text. And it does not throw into relief the sincerity of the married couples in their error. But is it not essentially aimed at contraception in marriage? And whence the arrogance of the sinners if not from a feeling that they are in the right?

As early as 1748, moreover, St Alphonsus Liguori, hostile to Jansenist practices, discouraged confessors from inquiring about the sins of married persons. For if the sinner did not confess on his own, it meant he was unaware that he was sinning. If the confessor destroyed this good faith and did not succeed in making him give up his sin, he transformed an unwitting sin into a mortal one.[8] What really is the theory of good faith, if not the awareness that other models of behaviour existed among Catholic peoples than those formulated by the theologians?

We know that theologians, under the blanket concept of the "sin against nature", included all sexual acts which do not result in the insemination of the woman, and that they considered this "sin against nature" as the greatest of sexual faults, even more serious than incest or the rape of a nun. Noonan does not hesitate to consider this ranking within the hierarchy of sins as the principal means by which contraceptive practices were discouraged.[9] But to accept this means also to accept without debate the theory that different social groups understood this expression in the same manner as the theologians, and that, like the theologians, they considered the acts it designates to be the worst sexual transgressions.

Must we therefore conclude that sincerity while sinning is a new phenomenon, characteristic of the eighteenth and even the nineteenth century? And must we say that during preceding periods a sin could be unwittingly committed solely because Church doctrine had not been sufficiently diffused? I do not think so. On the contrary, I believe that — with the exception of a few devout circles — the status given by theologians to the concept of the "crime against nature" was never fully accepted.

Indeed, the purpose of this concept seems to me to be twofold. On the one hand — and Noonan placed too little stress on this — it is polemical: it is a question of persuading those accustomed to practising sterile acts that these are a form of sodomy, condemned by St Paul on the basis of Old Testament texts and considered by him as contrary to nature. This procedure is an ordinary one and had already been used to group all sorts of fornication under the sixth commandment, concerning adultery. On the other hand, it is explanatory and rationalizing: the evil of these acts lies in their very opposition to the law of nature. I therefore interpret this position as being the antithesis of an interdict; and I doubt whether it succeeded in becoming a part of the moral conscience of the Christian masses in the Middle Ages.

Though I have not studied local customs and folklore, let us at least see whether the law includes this concept of a crime against nature. It is well known that judicial procedure sent sodomites to be burned at the stake and condemned to death all those guilty of bestiality; but though it was very strict about incest and adultery, there was no concern at all with other unnatural acts.

In principle, canon law shows more concern. It sets forth three penalties for husbands guilty of deceiving nature: denial of the conjugal bed, separation or divorce "*a toro*," and annulment of the marriage. But research in judicial archives would be required to find out whether these penalties were really applied before the nineteenth century, and at this point no one seems ready to confirm this. Even if they were applied, they would have been aimed at contraception within a marriage and not extramaritally.

While those involved in extramarital relationships were not punishable under canon law, they could still be chastised through the confessional, which had the authority to exert pressure on those committing unnatural acts by demanding greater penance than for other sexual sins.

During the early Middle Ages, the penance imposed for such sins is known to us through penitential. Noonan, who studied twenty of them dating from the sixth through ninth centuries, shows us that all penitentials, save one, were concerned with one or several contraceptive measures. Not only "poisons creating sterility" — apparently connected with the crime of sorcery — but two sorts of unnatural intercourse[10] were considered grave sins by all those mentioning them. Many authors imposed for these sins a penance equal to that for homicide; and all considered them more serious than aborting a fetus of less than forty days. This severity — as Noonan has clearly observed — suggests that these contraceptive measures were attacked in their own right and not in order to protect a potential human life. The penance for these sins points out the order of their magnitude: from three to fifteen years of fasting.

In the case of onanism, the penance was slightly less — two to ten years — but the order of magnitude of the penance was identical. And, in the only two works which mention it explicitly,[11] it was included in the same article as that dealing with contraceptive and abortive potions and was punished with the same severity. This information had eluded Noonan's predecessors, and it is of marked interest. I note, however, that this practice is only referred to in two articles which are in every way identical, and that no penitential mentions it alone. It is thus difficult to measure its real status at the time.

This is all the more true since a number of articles in the several penitentials I have read appear to contradict the works just mentioned in terms of the severity of the sin. It is first of all evident that solitary practices — which are also crimes against nature, according to later theologians — were viewed with great indulgence, even when they were committed by clerics, thereby profaning a church; the penance was from seven days up to fifty in the case of a bishop within a church.[12] It is thus a matter of minor sins, much less serious, for example, than sexual intercourse between married people during Lent,[13] than rape (punished by a year of penance),[14] and even less so than simple fornication.[15] But there is more: one wonders whether contraception was not encouraged in illicit relationships since the punishment was increased if the relationship was fertile, while on the contrary it decreased when the couple succeeded in sullying itself without a true copulation.[16] Hélène Bergues, who has pored over a similar test, has learned from it that scandal was penalized as well as the sin itself.[17] Agreed. But did this not implicitly orient the sinner toward measures which would avoid scandal?

Finally, a study of penitentials dating from the sixth through eleventh centuries reveals that the unitary concept of the "crime against nature," as later theologians would define it, was not current and that in any event certain acts later included under that heading were viewed with indulgence. *Coitus interruptus*, or onanism, the chief means of contraception in the modern period, still attracted little attention. Is this because it was practised, as they heavy penance prescribed by two penitentials would lead one to believe? Or is it, on the contrary, that in illicit relations it was deemed less guilty than complete and fertile copulation? In the present state of research, it is impossible to draw a conclusion on this point.

After the eleventh century, the confessor was much freer to choose the penance he would impose upon the sinner, and as a result it is more difficult for us to gain a concrete idea of the importance given to different sins. Yet we would be wrong to believe that the confessors were totally free and to imagine that the historian has no freedom at all. A certain number of sins was indeed reserved for absolution by the bishop, and the parish priest could not therefore pardon them. It is clear that this more-difficult-to-obtain absolution made those mortal sins thus set apart appear more serious in the eyes of the Christian population. And, according to whether or not a sin was reserved, the historian has the right to consider the resulting interdict as more or less serious. Now, we possess a great number of medieval and modern synodal statutes, and these statutes rarely fail to include a list of sins reserved for the bishop of the diocese. We therefore have in them a means of measuring the weight, the stability, and the variability of religious interdicts, across space and time.

It is not my aim here to analyze these documents in a chronological or comparative manner. I will limit myself to an arbitrary sampling of seventeen lists of reserved cases — all French — lists which stretch from the thirteenth to the seventeenth century.[18]

First let us examine the list of reserved cases in the diocese of Cambrai (1300–1310). It has the merit of indicating for us the sins reserved for the bishop, those which he could delegate to the penitentiaries-general sent out into the deaneries, and those which he turned over to the parish priests and vicars. Sins against nature are found in all three groups:

- *reserved for the bishop*: sins against nature by a man over twenty years of age;
- *reserved for the penitentiaries*: sins against nature perpetrated by women of any age and by men of less than twenty; "manual pollution" at any age;
- *jurisdiction of the parish priest*: "disordered copulation with women"; the sin of "voluptuousness" or autoeroticism [mollicies]; sins against nature during childhood, for boys up to the age of fourteen and for girls to the age of twenty-five.

By comparing these sins, we can deduce that those sins called simply "sins against nature" are in all probability homosexual acts. They were less serious for girls than for boys, and this appears to me to agree with what is known of judicial practice. We must still determine the meaning of the word "mollicies," since "manual pollution at any age" is referred to elsewhere.[19] As for "disordered copulation with women", this may mean simple fornication, which is not included elsewhere; it may also denote any intercourse which obviously renders conception impossible and other forms of intercourse deemed nonconformist solely on the grounds of position. Let me stress that disordered copulation, like autoeroticism, fell under the jurisdiction of the parish priest, while incest, when it involved close relative, was within the bishop's jurisdiction and, when the relationship was more distant, that of the penitentiary; sexual relations with nuns were considered a form of serious incest and were under the bishop's jurisdiction; adultery fell under the jurisdiction of the penitentiary, and rape under that of the parish priest.

In the sixteen other lists, the cases reserved for the bishop are not indicated. It is therefore not easy to dispel the ambiguity of the expression "sin against nature". But it is noteworthy that one of the sins against nature is condemned with unusual constancy; that is sodomy, which is explicitly mentioned ten times. Of these ten lists, only one uses the concept of "sin against nature", and its scope is restricted: "sodomy and any other even more grave sin against nature".[20] Six others include bestiality with sodomy.[21] In addition, no other sin against nature is specifically mentioned, with the exception of the autoerotic acts or mollicies cited by the most severe of our synodal statutes.[22]

Why is this equivocal sin of autoeroticism mentioned only once, and then on the strictest list? Why do they never openly refer to contraceptive intercourse with women? Why never to masturbation? Is it out of discretion? But the ten lists which mention sodomy seem to show little concern for discretion and yet make no further references to it. Is this because these practices were not very widespread? But who will insist, on the basis of that principle, that masturbation was less widespread than sodomy or bestiality? After examining all these questions in light of what we have learned from the statutes of Cambrai, I tend to think that only sodomy and bestiality are hidden behind the expressions "sin against nature" and "sins against nature"; all other acts which the theologians included under that blanket concept were undoubtedly sins within the jurisdiction of the parish priest.

In the improbable event that these other acts are also designated by the expressions in question, we would be obliged to note that they were, at the maximum, reserved for the bishop in only seven of the seventeen lists studied, while incest is explicitly listed all seventeen times, adultery nine, and rape eight. n short, a study of the lists of reserved cases confirms what we have learned from judicial practice: the great crimes were sodomy, bestiality, incest, and adultery, and not the sin against nature as such, and less still masturbation or coitus interruptus. The numerous attestations of theologians to the contrary are polemical and rationalizing. They are not as revealing of social pressure and the reality of the interdicts as are the lists of reserved cases or judicial practice.

Now let us see whether contraception is forbidden with equal rigor within marriage and without.

Noonan, in his study of the penitentials, observes that, when they punished women for using contraceptive drugs, they were more indulgent toward the poor woman overburdened with children than toward the lewd one who tried to hide her sin.[23]

Are we to conclude from this that contraception as we define it was a more serious offense outside marriage than within? I do not think so. For the use of contraceptive drugs is an act which is distinct from intercourse itself; it is not a sin of lechery but a crime involving infanticide and sorcery.[24] Thus one can consider poverty and numerous children as an attenuating circumstance. But here I am talking of the sin against nature, that is, the sexual act which is of its own nature sterile. Now, we have seen that — with the exception of sodomy and bestiality — the penitentials were more strict about illicit sexual acts resulting in the conception of bastards than about those which were sterile. It seems to me that the penitentials were implicitly pushing people toward extramarital contraception.

Established between the twelfth and thirteenth centuries, Church law devoted three canons to contraception.[25] The canon "*Si aliquis*", borrowed from the penitentials, likens the use of "sterilizing poisons"[26] to homicide, while the two others — "*Aliquando*" and "*Si conditiones*" — attack contraception as contrary to marriage.[27] Now we have already said that the only canonical punishments for any heterosexual copulation which was intrinsically contraceptive were aimed at a search for sterility in marriage, and not extramaritally. The stricter the enforcement of these canons, the clearer it becomes that contraception was considered an extramarital practice.

This is not surprising. These two canons, which came more or less directly from St Augustine,[28] have to do with the question of sexual behaviour in which, from the second to the nineteenth century, the doctors of the Church became totally engrossed.[29] Any attempt at carnal pleasure was condemned: the conjugal act was considered more than a carnal encounter; it was deemed an act of procreation desired by God and by nature. Indeed, St Augustine, to return to him, believed that sexual pleasure was inevitably corrupted by lust and saw the procreative act as the necessary legitimation of the conjugal act. Even when St Thomas Aquinas rehabilitated the notion of pleasure resulting from the marriage act, he firmly maintained that pleasure in the act should be condemned as an end.

Now, the characteristic end of any extramarital intercourse is the search for pleasure for its own sake. Arguing against concubinage, St Thomas wrote: "Whoever, therefore, uses copulation for the delight which is in it, not referring the intention to the end intended by nature, acts against nature."[30] Elsewhere, he shows that any act of lechery is a mortal sin because it is not done for procreation and the rearing of offspring.[31] "The human seed," he wrote, "in which man is in potentiality, is ordered for the life of man....And therefore disorder in the emission of seed concerns the life of man in potentiality."[32] This attack against potential life makes the sin of lechery a mortal one.

For St Thomas the lecherous act not only injures the potential individual child in the squandered seed, but the human species in general, whose preservation is thus threatened.[33] "The seed, although superfluous for the conservation of the individual, is yet necessary to the propagation of the species....Hence...it is also required that it be emitted to be of use in generation, to which coitus is ordained." And he concludes, "The disordered emission of seed is contrary to the good of nature, which is the conservation of the species."[34]

This argument is not aimed at contraception *per se*, but at fornication. For St Thomas, any extramarital intercourse, be it biologically fertile or sterile, is a disorder in the emission of semen, an injury done to the human species, and consequently to nature and to God. By the very fact that it is sought outside marriage, its aim is pleasure and it perverts the order of nature. On St Thomas' level of reasoning, contraception seems to add nothing to the sin of fornication, except, I imagine, a more concerted scorn for the laws of nature.

This disorder in the emission of semen can also occur within a marriage, and all theologians called the married couple's attention to this fact. Some considered the search for pleasure in marriage to be a mortal sin:[35] others a venial sin.[36] But all St Jerome's warning that the man who displays too much ardor while making love to his wife is an adulterer. Let us pause at the statement which Benedicti gave in 1584 concerning this warning:

> The husband who, transported by *immoderate love*, has intercourse with his wife *so ardently* in order to satisfy his passion that even had she not been his wife, he would have wished to have commerce with her, is committing a sin. And St Jerome seems to confirm this when he cites the words of Sixtus Pythagorician, who said that the man who shows himself to be an *uncontrollable lover* of his wife, rather than her *husband*, is an adulterer. And yet this is not to say that since the man has his wife's body at his bidding, he should take advantage of her as he pleases, for the proverb says, 'One can get drunk on one's own wine.' Which means that a man must not use his wife as a whore, nor the wife behave toward her husband as with a lover: for this holy sacrament of marriage must be treated with all honesty and reverence. Note this, you other married couples who make of your bed your god.[37]

Ariès and Noonan have already wondered about what might comprise that "immoderate love" denounced by theologians and preachers. St Thomas, St Bonaventura, Gerson, and St Bernardine of Siena take it to mean preferring sexual union with one's wife over union with God. Chaucer is also apparently criticizing this idolatry in his "*Parson's Tale*", leading Ariès to conclude that it is rather a question of amorous passion than of sexual depravity. Noonan observes that every mortal sin can be defined as a preference for a temporal end over the eternal union with God, and that unless this interpretation is understood to be particularly aimed at courtly love, it is inadequate.

Other theologians[38] — and Benedicti appears to agree — reproach the husband for having "commerce with his wife as if she were not his wife." Trying to arrive at a concrete meaning, Noonan conceives of only one solution: "Using one's wife as a whore" means preventing conception.

By its surprising parallel of the two words "lover" and "whore", Benedicti's statement permits us to move ahead in our thinking. By granting them the same value, he negates the dichotomy reached by Noonan and Ariès, both imprisoned in too contemporary a vision of things. Indeed, neither "lover" nor "whore" have the meaning and value which we give them today. The meaning of lover at that time was not very far from the current meaning, to the degree that, today as in the sixteenth century, the lover is animated by an emotion more limited than love for his neighbour. But the intent of the word in this text is completely different from today's meaning; contemporary Western civilization has given it a positive meaning,[39] and the Church today has accepted roughly the same connotation. Yet in the sixteenth century love was an extremely controversial subject and, on the whole, Christian morality denied its existence. The lover, in the Christian vision of that period, was a paramour, a wencher, a lecher, though at the same time he was what we today call a lover.

On the other hand, the word "whore", so abundantly used in that period, had the pejorative meaning which it still has today, but for reasons different from ours. We and our sixteenth-century ancestors both apply it to prostitutes; but we reproach them for playing the game out of love for money, while they reproached them for devoting their life to it. At that time, therefore, the word was properly applied to any woman who sought carnal relations out of passion or for pleasure; the honest woman was supposed to seek them only for the good of the marriage, in conformity to the duties of her position — we might almost say "from professional conscientiousness". This is a paradoxical about-face in the social values hidden behind a single word.

In short, the behaviour of married persons is systematically contrasted with that of lovers; the former are connected with procreation, the latter with the search for sterile pleasure. Similarly, the "natural" manner of intercourse is contrasted with unusual ones, which are called unnatural and are suspected of being sterile.

Indeed, the positions of sexual intercourse are a traditional subject for theological discussions. "Unnatural" positions have never been condemned on the basis of a personalist view of marriage, in which the individual is supreme, but in the name of the age-old marriage rite,[40] which has at its foundation certain notions regarding the relationship between a man and woman[41] that exclude the idea of excessive pleasure,[42] and which shows concern for procreation.[43] When theologians have tolerated certain of these forms of intercourse — as they frequently did in the sixteenth century — it is on the condition that they have been shown to be fertile,[44] and not for pleasure.[45] We might well wonder what impact this new example of theological rationalization had upon the faithful. In any event, a layman like Brantôme, who cannot easily be accused of excessive prudishness, mentions this opinion with obvious reticence:

> Other learned doctors say that whatever form is used is good, but that "*semen ejaculetur in matricem mulieris, et quomodocumque uxor cognoscatur, si vir ejaculetur semen in matricem, non est peccatum mortale.*"

> These disputes are to be found in the *Summa Benedicti*, the work of a learned Franciscan who has written very well about every sin and has shown that he had seen and read a great deal. Whoever reads this passage will find there are great number of abuses which husbands commit upon their wives. He also says that "*quando mulier est ita pinguis ut non possit aliter coire*" in any other position, that in such a case "*non est peccatum mortale, modo vir ejaculetur semen in vas naturale.*" Others say that it would be better for husbands to abstain from intercourse with their pregnant wife, as do the animals, than to sully their marriage by such outrages.[46]

Now, did he consider these "outrages" to be inadmissible in an extramarital relationship? This does not seem to have been the case, for he speaks lightly of those "positions of Aretino" in an extramarital context,[47] only becoming indignant when he contemplates them within a marriage. Though he is rather insensitive to the rationalizations of the theologians, he appears to have fully accepted the contrast between matrimonial and amorous behaviour which had marked the Christian doctrine of sexuality since the second century.

Doubtlessly the antinomy between pleasure and procreation inherited from classical morality[48] and carried on by ecclesiastical culture did not succeed in imposing itself completely. Brantôme himself reveals the existence of contrasting views;[49] and medical literature, nourished by other classical traditions, confirms this.[50] But in the same sentence Brantôme implies that this association of extraordinary pleasure with procreation is abnormal; and the medical profession, imitating theologians, expressed its suspicions that "overly ardent" love was sterile. Thus, despite the existence of an opposing viewpoint among some laymen, and despite the medical profession's Aristotelian mistrust of excess in general — an attitude which may be discerned in actual medical practice — it appears that the antinomy between pleasure and procreation was widely accepted by those outside ecclesiastical circles.

Pleasure, sterility, whims contrary to the order of nature — this is the associative context of extramarital sexual relations. But do we find texts which, speaking explicitly of contraception, make a distinction between married persons and fornicators?

First, in order not to mislead the reader who is unfamiliar with the moral and theological literature of the past, let us point out that all authors dealing with the subject unequivocally condemned contraceptive intercourse, and that this condemnation made no exception for intercourse extramaritally.

Nevertheless, when discussing the conjugal versus nonconjugal context of these relations, they condemned contraception with special vehemence when it occurred within marriage. For example, John Gerson, writing at the beginning of the fifteenth century, notes briefly: "And this sin is more grievous the further one strays from the natural law: be it outside marriage or — which is even worse — within marriage...."[51] And several sixteenth-century theologians insisted upon the fact that unnatural intercourse is more serious when committed by husband and wife than by two persons not united in marriage. In the latter case, the crime against the potential life is compounded by that of fornication or adultery, if one of the sinners is married. But when they are husband and wife, it is a double adultery. Thus Cajetan, Soto, Azor, and Sanchez, all important theologians, prescribe that the confession should state the aggravating circumstance "that the sin was committed with one's own spouse."[52]

Writing during the same period, Brantôme expresses a notion

indicating that this judgment was accepted by laymen who were not particularly devout. Concerning married persons, he says:

> ... of the thousand cohabitations which the husband may have with his wife during a year, it is possible, as I say, that she may not become pregnant once...from whence comes the erroneous belief of some unbelievers that marriage was not so much instituted for procreation as for pleasure: which is a wrong belief and an incorrect way of talking, for, although a woman does not become pregnant every time one takes her, it is owing to some will of God, to us unfathomable, and He wished to punish husband and wife, all the more so since the greatest blessing which God can send us in a marriage is a good progeny, and not through concubinage.

Then, immediately after this, he discusses the practice of coitus interruptus, and presents it as a part of the framework of adultery:

> ... There are a number of women who take great pleasure in having children by their lovers, and others not; the latter are unwilling to let anything be released within them, as much to avoid palming off upon their husbands children which are not really theirs, as to appear to be doing their husbands no wrong and not be cuckolding them since the dew does not enter them, no more or no less than a weak and upset stomach can be blamed when indigestible morsels are ingested, put into the mouth, chewed, and then thrown up.

> Likewise, after the name "cuckoo" borne by those April birds which are thus called because they lay eggs in the nests of others, men are by contract called cuckolds when others come and lay eggs in their nest, which in this case is their wife, which is the same as saying that they discharge their seed and make children for them. That is how some women think they are doing their husbands no wrong by taking in [a man] and enjoying him until sated, without receiving his seed; thus they are suitable conscientious....[53]

It is true that Brantôme does not unequivocally condone these ladies; but he obligingly develops their casuistic arguments; and nowhere does he become indignant at what is, in the eyes of the theologians, an unnatural practice. Not only will I conclude on the basis of this passage that coitus interruptus was practised in courtly circles in the second half of the sixteenth century — this has already been pointed out[54] — but also that it seems to have been practised extramaritally for moral reasons. For the argument — made with a touch of humour and paradox — is a moral one: "palming off children upon their husbands" was, in the mentality of that century, the principal crime of an adulterous woman, and contraception avoided committing it. How could a Christian civilization have given birth to such a morality? How could such an argument have been openly developed? I believe I have already made the answers clear: coitus interruptus was not considered as abominable a practice as sodomy or bestiality; it was surely less severely punished than incest or adultery; and since all extramarital sexual relations are normally sought for pleasure — and not for procreation — rendering them sterile did not increase the sinfulness.

It is true that this argument is not specifically found in the works of any theologians or casuists. That is doubtlessly because in plainly authorising extramarital contraception one could in practice have encouraged sexual disorders.[55] Nevertheless, while speaking of simple fornication, the great Sanchez went so far as to explicitly to uphold, with extreme prudence, an opinion concerning adultery akin to that described by Brantôme:

In fornicatory coitus, after the woman has emitted her seed[56] or the risk of emitting it has become inevitable,[57] is the man permitted to withdraw before his own semination? Certain learned men think...this is not permitted and that on the contrary he is obliged to expel his seed...and they say that there is no possible doubt, because after a woman has ejaculated, the man is obliged to expel his seed in order to avoid a greater evil and complete the act for a nonlibidinous purpose, and thus this semination is not strictly fornicatory, but only materially so: so that for this reason it is not intrinsically evil. And this opinion is credible.

But is much more credible not only that the man is not obliged to ejaculate then, but that in expelling his seed he becomes guilty of a new fault, and that this fault must be revealed in the confessional, unless it was not discerned during intercourse. Because in a licit act, nothing is illicit, and for that one must seminate; but there is something intrinsically evil in an illicit act which cannot be rendered honest in any eventuality.

And that does not prevent one from being obliged to choose the lesser of the two evils. Certainly, this nonsemination is in itself unnatural, and as a result more wrong than fornication. But fornication is absolutely and simply worse, since it is so intrinsically wrong that it is never permitted.[58] Now, nonsemination is not so bad and unnatural that it is not permitted for a very compelling reason, as we have proved in the previous paragraph.[59] This is what will be acknowledged here: that is to say, *in order that fornicatory intercourse not be consummated to the serious disadvantage of raising the child. And the fornicator will not be accused of error if, in withdrawing from the woman, he ejaculates involuntarily outside the vessel.* Because the involuntary pollution resulting from a just cause is necessary and absolutely innocent. Likewise exempt from guilt is the fornicating woman who, acting from repentance over the crime she has committed, moves her body away so as not to receive the male seed and not consummate the fornication which had begun. And the man will not be considered in error if he spills his seed outside. Because that is not his intention and she is doing a licit thing in tearing herself away from a crime which has already been begun.[60]

These arguments were just what was needed to assuage the consciences of the ladies portrayed by Brantôme. As for the pious motives which must justify the withdrawal, is not the anguish being felt a form of regret over the illicit act? Is not sin pushed away at the very same moment as the temptress? And why is the embrace broken, if not for fear of causing harm to a potential child or its mother?

But what is the authority behind this text? Let us stress that Sanchez in not a negligible author nor one whose orthodoxy is suspect. And in this century of Jesuits he was the Society of Jesus' greatest specialist in marriage; many of his contemporaries considered him a walking encyclopedia and viewed him as a saint — which Alphonsus Liguori would have the good fortune to become in the eighteenth century. Nevertheless, he had many enemies during the seventeenth century. Bayle, Jurieu, and the Protestants all held him in horror; Jansenist or rigorist theologians denounced him as lax; and Pierre de l'Estoile even tells how his book, which "had sold...publicly in Paris and everywhere, printed and reprinted with the name and reputation of the author, who was considered learned," was withdrawn from sale by royal order because it had created such a scandal.[61] It is obvious that on this point he was innovative: he, who habitually cited dozens of authorities to support his or contrary opinions, cited no one here to support this thesis. I do not, however, consider this sufficient evidence for us to ignore his opinion. I have no doubt that had the respectable ladies of Brantôme, and even their lovers, not found direct reassurance from the *De Matrimonio*, they would have found it through a carefully selected confessor.

Sanchez assuredly did not originate the ideas concerning contraceptive behaviour described by Brantôme, since the *De Matrimonio* came after *Livre des Dames*. Although no cause-and-effect relationship has been established, the fact that the quasi legitimation came later is of no small interest to the historian. But, and we have stressed this several times, the principles which permitted Brantôme and the ladies of his day to precede Sanchez on this question had already long existed in the doctrine of marriage and sexuality.

Therefore, I do not wish to suggest that the late sixteenth century witnessed a major step in a moral evolution. The idea of illicit relations has always involved the idea of sterility, and the penitentials had already indicated that contraceptive intercourse mitigated the guilt of fornication. Moreover, in lay tradition, long before the gallant ladies of Brantôme, did not the rules of courtly love tend in the same direction, separating love from marriage and procreation?

The relationship between the bards singing of this "pure love" and the Cathar heresy have often been stressed. But the crime of the Cathars, like that of the Manichees in the fourth and fifth centuries, or the Gnostics of the second century, was to attack the sacrament of marriage.[62] It is because they likened marriage to fornication — or adultery — that they recommended sterile intercourse within a marriage. By contrast, Sanchez or Brantôme, like the troubadours, pushed to the extreme the contrast between marriage and fornication which the Church Fathers had developed since the second century.

Under pain of heresy, contraception could not only be envisaged extramaritally. Under pain of scandal, illicit relations had to be sterile. And demographic statistics, within the limits of current research, indicate — only for the seventeenth and eighteenth centuries, and then only in France — practically no contraception in marriage, but a very low, indeed too low, illegitimate birth rate.

These statistics also indicate, during the same period, a late marriage age, on the average more than ten years after puberty. These late marriages are justifiably seen as a means of birth control, which was not — without going into detail — a manifestation of the collective will of a society struggling against the threat of overpopulation, but rather of the individual necessity, valid for women as for men, of having sufficient capital to start a family. To an extent which we still cannot document, this capital was acquired by domestic, artisanal, or agricultural labour, and took time to acquire. Are we to believe that the majority of these prolonged celibacies were chaste?[63] We may doubt it, when we recall the virulent hostility manifested in the early sixteenth century[64] toward ecclesiastical celibacy, a hostility which the Protestant reformers took up in their turn, or when we think of the difficulty the Catholic Counter Reformation encountered in imposing chastity upon the secular clergy.[65] Instead, I believe that those who could not afford to have children found an outlet for their sexual impulses in illicit and sterile practices, including both solitary practices[66] and fornication.[67]

In short, I believe that illicit relations were not the deeds of restricted groups on the outskirts of society, and that they involved contraceptive measures.[68] Before the massive introduction of contraception into marriage, these techniques were learned in "sin".[69]

One problem remains which is apparently more difficult to solve now than at the beginning of this article: if, for centuries, contraception was a characteristic of illicit relationships and if marriage itself was only for procreation, how can we explain the free consciences of those Christian couples which, without doubt since the eighteenth century, sinned in good faith? First let us recall that this contract between marriage and pleasure was found among both theologians and courtiers; we have not proved that it existed on all social levels and in every region of the Christian West. But, for those circles in which this dichotomy existed, the innovation was to behave in marriage as one did outside marriage. Through this innovation the husband behaved toward his wife as he would with a mistress, and the wife "behaved toward her husband as toward a lover". Good faith would therefore mean that marriage is an amorous relationship legitimized as such by the sacrament. And the sin lay in believing this a century too soon.

Chapter 8

Man and Wife in the Marriage Bed

MARITAL DEBT — THE EQUALITY OF THE SEXES

Although women used to have skills which were markedly different from those of men, which in fact gave them much responsibility and independence vis-à-vis their husbands, legally they were entirely subordinate to them. In all aspects of their life together, the husband was the head ["*caput*"], the wife the body. He was in all ways responsible for her behaviour, and had the right and the duty — within certain limits — to punish and beat her in order to prevent her from doing wrong, or simply to remind her of his supremacy. Like a child or a servant, she had to obey him in all that he commanded that was reasonable, and bear his reprimands or blows without replying. Abundant proof of this is provided by ecclesiastical moralists, jurists, proverbs and traditional popular customs.[1] There was, however, one place where women were theoretically their husbands' equals: in the marriage bed.

From the very beginning, the same St Paul who, in his letter to the Ephesians had sanctioned the subordination of wives,[2] had also established, in his first letter to the Corinthians, that wives had the same sexual duties and rights as their husbands: "But because of the temptation to immorality, each man should have his own wife and each woman her own husband. The husband should give to his wife her conjugal rights, and likewise the wife to her husband. For the wife does not rule over her own body, but the husband does; likewise the husband does not rule over his own body, but the wife does."[3] After him — or at least since the theological renaissance of the twelfth century — all the scholars who have written about "marital debt" have clearly and forcefully endorsed the equality of men and women in this area: "*in hoc, enim, pares sunt*", [they are equal][4], which phrase they contrasted with the conventional maxim subordinating women to their husbands in all other aspects of their life together, "*mulieres subjectae sint viris suis*" [let women be ruled over by their husbands].

This paradox was one which the faithful had difficulty in understanding and accepting and which theologians struggled to explain and justify.[5] The historian's attention must be drawn less to their explanations than to their stubborn assertion of this paradox. Granted, each society, each era, each social class usually retains from its religion only that which agrees with its attitudes and material situation. I would even be tempted to say that the theologian's role is still today what it was in the past: to make doctrine acceptable to the society of the day. This is not true for this particular point however: between the twelfth and twentieth centuries, in a society in which women were subordinate to men in all things, theologians unceasingly affirmed that the wife had equal rights over her husband's body to those of her husband over hers. This is no doubt because from the beginning that had been one of the characteristic paradoxes of Christian marriage.

As in practice wives were not used to experiencing such equality, theologians went even further: they favoured wives, by making the husband's obligation greater: "Because coldness and shame are stronger in women than in men, a wife has the right to wait for an explicit request from her husband [before giving him what she owes him], whereas a husband does not have the right to expect the same from his wife: he must consider even implicit requests, just as a doctor has to help a sick person even if he is the only one to see that the person is sick."[6]

Albert the Great appears to have established this privilege of women to be understood without having to go into great detail in the thirteenth century and this privilege appears to have been mentioned since then by the majority of theologians dealing with "marital debt". Some comment is called for. Firstly, the idea that the timidity of her sex prevents a woman from clearly claiming her due was never contested, and it therefore appears to me to be indicative of the *sexual status of women* in traditional Western society, no matter what the natural differences are between men and women in this respect and no matter what earlier female behaviour may actually have been.

Of course, for theologians, a woman's modesty was a natural virtue of her sex. Because it was natural, it was unchangeable. Because it was a virtue, it did not need to be changed. Hence, they could do nothing but think of how to compensate for its unfortunate effects. Within these limitations, one could say that they did everything possible in order to allow a wife to enjoy fully the rights over her husband's body given her by St Paul.

Thirdly, this tradition survived up until the twentieth century.[7] Not only did men continue to expect greater modesty from women — and were scandalized and unhappy when the reality did not live up to their expectations — but women often continued to expect men to be aware of their desires or even "to perceive better than themselves when women wish to make love"[8], as Thomas Sanchez wrote at the beginning of the seventeenth century.

In fact, the excessive attention demanded of men in order to re-establish equality of sexual rights between husband and wife definitely contributed to unequal relationships being perpetuated. By dint of interpreting a woman's desires, there was the danger of taking them away from her. This is suggested in Sanchez' words. Ultimately, female desire could even become almost unimportant, which was quite the opposite of the intended effect.

All in all, slavish devotion to the idea of "marital debt" would theoretically make women equal to men. However, if a wife did not dare to claim her rights and if her husband was left to discern her desires, obviously in practice she was only enslaved by it. This sexual enslavement of women certainly existed prior to Christianity. But Christian doctrine may have contributed to its being perpetuated.

THE ROLE OF MEN AND WOMEN IN SEXUAL INTERCOURSE

Equality of rights over one's spouse's body in no way implied the defining of sexual roles, nor even equality in the physical relationship. According to Viguerius, "in the marital act, the man is active [*agens*] and the women passive [*patiens*] and therefore the man's [role] is the most noble."[9] These different sexual roles were considered natural, in other words, desired by God. Adopting the opposite sex's role was therefore sacrilegious, a "crime against nature", a perversion of God's work. This comes across clearly in theological discussions of positions used by married couples during intercourse.

"The natural position consists of the woman lying on her back and the man lying on top of her, making sure to ejaculate into the vessel intended for that purpose".[10] This position is appropriate, explains Sanchez, not only "because it most favours the ejaculation of sperm as well as its being received and retained in the female vessel", but also because it "conforms better to the nature of things that the man act and the woman accept".[11] On the contrary, "when the man is underneath, by the very nature of the position, he accepts and when the woman is on top, she acts. Who cannot see how horrified nature is by this aberration?" In addition, "Methodius, in his commentary on the book of *Genesis*, said that the cause of the Flood was that the women, overcome with madness, had misused the men, the latter being underneath and the women on top." According to Sanchez, St Paul confirmed this when writing to the Romans: "Their women exchanged natural relations for unnatural".[12] It should be noted that theologians do not hesitate to take liberties with the Holy Scriptures in order to justify their condemnation of this position for sexual intercourse. I know of nothing in *Genesis* which would allow us to attribute this reversal of sexual roles to antediluvian society, nor to explain God's wrath in this way[13]; as for the unnatural practices denounced in Paul's letter to the Romans, it seems obvious to me that they were homosexual practices and that the passage had to be "pruned" in order for anything else to be read into it.[14]

But these incorrect commentaries on the Scriptures were not aimed at forcing the faithful to condemn practices which conventional morality would have accepted. Although those positions considered "against nature" appeared to symbolically pervert the natural order — either by imitating animals[15] or by reversing the male and female roles — theologians from the late Middle Ages and modern times have not categorically condemned them. Some have commented that they did not prevent procreation, the uterus being able to accept sperm equally well in either position. Others recognised that it might be necessary for couples to adopt one or another of these positions if they were too large to be able to have sexual intercourse otherwise, or when the woman was pregnant and they were afraid of harming the unborn child. This liberalism, far from moving towards conventional morality, seems to have rather scandalized lay people, even the least prudish.[16] Regarding equal rights over their partner's body, theologians upheld St Paul's paradoxical teachings against the prejudices of their time. As far as sexual roles and positions for sexual intercourse are concerned, on the other hand, they seem to have sometimes distorted passages from the Holy Scriptures in order to justify these prejudices.

WOMAN'S RIGHT TO PLEASURE

Theologians of the past often gave the impression of believing that any sexual act automatically gave the woman as much pleasure as the man. Yet, they did sometimes debate woman's right to orgasm — if I may use this anachronistic term — in marital sexual relations.[17]

According to Christian doctrine, it must be remembered, the purpose of sexuality is not pleasure but the reproduction of the species. Pleasure is there solely to entice us and it would be a grievous sin for us to resist this enticement and not to let ourselves be beguiled. Marriage gives each spouse rights over his or her partner's body, but as an instrument for procreation, not for sensual pleasure. For men, however, pleasure cannot be dissociated from ejaculation. The issue was whether female pleasure was also necessary for procreation.

Galen believed that, like the man, the woman emitted a "seed" and that this emission gave her, as it did him, pleasure. The mixing of these two seeds caused the embryo to be conceived and therefore procreation was not possible without shared pleasure.[18] In other words, any sexual act where the woman did not reach an orgasm was an incomplete act and ought logically to have been condemned by Christian moralists.

Aristotle's theory, however, was completely different. In his view, the woman contributed to conception only by her "menstrual blood", blood which collected in the uterus for this purpose, and was only finally discharged after a month when conception had not taken place. When, on the other hand, sperm from the man entered and remained in the uterus — and the best time for this was shortly after the menstrual discharge, at the time when the womb was supplied with new blood — it acted on the blood like a sort of fermenting agent. This fermentation resulted in the conception of an embryo after a certain period of time — a period of forty days was most often mentioned.[19] Thus, the woman played the same role in the process of generation as she did in the sexual act: her menstrual blood was a passive substance, whereas the man's sperm was an active principle which created and organised. But we are interested here in the fact that the blood which represented the woman's contribution to reproduction was discharged continuously and without pleasure, whether or not she had sexual relations. In short, female pleasure was not necessary for procreation.

It appears difficult to accept both of these theories at the same time and depending upon which one chooses, one would arrive at very

different moral codes for marriage. Whether because of the constraints of Christian morality or because, conversely, the choice made
between these theories reflected the sexual status of women in the
society in question, the evolution of theories of reproduction could
reveal a veritable history of the orgasm. Aristotle's theory seems to
have prevailed until the end of antiquity — St Jerome and St
Augustine are examples[20] — and to have still existed in the thirteenth
century in the works of Albert the Great.[21] Later, sixteenth and seventeenth century doctors preferred Galen and the majority of theologians — even though they rarely referred to medical treatises of their
time — again took up Galen's arguments, quite resolutely.

What is strange is that none of them seem to have been supporters
of Galen or Aristotle alone. Their respect for the Church Fathers and
the great thirteenth century doctors no doubt prevented them from
totally abandoning Aristotle. The fact that many women conceived
without pleasure — a fact of which confessors must have been aware,
although it was never mentioned in debates — perhaps also led to
this. In any case, sexual intercourse from which only the man derived
pleasure was never considered to be an incomplete act without any
chance of procreation and therefore a crime against nature. On the
other hand, they could not give up Galen either, since the existence of
pleasure for women could not be doubted, even if not all women who
conceived had experienced it. Such pleasure had to play a part in
procreation because there was no question that the sole purpose of
sexuality was procreation.[22] If one followed Aristotle's teachings too
scrupulously, it would undermine the basic tenets of Christian doctrine on marriage and sexuality. Theologians therefore looked for a
compromise solution, taking ideas from both Aristotle and Galen.
They generally accepted that the female seed — and therefore female
pleasure — was, if not necessary for conception, at least useful for its
accomplishment: the children of those mothers who conceived with
pleasure were more perfect, more handsome that those whose mothers conceived without pleasure.

It remained to evaluate the gravity of the sin of those couples who
conceived such imperfect children and to inform them how not to
commit this sin. This is the subject of the theological debates which I
shall try to summarise, while drawing attention both to the way in
which the questions were phrased and to the various answers given
in reply.

Firstly, must the woman emit her seed during sexual intercourse?
This question is part of the debate on contraception: it assumes that

the woman holds back her orgasm in order to avoid procreation. That could be tolerated if the man had also held his back, but the case under discussion is when he has not held it back and the woman wants to take away the procreative value from sexual intercourse.[23] Of fifteen theologians examining this case, eight think that the woman commits a grievous sin, four think it a venial sin and three conclude that it is not a sin at all, her behaviour having only decreased, not nullified, the chances of conception.

Secondly, must the man prolong intercourse until his wife emits her seed — in other words, reaches orgasm? Four theologians consider it his bounden duty. The others — the vast majority — judge that he is in no way constrained to do so. All of them, however, "allowed" the husband to prolong intercourse until his wife's orgasm. Oddly enough, this was a concession, although the importance of procreation should have resulted in either advice or a command.

Must the man and woman reach orgasm at the same time? This third question was also asked with a view towards the perfection of the child created. Indeed, Galen believed that reproduction was only possible if the two seeds were emitted simultaneously; and his disciple Ambroise Paré wrote in the sixteenth century: "Conception never takes place except when the two seeds are emitted at the same time".[24] However, of twenty-five theologians involved in these debates, only six dealt with this problem. And even though all six recommended that couples do their best to emit their seeds at the same time — the faster partner needing to arouse the slower partner by kisses and caresses before intercourse — it was only because simultaneous emission facilitated conception or made the children better-looking, not because they believed conception to be impossible otherwise.[25]

Nonetheless it must be noted that "shameful kissing and touching" were also discussed — not explicitly with regard to female seed and female pleasure — and that most theologians sanctioned them as preparation for sexual relations. When couples caressed with a different intention, on the other hand, they were committing a venial or mortal sin, because of the "danger of pollution". Only Thomas Sanchez allowed such caresses under all circumstances and despite this risk, "because they sustained mutual love".[26]

Despite wanting to minimise the difference between man and woman as far as "conjugal duty" was concerned, Christian moralists could not help but notice that the woman was generally the slower of the two to reach orgasm: "Because they are more lusty, men more often emit their seed first".[27] When the woman had been frustrated of her pleasure in this way, could she then, after the penis was withdrawn, reach orgasm by masturbating in order to emit her seed as well? Of seventeen authors who broached this fourth question, fourteen allowed her to do so and only three forbade it.

This division of the answers may appear surprising for several reasons and some comment is therefore in order. Men were strictly forbidden to masturbate, no matter what the circumstances; women were also forbidden to masturbate, except in this specific case. This prohibition, however, was not based on the selfishness of such sexual behaviour, as is the case today, but on the fact that it did not contribute to reproduction. It is therefore understandable that it was authorised when it could facilitate procreation.

It is true that the ability of such behaviour to aid in procreation could be challenged: Sanchez notes that, according to some writers, "as soon as the male organ is withdrawn, air gets in in order to avoid a vacuum" and that "the seed received is contaminated by it". Since it is emitted after the contamination of the male seed, "the woman's seed is therefore no longer of any use".[28] Is it not strange that so many writers tolerated this stratagem, the validity of which was debatable, while so few advised the men to prolong intercourse until the woman reached orgasm or to arouse her by caresses so that she would emit her seed at the same time as her partner? I confess that, for the time being, I am unable to provide a rational explanation for these apparent inconsistencies. Perhaps theologians were too conscious of their lack of knowledge about procreation to prescribe a definitive moral code, and so contented themselves with tolerating or not tolerating that which caused the greatest problems.

Moreover, other motives, generally less explicitly expressed than the importance of reproduction, were mixed up in the debate. Some theologians commented that "if women, after being aroused, were obliged to repress their nature, they would always be in danger of committing mortal sin, since men, being lustier, are more often the first to ejaculate". The idea was that it would be unfair for women, who have just as much right as men to find a means of preservation in marriage. This argument could have been used to justify post-coital masturbation, even if female seed emitted after the penis' withdrawal was shown to be completely useless. Alfonso de Liguori, who mentions this, rejects it immediately by commenting that, "in a case where the woman was faster than her husband, it would lead to the man being given the same right, which would cause him to commit a terrible sin".[29] But the lack of realism in Liguori's argument seems rather to emphasise the strength of the opposite argument. On the one hand, in fact, the man is faster than the woman "because he is lustier"; on the other hand, because he is the active member of the couple, it is he who decides on the beginning and the end of intercourse, as shown in all the debate over *coitus interruptus* and *amplexus reservatus*. The reasoning refuted by Alfonso de Liguori could therefore justify post-coital masturbation by the woman, in the absence of any proven scientific data as to the usefulness of the "female seed".

We must point out that Diana — one of the three theologians who did not accept this practice — considers it a mortal sin "if the woman is able to contain herself". When, on the other hand, she is not able to control the sexual desires awakened by intercourse, one can therefore assume that she would be committing only a venial sin, or even no sin at all.

Considerations unrelated to concern for procreation are even more clearly visible among reasons for condemning voluntary arousal after intercourse. Admittedly, Diana insists that "the female seed is not necessary for reproduction". But this is only a rhetorical argument, since all theologians acknowledged that point and since the debate centred on the usefulness of the seed, not on its necessity. The two arguments which are the basis for Diana's hostility to this practice were different in nature. On the one hand, "such touching, after intercourse with a man, is intrinsically bad"; on the other hand, if a woman emits her seed separately, she is not "one flesh" with her husband. Despite the old-fashioned expressions, there is the feeling of a new vision of sexuality evolving. If the German Theatine's arguments are less rational than those of other theologians, that does not mean that they are less modern. On the contrary, this irrationality is the manifestation of the inconsistencies in the Church's doctrine of which people were becoming aware. There was inconsistency be-tween the old "Augustinian" vision — inherited as far back as the second century A.D. from the Stoics and other philosophers from pagan antiquity — and the personalist vision, which still has not entirely prevailed today, as shown by the encyclical *Humanae vitae*, a fine example of this escape into irrationality.[30]

III. THE CHILD AND PROCREATION

"Childhood and Society", which appeared in Annales ESC (March/April 1964) is a review of Philippe Ariès' now famous book Centuries of Childhood (published originally in French as l'Enfant et la Vie familiale sous l'Ancien Régime and translated from the French by Robert Baldick). This book opened up a whole new field to historians, the history of childhood, and it is therefore natural that this review should begin this chapter.

"Attitudes Towards Young Children and Sexual Behaviour" takes up and develops a short presentation made in 1970 to the Société de démographie historique, at a meeting concerning childhood. The article was written up during the summer of 1972 and was published in its present form in the 1973 issue of Annales de démographie historique.

"Ancient and Modern Adages Concerning the Child within the Family" does not claim to draw very original conclusions on the history of childhood, but to show what historical lessons can be learned from studying proverbs. This is a difficult exercise, which has rarely been undertaken and even more rarely been successful. This article appeared in a special issue of Perspectives psychiatriques concerning the family (1976, 1, no. 55). "The Young Woman in Ancient French Proverbs", appeared in le Groupe familial, the quarterly journal of the Ecole des parents et des éducateurs (no. 80, July 1978). It is a less weighty article, since it is based on a more restricted corpus of proverbs.

Chapter 9

Childhood and Society
Review of a Book by Philippe Ariès*

The starting point for too much historical research is a collection of documents. The starting point of Philippe Ariès' research on the child and family life is a question, and, being a topic pertinent for today, therein lies its greatest merit.

For contemporary thought is obviously obsessed by childhood. This is adequately demonstrated by the interminable discussions on age and educational programmes, the proliferation of approaches and of safety measures for children and the particularly remarkable growth of child psychology; but perhaps even more so by the almost exclusive interest in childhood shown by Freudian psychoanalysis in its explanation of adults' psychological problems.

Thus, countless undeniably interesting studies exist, but studies which are generally lacking in historical perspective. Educationalists, psychologists, psychoanalysts, even sociologists find themselves, as a result of their methods, immersed in a topical issue with no depth and find it difficult to show the main strands of the evolution of childhood when its history is not yet written. My insistence on the necessity for a history of childhood is not simply that of a compulsive historian. Some psychologists also feel this need: the Dutch psychologist H. Van der Berg, in a book rich in ideas,[1] albeit controversial ones,

---

* Ariès, *Centuries of Childhood*, translated by Robert Baldick, London, Jonathan Cape, 1962. (Originally published in French as *l'Enfant et la Vie familiale sous l'Ancien Régime*, Paris, Plon, 1960; republished Seuil, "L'univers historique" collection, 1973; revised edition, Seuil, "Points-Histoire" collection, 1975.)

demonstrates the good use the psychologist can make of historical perspective.

As for Philippe Ariès, he is less ambitious, or at least less obviously so. While writing an existential history book, he makes too many concessions in his introduction to traditional psychology's fixed ideas. "Is the family," he writes, "a phenomenon any more subject to history than instinct is? It is possible to argue that it is not, and to maintain that the family partakes of the immobility of the species. It is no doubt true that since the beginning of the human race men have built homes and begot children...It is not so much the family as a reality that is our subject here as the family as an idea. True, men and women will always go on loving one another..."

No doubt he was wise to specify the nature of the research: it is the idea of childhood and family life and not their reality which is to be studied. But why limit possible extensions of the study? Why lock oneself in advance into psychological categories as questionable as instinct, and as badly defined as the love of men and women? Why accept so quickly the universality of the human tendency to "build a home"? Finally, why make such a great distinction between the idea of childhood (or of family) and its reality? Such caution borders on absurdity and is surprising, all the more so as the author, thank goodness, moves away from it during the study.

His investigation is organised into three parts: the idea of childhood, scholastic life and the family.

The idea of childhood, according to Philippe Ariès, has not always existed. In order for it to exist, it is necessary to have a clear idea of the different "ages of life". Until the fourteenth century, many ideas existed about the number of ages: sometimes there were twelve, related to the twelve months of the year, sometimes seven, sometimes five, sometimes four. It was not until the fourteenth century that the idea of the five ages was decided upon, which remains unchanged in iconography to this day: the age of toys, the age of school, the age of love or courtly and knightly sports, the age of war and chivalry and, finally, the age of men of law, science or learning.

In order for the idea of childhood to exist, its vocabulary must also exist. Throughout the Middle Ages, its vocabulary remains nebulous, emphasising dependency rather than biological development.

If childhood is noticed and attention paid to it, children must appear in iconography, yet they are rarely found in medieval illustrations. Up until the twelfth century, they appear with an adult's frame and differ from adults only in their height. They cannot be distinguished by their clothing until the fourteenth century.

In daily life, children lived an adult life with adults. At least until the seventeenth century, they shared the same games and the same working life, since from top to bottom of the social ladder children learned through apprenticeships. At school, the training ground for clerics, no distinction was made between age groups: ten-year-old pupils were mixed in with adults. Finally, no sexual secrets were hidden from children: until the seventeenth century they participated in all conversations, all jokes, and even in all forms of entertainment.[2]

In short, then, around the eleventh to twelfth centuries there was nothing to fundamentally distinguish children from adults. Philippe Ariès' major contribution is to mark the stages and forms of this differentiation.

Once the concept of childhood appears, what form does it take? Ariès distinguishes two forms: firstly, "coddling", in the sixteenth century and secondly, the attitude in the seventeenth century that children needed to be both safeguarded and reformed. This leads him into a history of education from the Middle Ages to the present. The ground seemed to have already been prepared for this research. In fact, great initiative was again necessary: on the whole, historians had contented themselves with using limited sources, being very careful to ask questions which the sources did not answer. They had studied Montaigne or Rousseau's educational ideas,[3] the organisation of medieval universities, or the Jesuits' educational initiatives.[4] But, to the best of my knowledge, nothing was available concerning the breakdown by age or by social background of the school population, about pupils' resources and life even, at school and away from school, except the recent work of P. de Dainville.[5] One would need to examine the sources available concerning educational methods, childhood or family life in order to fully comprehend the originality and the importance of Ariès' book.[6]

After painting a picture of early school life, he describes the introduction of colleges and of separate classes at school. He shows the trend towards dividing classes by age from the seventeenth to the nineteenth century, the changes in discipline, the development of boarding schools, the establishing of primary education and its significance for the society.

What is the result of this long study of schooling? On the one hand, the fact that medieval schools recruited hardly anyone but future clerics in order to give them professional knowledge, whereas modern schools are intended for all children, in order to educate them. In the seventeenth and eighteenth centuries, there is therefore an increase in the number of colleges, recruiting their students from all classes of society. On the other hand, the division into classes at school, which, in France, took place around the sixteenth century, contributes to the formation of a more marked distinction between age groups of children, which only became restricting at the beginning of the nineteenth century. The very slow development of boarding schools (which only became commonplace at the beginning of the nineteenth century) and also discipline at school, which appears as early as the end of the Middle Ages, separated school children from the world of adults and confined them to an inferior world, one with its own strict rules.

The course taken by this development is very different in France and in England. But, in Western Europe as a whole the result was the provision of schools for children, i.e. (although I go slightly beyond Ariès' conclusions) treating a sizeable proportion of the population as children.

In the third part of his book, Ariès researches the birth and characteristics of the concept of the modern family. He notes the gradual appearance of the family in examples from the sixteenth to the eighteenth century. His work is based on that of historians of medieval society and he concludes that there was a strengthening of bonds within the marital family as opposed to bonds of lineage in the last centuries of the Middle Ages. Religious history, after all, shows that the sanctity of the family barely dates back to before the sixteenth century.

Thus, the concept of the family develops parallel to the concept of childhood. They come together in modern times, particularly with the inclination towards family intimacy which appears in well-to-do classes in the eighteenth century. This inclination towards intimacy is shown in the fitting out of apartments and in the insistence on good manners and sociability. From now on, the family closes itself to the world and turns in on the child.

The historical importance of these conclusions must be stressed. Philippe Ariès touches on one of the most profound existential changes in Western society: the child is there to be loved and educated, and the modern family has become the basic unit of society surrounding the child and conscious of the *duties* of love and education. This transformation, while in itself fundamental, also explains the demographic revolution of the nineteenth century. Because the family was based around the child and because the couple felt responsible in every way for the child's future, they began to "plan" their families.[7]

Obviously there is no question of making this slow transformation the major reason for this demographic change and therefore for our history. There is no question of contrasting it in any causal hierarchy with the logic of economy. But it is certain that the use of contraception could not spread into society as a whole without a profound change in mentality. Describing this change was one of Philippe Ariès' initial ideas.[8]

However, his book could not be reduced to merely resolving this demographic question. He also describes the historical scene behind society's loss of demographic equilibrium. His vision of medieval and modern societies is often controversial, but always enriching, whether for the historian or for other social science specialists.

These are therefore some of the original theses which remain unexplored on a fundamental historical subject. Upon what documents and what methods of analysis are they based? It is a crucial question. Looking to ancient documents to satisfy contemporary curiosity is always a risk: they were not intended for that, they can never completely answer our initial questions.

I feel two contradictory sentiments when I examine Philippe Ariès' work: wonder and disquiet.

I feel wonder at the variety of documents used; the quantity and the consistency of the information they give; the way in which he looks for the answer to a well-defined question in each series of documents; and the way in which the question is adapted to the nature of the document, while still remaining within the framework of his research.

Sometimes the inquiries are extremely simple, such as could be carried out by machines: are there or are there not children in a given series of illustrations? At what date do children appear in it? Is the child alone, with other children or together with adults? This is similar to a sociologist's analysis of content.

But often the inquiry is more subtle and is guided more by the nature of the document. For example, when the author is studying genre paintings (pp. 37–8), he notes: "Painters were particularly fond of depicting childhood for its graceful or picturesque qualities..." Or again (p. 47): "The baroque painter depended on them [children] to give his group portrait the dynamism that it lacked." Obviously such assessments are not exhaustive since he is dealing with works of art whose main function was not the portrayal of childhood. Neither is the document distorted or incorrectly considered to portray child-hood. Its nature as a work of art is used to best advantage, and to the best advantage of the research.

The division of questions and the multiplicity of perspectives match the variety of documentary material. For example, in order to study the idea of age, Philippe Ariès considers in turn the registry office, inscriptions on paintings and family furniture, memoirs and account books, scientific treatises and medieval poems, calendar illustrations, and the use of vocabulary. Then, from similarly varied documents (sometimes the same ones), he considers games, costume, modesty and immodesty, pupils' ages, school discipline, etc. The results of all these studies agree that in the Middle Ages, childhood was little recognised, and that in modern times it is increasingly recognised.

Philippe Ariès uses the following methods very skilfully: a great variety and quantity of documentary material, the creating of series, dividing of the questions and their adaptation to the nature of the document, and research on the convergence of ideas. They are indeed the methods necessary for any regressive research into existential history.

Unfortunately certain weak arguments occasionally hamper the strength of an affirmation. For example (p. 67), based on Louis XIII's childhood alone, the conclusion is drawn: "It seems, therefore, that...there was not such a strict division as there is today between children's games and those played by adults." I am not questioning this conclusion: it is supported later on by abundant proof. But how can the childhood of a Dauphin be accepted as typical on the question of games, when it is considered exceptional on the question of educa-tion?

The author generally points out the convergence of ideas, although he seems to concern himself little with certain divergences. For exam-ple, as far as medieval schooling is concerned, the author only stresses the fact that "the medieval school was not intended for children: it was a sort of technical school for the instruction of clerics" (p. 330). Of course, the vast majority of children avoided school, and there were many older students. Yet, was education not linked in the medieval mind to the training of children as it was in ancient times and is in our time? Illustrations of the five "ages of life", unchanged since the fourteenth century, clearly prove it: after the age of toys comes the age of school. Why should this be forgotten when one is talking about the relationships between school and childhood?

Too often the author seems to be a prisoner of his initial question (is there a concept of childhood?), and perhaps also of preconceived ideas. Not only was it essential to research the existence of a concept of childhood and its stages of development, but also to explore the nature of this concept and to shed light on the characteristics of childhood in different periods. Too anxious to show the discovery and the segregation of childhood, Philippe Ariès seems to distort some evidence and not to make full use of other proof.

Thus, when he writes (p. 33): "Medieval art until about the twelfth century did not know childhood or did not attempt to portray it. It is hard to believe that this neglect was due to incompetence or incapacity; it seems more probable that there was no place for childhood in the medieval world", Ariès distorts the evidence provided by illustrations since they do not present an actual absence but only a scarcity (which ought to be clarified), and a summary characterisation of childhood: the children are "reduced to a smaller scale than the adults, without any other differences in expression or features". This concerns not the existence of childhood but the nature of the concept of childhood.

The same is true when, following Jean Calvet's lead,[9] he studies the child in medieval literature. Ariès notes only the fact that thirteen or fourteen-year-old children were present at battles; these children were presumably therefore already considered to be men. However, these texts have a reason for indicating the fact that these heroes are thirteen or fourteen: their young age intensifies the extraordinary character of their achievements, all the more so since childhood is characterised by its small size in a society where height and physical force are major assets.

When he turns to illustrations and modern dress, he seems to be prevented from going deeper into his thoughts on the nature of childhood. He is right to note (p. 44): "The taste for the *putto* corresponded to something far deeper than the taste for classical nudity, something which can be ascribed only to a broad surge of interest in childhood." But further research would have been necessary in order to discover what is shown by this love of naked children. The scene of the Dauphin and his sister frolicking naked in Henry IV's bed, as described by Héroard, is perhaps another manifestation of this concept, the nature of which remains to be explored.

Finally, it was interesting to note the characteristics of childhood dress, which became clearer in the seventeenth and eighteenth centuries (archaic, feminine, both martial and popular in character) because these characteristics of dress can give us information about characteristics of childhood. Why are little boys dressed so similarly to women? The author asks the question without making any attempt to answer it (p. 58). In order to explore this trend towards effeminacy, it would be necessary to study the history of costume more closely. Perhaps within this history a short period (that of the fashion) and a long period (that of the concept of childhood) could be discerned. But I am tempted to compare this effeminacy of dress to the fondness for naked children and to the "coddling" which Ariès notes as the first concept of childhood. Grace, beauty and delicacy of skin are recognised values of femininity: they are possessed by children as well as by women but this was perhaps only recognised subsequently. In any case, in the seventeenth century, children and women are both beings which one regards and embraces out of pleasure. It would be interesting to determine if this has always been so.

Another very marked characteristic, archaism of costume, seems to me to be equally rich in teaching material. Philippe Ariès concludes, perhaps somewhat hastily, that they wished children to be distinguished by their dress. On the contrary, did adults not project nostalgia for their own childhood onto their children, thereby coming closer to it by distinguishing it? But there again, it would be necessary to examine more closely the history of costume and to try to find out from the texts whether nostalgia for childhood exists.

Many other details could be discussed; I only wanted to show how the author is prevented from making the most of the gathered documentary evidence to explore other avenues by his obsession to prove that progressive distinction and segregation of childhood did exist. The reader is made too aware of this obsession and sometimes wonders whether certain converging results are not solicited.

This disquiet is even more disturbing because quantitative arguments remain vague and subjective. For example, we are told that references to children's jargon in literature are "unusual before the seventeenth century" and abundant after this period (p. 47). For that, one may provisionally trust the author. But when he claims that it cost less to keep a day pupil before the Revolution than a boarder in the nineteenth century (p. 307), it is more difficult to accept the absence of specific, concrete statistics by way of proof. The same is true when he sees schooling as a factor in the bringing together of child and family: "the length of time the student spends away from home...is not as long as the apprentice's period of separation" (p. 369). Further examples of this absence of objective details and statistical research could be cited.

This is true to such an extent that this book often seems more like a brilliant essay teeming with ideas than a scientific study.

Should Philippe Ariès be reproached for this? On such a subject, is it possible for him to do work as sound as that currently being done in economic history? Yes, I am sure it is. But that demanded toil which perhaps surpassed the capabilities of one man. In any case, it demanded more time than Philippe Ariès had available. Those involved in economic history know the length of time necessary for statistical studies. It is almost impossible to undertake such a task without material aid and moral support.

Thus, the particular merit of Philippe Ariès' book is that it opens the door to new research. His analysis of series of illustrations proves that it is possible to explore fields about which many historians are still sceptical. Yet the aim of this new research ought to be less originality of thought than greater scientific precision. It is now certain that the concepts of the past are different from those of today. But the concept of childhood clearly did not appear *ex nihilo*, no more than did Western love, as studied recently by Denis de Rougemont. We must avoid the obsession for establishing the date of their appearance; undoubtedly there are only changes in form and value, changes in rational and affective liaisons, changing of place in the structure of existence. One must, therefore, by means of exhaustive surveys of sources systematically divided into series, through purely statistical analysis, and through an even more astute qualitative study of the documents, analyse these concepts and determine their place in the personal and collective lives of the people of the past.

Chapter 10

Attitudes Towards Young Children and Sexual Behaviour

ANCIENT SOCIAL STRUCTURES AND THEIR DEVELOPMENT

Introduction

Despite the fact that, for years, there has been a move towards explaining the "Malthusian revolution" in psychological terms, little enthusiasm has been shown for exploring the psychology of traditional demographic behaviour and often there seems to have been poor comprehension of the changes in mental attitudes implicit in the shift to present-day behaviour. Why were couples formerly so prolific? Did they really wish to have families with eight, twelve or twenty children? Or did they instead resign themselves to the situation because — for technical or moral reasons — they were unable to make their conjugal relations sterile? Did they not have reasons for being Malthusians, as we do? And if so, why were they not Malthusian, or at least not to the same extent as we are?

The psychological changes which explain the advance of contraception in marriage between the eighteenth and the twentieth centuries are too numerous and too complex for me to undertake to examine them all in this article. I intend to examine only to what extent the introduction of contraception into marriage is the manifestation of increased concern for children — in short, a result of the increase in the concept of childhood — just as Philippe Ariès suggested more than twenty years ago.

Ancient Social Structures

CONDITIONS FAVOURABLE TO INFANTICIDE

Why Did Couples Formerly Have Many Children?

Given the economic and sanitary conditions of the seventeenth and eighteenth centuries, a much higher infant mortality rate than today was inevitable. Thus a higher birth rate was necessary to maintain society's demographic balance. Yet couples of that time did not rationalise like demographers nor even like patriots, as did some couples in the nineteenth and twentieth centuries. What then were the reasons for the high fertility rates, within each individual family?

Understandably, the high infant mortality rate encouraged men to father many children in order to perpetuate the strength of their families, in a society where family and blood ties were more important than today. But it is questionable whether this motivation was felt equally strongly in all social classes and it has never been proven that the birth rate in different social milieux was a function of the concern felt by families in each of these milieux for the perpetuation of their power. Noble or middle-class families were undoubtedly larger than those of peasants, but that can be explained mostly by the fact that noble and middle-class children were entrusted to paid wet nurses, which increased their mothers' fertility. As Maurice Garden showed recently,[1] shopkeepers and artisans in Lyons who also put their children out to nurse, produced just as many children as the nobility and the upper middle classes. Indeed, it is interesting to note that birth control was used by dukes and peers, who were thought to be particularly proud of their lineage, well before it was used by shopkeepers and artisans.

It has been claimed that children represented a form of wealth for those families who lived more from their work than from their possessions. And Maurice Garden's evidence as to shopkeepers' and artisans' reasons for putting their children out to nurse does indeed prove that financial considerations played their part in families' decision-making. Moreover, it is clear that in the past older workers could expect no pension other than that provided by their children. But these financial considerations required them to have the means and attitude necessary for such long-term investment. Thus it is difficult for me to imagine that this explains the fertility rates of artisans, who apparently had neither, and who really struggled to pay the wet nurses to whom they were to entrust the children born each year. Moreover, if children were such an investment, how do we explain the fact that parents did not visit every Sunday to make sure that they were well-fed and that their money was well-spent? As for the nobility and the middle classes, if ensuring that they had descendants was so important to them, why did they take so little care of their very young children?

The more we study couples' behaviour in the past, the more we have the impression that their behaviour was modelled on patterns which to us seem irrational. It is probable that these patterns, the logic of which escapes us, can be explained historically by the survival of various cultural elements from the past, many of which are unknown to us today.

It is possible to distinguish some of these elements however. There is, for example, the lack of concern counselled by the Church in its sermons. Together with other such ideas, an example of this lack of concern is found in the *Somme des péchés* by Benedicti, the preacher from Lyons: "A good man must never be afraid of having too many children, for he must think that it is a benediction from God and believe what David says: 'I', he says, 'have been young and now I am old, but never have I seen a just man abandoned nor his children looking for bread in great need', for because God has given them, so He will give him the means of feeding them, because it is He who feeds the birds in the sky; otherwise He would not give them to him..."[2]

This is a common theme for preaching, which can be found in various books of practical theology. One could comment on each phrase and expression in such texts, and I will return to this several times during the course of this article. For the moment, I will content myself with noting that the Church encouraged people to reproduce.

Noonan[3] has clearly demonstrated that, from antiquity to the end of the nineteenth century, the Church did not really have a demographic policy and that its doctrine on marriage in fact owed very little to Biblical populationism. At the doctrine's centre was the idea of chastity, an evangelical idea developed to a certain extent during the conflict against the Gnostics and under the influence of Stoic morality. For the Church of that time, the main point was that sexuality was given by God for procreation alone and that it should therefore never be used for other purposes. By forbidding all sexual activity for any but a procreative purpose, the Christian idea of chastity encouraged the faithful who were incapable of remaining continent to marry, and it encouraged married couples to reproduce as long as one or the other still felt the stirrings of physical desire. That is certainly one of the fundamental elements of sexual behaviour in ancient Christian society. However, there are many other, sometimes contradictory, elements: for example, strong Malthusians tendencies which I am going to try to highlight and explain.

The Feeling of Over-Population in Christian Society

Societies exist — in Africa for example — where children are always welcome. Such is not the case in ancient Western society. There, on the contrary, one discovers the feeling that the birth rate must be limited — not only in Greek and Roman times, but throughout the centuries when Christianity predominated. This feeling makes itself felt at two very different levels: in sociological thought and in behaviour.

At the ideological level, there is in fact a pseudo-Malthusianism in Christian society which, beneath the facade of thinking about the good of the world's peoples, has as its only goal the justification of certain theological positions. Indeed, theologians periodically demonstrated the need for a celibate clergy or for continence in marriage by Malthusian arguments, just as they denounced sterile pleasures by using populationist arguments. Noonan has stressed how much the Malthusian speeches given by St Jerome and other Church Fathers between the third and the fifth centuries occurred at an inopportune time demographically speaking,[4] and the same could be said of one of Gerson's texts, at the turn of the fifteenth century.[5] In fact, the Church at this time did not have a real demographic doctrine, nor genuine Malthusian concerns.

Aside from this false ideological Malthusianism — which took up themes developed by certain ancient philosophers — theological literature reveals the existence of another Malthusianism at the level of individuals' behaviour. For example, penitentials from the early Middle Ages, when they deal with infanticide, mention the poor woman who resorted to it because she could not provide for her children.[6] I do not know how important it is that this example almost disappeared in the twelfth and thirteenth centuries.

But at the beginning of the fourteenth century, for the first time, Peter de Palude suggests that the man incapable of providing for more children should resort to *amplexus reservatus*.[7] At that time, Malthusian tendencies are no longer only apparent in the fact that certain individuals are addicted to reprehensible acts: the problem of an overabundance of children is quite widespread and is important enough, at the family level, that a theologian with great influence looks for a solution which is acceptable to Christian morality and less demanding for the faithful than the classic solution of continence. It is hardly surprising that this takes place at the beginning of the fourteenth century, before the Black Death, when everywhere in Europe the population is reaching its medieval maximum. It seems impossible to me that the method proposed was really used from that time on as a means of regulating the birth rate: it is the fact that P. de Palude proposed it which is of interest, as a sign of an increasing sense of over-population. And the fact that fifteenth, sixteenth and seventeenth century theologians take up this proposal again will not have the same meaning as its initial introduction in the fourteenth century.

References to acts "against nature", and more particularly to *coitus interruptus*, are much more frequent, and are also evidence of Malthusian concerns. This is particularly true from the fourteenth century onward, since P. de Palude recommends *amplexus reservatus* to those who might be tempted by behaviour which is "against nature" for Malthusian reasons. Yet it is important to be aware of the fact that in principle acts "against nature" had other purposes than allowing sterile conjugal relations and that their existence does not always indicate Malthusian tendencies.

In popular thought in the sixteenth and at the beginning of the seventeenth century, various other corroborating indicators suggest that Malthusian influences become important again. Firstly, there are the efforts of Soto, Ledesma and Sanchez to release from their conjugal duty those couples who could no longer provide for any more children or bring them up in a manner appropriate to their status. Secondly, there is the greater emphasis on *amplexus reservatus* and *coitus interruptus* and on the problem of the Malthusian position on these discussions in treatises on moral theology. As for the new series collecting cases of conscience, which is more open to conjecture, there is little interest in the old debates on the necessity for periodic continence and much more in discussions on the means of, and reasons for, birth control. A quantitative study of all these series of documents remains to be made: these are just my overall impressions.

Finally, it is known that the age at marriage which, as early as the sixteenth century, was higher than in most non-Western societies, rose again between the sixteenth and the eighteenth century. This rise in the age at marriage was an efficient means of regulating a household's fertility, and, in some families at least, it seems to have been consciously used for the same.[8]

The Family Institution and the System of Property Inheritance

The feeling of there being an excess of children appears at the level of individual families and not at a political level, obviously because in Western society it is the family, not the State which has the job of feeding and raising children. In these countries, wealth is apportioned through the inheriting of property, with no consideration taken of the financial burdens of raising a family. As a result, a great many parents are too poor to be able to raise a large family.

In antiquity, fathers were able to adapt their burdens to their wealth: they were free to refuse the children presented to them by their wives, and it appears that they did in fact refuse many at birth. In Christian society, on the other hand, parents had to bring up all the children they produced. Yet the question must be asked whether, by changing the moral code without changing the system for the division of wealth other than by encouraging charity, Christianity really changed the situation.

It is true that in practice, if not in law, economic conditions were agreed upon at marriage. In those classes where wealth was for the most part inherited, a great number of younger brothers and sisters were thus destined for celibacy. In those classes in which it was earned through work, the age at marriage was higher as a result. But these temporary measures — as well as posing a risk to chastity and taking away from marriage the purpose as remedy for fornication attributed to it by St Paul[9] — were not enough to cause the disappearance of families which were too large or too poor.

Christianity offered only one way of limiting the burdens of family life to parents too poor to raise a large family: continence. Can we believe that they could really be content with this solution? And if not, what immoral solutions did they resort to?

Contraception and Infanticide

Contraception was not forbidden either by ancient laws or by the pagan religions, and many contraceptive methods were known to Graeco-Roman civilisation. We do not have much information as to who used the various methods, and it is particularly difficult to know to what extent married couples made use of them and to what extent they turned instead to abortion and infanticide. However, it is possible to consider certain facts and to put forward some hypotheses.

Firstly, there is the fact that, long before the arrival of Christianity, ancient writers frequently contrasted two types of sexual behaviour: marital and extramarital behaviour. The purpose of each was different: the former was aimed at procreation, the latter at the pursuit of pleasure. There were religious differences too: the former was watched over by Ceres, the goddess of the harvest, the latter Adonis, the god of wild plants, both sterile and aromatic.[10] The forms of sexual intercourse were different as well: marital intercourse took place in a way symbolic of fertilisation, the wife on her back on the ground allowing herself to be passively fertilised by her husband; whereas extramarital intercourse took place in various other positions, the woman generally being very active in order to give the man pleasure.

Of course these are only archetypes of behaviour. In actual fact, it is obvious that the majority of married couples also sought some pleasure in marital intercourse and that they often refused the children which resulted from it. For all that, can it be said that there was in fact no difference between marital relations and those that a man had with prostitutes? That would mean assuming that married women had the same knowledge and skills as courtesans, whereas we know that they did not. The future courtesan was taught everything that would allow her to attract men, to give them pleasure and to avoid pregnancy; whereas a young woman who was intended to get married was trained only in household skills, and was kept scrupulously ignorant of the secrets of sexuality. In *l'Economique*, Xenophon writes of the ideal wife as an innocent young thing; and although the Athenians undoubtedly carried things to extremes, we have no reason to believe that elsewhere in the Roman world young women were — as in ancient Japan — taught the art of giving pleasure to their future husbands.

The contraceptive methods used in antiquity — many in number and not all effective — were women's methods. Even applying balms to the penis could be done by the woman and did not imply initiative on the man's part. It must particularly be stressed that *coitus interruptus* is mentioned nowhere in Greek or Roman literature. No doubt that is logical, if men were entirely selfish about their pleasure.

In relations with prostitutes, it was obviously not up to the client to think about contraception. But, in marital intercourse, it was in principle left to the husband to decide whether or not he wanted children. Thus, within marriage, *coitus interruptus* would have been essential as a means of birth control, because of its simplicity and effectiveness and because it is the man who initiates it. In actual fact, we find no mention of *coitus interruptus*, whereas in the same period, in the Graeco-Roman world, Jews of the Diaspora were familiar with and made use of it. Might this not indicate that contraception was un-known in conventional marital behaviour? One does sometimes hear of married couples who, in order not to conceive, had intercourse in a way which was contrary to the standards of the time,[11] but nothing proves that this referred to *coitus interruptus*. Moreover, such refer-ences are very rare and show such practices as being atypical.

If the husband had wanted his wife to practise birth control as prostitutes did, he was probably inadequately qualified to instruct her effectively. Most of the methods suggested by doctors seemed inef-fectual, whereas prostitutes used safe methods of necessity, in order to be able to ply their trade. But were they prepared to divulge their secrets? And moreover, did husbands' attitudes allow them to have their wives introduced to these secrets? It is doubtful. It was one thing to refuse a child when it arrived, in accordance with well-established customs, and another thing to have one's wife trained like a courtesan, in a civilisation in which the conflict between the idea of wife and the idea of courtesan was so strong. It is probable that, in the Roman world, as ancient moral structures disintegrated, a certain number of married couples practised birth control and imitated extramarital behaviour; but it can be assumed that they were few in number and that such behaviour was never normal for Malthusian couples.

As for abortion, Wrigley[12] saw clearly that it was more dangerous for the woman than giving birth and that, if it had been the only method used, women would have needed to make use of it much more often than infanticide. There is no doubt that it too was used mostly outside of marriage when a form of birth control had not worked. Thus, the hypothesis could be proposed that, in antiquity, infanticide was normally used by Malthusian married couples, whereas contraception and abortion were ordinarily used by slaves, concubines and prostitutes.

In Christian society, did those couples forced to the Malthusian limiting of the size of their families, and who were incapable of escaping through continence, resort to contraception or to infanticide?

If, as I have just hypothesised, infanticide was traditionally more characteristic of behaviour within marriage, it can be assumed that this tradition continued for a certain period of time after conversion. It is true that civil laws do not appear to have considered contraception as such, whereas they severely condemned infanticide.[13] However, before attaching great significance to this fact, one must wonder whether those guilty of infanticide were very likely to get caught — this question will be considered later — and whether effective birth control methods existed and were available to married couples.

Penitentials from the early Middle Ages mention three types of practices capable of yielding Malthusian results. Firstly, there were "acts against nature". Some of these, such as masturbation, homosexuality and bestiality, are typical of relations outside of marriage. It seems that the same could be said of intercourse which was *inter crua* [between the legs] or *inter fermora* [between the thighs], which must be distinguished from *coitus interruptus*: it was generally considered less serious than full intercourse out of wedlock. I expect that it was the practice especially among adolescents or in acts of violence in which it had the advantage of not sacrificing the woman's virginity.

However, some "acts against nature" were mentioned in the context of marital relations. Of these, *coitus interruptus* is the only one which married couples could turn to and obviously have contraception in mind. Noonan has found three examples of this, which is not insignificant.[14] But, of the approximately fifty penitentials which I have studied, I do not remember having found any further examples, even though the majority dealt with "acts against nature" within marriage. I conclude from this that it was a very unusual practice at that time.

As for the other "acts against nature", not all were sterile,[15] and they were indicative of sexual depravity rather than of Malthusianism. This is true not only in the ideological structures of the time — in which the two acts were closely linked — but also according to our own: we would consider it perverted behaviour to regularly and exclusively give oneself over to either of the two practices which are sterile. I do not conclude from that that such behaviour was also rare — for sexual repression favoured various kinds of aberrations in the age when behavioural patterns were formulated — but I find it hard to imagine that couples who originally engaged in normal behaviour subsequently abandoned it completely in order to give themselves over exclusively to such practices once they no longer wanted children. That is really what it comes down to, since turning to them occasionally would not have guaranteed effective contraception, given their ignorance of periods of fertility.

Abortive and sterilising potions provided another means of birth control. The penitentials speak of them often enough that we cannot regard them as having been rarely used, and nothing indicates that they were used by prostitutes alone. Moreover, it seems that in Christian civilisation prostitutes did not have the professional training which they had in antiquity and that the profession lost its technical knowledge. The technical experts in this period are the witches who are familiar with the potions' secrets, not the women who use them.

However, nothing proves that sterilising potions from the early Middle Ages were as effective as the contraceptive techniques used by the courtesans of antiquity, and that they could be successfully used by married couples who did not want any more children. I am not even convinced that these "sterilising poisons" were intended to prevent conception in the sense we understand today, for what was called conception, i.e. the transformation of the sperm into an embryo, was seen as a slow process which lasted forty days.[16] Thus, the purpose of these drugs might have been to cause an abortion in the period shortly after conception, and they would therefore have been more appropriate for women who had illicit relations from time to time than for married couples having intercourse on a regular basis. Moreover, it must be noted that for the time being only one, quite late reference to their use for economic reasons is known, whereas many penitentials mention these economic reasons among those which lead to infanticide or to abortion.[17]

But, both in antiquity and the early Middle Ages, abortion does not appear to me to have been more convenient a method than infanticide for those married couples wanting to limit the number of their offspring. Thus, unless the life of the new-born was truly sacred for the people of that time, I would assume them to have resorted to infanticide rather than abortion.

The Psychological and Cultural Chances of Infanticide

Certain passages describing a mother or father's love for their young children in France in the Middle Ages could lead us to doubt that infanticide could have still been common. At the end of the sixth century, for example, Gregory of Tours, recounting an infant's miraculous recovery from the point of death, writes: "His father's only child, he was for him like a memorial of the love that he had had for his wife...As soon as the inflammation took hold of the child, the father hurried to the Church so that his child would not die without having been regenerated by baptism... The child was placed on the blessed sepulchre to the sound of his father's cries of anguish..."[18]

Another miracle by St Martin gives rise to an even more tragic description. Cardégisile, a pious citizen of the town of Saintes, is said to have recounted the following: "...My young son who you see here was still at his mother's breast when he fell ill; for thirty days or even more, he was carried in our arms, with no little fatigue; finally, he was so weak that he could no longer suck the breast...On the sixth day after the illness got worse, he fell unconscious and we placed him before the altar, crying and waiting for his death. Unable to bear the anguish, I left the house and left instructions for my wife to bury him as soon as he died. The child remained there until the evening, while his mother cried..."[19]

Finally, reporting on the death and resurrection of a three-year-old child, Gregory of Tours writes: "He had been in danger for three days, cradled in the arms of those who loved him, when one of the servants said: 'It would please God if this child were taken to St Maximus' tomb...' While he was carried in the arms of those who loved him, he died. Seeing this, his parents, amidst their crying and screaming, placed him on the ground in front of the sepulchre of the blessed Maximus...The night was spent in lamentations. When day broke...the child was seen standing up... The parents were lost in wonder and jubilation, the grieving mother picked him up joyously and carried him back home, cured."[20]

Such passages must be taken into consideration in order not to exaggerate ancient society's indifference towards the life of the young child, and to comprehend the place of psychological and cultural changes. Throughout the whole of the Middle Ages, one could find numerous miracles which make clear parents' attachment to their offspring. Special sanctuaries even existed which specialised in curing children or in reviving them for long enough to be baptised. Indications as to the development of concern for the health, life and salvation of the child could be obtained from a serial study of these sanctuaries or of the miracles traditionally reported.

But we must also note that these examples of paternal love are quite different from those which could be found today. The children discussed are never daughters: as though they were loved less for the innocence of their age than for what they would later become. The first passage speaks explicitly of an only son, even more precious because the mother was no longer there to give the father other heirs.

In the second text, the father's love for his son is expressed in a selfish manner which would no longer be accepted today. Lastly, concerning the third child, one may wonder whether "those who loved him" were indeed his parents; whether it was his parents who cradled him in their arms and carried him to St Maximus' tomb. In any case, there is no doubt that a servant suggested that course of action.

Moreover, the fact that paternal or maternal love could be very much alive in some cases does not mean that Frankish society rejected infanticide to the extent that ours does. We have no reason to think that such bonds were impossible in societies which openly practised infanticide at birth. Once children were accepted, it is probable that they carried their parents' hopes and that the very care lavished on them led to the creation of a bond. It is even possible that many mothers in these societies despaired when, after their sufferings in childbirth, they saw the father seize the new-born in order to abandon it. It is important to find out how sacred the life of a new-born was in Christian society of the early Middle Ages; whether it was as sacred as that of an older child or an adult; whether one was expected to sacrifice everything for him; what actually was sacrificed for him; and whether, on principle, the child was an object of particular tenderness, because of his age, his frailty and his innocence.

Did the writers of the time really accept this innocence, which Christianity delights in emphasising? In speaking of a man who "from his birth" had "hands which were closed and unsuited for work", Gregory of Tours wondered: "Where did that come from? Was it because he or his parents had sinned, that he was born maimed in this way? We could not be the judge of this."[21] That last sentence shows unusual humility and prudence for such a situation. Ordinarily it was accepted with no apparent hesitation that man's body could only be affected by God and only with just cause, and that this usually was punishment for his sins. Thus Gregory of Tours does not reject the theory that a child may be born a sinner having been born maimed.

The other theory, that of the parents' guilt, was much easier for a religion based on the existence of original sin to accept. Any deformity in the child at birth usually indicated the parents' sin, and more specifically sin against chastity, since the child is the physical result of sexual relations between his parents.

A passage attributed by medieval theologians to St Jerome[22] shows clearly the mechanism for this immanent justice, using the example of married couples who engaged in intercourse while the wife was menstruating, despite the strict ban in Leviticus: "Therefore men must abstain from their wives because the [children] conceived will be without limbs, blind, lame or leprous, *so that,* the parents not having been embarrassed to have sexual intercourse in the conjugal bed-chamber, their sins will be made manifest to all and reviled in their children".[23]

At the beginning of the sixth century, St Caesarius of Arles confirmed in one of his sermons that: "If someone has known his wife while she is menstruating, or if he has not wanted to contain himself on Sundays or at any other formal occasion, those who are thus conceived will be born leprous or epileptic or perhaps possessed by the devil".[24]

And, towards the end of the century, Gregory of Tours recounts the story of a man "crippled in every limb" because his mother had conceived him on a Sunday night. He concludes, "since that happened because of his parents, for their sin in desecrating Sunday night, take care, oh men, who are married to women. It is enough to become attached to sensual pleasure on other days: on that day, hold back, in honour of God the unpolluted. Because those couples who have intercourse on that day will give birth to children who are crippled, or epileptic or leprous as a result. And may what we have said serve as a lesson to you, so that you do not suffer for a great many years because of a wrong committed one night only."[25]

Throughout the following centuries, many other writers preached on the same theme.

How was it possible that society in the Middle Ages considered it right that children be thus made to suffer through physical handicap for their parents' sin?

One possible explanation might be that Christians of that time were contemptuous of life on earth. Their attitude was: Suffering down here is of no importance — only eternal salvation matters. Moreover, no one is without sin and the suffering sent by God is always fully justified, even if after the event. It is a sign of his indulgence to make us suffer in this world rather than in the next. Furthermore, plainly the child was never made to suffer in the next world for his parents' crime: when the parents' punishment was the child's death and not his deformity, the death only ever took place after baptism.[26]

Yet this reasoning concerning eternal life was not very widespread in medieval society. The Church did indeed take pains to have children baptised before they died,[27] but did not consider infanticide before baptism or the abortion of an animated foetus to be more serious than the murder of an adult or an already-baptised child.[28]

The Church had to take into account an already-existing value system which accorded higher value to life in this world.

Indeed, the purpose of immanent justice is to instruct more than to punish. Therefore it had to conform more to man's idea of justice and to the ideas of the time than to eternal justice. The fact that God visited the parents' sins upon the child means that, whether in Frankish society, among the Hebrews of the Old Testament or among the Greeks in mythology, in man's eyes the child was seen as nothing more than his parents' possession. It is extremely rare nowadays — either in fact or in fiction — for someone to wreak vengeance on a man's descendants. And kidnapping, which does however show that parents would be affected by such an act, is universally censured. For not only do we increasingly feel a sense of individual responsibility, but we regard the child as sacred and do not accept his being used as a means of punishing his parents.

Conversely, sixth century Frankish society tended to the idea of collective responsibility and did not consider the child as sacred. Indeed, that society seems to have been particularly insensitive to the hardships of other people's children. For example, Gregory of Tours wrote, on the subject of the "man crippled in every limb": "And because [during his childhood] he was regarded by many with contempt and because his mother was blamed for having had such a son, she confessed in tears that he had been conceived on a Sunday night".[29]

What is interesting in this text is not the lack of charity towards the mother — we could find examples of this closer to home — but the absence of pity towards the crippled child. The contempt of which Gregory of Tours speaks is probably shown by adults, since it leads to the mother confessing. Neither the remainder of the story nor the writer's comments condemn their attitude. It seemed completely normal and is actually logical if it was considered right that God punish the child for his parents' mistake.

In fact, I am not questioning the fact that some paternal or maternal love existed in the Frankish society of the early Middle Ages, but I do believe that such feelings do not necessarily imply affection for the child as such and that they could just as easily be found in societies which openly practised infanticide at birth. Moreover, it is obvious that both God and civil laws imposed duties towards their children on the parents of that time and that they did not have the right to kill or to abandon them. Yet the passages cited suggest that society's attitudes towards children were archaic and more similar to those of pre-Christian societies than to ours. If parents did not make an attempt on their child's life, it must have been more out of respect for divine or human laws than out of a real respect for its person or a particular affection for babies.

THE INTENTIONAL KILLING OF CHILDREN IN CHRISTIAN CIVILISATIONS

Infanticide at Birth

In some regions of Europe, the tradition of infanticide was so well established that it was able to continue openly for several centuries after conversion to Christianity. One example is that of the Scandinavian peoples about whom Lucien Musset wrote: "the abandonment of children, reserved in 1000 by the Icelandic Altig, when conversion took place, is still accepted by twelfth century Norwegian canon law when the new-born is not viable or is malformed".[30]

Although infanticide was no longer officially accepted in Frankish society in the early Middle Ages and was condemned by civil and religious laws, we have nonetheless found many reasons to believe that it was still practised and was significantly common: because the Malthusian structures of the society survived; because the cultural traditions did not offer couples any other methods of limiting the number of their children that were equally practical and efficient; because the child was not yet really considered sacred and because in principle, the child did not yet arouse respect and love. And in point of fact the penitentials do often mention infanticide and those who commit it.

Firstly, there is infanticide for economic reasons, as we have seen. Yet one may wonder why the penitentials always mention poor women and not poor men in connection with this. There was probably a change from the practice of infanticide in antiquity: then it was the father who made the decision as to whether to keep the child or to reject it. What is the significance of this apparent transfer of responsibility?

The poor women mentioned are probably not all widows. If their husbands are not mentioned, it is firstly because they no longer have the right to decide on their own child's life or death. Secondly, it is because in practice it is the mother and not the father who took care of the small child up to a certain age. It even seems that this responsibility led in practice to a kind of legal responsibility, at least before the confession tribunal. This is suggested for example by article 174 of Burchard of Worms' interrogation: "Did you put your child near a chimney and did another person come and spill a cauldron of boiling water on the fire so that the child died, scalded? *You who were to look after your child carefully for seven years*, you will fast on the designated days for three years. She who spilled the cauldron of water is innocent".[31]

This article is found along with others which all concern sins committed by women. In addition, towards the end of the century, Ivo of Chartres explicitly entitles a similar article: "Concerning the mother whose child died through her negligence because she placed him near the hearth".[32]

It is not impossible that this transfer of responsibility might have resulted in a noticeable decrease in frequency of infanticide in Christian society, if one accepts that, for natural and cultural reasons, the mother's attachment to the small child was usually stronger than the father's. But, conversely, it seems that Christian morality gave rise to new, non-economic, reasons for infanticide at birth.

In principle, the Christian value of chastity was favourable to the child's life because it made intentional procreation the purpose of sexual activity. For a long time, marital intercourse was only really considered legitimate if the spouse who demanded it was thinking of reproduction.[33] And what Christian theology calls "the good of procreation" includes the child's feeding and upbringing as much as his generation.[34] Hence chastity demanded that those couples who did not want any more children or who were not able to provide for any more, remain continent for ever more. Furthermore, moralists from the early Middle Ages claimed that there is no chastity within marriage without periods of continence; and the periods of legal continence were so numerous that they must have significantly decreased the chances of conception. But in certain statistically unavoidable circumstances in society, this requirement of chastity had the reverse effect of encouraging infanticide, for the birth of a child could reveal his parents' sexual sin to the world and dishonour them.

Two groups of children fell into this category: handicapped children who we have discussed, and bastards, who still today harm their mothers' reputations. In both situations, the parents could be tempted to get rid of the child at birth, even before its baptism. Numerous passages report that a certain number of sensual parents chose such criminal behaviour in order to hide their sin.

Gregory of Tours, telling the story of the "man crippled in every limb", explains that his mother, "not daring to kill him, *as is the custom among mothers*, had fed him as she would do a healthy child". Thus, according to the most widely-accepted interpretation of this passage, mothers habitually killed their handicapped children.[35] If on the other hand we are to understand that mothers habitually showed a particular repugnance against getting rid of their children, even if they were handicapped, this second interpretation, implying that mothers were in that way abnormal in sixth century Frankish society, would suggest even more worrying possibilities as to the frequency of infanticide.

Did Christianity really create the conditions which encouraged infanticide at this time? We must not forget that, in the pagan societies which we have discussed — Greek, Roman and Scandinavian society — handicapped children were already abandoned. This custom is generally attributed to concern for eugenics which could have existed in the case of Sparta. But when the abandonment of children was carried out by parents, and not by the State, it is likely that their behaviour could be explained, at least at a certain level, by the shame that they felt for their child. Even today, this shame partially explains parents getting rid of their handicapped children, either by abortion or by sending them to special institutions.

These comparisons give rise to the thought that the killing of handicapped children, in society in the early Middle Ages, was done within Christianity's ideological framework for conscious reasons which were part of Christianity, but that such killings already existed before Christianity. Thus, Christianity cannot be primarily held responsible for such infanticide. It must be stressed that early medieval Christian ideology allowed the survival of this form of infanticide at birth, despite the fact that Christianity condemned infanticide.

As for the killing of bastards, it must also be observed that this stemmed more from how the society was organised than from Christianity: a child did not have much chance of surviving outside of the family framework, even when morality did not forbid extramarital relations. Moreover, it must be noted that illegitimacy was a taint in pagan Rome as well as in Christian society. Once again, however, Christian values intervened at the level of conscious motives and encouraged infanticide at birth when neither birth control nor attempted abortion had succeeded.

Although the penitentials generally attribute infanticide and abortion to women and the character of the female fornicator who wants to hide her sins is always set against that of the poor woman who cannot feed her children, one male character does also appear: the fornicating clerk who makes the results of his guilty love affairs disappear in order to avoid scandal. For him, infanticide is such a logical consequence of his first crime that it hardly seems to make it worse. This is suggested by comparing for example articles 11, 12 and 13 of Finnian's penitential: article 11 severely punishes the clerk who habitually commits the sin of fornication, albeit without scandal; article 12 punishes even more severely the one who conceived a child and killed it in order to avoid scandal; article 13 is as follows: "If the clerk does not kill his child, the sin is lesser, but the penance remains the same".[36] Since the penance is always proportional to the gravity of the offence, one can assume that the second sin was only slightly less serious than the first, and that scandal made fornication almost as serious as infanticide did.

It seems that after the early Middle Ages, obvious infanticide at birth was only rarely found within legitimate families. Indeed, we will see that couples had many other less dangerous ways of getting rid of unwanted children. Yet infanticide at birth continued in cases of illegitimate births, and I see a notable indicator of its frequency in the sixteenth century in Henry II's edict "which pronounces the death penalty against young women who, having hidden their pregnancy and their confinement, let their children die without having been baptised".[37] Indeed the introduction to this edict, dated February 1556 — in fact 1557 according to the way we now calculate dates — states: "...Being duly informed of a very great and atrocious crime, *frequent in our Kingdom*, which is that several women, having conceived Children by dishonest means, or otherwise persuaded by bad will and counsel, disguise, obscure and hide their pregnancies without them being discovered and registered; and the time arriving for the delivery of their children, they secretly deliver themselves of them, then suffocate, bruise and otherwise kill them, without having given them the sacred Sacrament of Baptism; this done, the women throw them into secret and squalid places, or bury them in profane land, thus depriving them of a Christian's customary sepulchre ..."

This frequency of infanticide at birth is not only explicitly confirmed by the introduction, but is implicitly proven by the edict's pronouncement and by its measures of application: "...That all women who find themselves duly affected and convicted of having hidden & obscured, either her pregnancy or her confinement without having announced either, & having taken enough evidence of one or the other, even of the life or death of her Child, at the time of its birth, and after the Child is found to have been deprived, either of the holy Sacrament of

Baptism or of the usual public sepulchre, *then let such a Woman be considered & reputed to have killed her Child*, & by way of reparation let her be punished by death and execution..."

The law's authors apparently consider that most young women who found themselves in the conditions described had intentionally killed their children. If that were not so, the tyrannical character of this law would be reinforced. For, at that time as today, it was usually up to the prosecution to provide proof of the crime — or to obtain admission of it — whereas here it is up to the accused to provide proof of her innocence and even to guard against possible accusation. The law's exceptional character is justified by the gravity of the crime of infanticide at birth in Christian society: to deprive a soul of baptism and a body of a Christian sepulchre is to deprive a human being of eternal salvation and of resurrection, whereas an ordinary murder only brings forward the time of an inevitable death.[38] It is also justified by the difficulty faced by judges in proving the guilt of the accused,[39] which must naturally have encouraged the criminals. But despite the validity of these two explanations, I do not believe that the legal systems would have resorted to such exceptional measures if infanticide at birth had been as rare in the sixteenth century as it is today.

This is particularly true because the edict mobilised considerable forces in the fight against this scourge: not only the royal and seigniorial officers — in particular the procurator fiscal of each seigniory — but all the parish priests in France, each of which had to read out the edict from the pulpit every three months to all his parishioners. And many times between the sixteenth and the eighteenth century, Henry II's successors reminded the people that this movement would continue. Would they have spent so much energy, with so much perseverance, if young women and widows who became pregnant outside of marriage had not always been tempted to commit infanticide in order to hide their mistakes?

In actual fact, the more society was concerned with commanding respect for sexual morality, the harsher it was on unwed mothers and illegitimate children, and the less it allowed a guilty mother to become attached to the child which was the tangible sign of her downfall. Logically, sexual repression meant an increase in infanticide, and Henry II's edict appears to be a desperate attempt to curb this logical progression by increasing the repression. However, one may wonder whether this coercion was effective, in a society which was pleased to believe that honour had a higher price than life did. Undoubtedly measures which were preventive and no longer merely repressive were necessary in order to bring about an end to this evil, i.e. the registering of pregnancies, which did not become widespread until the eighteenth century.

Abortion

Well before the State threw itself into the vicious fight against infanticide at birth, the Church had undertaken a vigorous fight against a crime equally as serious in its eyes: abortion. We can see this from studying the "reserved cases", those sins for which the bishop reserved for himself the right to absolution. These were not always the sins which were the most reprehensible in theory. Masturbation, for example, which theologians considered to be worse than incest, was much less often a reserved case, no doubt because it was too common a sin. Conversely, other serious sins were not mentioned in the lists of reserved cases because they were too rare and did not attract the ecclesiastic authorities' attention. Those which are commonly found in these lists are those which the Church decided to oppose particularly energetically. This is true of abortion: of thirty-seven lists studied, during a period from the thirteenth to the eighteenth century, it is mentioned in thirty-one.

Abortion is considered to be an even more horrific form of homicide because it deprives an innocent soul of baptism and eternal salvation. But it must be noted that none of the thirty-one lists confines the reserved case to what can be considered as homicide, i.e. aborting the foetus after animation. On the contrary, several specify: "whether the foetus be animated or not". If one adds that to the fact that abortion is often mentioned in the same article as the use of sterilising potions, or indeed — until the sixteenth century — in the same article as various practices of witchcraft, one can see that as a reserved case, abortion is considered to be different from homicide as a means of birth control. Indeed it is probable that before the spread of *coitus interruptus*, it was the most efficient means.

Infanticide would not be mentioned because it is obviously intentional homicide, a crime for which almost all bishops reserve absolution for themselves. On the other hand, even when abortion is seen as homicide in the eyes of the Church, it may not appear as such to the faithful, which is why it was necessary to mention it explicitly in the lists of reserved cases. Moreover, infanticide was perhaps less frequent than abortion, particularly if one includes failed and collaborative attempts. Finally, abortion was probably less easily controlled by civil laws, and the confession tribunal was probably better armed to quell it than the royal tribunals. All these reasons are found more or less explicitly in a pastoral from the Archbishop of Paris in 1666.[40] In addition, Guy Patin provides us with other indicators for assessing the frequency of abortions and the relations between the Church and State towards it. Indeed, in 1655, when an abortionist midwife who had inadvertently caused the death of a young lady of the Court who had been made pregnant by the Duke of Vitry had been hung, the famous doctor wrote: "On this subject, the vicars-general went to complain to the First President that, over the past year, six hundred women in all have confessed of having killed and smothered their children".[41]

Obviously the State did not embark upon the same struggle against abortion as against infanticide because that was much more difficult. It is likely that the requirement for pregnant young women to register their pregnancies — which seems to have gradually been introduced from the mid-seventeenth century — was intended to prevent abortion as much as infanticide. But that could only be claimed for those regions where registrations were made in the first months of pregnancy and these appear to be in the minority.

In any case, it can be assumed that, in modern times as in antiquity and in the Middle Ages, intentional abortion was not generally the Malthusian weapon used by legitimate couples. Like contraception and infanticide at birth, abortion must have been used particularly in extramarital relationships in order to protect the mother's honour. For a long time, legitimate couples had had others means of disposing of their unwanted children without falling foul of the law.

The Smothering and Suffocating of Children

No doubt smothering or suffocating children is one of these means. In principle, it was unintentional infanticide: the mother put the child to bed beside her in the marital bed, and she crushed or smothered it beneath her during the night. Thus it at first seems surprising that the Church paid so much attention to it, from the early Middle Ages to the nineteenth century. Not only did penitentials from the early Middle Ages often speak of it, but they imposed harsh penances on the unhappy parents: three years of penance, one of which on bread and water in St Colombanus' penitential, which is distinctly more than for those who caused abortions using magic spells;[42] three years of fasting on bread and water on the specified days according to

Burchard of Worms, which is as much as for the abortion of a foetus
after animation.[43] Later, from the thirteenth century to the eighteenth,
this "crime" was very often a reserved case, since it is to be found in
twenty-six of the thirty-seven lists I studied.

Moreover, it will be noted that the words "smothering" and "suffocation" sometimes refer to something other than this well-defined
accident. One example is the death of the embryo in its mother's
womb, which was attributed to the sexual relations that the mother
allegedly had at too advanced a stage of pregnancy. Thus the synodal
statutes of Amiens, in 1454, reserve for the bishop the sin of "he who
smothers and causes the death of his child...*before birth* or after". We
have also seen that Guy Patin, no doubt speaking of mothers who had
intentionally aborted their children by completely different means,
says that they were accused of having "smothered their children".
This misuse of language shows us how the concept of suffocation of
children was widened, from one specific type of unintentional infanticide and abortion to all kinds of infanticide and abortion. Why did
the expressions "smothering of children" and "suffocating of children" change in meaning, if they originally referred only to a banal
accident?

Several lists of reserved cases clearly state that it is not always an
accident: ten out of twenty-six speak of intentional smothering or
suffocation, and this intent is not denied by the other, more concise
lists. Moreover, it is understood that parents who wanted to get rid
of an unwanted child — but who did not need to hide its birth —
found that a useful method for doing so without falling foul of the
law. And there again, the Church was in a much better position than
the State to obtain confession of the crime and to curb it. Moreover
the Church seems to having become increasingly concerned about the
issue since, from the thirteenth century to the eighteenth, it led an
increasingly harsh campaign against the smothering of children.

The two thirteenth century lists do not make the smothering of
children a reserved case. Is this by chance or did the ecclesiastic
authorities not yet consider it a serious scourge? At the beginning of
the fourteenth century, the synodal statutes of Cambrai reserved
intentional smothering for the bishop and "unintentional and accidental" smothering for the assistant penitentiaries in the deaneries.[45]
Then, from 1411 to 1696, nine lists reserve absolution for smothering
or suffocating children for the bishop, without specifying whether the
act was intentional or unintentional.[46] Probably both were reserved
cases, as is specified in the 1454 statutes for the diocese of Amiens,

which are more explicit that those of 1411.[47] But the failure to stipulate seems to me to be significant: from 1454 to 1696, only four lists in all mention smothering by negligence or accident explicitly.[48] In contrast, that becomes the rule in the eighteenth century. From this one must not conclude that intentional smothering ceased to be considered possible or frequent — eight lists still mention it[49] — nor that accidental smothering became more common, but that the Church was fighting with increased determination against these accidents and crimes.

From the end of the seventeenth century, the Church added preventive measures to the repressive ones. In 1687, the Bishop of Arras wrote: "The danger in which fathers and mothers, wet nurses and other people place children by putting them in the same bed as themselves when still at a tender age, is so great and *the resulting suffocations are so frequent, that we do not believe it possible to apply too strong remedies to such a great evil*: that is why we believe that in order to prevent it, we must explicitly forbid, on pain of excommunication, all fathers, mothers, wet nurses and other people generally to put children in the same bed as themselves, until they are exactly one year old: and in the case of suffocation of said children, we forbid all priests to absolve them of this misdeed, except when absolutely necessary, if they do not have the right to absolve reserved cases".[50]

Had this preventive measure been the subject of discussions within the French episcopate? In any case, there seems to be a large number of bishops who took the same measure at the end of the seventeenth and in the eighteenth century.[51]

Not all of the bishops went quite as far. In 1789, the Bishop of Langres wrote the following in his ritual, concerning homicide, the fifth reserved case: "A murder committed by accident is not a crime...In order to decide whether it is a reserved case, one must look at whether the action is of a kind which ordinarily kills...It is because of this principle that we do not classify with reserved cases the very serious sins of mothers, wet nurses and other people who put children to bed in their bed when less than two years old. To put a child in bed beside its mother is not an action which ordinarily kills; but we strongly recommend to all *Curés*, Vicars and Confessors to warn mothers and wet nurses of the risk they run and of the sin which they commit when they put children under the age of two in bed with them".[52]

This passage necessitates several comments. Firstly, in those dioceses in which they had qualms about including the simple fact of sleeping with one's child among the reserved cases, there was a need to justify it, and they insisted that the *curés* denounce the custom from the pulpit and in the confessional. Secondly, its inclusion among the cases reserved for the bishop constituted an exceptional measure which might have been called "unjust" and "despotic", were it not justified by the gravity of the problem.

Another example of these tyrannical measures is Henry II's edict, and there were other, well-known examples, aimed at getting rid of the custom of fighting a duel. The ecclesiastical authorities believed themselves justified in employing such tyrannical methods because the smothering of children could be considered a scourge, because of its frequency and its effects — just like infanticide at birth or duelling. Undoubtedly these measures were used successfully: the mother who smothered her child in her bed could not claim it was an unforeseen accident if the mere fact of sleeping in the same bed as the child was a crime regularly denounced in the pulpit and the confessional. From that time smothering was no longer a good method for getting rid of an unwanted child without danger. The Bishop of Langres does not seem to face the same situation as the Bishop of Arras a century earlier. On the one hand, he speaks of children of less than two years old, whereas previously bishops spoke of children under one year of age: as though the number of children smothered under one year of age had fallen to the same frequency as the smothering of children between one and two years of age. On the other hand, whereas the Bishop of Arras considered the danger so great that he could not apply too harsh remedies, the Bishop of Langres, a century later, thinks that "putting a child in one's bed...is not an action which normally kills": can this change of opinion not also be explained by the change in circumstances?

The Exposure and Abandonment of Children

Parents had another, radical, method for limiting the number of children in their families: abandoning their children, whether at birth or later on.

At first glance, abandonment at birth is a form of infanticide which is more obvious than the smothering of a child, and indeed it was condemned as such by civil laws.[53] However, its nature had changed since antiquity. For the Greeks and Romans, the exposure of newborns was generally a hypocritical way of causing the death of an unwanted child: it allowed the final responsibility for its life or death to be left to the gods. In actual fact, when abandoned in the wild, a baby had almost no chance of surviving. I assume that malformed new-borns in Scandinavia in the eleventh and twelfth centuries were still subjected to such exposure.

In Western Christian society, the psychology of abandonment un- doubtedly remained similar to what it was in antiquity: a desire not to dirty one's hands with the blood of one's own child[54] and giving back the child's destiny into the hands of God, who was already responsible for its birth.[55] But there was also a reliance on the charity of others. One hoped that the child would be taken in and that it would survive and those who found the child were obliged to show charity or to commit an equally serious sin themselves. Of course it is difficult to know what proportion of abandoned children really were able to survive, but the fact that they were abandoned in inhabited regions and no longer out in the wilds is evidence of this consideration and this hope.

In reality, not much could be hoped for from private charity: from a very early date, the history of abandoned children was associated to that of public charity. Parents' lack of concern seems at first sight to have evolved in an opposite direction to that of society. Yet it is important to understand which of these developments depends on the other: various indicators lead us to believe that it is the increased capacity of specialised institutions which explains the increase in the number of abandoned children recorded.

Firstly, one could stress that, for a long time, hospitals refused to take in all foundlings. In the seventeenth century, it sometimes hap- pened that a draw was held to decide which of the children would be reared:[56] a practice unknown in Christian society and one which indicates embarrassment and a transient situation. The significant fact is that in the fifteenth and sixteenth centuries, it was known which children to take in and which children to reject: French hospitals then were intended for the children of poverty and not for those of sin. That is essentially what Benedicti wrote in 1584, when examining what an adulterous women who has conceived a bastard should do in order not to damage her husband's interests and those of her legitimate children: "The fifth opinion says that the mother should abandon it or take it to the Hospital. But at whose expense will it be fed? The Hospital's possessions are for the poor, and are not intended for feeding bastards, except in a hospital intended for the purpose of feeding abandoned children, as there is one such hospital in Florence, with an income of more than five thousand *livres*".[57]

The letters patent given by Charles VII to the Hôpital du Saint-Esprit in Paris in 1445 states: "If one were to receive illegitimate children indiscriminately, it could happen that there would be a great number of them because many people would abandon them and would show less restraint in giving themselves up to sin, were they to see that such children would continue to be fed and that they would not have the chief responsibility nor the care of them, that such hospitals would not be able to bear it nor maintain it".[58]

Obviously there is a contradiction between the admitting of illegitimate children into hospitals and the protecting of chastity, and for a long period of time people seem to have chosen to protect chastity to the detriment of children's lives. I am not even sure that in the seventeenth and eighteenth centuries the opposite choice was made consciously and deliberately, for religion and the social system seemed to have been opposed to it.[59]

Indeed, according to Lallemand,[60] they continued well into the eighteenth century to believe "that the majority of these poor children were legitimate children who had been abandoned by parents forced to such extreme action by poverty". There were those at that time who, like Abbé Malvaux, believed the opposite and wanted the hospices to be closed to children who were the products of sin: "*Under the pretext of relieving poverty*, our hospitals for Foundlings are increasing concubinage...*Recently*, it has become too easy for libertines to hand over to society the job of feeding the results of their debauchery. This has greatly increased the amount of libertinage in all the towns and almost all the villages. It should be restricted...We should feed only the children of those who would not be able to feed them themselves..."[61]

The flood of new-borns from the provinces into Paris or from some foreign countries to those French provinces having hospices for foundlings proves that it is the hospice which attracts foundlings rather than the foundlings necessitating the establishment of hospices. Indeed, a pronouncement by Louis XVI in 1779 reported that "every year, more than two thousand children born in distant provinces came to the hospice for Foundlings in Paris".[62]

And in the *généralité* of Soissons where an official enquiry had been undertaken in order to find out why, in a period of eight years, three thousand two hundred and forty "illegitimate or abandoned" children had entered the hospices, the report is said to have shown that "586 children foreign to the kingdom were put in hospitals within the *généralité*. The greatest number come from the region of Liège. That free city, peopled with the dregs of nations, does not have establishments to take in abandoned children".[63]

Another indicator which corroborates this is the noticeable decrease in the number of foundlings during the Revolution, when the mortality rates in the disorganised hospices were frighteningly high. When they no longer had any hope that their children might survive, mothers were more and more reluctant to abandon them.

Finally, attention must be given to the ecclesiastic authorities' attitudes towards these abandoned children. Certainly, they did not encourage, and even condemned the majority of such cases; but much less vigorously than abortions — even before animation — or than the smothering of children, even accidentally. Of the thirty-seven lists of reserved cases studied, thirty-one mention abortion, twenty-six the smothering of children and only two the "exposure" or "clandestine abandonment" of children. Even then, neither of these two lists are from the eighteenth century, the period when the abandonment of children reached worrying proportions; and both condemn the clandestine nature of such abandonment, not the abandonment itself.[64]

Among confessors, theologians and casuists, there is the same ambiguity. Fromageau, wondering whether to counsel a woman to abandon her child in order to save her reputation or because she cannot feed it, replies in the negative, agreeing, it would appear, with eighteenth century theologians. He points out that "If women were free to expose their children, that would open the door to the dissoluteness of all kinds of people, most of which do not sin only because of their fear of reprisals and of the upset caused by such behaviour".[65] Moreover: "If her fear of poverty or inability to feed her child leads a mother to abandon it, the confidence she must have in Providence and the Charity of the Faithful ought to prevent her".[66] When he then adds: "God does not fail to help those who serve Him", one has the feeling that the attitudes towards children of the Sorbonne doctors in the eighteenth century remained very close to those of writers in the early Middle Ages: the life or the death of the child in this world was always decided by God by way of reward or punishment for the parents and not in the interests of the child itself.

However not all theologians were — nor had they always been — of Fromageau's opinion. From the very beginning of his reply, he himself stipulates: "There are two feelings among the Doctors. There are those who say that a woman can abandon her child in either of these two situations...provided that the child is not exposed to the danger of dying of hunger or of cold".[67] And in support of this opinion he cites reputable writers of the sixteenth, seventeenth and eighteenth centuries: Sylvestre, Azor, Layman, Bassaeus.

If the Church remained moderate in its condemnation of the abandonment of children, it is because it saw it as a lesser evil — as it does
today with the question of birth control. As far as illegitimate children
are concerned, the ideal would have been for the mother herself to
raise the child and for the snubs which she would have to endure
throughout her life to make her repent her sin. But many unmarried
mothers did not hesitate to preserve their honour through crime: if
the child could not be discreetly sent to a hospital, it ran a great risk
of being killed at birth. The Church was conscious of this, and had
been for a long time. It was apparently in order to "prevent parents
from killing those children whose births they did not want to divulge"
that archpriest Dathaeus of Milan created an asylum for foundlings
as early as 787.[68] The establishment of the foundling hospital in
Florence is obviously a response to the same concern. And when, in
the eighteenth century, Abbé Malvaux discusses the advantages and
disadvantages of French charitable institutions, he writes: "You say
that in this way mothers are diverted from smothering their offspring... Must we then, under the specious pretext of preventing two
or three mothers from being monsters, risk a hundred thousand
becoming cruel and unnatural mothers".[69]

Obviously the juxtaposition of "two or three" against "a hundred
thousand" is rhetorical. Moreover, even if the moralistic abbot had
wanted to know the exact number of infanticides in the years 1770–
1780, and had he had the means to do so, it would have taught us
nothing about the extent of infanticide before the increase in the
number of hospices and before they, either legally or actually, took in
illegitimate children. The only fact allowing us to assess this is that in
the sixteenth century Henry II was confronted with the problem of
the infanticide of bastards at birth, whereas towards the end of the
eighteenth century, Louis XVI is faced with a dramatic increase in the
number of foundlings.

As for those legitimate parents who abandoned their children
because of poverty — the numbers of which seem to have been
alternately exaggerated and underestimated in the eighteenth century[70] — the Church hardly dares to condemn them. In the sixteenth
century, Benedicti wrote: "He who, *having the means to feed his children*,
exposes them, whether in a private place or public, sins".[71] The austere
Franciscan from Lyons says nothing about those who were not able
to feed their own children.

NEGLECT AND LACK OF CONCERN
Lack of Concern in Procreation and Infant Mortality

We should specify exactly what being able or not being able to feed one's children meant in ancient Western society. We could specify from what age poor children began to help their parents or to work outside the family in order to provide for its needs — theologians suggest that this began at seven years of age — what they ate before that age and how much of a strain that was for their parents; how many children there could be completely in their parents' charge, given the usual periods between births and without taking the infant and juvenile mortality rates into consideration. That would give us an idea of the financial conditions necessary for raising a family, and enable us to know what proportion of young married couples found themselves in such conditions.

In the absence of such research, I have the impression that a great many married couples did not have the financial means for raising all the children which were the inevitable result of marrying — even marrying late. Thus, when they did not decide to get rid of their children by abandoning them or by infanticide, for simple economic reasons, they were condemned to providing for their children through charity or pilfering, or to letting them die around them, of hunger, intestinal diseases or other causes. The Church exhorted them to believe in divine Providence and in the charity of the faithful right up to the last moment; and obviously there were ways of saving at least a certain number of the children dying of poverty in seventeenth and eighteenth century society. But, at family level, where the problem actually existed, abandoning the child was often the lesser of several bad options, and the Church was very conscious of this.

However it appears very probable to me that most of the children condemned to death by their parents' poverty and the number of brothers and sisters they had, were neither abandoned nor victims of blatant or concealed infanticide. Most of these children died near their parents, and it is this — more than the number of children killed at an early age — that distinguishes ancient Christian society from the pagan societies which preceded it. We must therefore try to explain why married couples reproduced without worrying about their children's futures and why they ordinarily refused to resort to radical means of getting rid of them. I will of course look for these reasons in the moral code of the time, or at least in that which comes down to us through the preachers, confessors and theologians.

"A good man must never be afraid of having too many children", said Benedicti. This apparent optimism is even more surprising since in the chapter concerning the abandonment of children he seems to recognise that it is possible not to be able to feed one's own family. In fact, this optimism does not hold true for the whole of society, and that is what prevents him from being too cruelly disappointed by the experience of the faithful. His optimism refers only to "the good man" or "the just man", which all might be but which not everyone is.

We shall not emphasise again the underlying conviction which that implies — inherited from the Old Testament and from attitudes in the late Middle Ages — that God lets children live or die in order to reward or punish their parents. What must be stressed is the sense of irresponsibility that such words risk encouraging in fathers: "Since God has given them, He will *therefore* provide the means of feeding them, because it is He who feeds the birds in the sky; otherwise He would not give mankind children".

Western society had known for thousand of years that procreation was a result of sexual intercourse. But, because neither the details nor even the fundamental organs of reproduction were known, and because it was noticed that sexual relations were not always fertile, one could believe that conception always depended directly on God's will. During intercourse, the parents gave the material for a future child, but God Himself decided whether or not to make a child from this seminal material, and in any case added the soul at a certain state of the gestation. Those couples who hoped for years for a conception which never came, could not doubt this; any more so than those who, despite having a normal sex life, were weighed down with more children than others.

Though economic and social structures encouraged the limiting of family size, this transfer of responsibility explains why infanticide and birth control were so rarely used within marriage. God sent children to those to whom He wished, in as great number as He wished and when He wished, and the partners did not believe that it was up to them to increase or decrease their fertility. Most writers were even in agreement in recognising that fertility did not depend on the frequency of marital relations. On the contrary, the Greek idea of moderation and the Christian idea of chastity reinforced each other on this point. Moreover, if the partners did not commit infanticide, it was because the children were sent by God, more than because of an abstract respect for life or for a love of children. But this respect for the child's life did not preclude very human examples of neglect, which will be discussed later; and it precluded to an even lesser extent parents abusing the rights recognised as theirs by the Church.

In a society in which death mowed down half of all children born, more in some families than in others, resignation was a psychological necessity. It was expressed by a formula found as often among doctors and ecclesiastics as among fathers with their account books: "God has given and God has taken away". This idea can be considered as eminently religious; but it cannot be denied that it favoured a certain fatalism towards procreation and children's deaths, a fatalism which is not particularly characteristic of the Christian religion. It was the powerlessness to fight against death and the ignorance of the progress of reproduction which stained the religion of the time with fatalism. Now that we understand the process of reproduction and illness better and can to a great extent control them, the Church stresses parents' responsibilities in reproduction and in keeping their children alive.

It may seem paradoxical that the principle of responsible parenthood was accepted at a time when, in Western Europe, almost all married couples could provide for a large family. In ancient society, when a great number did not have such means, one can suggest that infant mortality was partially due to parents' irresponsibility in their procreative activities. I will return to this argument in the final part of this chapter, by analysing the transition from the old demographic system to the new one; but it already seems to me to be difficult to question it in theory.

Before that, I wish to show how the old attitudes encouraged a certain amount of neglect on the part of parents towards their children, and how such neglect also explains, to a large extent, the remarkably high infant mortality rate in France in the sixteenth, seventeenth and eighteenth centuries.

Neglect and Various Accidents

From what has been said concerning the smothering of children, the conclusion must not be drawn that it was intentional in the majority of cases. On the contrary, smothering children in the marital bed can only have been used as a means of intentionally trying to kill unwanted children because it was usually accidental. Such accidents not only highlight parents' ignorance, but can also be explained by their neglect. While conscious of the fact that it is dangerous to put an infant to bed in their own bed, many seem to have taken the risk in order to avoid expense or fatigue. Benedicti, as an example, criticises them for this: "The mother or the wet nurse who puts a child to bed at her side, not wanting to leave it in the cradle for fear that its crying would prevent her from sleeping, or so sensual that she prefers putting it to bed near her to enduring the cold to nurse it, she commits a mortal sin: for she runs the risk of suffocating it...Mothers must look to this, and see at least that the bed is big and wide, and that something is between her and the child, if they are not able to put children to bed elsewhere in order that, being further away, they be out of danger. There are certain Doctors, who seem in no way to excuse those who are so poor that they do not have the convenience of having big beds, or cradles and other necessary things. As to that, I leave it to their consciences, Mortal Sin".[72]

The Church also pursued, although less stubbornly, various other examples of neglect which were dangerous for the child's life. We have seen, for example, that Burchard of Worms in the eleventh century, Ivo of Chartres in the twelfth, and many other writers in previous centuries, severely punished the mother alleged to have left her child too close to the hearth or to a cauldron of boiling water. Similar articles are found in certain synodal statutes from subsequent centuries. So, at the beginning of the sixteenth century, the synodal statutes of Cambrai concerned the "negligence of those parents who have lost in fire or in water those who were born to them".[73]

One could note that still today it is rare that parents who lose a child through an accident do not have some similar neglect to reproach themselves with. One cannot predict everything, nor live permanently in obsessive fear of possible accidents. One understands perfectly that a mother with too many children could not look after each one with as much care as an only child, particularly when she was poor and had to contribute to the household income. But it seems to me — as it does to Philippe Ariès — that, for not only material but also cultural reasons, parents were less careful of their children in the past than they are today; and that this mental attitude was linked to the old demographic system. In a society where children were very plentiful, they were less precious that in our society with its methods of contraception.

These arguments, which Philippe Ariès based on reasoning and on the history of the concept of childhood, are confirmed by analysing certain contemporary facts. Thus, the current high mortality rate in the northern region of France is not explained by the climate, as was at first believed; nor by the standard of living, which is now higher than that in many other regions of France; nor by the real shortage of medical equipment, since, in the same material and sanitary conditions, the children of foreign labourers living in the region have a much lower mortality rate. After eliminating all these explanations, a cultural factor must be considered: the traditional lack of concern for children's health which characterises all the working classes in the region, including peasants, employees and labourers.[74] There is no obvious correlation between the mortality rate in the northern region and its birth rate: many regions of France with lower infant mortality rates have higher birth rates. Yet, the study shows us that infant mortality is markedly higher among blue-collar workers than among white-collar workers, and that while wives of blue-collar workers are less likely than wives of white-collar workers to want another child, they are more likely to have more children. Thus, aside from the ideologies common to the working class, there is the additional factor of neglect among French blue-collar workers: there is a greater number of unwanted children.

Studying the patterns of order of birth also shows us that, overall, the probability of death is less among first-borns than among children born later in the family. This is in part due to the order of birth, but particularly to the fact that by definition there are more children in a large family and infant mortality is markedly higher in large families than in Malthusian families.[75] It is entirely probable that such high mortality rates among large families can be in part explained by practical factors, the number of children creating serious economic difficulties, particularly at a time when family allowances did not exist. Such difficulties have obvious psychological results: neither parent could pay as much attention to each child as Malthusian parents. In addition, to the extent to which the probability of death depends more on the *future* size of the family than on its size at the time of the child's death, such a death is obviously explained by yet another factor other than the economic difficulties of a large family and the psychological attitudes resulting from it. Parents of a large family are, from the outset, more careless than others of their children's health.

One might suppose that such carelessness with regard to children, which is today a characteristic of northern France in comparison with the rest of France, or a characteristic of large families in comparison with Malthusian families, was a characteristic of society in the past in comparison with our own. Indeed, it must be accepted that some of the appalling infant mortality of the seventeenth and eighteenth centuries was due to such carelessness.

Paid Wet Nursing

The neglect involved in the wet nursing of infants was undoubtedly much worse than the neglect which we have already looked at. In the sixteenth century, Benedicti reproached mothers for "giving" their children to "paid wet nurses, knowing full well that a child is never as well fed with a stranger's milk as with that of his own mother". Taking them to task, he exclaimed: "Why did nature give them two breasts shaped like two little bottles, if not for that reason? Yet cruel and unnatural as they are, it is enough for them to have given birth to their children out of their wombs and put them on earth, and then to send them to dreary villages to be fed by unfamiliar, unhealthy and bad-tempered women".[76]

Maurice Garden has recently provided information about these "dreary villages" in the provinces surrounding Lyons, in the eighteenth century. In 1771–1773, 62.5% of the infants from Lyons sent to the villages of Savoy by the Hôtel-Dieu died there; among those in Dauphiné, the average mortality rate was 63%; among those in Bugey, Franche-Comté, Bresse and Vivarais, it was 67.6%, 70%, 71% and 75% respectively. No doubt the mortality rate of children in families was less than that of children at the Hôtel-Dieu, to which these statistics refer, but the difference would not have been great.[77]

Paid wet nursing involved not only foundlings or children from noble or bourgeois families, but also those from artisans' or shopkeepers' families. In all the professions in which the woman was involved in her husband's work, it seems to have become the rule to put the children out to nurse in the eighteenth century. "Sending the children to a wet nurse", writes Maurice Garden, "is clearly seen as a necessity in labourers' and artisans' households."[78] Eighteenth century reformers also said: "Labourers' wives are as tenderhearted as we are, yet despite their tears, they take their children to be fed by others, for they need to begin to feed themselves".[79]

Since I am attempting to show the connection between attitudes towards children and the infant mortality rate, I will go beyond this indulgent assessment of the situation. I have already highlighted the influence of economic and social structures on the infant mortality rate; now the influence of psychological factors and individual responsibilities must be emphasised. One must be aware of the absence of scruples in peasant women who, in order to better their miserable lives, took on more children than they could feed. Maurice Garden tells us of one wet nurse who, over a period of twenty years, took in twelve infants and never returned one alive.[80] He shows us a village where there were only sixteen baptisms in 1759, and yet in which twenty-six infants were accepted in that year, to be divided between twenty-one families. And the number of infants rises again in times of crisis: thirty-nine in 1767, thirty-five in 1772, thirty-one in 1775,[81] whereas the women of the village probably had less milk than usual at that time.

As for the parents who endangered their children's lives in such a way, could they really not avoid it? It seems that, among the poorest classes, the mothers did their own breast-feeding, because their income was barely above that of a wet nurse.[82] If the silk artisans and shopkeepers sent their children to the "dreary villages", it was because they preferred risking the new-born's life to reducing their profits. The financial sacrifices they made by paying for a wet nurse out of their meagre income shows to what extent they were more concerned about the survival of new-borns in eighteenth century Christian society than in Graeco-Roman times. But if this concern had been more important than any other, paid wet nursing would probably have been less widespread, more strictly supervised and less dangerous. This is even more true in the case of the bourgeoisie, whose children were "affected almost as much as the others".

Even though ecclesiastic moralists seem to us to be sometimes unconscious of society's responsibilities and too harsh on individuals, we cannot find fault with them for having urged mothers to nurse their children themselves when that was physically possible, and for having drawn a comparison between sending a child to a wet nurse and abandoning it.[83] For putting children out to nurse, which in itself seems to indicate a certain amount of indifference towards one's children, definitely caused an increase in such indifference. The child was often left in the country for several years — sometimes until the age of ten, in middle-class families — and it is understandable that this separation did not encourage parental and maternal sentiments to crystallise. In addition, some parents never even asked for news of the infant, even when it was in a village near to their home.[84]

Premature Weaning

Yet it might seem odd and excessive for moralists to have called for mothers to nurse their children for three years. For example, Benedicti writes: "Those mothers sin who do not care to nurse their children or at the very least to provide them with good wet nurses, *up to the age of three* — after which time fathers are expected by natural law to advance and give them the necessary."[85]

Similarly, the Portuguese theologian Fernandes de Moure wrote: "They sin when they refuse to nurse their children *for three years,* being able to do it, according to the same Navarrus. The reason for this is taken from nature, which teaches us to take care of our children for as long as they cannot feed themselves, as animals do, who have no reason".[86]

Sanchez, no longer prescribing, but rather referring to the reality of nursing, speaks of a period of two years only.[87] Yet Gregory of Tours, in the sixth century, spoke of a child in its third year who was still breast-feeding;[88] and Catherine de Médicis' correspondence, in the sixteenth century, shows us that, when possible, children were still breast-fed after the age of two.[89] We must remember that, until Pasteur, sterilisation and most principles of hygiene were unknown; that water was usually polluted and that children, once they consumed anything other than their mother's or their wet nurse's milk, were therefore subjected to much greater risks than today. The seasonal infant mortality rates, with the highest levels in the summer, suggest moreover that most young children died of diarrhoea and other intestinal disorders. Under these circumstances, was it not wise to breast-feed them for as long as possible?

Obviously, breast-feeding was, in general, continued for much less than three years in France during the seventeenth and eighteenth centuries: studying the intervals between pregnancies proves this. We must therefore wonder whether such a long period of breast-feeding was a physical impossibility, at least for the average woman. Yet we know that, in some non-European countries, mothers breast-feed their children much longer than they do in Europe.[90] Are there physical differences between them? And, if it is a physical impossibility for European mothers to breast-feed for such a long period, where did western theologians get their dictates from?

Thus, given the current state of research, it appears reasonable to me to explain the length of time breast-feeding was carried on in ancient France by cultural rather than physiological factors: it is because women quickly returned to conjugal relations and became pregnant after several months that European mothers could not breast-feed their children for two or three years as did the American

Indians. When the infant dies, the fact that the intervals between pregnancies was so short is always explained by its death which, by interrupting breast-feeding, would have made the woman fertile more quickly. But should we not surmise that on the contrary — in a certain number of cases which would be easy to identify from family records — the infant's death followed the conception of a new child, and therefore was due to the child's being weaned prematurely as a result? This hypothesis has been proposed by those demographers working with non-European societies;[91] it would need to be systematically investigated for ancient Western society.

In the absence of such research, one can however make several comments likely to support this theory. For example, when Pierre Goubert shows us the Decaux-Crosnier family in order to illustrate the influence of breast-feeding on the interval between pregnancies,[92] it is noticeable that any interval of less than fifteen months implies the death of the previous child before the age of six months. Yet on the other hand, when breast-feeding stopped because of the death of the eighth child before the age of six months, this did not shorten the interval between the eighth and the ninth births. It seems to me to be very probable that the lengthening of the intervals after the fifth birth can be explained by the slowing down of sexual relations between the partners after seven years of marriage, and that this allowed five of the last six children to survive, whereas, in the first years of marriage, three of the first four had died.

Moreover, J. Dupâquier and M. Lachiver show us that in Meulan between 1660 and 1739, 22.6% of penultimate children died before the age of one year and 41.3% before the age of five, whereas of the last-born children, only 14% died before the age of one and 28.7% before the age of five.[93] Given the time period, this cannot be indicative of the voluntary limiting of births; particularly because, when contraception within marriage became common between 1790 and 1839, the mortality rate of last-born children was on the contrary slightly higher than that of the penultimate child. The lower mortality rate of last-born children between 1660 and 1739 must therefore be interpreted in a different way: it is a result of the fact that they were never the casualties of premature weaning because their mothers conceived while they were breast-feeding. In other words, if parents had avoided conceiving in the two or three years during which a child ought to have been breast-fed, the mortality rate of the penultimate child would have been the same as that of the last-born child, or perhaps even lower — as we observe between 1790 and 1839 — since the physiological risk of being short of milk is lesser in a younger mother than in a mother who is approaching the menopause.

Finally, if weaning before the age of two or three was considered premature, as theologians tell us, such premature weaning should be held responsible for the majority of deaths caused by intestinal disorders before the age of two or three. It would therefore appear that, in the medical and sanitary conditions of the seventeenth and eighteenth centuries, a considerable proportion of children died because their parents did not believe that they had to avoid conceiving before the normal end of breast-feeding.

Marital Morality and the Breast-Feeding of Infants

Yet the risks which a new pregnancy posed to an infant were not unknown. Doctors in ancient, medieval and modern times generally considered that milk is only the mother's blood, a specially pure and specially "cooked" blood. When the woman was breast-feeding they believed that all her "surplus" blood was changed into milk instead of being discharged at regular intervals and that this explained the disappearance of her periods. Sexual relations were thought to result in blood being drawn towards the womb and to cause her period to start again; thus this would cause less milk to be produced. If, by misfortune, conception took place, there was a risk of the milk supply stopping completely: for the embryo, ensconced in the womb, could suckle its mother's blood at source and prevent a single drop from getting to her breasts. If the mother did conserve some milk for a short time, it was a rancid, thick milk which was deprived of its purest component and thus difficult for the infant to digest. In any case, a new pregnancy during breast-feeding entailed weaning the infant. This was more dangerous the sooner it occurred after the birth.

It is known that certain societies took steps in order to avoid such premature weaning. Some forbade sexual relations with nursing mothers and the situation was made more bearable for the man by polygamy or extramarital relations.[94] Others advocated using contraception for conjugal relations during breast-feeding. It must be noted that several rabbis from antiquity recommended this solution without being restrained by the taboo which others believed was the moral of Onan's story.[95] Among Christians, who accepted neither polygamy nor extramarital relations, and were even more strongly against contraception within marriage, the only orthodox solution must have been the couple's complete continence.

In the sixth century, Pope Gregory the Great actually wrote to Archbishop St Augustine of Canterbury: "In truth, the husband must not have intercourse with his wife until the new-born has been weaned".[96]

In the sixteenth century, the jurist Tiraqueau explains in detail why "women who are breast-feeding their children must refrain from intercourse".[97] And Benedicti, who was always strict, wrote: "There is even a law which says that the husband must abstain from his wife until such time as she has weaned the child from her breast: a belief which you could equally hear from those Patriarchs whose wives were wet nurses or from Anne, mother of Samuel and from Oseas' wife. And it is also reasonable: for incontinence and copulation often cause wet nurses to lose their milk, not without damage to the children. Were the mother to lose her milk in this way and the child to die as a result, that would indeed be a mortal offence".[98]

The law mentioned in this text is Gregory the Great's short sentence which became the first sentence of the canon *Ad eius*, in Gratien's *Decretum*. This canon has been commented upon by an infinite number of theologians and canonists. However, almost none of them take up his idea and rare indeed are those who even agree to discuss it:[99] most of those who comment on this canon — which goes on to deal with another problem — act as though they overlooked this particular point. Why is this?

At the beginning of the seventeenth century, Thomas Sanchez, among several other justifications of his opinion, gives what is, in my opinion, the fundamental explanation: "I actually consider that there is no harm in not abstaining from asking one's due. This is because the harm [caused to] the child who is nursing — when another child is conceived from such intercourse — can be remedied if during that time he is given to a wet nurse to be nursed. And if the parents are poor, experience shows that they observe no such waiting period — during which they would abstain from intercourse — and that [neither] do they give their child to a wet nurse. In spite of this, we do not perceive noticeable damage in the child. For a rare and uncertain occurrence, *it would therefore be very hard* [and] *morally impossible to force couples to abstain while still sleeping in the same bed during the two years that the child is nursing*, then for another two years when the mother has again given birth. In these circumstances marriage would not be a remedy for concupiscence for the poor, but rather a trap and the cause of much sinning".[100]

Indeed, the theologians of that time believe it to be practically and theologically impossible to force couples to abstain from physical pleasures for a long time: by definition, married people are not suited to continence.[101] It would be acceptable to recommend continence to them for brief periods — holy days, before communion, or during menstruation; but to demand it! and for two years! that would be contrary to the institution of marriage as St Paul defined it. In practice, that would drive husbands to look for sexual satisfaction outside of marriage, thus to sin mortally.

This being so, theologians prefer not to discuss the problem of the consequences of marital relations during breast-feeding. And when they do discuss it, they tend not to face up to reality: either they assume that all parents can afford to pay a wet nurse should the mother's milk dry up, or can arrange to have one paid for them by a charitable person; or they claim that, among the robust people in the country, a new pregnancy is only very rarely dangerous for the infant. A humanist faithful to the ancient traditions obviously describes the reality in a completely different way: "*It is frequently lethal*" — writes Tiraqueau — "not only for the infant who is nursing, but also for the embryo in the uterus, *as we learn from daily experience*, and as we have heard from our traditions and from almost all those who have written of these things".[102] In the current state of research, the evidence provided by historic demography does not contradict such pessimism.

Moreover, we know that a certain number of parents really did believe in this danger and that they gave their children to wet nurses for this reason. In the sixth century, when the Church was stressing continence within marriage under all pretexts, Gregory the Great wrote: "A depraved custom has arisen in conjugal morality: women scorn to nurse the children to whom they give birth and instead give them to other women to nurse. *This appears to have been devised for one reason alone: incontinence*. Because they do not want to restrain themselves, they scorn nursing those whom they conceive".[103]

We must not believe, on the basis of this text alone, that putting children out to nurse suddenly began in the Pope's lifetime: he himself would have been brought up by a wet nurse;[104] and he obviously pretends to believe that this custom is new in order to be able to better condemn it. It must be remembered that he condemns it because people resorted to it in order to avoid being continent within marriage. Conversely, most sixteenth century theologians consider wet nursing to be beneficial because it seems impossible to them to force married couples to be continent for a period of two or three years.

Putting a child out to nurse could have been done for other reasons or conscious motives than merely permitting its parents to continue their intimacy without endangering the child's life; but it is that reason which is given by theologians, as much in the sixth century as in the sixteenth, as much when they condemn it as when they recommend it.

Moreover, parents were so conscious of the risk which a new pregnancy could constitute to the child that those who were rich enough and anxious enough about their children's health to have the wet nurse living with them forbade her to see her husband, out of fear that she might conceive and that their infant would suffer as a result.[105] Those who sent the child to the country and could not supervise the wet nurse in that way, often reproached her for getting pregnant during breast- feeding, when they started proceedings against her for having "spoiled" or lost the child which had been entrusted to her.[106]

The way in which theologians and doctors speak of the country as though it were a separate world with its own customs, might lead one to believe that the rural masses were ignorant of the danger which conceiving during breast-feeding constituted for infants. If that were so, one could not speak of neglect in such cases. It is the Church which would shoulder the moral responsibility for the higher infant and juvenile mortality rates because of premature weaning, since it had the means of knowing and it seems to have done nothing to make peasants aware of the dangers of sexual relations during breast-feeding. On the contrary, we have seen that the Church did not specifically criticise such sexual relations when talking to married couples who worried about not being able to exercise their marital rights without endangering their child's life. A quotation from another of Sanchez' passages is very characteristic of theologians' lax attitudes at that time: "However I will not condemn the man who demands [marital intercourse]. *Because it is just to risk* [the life of] *one's child if one* [risks it] *in order not to be forced to abstain for such a long time,* which is so difficult, or even morally impossible".[107] Such an idea was not shocking at that time, for the Church's doctrine did not offer any solutions other than risking their infant's life to couples unable to remain continent for a long period of time.

There are other examples of the Church's attitude towards this, which is in stark contrast to its struggle for centuries against infanticide and against parents' neglect, which we shall look at. True, people's fears concerning conception during menstruation or conjugal relations during pregnancy are considered by doctors today to be mistaken, whereas the possible tragic consequences of conception during breast-feeding are not. However, for people at that time these three risks all seemed equally real, and theologians accepted that in these three cases the physical good of the child should be subordinated to his parents' conjugal rights. We must try to understand how theologians from the late Middle Ages and modern times arrived at this decision and to find out whether changing opinions concerning conjugal chastity was to the disadvantage of the child or to his advantage.

Changing Attitudes

CONJUGAL CHASTITY AND THE GOOD OF THE CHILD IN THEOLOGICAL DEBATES

In antiquity, Christian rhetoric condemned patterns of behaviour considered to be "against nature" because of their resultant cruelty to the child, and condemned infanticide as the result of lust: the interests of the child and the interests of chastity, far from being mutually exclusive, were mutually dependent. Basically, sexual relations seemed permissible only when their purpose was the good of the child.

Like the Church Fathers, the clerics of the early Middle Ages considered only regular sexual intercourse to be conjugal behaviour, by which they meant — among other things — intercourse interspersed with periods of continence. But whereas the Fathers, following on from the Stoics, had considered the good of the child to be the rule, the clerics seem to have been particularly aware of the need for periods of sexual intercourse to be appropriate to the liturgical calendar. They spoke of the child only rarely except as the vehicle — in actual fact the victim — of immanent justice when it struck overly lustful couples, as we have seen.

Signs of Increasing Interest in the Child

With the theological renaissance of the twelfth century, debates concerning periodic continence become more animated, and concern for the child begins to play a major role.

For writers in the early Middle Ages, sexual relations were forbidden during menstruation because *Leviticus* and the Church Fathers had forbidden them; and the handicaps of children conceived at such times were obviously sent by God in order to punish the violators of the taboo. Intercourse on holy days was thought to have the same effect as intercourse during menstruation. In the thirteenth century, on the other hand, it is no longer thought that handicapped children had been conceived on a Sunday or at another holy time. And the handicap of a child conceived during menstruation is attributed to the natural action of the tainted blood from which it was formed.[108] The prohibition in *Leviticus*, formerly considered sacred, is now considered to have been nullified. If, however, couples should break off their sexual relations during that time, it is merely out of charity towards the child which might be conceived.[109]

In this debate, the Church Fathers' attitudes were closer to those of twelfth and thirteenth century theologians than to the theologians of the early Middle Ages. But changes were certainly made in medieval times as to the justifying of continence at other times.

The breaking off of relations during pregnancy had not been commanded by the Old Testament: it was, above all, the logical result of the condemnation of sterile sexual acts, which the Church Fathers had retained from the philosophers of antiquity.[110] Following Albert the Great and St Thomas Aquinas, thirteenth century theologians and their successors accepted that couples could have intercourse for reasons other than procreation, because the purpose of marriage, according to St Paul, is to avoid fornication:[111] since neither the husband's nor the wife's sexual urges disappear during this time, the remedy of marriage could prove necessary. Thus, from that time on, sexual intercourse during pregnancy is only cautioned against to the extent to which it could be dangerous for the embryo.[112]

Could we then say that the thirteenth century was the time of a major transformation in the development of the concept of childhood? Noonan encourages us to believe this, because he discovers the ancient doctrine again in Gratien and Peter Lombard, in the twelfth century, and Albert the Great seems to him to be the first to have expressed the new opinion. However, careful study of minor writers, from the sixth to the thirteenth century, leads me to believe rather that there was a slow evolution beginning in the early Middle Ages. Indeed, the penitentials differ considerably when establishing the stage of pregnancy at which couples should break off relations. Only the Irish penitentials — and those penitentials from the Continent which derive their inspiration directly from them — express the requirement, practically unenforceable, of breaking off relations from the day of conception. The more realistic Anglo-Saxon penitentials take into account the length of time necessary for couples to become aware of the pregnancy, and recommend that conjugal relations be broken off once the pregnancy becomes apparent. Thus in total, only fifteen or sixteen penitentials apply the Fathers' doctrine, and with varying degrees of realism. But eighteen others require continence only in the last three months and six pay special attention to the last forty days. Why would such time periods be specified if intercourse was forbidden because of its sterility and not for the danger which it posed to the embryo? We must note that this reduction in the period of continence appears very early: the first mention of the period of three months is found in seventh century English penitentials and the first mention of the period of forty days in penitentials from the Continent at the beginning of the eighth century. Obviously, one could claim that this merely demonstrates the laxity of the second generation of penitentials, and emphasise the fact that the embryo is not mentioned anywhere. But there are also penitentials which command couples to break off relations as soon as the embryo begins to move. I have found eight examples of this in all, dated between the ninth and the twelfth century.[113]

It was not until the theological renaissance of the twelfth and thirteenth centuries that these early instructions were explicitly discussed and the new opinion explicitly formulated. But it does seem as though this opinion was discreetly developed between the seventh and the twelfth centuries, and certainly from the ninth century onwards.

The debates on conjugal chastity offer many other indicators as to increasing interest in the child, and it is possible to trace the development of this interest. At the beginning of the fourteenth century, as we have seen, Peter de Palude suggests that the man who could not feed more children than he already had turn to *amplexus reservatus* in order to satisfy his concupiscence or in order to pay his marital debt without risking pregnancy. He is also the first — or so it seems to me at this stage of my research — to have allowed couples to have intercourse in positions previously considered to be "contrary to nature", when conventional intercourse posed dangers for the embryo:[114] "If the wife is pregnant and one is afraid of suffocating the foetus, and if because of that one does not dare to enter her from the front, one does not sin mortally in entering from behind, provided that the small female vessel is not used inappropriately and that semen is not spilled outside".[115] On this point, as on the previous one, Palude is supported by many subsequent theologians.

From the fifteenth until the eighteenth century, theologians can be found who consider it not permissible for the marital debt to be demanded during the period of breast-feeding, when it is possible that a pregnancy could be fatal for the infant. Between the seventh century and the end of the fourteenth, no one had supported this opinion, and in the thirteenth and fourteenth centuries, some theologians even supported the opposite opinion.[116]

In the sixteenth century, Dominic Soto, Peter de Ledesma, Luis Lopez and Thomas Sanchez authorised couples to shirk their conjugal duty when they feared harmful effects on a child soon to be or already born. Thus Ledesma wonders: "What must one do when afraid that the rendering of the debt would be dangerous to the child's health? What must one do for example if the woman...is nursing a child who is already born and if, as she is poor, she has no wet nurse who can breast-feed the child, knowing that the rendering of the debt results in the wife's pregnancy, while the milk of pregnant women is very harmful and noxious for children and that sometimes pregnant women have no milk at all? The answer to this question is obviously that it is sufficient to excuse the spouse from the rendering of the debt...because intercourse at such a time is against the interests of the child which marriage is particularly designed for."[117]

In the middle of the century, Dominic Soto had already accepted that duties towards the child were more important than conjugal duty, "particularly when the parents are dogged by poverty which makes it impossible for them to feed so many children".[118] And, in 1592, Ledesma extends this principle to families who are relatively and no longer absolutely poor, maintaining that one could shirk conjugal duty when further births would prevent those children already born from being given the upbringing required by their social condition.[119]

Signs of Developing Attitudes Which Are Harmful to Children

This increase in interest in the child must not mask the fact that theologians usually subordinated the good of the child to that of his parents. Believing that children conceived during menstruation were born lepers or handicapped did not prevent them from advising couples to run the risk of pregnancy at such times in certain circumstances. If, for example, the husband demanded his conjugal right from his wife, she had the duty to grant it to him irrespective of her indisposition, because her body belonged to her husband and it would have been unjust to refuse him. Moreover, by refusing him the remedy of marriage, she might have caused him to turn to fornication and would thus have put his soul in grave danger. As for the husband, if he feared he might be tempted to commit adultery, theologians allowed him to demand this remedy of marriage from his wife, even when she was menstruating. For example, Angelus de Clavasio writes in 1486: "... Neither he who demands nor he who renders it commits a mortal sin, *because it is more important to devote oneself to one's own salvation* or that of the next person [i.e. of one's spouse] *than to the physical good of the next person* [i.e. of the child]".[120]

And in 1514, Sylvester da Prierio writes: "It is not a mortal sin for the man to demand [his conjugal right] when he fears illicit corruption for himself and he cannot easily satisfy it [through other means]; because he is *more obliged to take care of his soul than of the body of the child to be conceived*".[121]

The subordinating of bodily needs to spiritual concerns, which partially explains this choice, does not explain everything. Indeed, St Thomas and subsequent theologians accepted that the wife was not obliged to make her indisposition known to her husband if she feared that it would horrify him, make him angry, or that he might take a sudden dislike to her. When her husband tried to have intercourse with her, she was to invent some clever pretext to distract him from his intentions. If she did not manage to do this, she was to give in to him, without having revealed anything to him: "Finally, if the man persists in his demand, she must pay the due to him who demands it; moreover it is not prudent to make one's indisposition known — for fear that the man begin to loathe her — unless one assumes prudence on the man's part".[122]

In short, Dr Angélique and all subsequent theologians advise the wife to run the risk of conceiving a leprous or handicapped child rather than that of suffering her husband's temper for having revealed to him that his wife is menstruating.

In the same way, theologians played down the risk which relations with a pregnant woman seemed to pose for the embryo and the risk which relations during breast-feeding posed for the infant. We now consider them to have been mistaken in the former, but they merely underestimated it for the sake of convenience.

In the thirteenth century, when theologians upheld continence during menstruation and pregnancy for the child's good, was it really because they were more concerned about the child than their predecessors? This is doubtful when one considers that they were also the first to have suggested that one could have intercourse during these periods without committing a mortal sin. From the twelfth to the seventeenth century, a distinct evolution of morality concerning these two questions can be seen. But this evolution is a move towards greater indulgence towards couples unable to respect the times for continence, hence is a move which can only harm the child.

As for the innovations of the fourteenth, fifteenth and sixteenth centuries which appeared to indicate greater concern for the child's health, life and upbringing, they too may all be interpreted in the same way. When P. de Palude suggests *amplexus reservatus*, does he do so out of charity for a child who cannot be fed, to avoid the father having to remain continent from then on or even to avoid sins against nature being committed? When he authorises certain positions which until then had been considered "contrary to nature", it is perhaps in order to avoid couples from suffocating the embryo, but also in order to help them avoid continence; in any case it is a broadening of the accepted patterns of sexual behaviour.

As for refusing to render the marital debt, which women are authorised to do when they are menstruating or nursing or when their husbands do not provide for the household expenses, this is again a liberal attitude in relation to ancient sexual morality; for it was as constraining for couples who were disgusted by conjugal intercourse as for those who desired it at inappropriate times.

The Growth of Contradictions Between the Good of the Child and Conjugal Chastity

All things considered, must it be concluded that theologians thought only of liberating conjugal relations from their ancient shackles and were no more interested than before in the life or health of the children? I get the impression rather that there are two evolutions, independent of each other and sometimes contradictory: one in favour of children, the other in favour of freer conjugal intercourse.

Sometimes, the two trends led to the same innovation: for example when *amplexus reservatus* is suggested or positions "contrary to nature" are accepted; or again when one of the spouses is allowed to shirk his or her conjugal duty. At other times, they were contradictory: in the case of intercourse during menstruation, during pregnancy, or during breast-feeding. But careful study almost always allows us to discover both trends in the evolution of each of these debates.

Let us consider the question of intercourse during breast-feeding: from the seventh to the fourteenth century, the trend towards liberating couples' sex lives is particularly evident; then, from the fifteenth to the eighteenth century, the trend for protecting the child's life makes itself felt. Paradoxically, perhaps, it makes itself felt from the thirteenth century onwards. For — to my knowledge — no text from the early Middle Ages justified the forbidding of sexual relations in that period by citing the risk to which they exposed the embryo. Writers of this time seem to have favoured continence for its own merits, and rarely to have been concerned with the child in this sort of debate. If they did not adopt the same attitude as Gregory the Great — whose letter to St Augustine of Canterbury was known from the eighteenth century onwards — it is because a period of continence lasting one, two or three years seemed to them to be rather excessive. Thirteenth and fourteenth century writers who have misgivings about imposing self-restraint on couples must have found it even more excessive. And yet, they cite that passage by Gregory the Great and comment upon it much more often than their predecessors. They are the first to note that there is a contradiction between the couple's right and the interests of the child. Even though they still subordinate the child's good to that of the couple, they were the first to confront the problem, which was resolved in the child's favour by certain theologians in the period from the fifteenth to the eighteenth century. Moreover, it must not be forgotten that the latter hesitate a good deal before forbidding conjugal intercourse during breast-feeding. This is because, to an even greater extent than thirteenth and fourteenth century theologians, they are opposed to compulsory continence within marriage, as they show in other debates, for example on the subject of continence during holy periods.

No doubt it is because they were more aware of the contradictions between the rights of marriage and concern for the child than their predecessors, that some of them arrived at the truly revolutionary solution of refusing conjugal rights. It was all the more revolutionary as their doctrine was more Pauline and less Augustinian than that of theologians before the mid-thirteenth century. For the mandatory nature of conjugal debt has always been one of the most uncontested and most fundamental elements of Pauline doctrine. To accept one of the spouses shirking conjugal obligation though the other is asking only for something permissible, is to show the intolerable contradictions between the good of the child and the right of the partners.

Such passages give us, sometimes indirectly, information as much about the attitudes of the faithful as about those of theologians. For example, Thomas Sanchez, who recognises the husband's right to demand the conjugal right even when that means a serious risk for the child, does however allow the wife to shirk her duty: "I recognise however with P. de Ledesma...that the mother who is breast-feeding her child and is so poor that she cannot pay for a wet nurse to nurse it and has discovered that her breasts go dry when she conceives or that her milk becomes very harmful for the child is dispensed from the obligation to pay the duty...The mother is not obliged to expose herself to such pain, to suffer such a loss and [to expose herself] to so great a danger".[123]

In fact, while less attentive than Ledesma to the good of the child, Sanchez is particularly conscious of the impossibility of asking a mother to risk her child's life. He already gave a similar lecture at the end of the chapter concerning sexual relations during menstruation, refusing to force a woman to fulfil her duty as a wife when she believes that as a result she will conceive a handicapped child. Does this reflect a change in the theologian's sensibility or the growth of maternal love?

When continence was strictly demanded within marriage, on pain of mortal sin, many husbands rejected by their wives — or perhaps wives deserted by their husbands — looked outside marriage to satisfy their sexual appetites. Theologians seem to have gradually renounced compulsory periodic continence in order to turn them away from adultery and to help them to understand better the hierarchy of sins.[124]

In so doing, they logically — if not consciously and actually — acted in the interests of the child. For all fornication — as St Thomas asserts very explicitly — can be defined as a crime towards the child: a child can only be brought up, educated and become an honourable adult if he is conceived within a legitimate family.[125] Indeed we have seen how bastards were doomed to die by blatant infanticide or other means much more often than legitimate children. Thus one could claim that, if thirteenth century theologians came to consider charity towards the child a new justification for ancient taboos, it is still — indirectly — in the interests of the child that they progressively abandoned them.

But this is not the most important point. As long as Christian morality, totally ignoring the realities of human life, only accepted sexual intercourse for the good of the offspring, such sexual morality was consistent, but stood little chance of being widely practised. The contradictions were to be found between the doctrine and the behaviour of the faithful. From the time when, in order to minimise these contradictions, theologians returned to Pauline doctrine, the contradictions became inherent in the morality of marriage: if one could legitimately have sexual relations for other reasons than for the good of the child, it became possible for such relations sometimes to be against the interests of the child. Theologians and the faithful seem to have become more and more conscious of these contradictions — an inherent factor in any evolution — from the thirteenth to the eighteenth century. Because these contradictions finally became untenable — for those of the faithful who were assimilating Christian values, which made them increasingly mindful of the physical and moral good of the child — a solution was provided: contraception. Only contraception safeguarded a couple's right to engage in intercourse at all times, throughout their entire married life, while avoiding the procreation of children for whom they could not provide.

I am not suggesting that all married couples who used contraception used it for that reason; nor that other historical changes did not equally lead to this change in married behaviour. In fact, I am convinced that the opposite is true: there were other conscious motives, a new understanding of marital relations and of marriage, and techniques available to protect human life more effectively, and hence for people to become more attached to their children. But introducing contraception into marriage was the logical solution to the moral contradictions which we have seen worsening between the twelfth and the eighteenth centuries.

The reasons why the contraceptive method adopted was *coitus interruptus* — introduced to the West during the Middle Ages — and not other simple and effective methods such as the woollen tampon used by prostitutes, are yet to be discovered. We would have to know whether contraception using *coitus interruptus* spread first inside marriage or in extramarital relationships; in which time period and in which milieux. I cannot elaborate on the question here and will stress only that Benedicti's exhortation not to fear having too many children suggests that in France, at the end of the sixteenth century, some couples were already turning to solutions unacceptable to the Church at that time.

Finally, let us examine how attitudes towards children evolved and the relationship between this and the change in the demographic system in France in the eighteenth and nineteenth centuries.

DEMOGRAPHIC CHANGES AND CHANGING ATTITUDES TOWARDS THE LIFE OF THE CHILD

The evolution of moral theology may have followed its own system of logic, with no relation to generally evolving attitudes, or it may even have developed against the current, resisting the development of ideas judged dangerous. Whatever the reason, the Church has never fought so relentlessly against contraception as at the end of the nineteenth century and in the first half of the twentieth, while more and more couples considered its use justifiable. Is it not possible that theologians showed themselves to be increasingly concerned for the health of the child because its fate became much worse between the eleventh and the eighteenth century, and because adults' interest in the child's life decreased?

There are two statistically verifiable facts which have led to this belief, despite the increase in writings devoted to children in the seventeenth and eighteenth centuries: the continuous and considerable increase in the recorded number of foundlings between 1640 and 1772; and the decrease in the number of children born in France in the eighteenth century. The growth of paid wet nursing could also be added, being not only a consequence of the increase in the number of children abandoned, but also another means of losing interest in them.

The Development of Methods for Getting Rid of Children

We know how gravely a child's life was in danger when he or she was abandoned, in spite of the increasing numbers of charitable institutions, and everything seems to prove that the mortality rate of foundlings rose during the eighteenth century.[126] As for their increasing numbers, most contemporaries attribute this to the decline of morals and the weakening of paternal or maternal feeling. But no one seems to have claimed that debauchery began to gain ground in the first part of the seventeenth century. On the contrary, it is agreed that rigid moral standards spread throughout that century and even to a certain extent into the eighteenth. And yet, the rise in the number of foundlings in Paris is constant from 1640.[127] Neither does anyone seem to think that debauchery decreased after 1772 or during the Revolution. Yet the number of foundlings in Paris decreases slightly after 1772 and much more markedly during the Revolution. Thus there is no automatic and absolute correlation between the number of foundlings and the frequency of extramarital relations.

In the current state of research, it seems reasonable to accept that the growth in the number of hospices during the seventeenth and eighteenth centuries had consequences which were both varied and, whether from a Christian viewpoint or indeed from our own, contradictory: it undoubtedly encouraged extramarital relationships and allowed both legitimate and illegitimate couples to escape their duties towards their child more easily; but it also allowed unmarried mothers not to commit infanticide and legitimate parents not to let those children die which they were not able to provide for. This increase in the number of hospices seems to be explained more by the growth in charity towards the child than by an increase in the number of children abandoned. Indeed, as we have seen, hospitals in the fifteenth and sixteenth centuries do not appear to have been particularly concerned about illegitimate children and it is only in the seventeenth or eighteenth century that, in practice or in law, they accepted them as legitimate. For that matter, it is known that during the three modern centuries, public charity has increased: whether middle-class charity, political charity, or charity created by the Catholic Reformation. Paradoxically then, the increase in the number of children abandoned can be explained by the trend towards public charity which increased during these three centuries along with interest in the child, the development of which Philippe Ariès has shown for the social elite.

At the same time as a means of lodging undesirable children was being organised, the Church and State seem to have found effective means for preventing infanticide.

I do not know how immediately effective the readings from the pulpit of Henry II's edicts were and the convictions which they led to. But in the second half of the seventeenth century and in the eighteenth century, the local authorities were effectively supervising pregnant young women, who were required to come forward and register their pregnancies before confinement.[128] In the sixteenth century, the police registered such declarations during roundups of young women of doubtful morality.[129] In the eighteenth century, it appears that pregnant young women got into the habit of coming forward of their own accord or on the advice of vigilant relatives. For these women, it was at one and the same time an opportunity for making a complaint about a seducer who abandoned them and obtaining an allowance in order to feed the child; a guarantee of not committing a statutory offence under Henry II's edict; and obviously a way of preventing them from doing anything silly after giving birth alone and in secret, since they were immediately placed under the care of an authorised midwife.

We cannot be sure that the practice of registering pregnancies was as effective against abortions, for registration generally took place late and, undoubtedly for a certain number of young women, after attempts at abortion had failed.

But we have seen that the Church took Draconian measures against the smothering and suffocation of children, measures quite similar to those taken by the State against infanticide. There can be no doubt but that these measures contributed greatly to the disappearance of the problem.

Of the three radical means at mothers' disposal for ridding themselves of children who had already been born, two seem to have almost disappeared during the eighteenth century, whereas the third on the other hand increased dramatically. Thus, one can assume that the increase in the number of abandoned children is explained in part by this means being used in preference to the other two methods. Moreover, contemporaries recognise that it became more common to abandon illegitimate children than to commit infanticide. I am not only claiming objectively that previously parents killed more children than died at an early age in hospices or on their way to the hospice in the eighteenth century. I am stating rather that by abandoning their children, eighteenth century mothers demonstrated less disregard for their lives than those in previous centuries who killed their children.

Changes in Parental Neglect: Paid Wet Nursing

These things considered, what are we to think of the increase in paid wet nursing among the working classes, at a time when so many people in the upper classes were decrying its harmful effects? Even if it was not caused by decreasing maternal or paternal feelings, it would be strange if that were not its result: the child's absence must have prevented such feelings from crystallising, and that would hardly compensate for any bad treatment which the infant might formerly have received from a mother burdened with too many children and exasperated by their crying. This is even more true since, although the child was a significant source of income for the wet nurse, that did not protect it from her impatience, if she herself was the mother of a large family and lived in her own village. Although some children received more warmth and affection from their wet nurses than from their mothers, as literary tradition leads us to believe, Maurice Garden has shown us that not all were so lucky. Moreover, his statistics prove that the mortality rate of unweaned infants rose considerably between the beginning and the end of the century.

But why was there this increase in paid wet nursing among the working classes, against the tide of what appears to have happened in the upper classes? Undoubtedly the question must first be examined in relation to the growth of towns. Equally, one could surmise that artisans and shopkeepers were aping the bourgeoisie and the nobility somewhat by putting their children out to nurse. If such were the case, the increasing opposition to paid wet nursing in those classes would have been a more important historical fact for the future — albeit quantitatively less for the time being — than the increase in the number of children put out to nurse. Finally, it is possible that, in the working classes, more mothers put their children out to nurse when they had no milk or feared not having any because of their conjugal obligations than had done so previously. In that case, the increase in paid wet nursing might then have been caused by greater concern for the child's health and it might have actually saved a significant number of young children from death.

Moreover, no matter what the advance of paid wet nursing, and its merits and harmful effects might have been, it obviously involved only a minority and the vast majority of babies continued to be breast-fed by their mothers. It is known that, even among these children, the mortality rate was high, and I have suggested that a significant part of this mortality rate could be explained by parents' neglect, particularly when weaning a child because of a subsequent premature pregnancy. Lastly, in order to discover whether their fate became better or worse, we must examine the changes in the infant mortality rates.

The Growth of Parental Lack of Concern: Infant Mortality and Birth Control

It does not seem to me to be useful to emphasise figures with which everyone is familiar: even though infant mortality seems to have increased or remained the same in a certain number of villages or even regions — for example in Brittany — it is generally agreed that on the whole it decreased, at least after the middle of the century, and often to a significant extent. Yet this fall in the infant mortality rate is not generally explained as anything other than the fall in the mortality rate generally: because of the disappearance of the plague and periods of famine, and because of the advances made in medicine and hygiene. It seems to me, however, that, given the current state of research, explaining it by one or the other of these two great advances, economic progress or the progress of medical "science", belongs more to the sphere of political eloquence than to scientific reasoning. What did young children actually die of? It has never been explicitly proven how the invention of vaccines or other eighteenth century medical advances were able to cause the mortality rate of children under one year of age to fall. If, as I believe, infants weaned too early died particularly of intestinal diseases due to the lack of hygiene, I don't really see what in the way of medical advances could have decreased their mortality rate before the popularising of Pasteur's principles. The latter did not occur until the last decade of the nineteenth century, and is clearly reflected in both English and French infant mortality statistics.

The "demographic revolution" has for a long time been distinguished both by the fall in the mortality rate — particularly of infants and children — and by the fall in the fertility of marriages. Some have claimed that, in a society in which the *general mortality rate* declined — as a result of advances in medicine or of economic progress — it was natural for the birth rate to decline also. But such Malthusian reasoning, applicable to a farming economy in which all arable land is being cultivated and without the benefits of technical progress, seems to me to be doubtful in a rapidly expanding industrial society, able to win huge pieces of land from militarily inferior peoples. It is even less likely to be true in a capitalist society geared to selling abroad and needing a cheap, and therefore plentiful, work force. Moreover, it is known that, throughout the nineteenth century, the English fertility rate remained the same or even rose despite the very noticeable decrease in general mortality; and that currently in Third World countries the fall in the mortality rate does not imply a noticeable and spontaneous fall in the fertility rate, even in agricultural societies with no chance of either colonising or being colonised and with slow technical progress. The fall in fertility is therefore not automatically linked to the fall in general mortality.

Other people do their reasoning at family level. They stress that, due to the fall in infant and child mortality, couples had to limit the number of births so that the number of their children living did not increase. This reasoning, which His Grace Bouvier had applied to Christian couples practising contraception, is not insignificant. But is it not *a posteriori* justification? Because there are few studies of family types in this period, there is nothing to prove that the gradual fall in average fertility cannot be interpreted as reflecting a gradual increase in the number of very Malthusian families. J. Dupâquier and M. Lachiver's article — the only one in existence to my knowledge — proves the opposite to be true in Meulan.

Such explanations always consider the fall in mortality to be the cause and the fall in fertility the consequence. Yet that has not ever been proven either.

In the eighteenth century, although the majority of researchers seem to have been little concerned with pointing out the correlation between the two phenomena, it appears quite clearly. In Saint-Méen-le-Grand, where, exceptionally, the mortality rate of children up to ten years of age is shown to have increased, the fertility rate is shown also to have increased. The opposite is true of Sainghin-en-Mélantois, Tamerville or Meulan, where infant mortality and marital fertility rates both fell significantly.[130] In the absence of general statistics, we can thus accept that both rates fell in France, but without knowing which of the two declines occurred first and thus caused the second.

If we try to examine closely the evolution of these two rates between 1770 and 1938, according to the figures offered by J. Bourgeois-Pichat[131] (see graph p. 195), we note that the two curves indicate a constant and similar decrease, whereas the child mortality curve is more uneven. It seems evident to me that this curve is affected by the same changes as the fertility curve, but fifteen years later: a marked drop from the second half of the eighteenth century to the beginning of the nineteenth; then the decline slows down, and there is a period almost of stagnation in the third quarter of the nineteenth century; finally, a marked drop in the fertility rate from approximately 1880 to 1938, and an even greater fall in infant mortality from 1895 onwards. If there is a causal relationship between these two phenomena, it is the fall in fertility which explains the fall in the infant mortality rate.

This connection at first seems to be confirmed by examining English statistics. In England, where the fall in fertility does not begin until 1880, there was no fall in the infant mortality rate until 1895.[132] Does this not prove that in France the fall of the infant mortality rate in the mid-eighteenth century can only be explained by the use of birth control? For if it could be explained by advances in medicine or in the

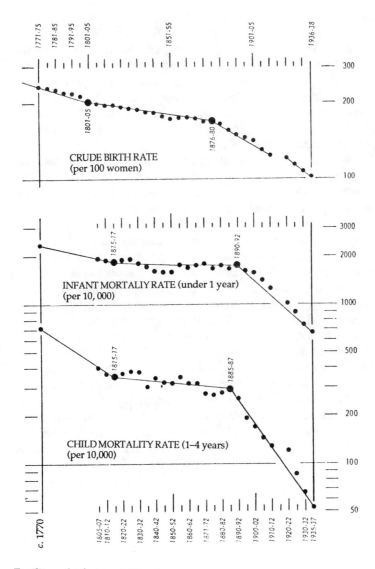

Fertility and infant mortality rates.

economy, it would have been obvious in England even earlier than in France.

However, one fact complicates this evidence and limits the significance of what I have recognised: when infant mortality begins to fall in England, *c.* 1895, the rate is approximately 150 per 1,000, whereas in France at the same time, where is has been falling for more than a century, it is still 161 per 1,000. Thus, either infant mortality in the eighteenth century was as high in England as in France but was concealed by the custom of baptising babies later, and in which case the stagnation in the nineteenth century is an illusion; or else infant morality in England actually was lower than in France, and my comments about higher infant mortality being attributable to lack of care, to neglect and getting rid of children must be limited to France, or at least not applied to England.

It is always possible that contraception within marriage was introduced in France a century ahead of other European countries because, as Fernand Braudel hypothesises, in the pre-industrial period France was over-populated in relation to the other countries; or because it had a particularly high infant mortality rate, which can be explained more by cultural than material factors. But in that case, the fall in infant mortality in France in the eighteenth and nineteenth centuries, which I explain by the use of birth control, would not mark the beginning of the great change, but simply France catching up with her neighbours.

Nevertheless, the fact remains that — in spite of significant facts which appeared to indicate a lack of interest in children in the eighteenth century and a worsening of their fate — their lives were safeguarded better than in the past, as shown by the decline in infant mortality. There are many reasons for believing that this improvement is the result of a change in attitudes towards children, as much in society as a whole as in individual couples. It is probable that the increase in the number of abandoned children and the growth of paid wet nursing, as well as the increase in the harmful effects of both, led to a beneficial realisation which combined with those which resulted from theological debates. Thus, birth control may have been a consequence of all these realisations; and for a century, it may have been the main means of reducing infant mortality.

CONCLUSION

If one examines the situation from a distance, it appears that because of the economic and social structures of European society, Malthusian tensions are always felt within couples and that such tensions probably even existed when there was no actual over-population, relative to the capacity of the land and technical possibilities. No doubt this is why, from antiquity to the present time, couples are always found who try to limit the number of children they have, even when the moral code condemned this attitude and states were populationist.

It is the attitude towards the new-born baby's life which has changed in the period between antiquity and today and not couples' desire to limit the number of their children.

Christianity seems to have played an important but ambiguous role in this evolution. How can we explain the legal ban on infanticide in the fourth century and its gradual disappearance since then, if not by the Church's fight against it? Yet on the other hand, the Church, by condemning all sexual relations whose purpose was not procreation or which had been dissociated from their procreative purpose, encouraged couples to conceive more children than they could provide for. Infant and child mortality due to ancient sanitary conditions was added to by mortality due to neglect and lack of concern: parents' inability to provide for all their children, children being abandoned to public charity, weaning children too early, etc.

A certain Christian moral code, dominated by the concept of sin, undoubtedly contributed to making this state of things psychologically possible, and to perpetuating it. This code insisted that parents did nothing which was directly and obviously contrary to the good of the child — killing it, abandoning it, refusing it food that they were capable of giving — but it did not forbid them from putting an infant's life in danger by taking the risk of conceiving before weaning, and it encouraged them to procreate with no fear of not being able to provide for their children.

Between the twelfth and the seventeenth century, theologians are seen to become increasingly concerned about the good of the child and increasingly conscious about possible contradictions between that good and couples' sexual rights. It is not known whether it was theologians who preceded and instructed the laity or whether it was the laity who instructed theologians about their own problems. In spite of St Paul's teachings, theologians took a long time to comprehend the risk which continence imposed for long periods could pose to marital fidelity; and similarly they understood two centuries later than the laity that contraception could be a way of showing parental love. Must we then think that parents were made aware of their duties towards the child by something other than Christian preaching? In the current state of research, I do not see what that "something" could have been.

The extent to which couples turning to contraception — which was a significant tool in the struggle against infant mortality — indicated increased interest in the child's life, it seems to me to be paradoxically the result of two thousand years of Christian preaching. But I am not forgetting that its use is also the sign of a certain liberalising of marital relations, of a new understanding of marriage and love and the consequence of many other historical changes which equally deserve to be studied and which themselves were not Christian in origin.

Appendix I

PASTORAL FROM HIS GRACE THE ARCHBISHOP OF PARIS AGAINST THOSE WOMEN WHO CAUSE THE DEATH OF THEIR CHILDREN*

HARDOUIN OF PEREFIXE, by the grace of God & of the Holy Apostolic See, Archbishop of Paris, to the Archpriests of St Mary Magdalene & St Severinus, Hail to thee in the name of our Lord. It is the ordinary result of a crime to hide oneself & to defend oneself by other crimes. Through experience we see this in those unhappy women, who lower themselves to the vice of immodesty, to disorder & to debauchery, who most frequently believe they cannot cover up the shame of their dissoluteness other than by parricide & who, in order to preserve that honour in men's eyes which they have lost in God's, feel it necessary to destroy innocent creatures, whom God has made in His image and likeness, to lose Souls which He redeemed with His Blood & to be the murderers of their own Children, almost before being their Mothers. And because the severity of divine and human Laws, which demanded the most serious chastisement in order to punish this sin, has not yet been able to completely suppress the frenzy produced now and again by these monsters of cruelty, we have good reason to fear that either the people are ignorant of the enormity of this crime & of the severity of said Laws, or that the guilty parties too often find indulgence in the Tribunals of Penitence, or that they too readily cherish a false hope of not being found guilty. This is why we believed it was important to repeat the ancient Edicts and Statutes of this Diocese, in order that the magnitude of the punishments make it clear with what abhorrence this crime must be viewed & that even should one be able to conceal it from man's knowledge, he would not be able to avoid the anathema of the Church, nor the anger of God who will punish such a sin terribly for Eternity, if it is not erased by a great & sincere penance. BECAUSE OF THIS, We forbid all Curés, Curates & other Priests, both Secular and Regular, no matter what power they claim to have, if they do not have Our permission to absolve reserved cases, to give absolution to any women or young women who by potions, or by other illicit means, caused the death or tried to cause the death of their offspring, animated

---

*   According to a notice printed in Paris by F. Muguet and preserved in Grenoble library under the reference D.5385.

or not, even when death did not take place, which We equally want to be observed with regard to all persons who consciously gave or prescribed said potions & means. And if there are any Mothers unnatural enough to spill the blood of their already born Children, to suffocate them, or to cause their death by any other manner, We command that they incur the penalty of excommunication & we reserve for Ourselves alone, our Vicars-General & Penitentiaries of our Church the power of absolution, whether for murder & parricide of said Children or for the Excommunication incurred for them. But because these hardened Souls, who scorn the Laws of Nature, also more often than not scorn also those of the Church & easily forget those of our very Christian Kings, and who, through fear of their punishment, could suppress their debauchery, we command that Henry II's Edict, attached hereafter, be read out during the Sermon of Parish Mass, after the present Pastoral, so that no one is unaware of it. THUS WE COMMAND YOU that by these presents you Deans, Abbots, Priors, Curés, Curates and other Superiors of Secular and Regular Communities understand this, so that they turn their hand to the execution of this task, as much for the publishing of them which We command to be done in their Sermons, as for taking them into consideration in Confessions. PRESENTED in Paris under the Seal of our Arms this tenth March sixteen hundred and sixty-six. Signed HARDOUIN, Archbishop of Paris.

Appendix II

*WOMEN WHO ARE NURSING THEIR CHILDREN MUST ABSTAIN FROM INTERCOURSE**

On the subject of intercourse, we also warn, insofar as possible without risk to modesty, that men should not have intercourse with women who are nursing their children. For that too is prohibited in the canon *Ad eius vero concubitum*, at the beginning of point 5. Indeed, of all things, nothing is more harmful for children who are breast-feeding, as we are told by Dominicus,...and, from among the doctors, Oribase... and Paul Eginète... and Alexandre Trallianus... And, before then, Galen said in book I of his *Protection de la Santé*: "I warn anyone who is nursing to abstain completely from intercourse. For intercourse with a man brings about the monthly cycle and her milk changes its charming smell for a bad one. What is worse, some women conceive in their womb, as a result of which, unfortunately, nothing remains for the child who is breast-feeding. Thus, in effect, all the blood is absorbed by the foetus. Truly, the foetus, since he (already) contains within himself his own principle for life, acts only in his own interest and continuously draws in the food he needs, cleaving to the uterus as to a root and separating from it neither by day nor by

---

*   Tiraqueau, *De legibus connubialibus*, book XV, no. 139, 1574 edition, p. 342. I abridged the passage myself.

night. Truly, during this time, the blood of the pregnant woman is logically made not only less plentiful but also of poorer quality, which means that the milk itself, which concentrates in the breasts, is as poor in quality as it is not plentiful. This is why I myself strongly advise that, should a woman who is nursing conceive a child, a wet nurse should be engaged."

That is what he says. And Pline says, in book 28, at the beginning of chapter 9: "Wet nurses, to conceive is fatal..."

And you will add to the above that it is also frequently lethal for the embryo in the uterus, not only for the child who is breast-feeding, as we learn from almost daily experience, and as tradition and almost all those who have written about such things pass on...

Appendix III[*]

The other cause of inflammation[†] is love, in which mothers who are feeding their children often make a mistake, in the way in which I will point out. If the wet nurse is married, mothers do not wish her husband to know her in any way: and this, for fear that it harm her milk. They are right to a certain extent, but do not have all the reasons. For it is much better for the wet nurse to have her husband's company, wisely and moderately, than if she is burning with desire. Unsatisfied desire is the main thing which harms the milk, as is seen in very amorous wet nurses, who chase their husbands like bitches on heat. Would it not be better for them to have some quenching of this great appetite, rather than forcing them to burn slowly? You will sometimes see them so distressed by amorous passion that they lose all composure as a result, even for sleeping and eating. Who can doubt that their milk will not also be affected, and their breasts in danger of drying up? The wet nurse must be well fed, sleep long into the morning, and do hardly any work. Such a pattern encourages acts of the flesh, arouses the senses and encourages lust. If a well-treated and healthy woman of leisure, tempted by this feeling, is forced to abstain totally, I believe that her milk will not be better as a result, overheated and harmed in this way, it will smell, just as she herself will. Thus it would be better that she enjoy her husband in moderation, as has been said, than to be totally deprived of him and sequestered. And why? Are the wives of labourers, artisans, shopkeepers and others who commonly nurse their children excluded from their husbands' beds? or do their husbands never embrace them, when they are wet nurses? It is well known that they do not. And are their children

---

[*]   Laurent Joubert, *Erreurs populaires*, vol. I, p. 226 and following.
[†]   The author has been speaking of another humour which dries up the milk: choler. He is reasoning within the framework of medical beliefs explained by humours and temperatures.

less well fed: are they more delicate or sickly than those of beautiful middle class women, of affected Damsels or of precious Great Ladies: who do not wish to lower themselves so much as to carry out their duty to nature by nursing their children with the milk given to them by God as He gives it to all mothers? Far from it: on the contrary the children of poor women, fed by their mothers, are commonly stronger and more lively. But it is feared — this is the strongest reason — that the wet nurse might become pregnant through intercourse with her husband: and that the child would be fed with bad milk. Which it undoubtedly would be, because of the pregnancy. And it is to be feared that the wet nurse might not announce that she was pregnant before the infant is affected by it. For most women do not menstruate while they are nursing and thus, do not realise they are pregnant until their milk is bad. And the others who do menstruate are very often one month pregnant before they notice it. What is worse is that there are wet nurses who, knowing full well they are pregnant, say nothing of it as long as they have a drop of milk, fearing to be given notice. And so the child is ill-treated, which in the Languedoc they call "*enganar*" ("deceiving"), from the Italian "*ingannare*". These are the main reasons given by honest women why they do not wish to allow their children's wet nurses to know men.

But the disadvantages that I put forward above counter-balance these reasons, and — in my opinion — are of equal value, being more momentous: for the overheated milk of a woman with a passion for loving is much worse and more damaging than that of a pregnant woman. And why? do we not see — as we said in the second chapter of this book — that women from villages have no difficulty in nursing their children, even though they are pregnant, as long as there is a drop of milk left in their breasts and the child can suck on it. Were that to last until the ninth month, they would continue to feed the child with no difficulty: and then would wean it, although it is only just over a year old. Are they more loutish and inept at work as a result of this? We can clearly see that they are more robust and patient at work than city dwellers. The poor say that if a child has drunk the best of the liquid, he must finally drink the dregs: just as they do themselves with wine. For they drink the bottom as well as the top, as long as the vessel will pour, right to the last drop. But people who are more indolent and delicate, those who are well-off and precious, leave the wine as soon as it has passed the halfway mark of the barrel, and say that it smells of the bottom of the barrel, so that the servants and chambermaids drink the rest right down to the dregs. So may it be for children who are nursed, whose wine is their mother's milk: just as conversely we say that wine is the milk of old people, which comparison is very appropriate.

Ladies who do not really hear what I am saying will say that I am recommending that children be nursed with the milk of a pregnant woman. But, with all due respect, I am not saying this by way of advice, but rather I am demonstrating again how the children in villages and of poor people who are roughly fed and that their pregnant mother's milk is not dangerous to them. I am not saying that it does not harm delicate children from good homes: as much as if they come from parents who are fed preciously as if it is their mother's milk. For it must be understood that there is such an affinity between the child and its mother's blood that it will be fed better by the worst of its mother's milk than by the best of another woman's. Well I know that this idea will be considered strange: but it is the truth, and I will prove it sufficiently in the sixth book, which will deal with this custom. And if I manage only to convince you that the milk of a pregnant woman is not as bad for a child as that of a woman like a bitch on heat, wanting very much the company of her husband or boyfriend, I will have sufficiently convinced of their error those women who find it strange that a wet nurse should enjoy physical love. By this I mean that she enjoy it modestly and soberly as one does when one is completely free to do so. For if it must be done in hiding and surreptitiously, they go at it like unsaddled donkeys, and they get so hot that the evil which results is doubly bad. Firstly, the milk is even more affected and secondly, wet nurses are more likely to become pregnant as a result. For it is as though one keeps wine locked up away from a drunkard. If he finds the key to the cellar, he takes as much as he can. Leave him the wine openly, when he himself is in control, he will drink less of it and will be more sober as a result. Wet nurses will say, many thanks, when they see this, you speak for us very well. This is a good formula: we will carry it out willingly. And their mistresses will think on the contrary that I am in love with wet nurses and that I like to caress them. Admittedly, it is true that I like wet nurses and that the woman whom I cherish the most in this world nursed all my children for as long as she had milk, and I did not stop sleeping with her and making love to her because of that, like a good partner to his good other half, according to the union of marriage: and — thank God — our children have been well fed and have survived very well. I do not give advice to others which I do not follow myself.

Chapter 11

Ancient and Modern Adages Concerning the Child Within the Family

Proverbs and other adages have rarely attracted the interest of historians, being often ambiguous, sometimes contradictory and always difficult to date. Despite these drawbacks, they do however represent an invaluable source for studying the history of human attitudes, since they provide almost our only evidence of the oral traditions of the vast majority of people in the past.

. This article will deal with early attitudes towards children and the upbringing which families did their best to give them. Admittedly these could have been determined by examining doctors' and teachers' prescriptions, sermons made to parents or the questions which they were asked in confession.

But ecclesiastic writers were too obsessed with the saving of souls and too bound to Christian doctrine, and doctors and teacherss were addressing too restricted an audience for them to be reliable witnesses of ordinary attitudes and practices. Proverbs, on the other hand, can be considered to express "common wisdom", even if one is not entirely familiar with the background to each saying, the extent of its currency and its influence on ways of thinking. This is, of course, assuming that one does not arbitrarily choose this or that adage, but carries out an exhaustive inventory of the subject under consideration.[1]

CHILDREN, A SOURCE OF WORRY FOR THEIR PARENTS

Proverbs, being adults' sayings, are indulgent expressions of the worries which parenthood gives rise to:

> *Autant d'enfants, autant de plaies* [As many little nuisances as you have children] (Provence, 1965).

> *Argent et enfants, moins il y en a, moins de tracas* [The less money and fewer children there are, the fewer worries there are] (Catalonia, 1969).

> *C'est la chasse à Saint-Grimaud, plus y en a moins ça vaut* [It's like St Grimaud's reliquary, the more there are, the less value each has] (Aube, 1904).

Even when proverbs are meant to be comforting, they are really no less pessimistic:

> *Mieux vaut enfants que maladies* [Better to have children than illness] (Catalonia, 1969).

Those found in recent collections are mostly concerned with the wear and tear on mothers:

> *Gros bébé, mauvaise année pour la mère* [A big baby means a bad year for the mother] (Catalonia, 1969).

> *Triste mère! trois enfants, quatre chats!* [Unhappy mother! three children, four cats!] (Catalonia, 1969).

Formerly, the fact that parenthood enslaved the father too was also made clear in such sayings. There was a proverbial joke in the Basque country in the seventeenth century, in which one asked a father: "*Pour qui travailles-tu?*" [Who do you work for?] and he replied: "*C'est pour celui qui dort*" [For the one who is sleeping, in other words, the baby in the cradle]. Aside from the contrast between work and sleep, the essence of the joke was the fact that at the time it was very paradoxical to see a superior — here, the father — working for his inferior. Proverbs also pointed out that "*celui qui a des enfants ne mange pas les meilleurs morceaux lui-même*" [he who has children does not eat the choicest morsels himself] (Basque country, seventeenth century), which was equally paradoxical at that time. As this would no longer be paradoxical today, the modern equivalent is: "*Quand on a des enfants, tous les morceaux ne sont pas vôtres"* [When you have children, not all the pieces are yours] (Provence, 1965).

In addition, children were reputed to dirty the house and their parents' bed:

> *Enfants, poules et les coulombs embrennent et souillent les maisons* [Children, chickens and doves make houses dirty and soil them with their excrement] (Le Roux de Lincy, sixteenth century).

> *Ehans, poules é couloms ensalissent les maisons* [Children, chickens and doves make houses dirty] (Gascony, 1607).

> *Celle qui couche avec les enfans n'a pas toujours la chemise nette quand elle se lève* [She who sleeps with children does not always have a clean nightdress when she arises] (Basque country, seventeenth century).

> *Qui avec ses enfants se couche, merdeux se lève* [He who sleeps with his children arises filthy (literally, covered with faeces)] (Hautes-Alpes, 1845).

> *Celui qui dort avec ses enfants, merdeux se lève* [He who sleeps with his children arises filthy (literally, covered with faeces)] (Armagnac, 1879).

This theme seems to disappear after the 1880s: all attempts to find it in subsequent collections have so far remained unsuccessful. Did they then make the best of what they previously considered dirty? The explanation is rather to be found in the way in which children were toilet-trained after the beginning of the nineteenth century. Before that time, as we know, children ran around without underpants — dressed only in a vest or a child's robe — and relieved themselves freely in the house or outside, like chickens in eighteenth century paintings of the interiors of houses, which are shown pecking away at the hard-packed ground which formed the floor. Until the nineteenth century and before the West became obsessed with cleanliness, children's dirtiness was considered an inevitable annoyance. True, this obsession goes back a long way: as early as the fifteenth century, war was waged on excrement and insects in order to ward off the plague. For example, there is an old (undated) proverb: *"Netteté nourrit santé"* [Cleanliness fosters health]. But I have not found any trace of this in proverbs referring to children which are dated before the end of the nineteenth century: *"Etre propre, c'est la moitié de la santé"* [Being clean is half of being healthy] (Béarn, 1892). There is an adage which refers mockingly to a dirty child: *"Il fait honneur à la propreté de sa mère"* [He is a credit to his mother's cleanliness] (Aube, 1932).

Thus, although children still cause much annoyance and worry today, it is because of their tears and shouts, rather than for the same reasons as in the past. Indeed, I am struck by the lack of references to their noisiness, found in only two proverbs: "*Pour bien se porter, un bébé doit pleurer deux heures par jour*" [To be in good health, a baby must cry for two hours a day] (Aube, 1932); and: "*Quand les enfants se mettent à pleurer, les mères se mettent à chanter*" [When children begin to cry, mothers begin to sing] (Alsace, 1966). Both of these were found in recent collections. That does not however mean that men were impervious to shouts and tears: numerous proverbs complain about women doing so, e.g.: "*Pleurs de femme crocodile semble*" [Women's tears are like crocodile tears] (LRL, sixteenth century); or: "*A toute heure, chien pisse et femme pleure*" [At any time, a dog is peeing and a woman crying] (LRL, sixteenth century). Could it be then that children, including infants, were quieter in the past than nowadays? Indeed it is known that wet nurses used to rush to suckle infants at the first cry, whereas, from the beginning of the nineteenth century, paediatricians have prescribed feeding them at set times. Thus, the image of children in proverbs seems to have substituted crying for dirtiness. This might be as a result of the changes in their routines.

Once the children had grown up, did parents regain their former tranquility? From the seventeenth to the twentieth century, proverbs have also been unanimous in warning against this illusion:

> *Au moment que les enfans sont achevez de nourrir, nos peines et soucis commencent à venir* [Just when we have finished providing for the children, our sorrows and troubles begin] (Basque country, seventeenth century).

> *Petits enfants, petits soucis; grands enfants, grands soucis* [Little children, little cares; big children, big cares] (Champsaur and Gapençais, 1885).

> *Petits enfants, petits maux; grands enfants, grands maux* [Little children, little troubles; big children, big troubles] (Aube, 1932).

> *Quand les enfants sont petits, petits tracas; quand ils sont grands, grands tracas; quand ils sont mariés, tracas doublés* [When children are little, little worries; when they are big, big worries; when they are married, worries are doubled] (Catalonia, 1969).

These proverbs, and a great number of similar ones, are particularly true with respect to the hope parents cherished of getting away from the disagreeable side of parenthood once their children were no longer small. It is this hope — no doubt not alway mistaken — which is the essential idea behind these paradoxical sayings.

Even more numerous are those proverbs which enlarged upon the theme of children's ingratitude. Emotional gratitude was emphasised in a bourgeois collection from 1861 and, in another way, in some subsequent rural proverbs:

> *L'amour des parents descend et ne remonte pas* [Parents' love is given and not returned] (Quitard, 1861).

> *Le coeur d'un père est dans son fils, le coeur d'un fils est dans la pierre* [A father's heart belongs to his son, a son's heart belongs to no one] (Quitard, 1861).

> *Quand le père donne au fils, rient le père et le fils; et quand le fils donne au père, pleurent le fils et le père* [When a father gives to his son, both father and son rejoice; and when a son gives to his father, both father and son weep] (Armagnac, 1879).

> *Quand le père donne au fils, rit le père, rit le fils; mais quand le fils donne au père, pleure le fils, pleure le père* [When a father gives to his son, the father rejoices, the son rejoices; but when a son gives to his father, the son weeps, the father weeps] (Provence, 1965).

Children's material ingratitude is shown in proverbs such as:

> *Un père nourrirait cent enfants, cent enfants ne nourriraient pas un père* [One father might feed a hundred children, a hundred children would not feed one father] (Provence, 1965).

> *Un père entretient beaucoup d'enfants, beaucoup d'enfants n'entretiennent pas un père* [One father provides for a great many children, a great many children do not provide for one father] (Catalonia, 1969).

> *Une mère nourrit plus facilement sept enfants que sept enfants une mère* [One mother provides for seven children more easily than seven children provide for one mother] (Alsace, 1966).

> *Jamais chaton n'apporta rat à sa mère* [Never has a kitten brought its mother a rat] (Provence, 1965).

Yet that which today seems to be almost a law of nature is only mentioned in recent collections. Is this a coincidence or is it because previously children's ingratitude to their old parents seemed less natural? Indeed, because there were no pensions, old people who did not have enough money could only survive on what their children gave them. Those who did have enough money were warned not to hand it over to their heirs too early:

> *Celui qui donna son bien avant que d'estre prest à mourir, passa fort à mal aise le temps de sa vieillesse* [He who gave away his goods before he was ready to die, spent his old age in much discomfort] (Basque country, seventeenth century).

> *Celui qui donne son bien de trop bonne heure connaîtra une mauvaise soirée* [He who gives away his goods too early will know need in the evening of his life] (Basque country, seventeenth century).

> *Faut pas se deshabiller avant de se coucher* [You mustn't get undressed before you go to bed] (Champsaur and Gapençais, 1885).

> *On ne se deshabille que pour se coucher* [One only gets undressed to go to bed] (Aube, 1932).

> *On ne doit pas se deshabiller avant de se mettre au lit* [One must not get undressed before getting into bed] (Alsace, 1966).

The fact remains that, once peasants and artisans could no longer work, they only survived if they had children to support them. That was the main benefit which they gained from parenthood.

WAS IT PROFITABLE FOR POOR HOUSEHOLDS TO HAVE CHILDREN?

I ask this question because it has often been raised with respect to nineteenth century working-class families, whose children worked in factories, and with respect to Third World countries which pay family allowances. More recently, some demographers have wondered whether the high fertility rate of poor families in pre-industrial society could not also be explained by the fact that children were profitable. They have been able to base this theory on an old proverb still in circulation today in various forms:

> *Enfans sont richesse de pauvres gens* [Children are the wealth of poor people] (LRL, sixteenth century).

> *Les enfants sont la richesse du pauvre* [Children are the wealth of the poor] (Champsaur and Gapençais, 1885).

> *Enfants, richesse du pauvre* [Children, wealth of the poor] (Provence, 1965).

Enfants et rire, richesse de pauvre [Children and laughter, the wealth of the poor] (Provence, 1965).

This last proverb is ambiguous and undoubtedly had different meanings in different periods. In the nineteenth and twentieth centuries, it indicates above all the higher fertility rate of the poor. When spoken by a Christian or a populationist at that time, it suggests that a large number of descendants is a gift which God gives to the poor to compensate for their poverty; children being a form of wealth, if only a spiritual form. But statistics prove that before the nineteenth century poor families did not have more children than rich families. In fact quite the opposite was true: the fact that children of wealthy families were given over to a wet nurse — and that contraception did not exist — significantly increased the fertility of wealthy mothers. Thus, children did not represent a form of wealth which rich people would usually have done without. The proverb only meant that in terms of wealth, the poor had only their children.

It is also appropriate to ascertain whether or not children did in fact represent wealth for them. Cotgrave questioned this in his French-English dictionary in 1673: "In other countries, where people are industrious, they may perhaps; but in ours [England], the great numbers of children reduce the majority of poor people to begging." Moreover, if it was profitable to raise children, why would it have been said of a miser: "*Il n'aura jamais enfant qui vive*" [No child of his will ever live] (Oudin, seventeenth century)? Children were a particularly heavy burden for the poor and people were indignant at the examples of injustice such as "*à un pauvre homme sa vache meurt et au riche son enfant*" [a poor man's cow dies and a rich man's child] (LRL, sixteenth century; Lagniet, 1657). In the nineteenth century, peasants from Trièves were still grumbling at the sight of too many lively and useless young people: "*Il mourrait plutôt l'âne d'un pauvre homme qui en aurait besoin*" [A poor man's donkey, which he needs, is more likely to die]. A cow or a donkey was useful to a poor man in his misfortune, not a plethora of children.

One proverb which until now I have only found in a recent collection, "*père pauvre n'a pas d'enfant*" [a poor father has no children] (Catalonia, 1969), expresses the old situation very well: the further down the social ladder one went, the fewer children were found living with their parents. This was not only for the demographic reasons I have mentioned, but because those who survived childhood and reached the age of about ten were placed as servants in rich people's houses.[2] A poor man bore the whole burden of raising his children until they could be put to work, then made a present of them to wealthy families — without charge in our Christian civilisation — because there was no work for them in the family business. He would only see them again subsequently if there was an inheritance of some kind to leave to them. In short, because children were sent out to work much earlier than today, and because, in pre-industrial society, a worker usually lived in his employer's house, the reality of family life was very different from what it is today, especially in regions where the rich had taken over the land and had it cultivated by farmers or tenant farmers. In England, or on the rich plains of the Paris basin, and even on the indifferent soil of the marshlands around Poitiers, or the positively terrible lands of Sologne, one would find both large families which included relatively large numbers of servants and poor families who only kept the youngest of their children.[3]

Under these circumstances, how can we explain the popularity of the proverb *"Enfans sont richesse de pauvres gens"* [Children are the wealth of poor people]? It was only justifiable within the financial and political framework of social classifications in antiquity. In Roman society, non-property-holders were called "proletariat", not because they had more children than the rich — at least not originally — but because, through lack of any other form of wealth, they only contributed to the common good by raising offspring — *proles* — who then swelled the ranks of the republic's armies. It therefore seems probable to me that this proverb, found in a scholarly sixteenth century collection, is of scholarly rather than popular origin and that it reflects the State's point of view — indeed that of the wealthy who were looking for manpower — rather than that of the poor. This saying may have been in circulation for such a long time because, as we must not forget, the French republican State, like the Roman republic, claimed, until the Second World War, that poor families provided its future soldiers.

ATTITUDES TOWARDS PROCREATION AND INFANT MORTALITY

The difficulties of parenthood, the non-profitabilty of children and their "ingratitude" all explain why numerous nineteenth and twentiety century proverbs warn married couples against reproducing:

> *Tant qu'ils ne seront qu'un ou deux, ils ne seront pas bien malheureux, mais*

quand ils seront une demi-douzaine, ils seront prou dans la peine [As long as there are only one or two, they will not be very unhappy, but when there are half a dozen, they will be miserable] (Champsaur and Gapençais, 1885).

Un: pas un morceau pour chacun. Deux: on n'est pas jaloux. Trois: la charge est là. Quatre: de quoi se battre. Cinq: c'est un assassin [One: not enough for everyone. Two: Nothing to be jealous of. Three: Something of a burden. Four: Something to fight about. 5: Enough for a murder] (Provence, 1965).

Je t'attends au troisième berceau [I await you at the third cradle, meaning after the third birth, you will have difficulties] (Provence, 1965).

Quand on se marie le lundi, au bout de l'an on est trois ou un [When you marry on a Monday, by the end of the year, there are either three or one of you] (Provence, 1965).

Mettez deux fous ensemble: au bout de l'année ils seront trois [Put two fools together: by the end of the year there will be three of them] (Provence, 1965).

Se marier ne serait rien si au bout d'un an on ne se retrouvait trois [Marrying would be nothing if by the end of a year there were not three of you] (Catalonia, 1969).

Qui a trop d'enfants ne meurt jamais grasse [She who has too many children will never die fat] (Catalonia, 1969).

Argent et enfants, moins il y en a, moins de tracas [The less money and fewer children there are, the fewer worries there are] (Catalonia, 1969).

In a more general way, young married couples were warned that *"qui donne à naître, qu'il donne à paître"* [let he who gives children, give food for them] (Provence, 1965), that *"oeuvre de nuit se voit de jour"* [work done at night is seen in the day] and that *"ce que fait de coucher t'en repends de jour"* [you will repent during the day for what you have done at night] (Champsaur and Gapençais, 1885).

Other proverbs, which are in favour of procreation, reply to these Malthusian ones:

Qui élève des enfants en a de la joie [He who raises children gets joy from it] (Catalonia, 1969).

Le petit enfant né, les douleurs sont oubliées [Once the baby is born, the pain is forgotten] (Alsace, 1966).

Femme qui n'a pas d'enfant s'ennuie [A woman with no children gets bored] (Gascony, 1916).

A qui Dieu ne donne pas d'enfant, le diable donne des neveux [To those to whom God gives no children, the Devil gives nephews] (Catalonia, 1969; Gascony, 1916).

Un vice, à nourrir, coûte plus qu'une foule d'enfants [It costs more to feed a vice than a pack of children] (Gascony, 1916).

A qui donne naissance Dieu donne nourriture [God gives food to those who have children] (Gascony, 1916).

Dieu donne l'habit selon le froid [God gives clothing appropriate for the temperature] (Gascony, 1916).

A brebis tondue, Dieu mesure le vent [God tempers the wind to the shorn lamb] (Aube, 1932).

Plus on est de fous, plus on rit [The more the merrier] (Gascony, 1916).

The last proverb, when considered together with the others, indicates above all the populationist beliefs of the author of the Gascon collection, which was published right in the middle of the First World War. But the others are all unequivocally in favour of large families. It is interesting to note the diversity of arguments presented and the religious tone of several of them, in a society which was Malthusian and in the process of dechristianization.

Added to these are at least one proverb against abortion: "*Les enfants sans os jettent les mères au tombereau*" [The mothers of aborted babies (literally, "babies without bones") condemn themselves to the tumbril] (Catalonia, 1969), and several against families with only one child:

Enfant seul, enfant évaporé; enfants nombreux, enfants heureux [An only child is a scatterbrained child; many children are happy children] (Gascony, 1916).

Celui qui n'a qu'un enfant n'en a aucun [He who only has one child has none] (Gascony, 1916).

Ceux qui n'ont qu'un enfant n'en ont pas [Those who only have one child have none] (Aube, 1904).

Un seul enfant n'est pas un enfant [An only child is no child] (Alsace, 1966).

Lastly, other adages are in favour of fertility, but only up to a certain point:

> *Deux enfants à nourrir coûtent moins cher qu'un vice* [Two children to feed cost less than a vice] (Provence, 1965).

Earlier in the nineteenth century, proverbs dealing with fertility are neither explicitly for or against, as though it was no longer an issue at that time:

> *Femme jeune et homme vieux font d'enfants une pleine maison* [A young woman and an old man make for a houseful of children] (Hautes-Alpes, 1845; Briançonnais, 1877; Trièves, 1887).

> *Femme jeune et homme vieux, d'enfants une pleine maison* [A young woman and an old man, a houseful of children] (Champsaur and Gapençais, 1885).

Sterility (meaning natural sterility as opposed to one of the partners being sterilised) was the issue in proverbs from before the eighteenth century and was not preached against: "*Il est heureux qui a des enfants, et n'est pas malheureux qui n'en a point*" [He who has children is happy and he who has none is not unhappy] (LRL, fifteenth century). It was pointed out to parents overwhelmed by family worries that "*celuy qui a des enfans a besoin de beaucoup de choses, mais aussi celuy qui n'en a pas a l'esprit en soucis*" [He who has children needs a great many things, but he who has none also has a worried mind] (Basque country, seventeenth century). Married men who were upset not to have any descendants were told: "*Celuy qui n'a point d'enfans est exempt des soins qu'on a pour les enfans*" [He who has no children is exempt from the care and attention necessary for children] (Basque country, seventeenth century); and barren women were told: "*Si la mule ne porte pas de poulain, aussi est-elle exempte des soins qui travaillent les bestes qui en ont*" [The mule which has no foal is therefore exempt from the cares which torment those beasts which do] (Basque country, seventeenth century).

Fertility was unquestionably considered a grace or a virtue — in the old sense of the term — and sterility a misfortune or a vice: "*L'ormeau a le branchage fort beau, mais il ne porte pas de fruit*" [The elm tree has very lovely branches, but it carries no fruit] (Basque country, seventeenth century.) Consequently, women were proud of their fertility: "*Toute accouchée est vaine*" [Every new mother is vain] (Basque country, seventeenth century). But no proverb urged married couples to reproduce and, despite the inconveniences of parenthood, none warned against repeated births.

Malthusian debate does not therefore appear in proverbs until the end of the nineteenth century, at which time birth control was being used all over France, and Church and State are just beginning to get worried about it.[4] Thus, these proverbs, which might have been considered archaic and fossilized, are still alive: they have recorded major changes in attitudes and can give us information about these changes, if not about their exact chronology.

The fact that, prior to the end of the nineteenth century, there are no proverbs which urge couples to reproduce is because, up until the "Malthusian revolution", their fertility was less the result of their virtue than of their inability to control it. This was not a technical inability — since the "Malthusian revolution" was achieved in France, in the eighteenth and nineteenth centuries, without contraceptive pills or other "gadgets" — but a psychological one. Parents did not consider themselves responsible for the number of children they had nor for the deaths of those they could not provide for. They shifted the responsibility to God and moreover, were encouraged to do so by the Church, from the sixteenth century to the Second Vatican Council.[5]

I am not questioning the desire of most couples to have children: the above proverbs show that, for rich people in particular, this desire was stronger in the past than nowadays, in spite of some disagreements over paternity or some, even stronger but more hidden, over maternity.[6] But I do not believe that in general they wanted to have as many children as they conceived in those cases where the wife did not die or become pathologically sterile after several years of marriage. It was not by choice that labourers or poor artisans — see for example the Lyons silk workers in the eighteenth century[7] — brought ten, twelve or eighteen children into the world. Such children put a heavy strain on their meager budgets and they got rid of them as soon as possible. Even if they needed children in order to survive when they reached retirement age, the poor did not have the financial means to make such long term investments by choice, nor did they have the necessary outlook: they lived one day at a time and in the immediate future a cow or donkey had greater value for them than a child.

When it was said of a miser that "*il n'aura jamais enfant qui vive*" [no child of his will ever live], the reference was not to whether or not he wanted the child to be conceived but rather whether or not he wanted it to survive. It was God who caused children to be born; man was expected to assist His designs by feeding the children which were sent to him. Parents' duty towards their children did not result from the responsibility they had taken on by conceiving it: it was imposed on them by God in sending them children. Sexual intercourse was — usually — necessary in order for conception to take place, but was never in itself enough, as daily experience showed. "A husband may make love with his wife a thousand times in a year, yet it is possible...that she may not once in her life become pregnant...because of some will of God which is hidden from us".[8] God was really the one responsible for the conception of a child.

It is not until the end of the nineteenth century that this responsibility is related to the duty to feed the child that has been born. In Armagnac in 1879, God's responsibility was still mentioned: "*Que Dieu qui nous donne à naître nous donne de quoi paître*" [It is God who has given us this child, let Him also give us food for it]. After this time, it is more or less explicitly the parents' responsibility:

Oeuvre de nuit se voit de jour [Work done at night is seen in the day] (Champsaur and Gapençais, 1885).

Qui a fait la gerbe la lie [He who has made the sheaf binds it] (Trièves, 1887).

C'est les enfants d'la balle, ceux qui les font les portent [Let those who conceive children in the hay carry the consequences] (Aube, 1904).

Au diable la hotte, que ceux qui les font les portent [Devil take the basket, let those who make them carry them] (Aube, 1912).

Qui t'a fait te berce [Those who produced you rock you] (Aube, 1912).

Qui fait l'enfant doit le nourrir [Those who produce the child must feed it] (Aube, 1932).

Qui fait l'enfant le nettoie [Those who produce the child clean it] (Provence, 1965).

Qui donne à naître, qu'il donne à paître [Let He who gives children give food for them] (Provence, 1965).

As we have already seen, it is true that, during the same period, many proverbs also guaranteed parents that God would give them food for as many children as he gave them. These proverbs are obviously answers — decreasingly convincing ones in a society moving away from Christianity — to the growing awareness of parental responsibilities. Although several similar remarks were made as far back as the sixteenth century by preachers and confessors grappling with the first signs of the modern understanding of parental responsibilities, no proverb dealt with this subject before the end of the nineteenth century. Moreover it is known that the birth rate in France did not rise again until family allowances had been set up, which changed the situation.

Formerly, parents not only considered themselves to be not reponsible for their fertility, but also not responsible for the deaths of their young children, which they appear to have accepted "philosophically". "I lost two or three of them, albeit at an early age, if not without regret, at least without anger", wrote Montaigne. The strength of his testimony, often cited, is attenuated by the context: "Thus it is chance which decides what strikes a man to his heart. I see enough other common causes of affliction, which would hardly touch me if they happened to me and which I have scorned when they did. Even troubles which the world generally considers atrocious, I would not be able to boast about without blushing".[9] Thus, Montaigne's stoicism, on this occasion, would indicate the moral strength given to him by his reading of ancient writers and perhaps also the hardness of heart of the upper classes, rather than the feelings of the common people. However, the proverbs of the time — would they all have come from antiquity or would they be of aristocratic origin and usage? — suggest that such tranquillity of spirit before the death of young children was normal: "*De petit enfant, petit deuil*" [For a little child, little mourning] (LRL, sixteenth century; Cotgrave, 1673). In general, as recent studies show[10], death was accepted with much more resignation than today and particularly the deaths of one's close relations. Furthermore, infants' deaths were so common that people had to accept them to maintain their mental balance: in northern France, two to three hundred children died in their first year for every two thousand births and only one of every two children reached the age of twenty. Proverbs have recorded this high mortality rate right up to the twentieth century:

> *Qui voit enfant, il voit néant* [He who sees a child, sees nothing] (LRL, fifteenth century; Cotgrave, 1673).

> *Qui enfant n'est pas mort ne sait de quelle mort mourir* [He who hasn't died as a child does not know how he will die] (Champsaur and Gapençais, 1885).

Il va plus au marché de peaux d'agneaux que de vieilles brebis [More lamb skins than old ewes' skins go to market] (LRL, undated).

Il va beaucoup d'agneaux à la boucherie [Many lambs go to the butcher's] (Béarn, 1892).

On tue plus de veaux que de vaches [More calves than cows are killed] (Aube, 1912).

In that Christian society where infanticide was forbidden and God alone had the right to take back the life He had given, the death of young children was not only accepted, but was sometimes hoped for in families which were too poor and had too many children. When, in the sixteenth century, it was said: "*A un pauvre homme sa vache meurt et au riche son enfant*" [a poor man's cow dies and a rich man's child], were they not hoping that the opposite would take place? And the saying from Trièves: "*Il mourrait plutôt l'âne d'un pauvre homme qui en aurait besoin*" [A poor man's donkey, which he needs, is more likely to die], even if it was spoken in jest, still reveals the conflict between poor parents' wishes and the fact that too many of the children Heaven gave them did survive. In fact, they did not hesitate to say in Gascony, by way of consolation, "*Si l'un meurt, il y a plus de pain pour un autre*" [If one dies, there is more bread for another].

Given the demographic and ideological structures which have just been briefly described, it was logical that people were resigned to seeing their children die at an early age and that, more or less consciously, people hoped for the deaths of unwanted children. It was the psychological side of a consistent practice. However, historians have not yet found the key to this practice. Is it to be found in economics, hygiene, medicine or in attitudes towards life and death? Did the old social structures collapse because of the "industrial revolution" or the expansion of medicine and progress made in the field of hygiene? Or was it that from the mid-eighteenth century onwards, French parents increasingly felt themselves to be responsible for the lives and deaths of their children; refusing to let them die, they refused to give them to wet nurses and thus avoided the excessively high fertility rates which resulted from it?[11] In order to be able to see this issue clearly, we would need to be able to look closely at the chronology of these changes, which it is not possible by examining proverbs.

THE STATUS OF THE CHILD

What we can still discover through studying these proverbs is more information about the status of the child in ancient society and in our own. In order to be able to endure the infant mortality rates, people not only attributed the responsibility to God, but also questioned the child's whole humanity. "*Qui voit enfant, il voit néant*" [He who sees a child sees nothing] does not only mean that the new-born's chance of survival was slight, for this idea could have been expressed in many other ways. Around 1912, when a child had just been baptised, the inhabitants of Champagne still used to shout: "*Ah! maintenant, s'il tombe, je le ramasserai!*" [Ah! now if he falls, I will gather him up!] Baptism was however only the first step towards the slow and difficult process of becoming human: in the fifteenth century, it was so problematic that its potential had to be confirmed by the maxim, probably legal in origin: "*Enfants deviennent gens*" [Children become people] (LRL, fifteenth century), which became in the seventeenth century: "*Enfants deviennent grand gens*" [Children become fully-grown people] (Cotgrave, 1673).[12]

The wisdom expressed in proverbs is that of adults: children are never thought to express themselves through proverbs and they are never addressed to children, but always to other adults. In such proverbs, children are only shown as something which adults discuss between themselves, which is indicative of their social status, as much as of the nature of proverbs: children are other people, those who are not well known, who are sometimes feared and whom parents must learn to control.[13] Admittedly this does not exclude the possibility that children used these proverbs, including those relating to childhood. But, by so doing, they were perceiving childhood through adults' eyes. In ancient oral culture, it was no more possible than in ancient written culture for the child to define himself in relation to adults, or to express his point of view about adults,[14] whereas today efforts are made to allow this or to give the impression of allowing it.

In ancient society, it was insulting to call an adult a child, which clearly indicates the inferiority of children's status:[15]

> *Il dit grand villenie à l'homme, qui enfant l'appelle* [It is great villainy to call a man a child] (LRL, fifteenth century).

> *Je ne suis plus un enfant* [I am no longer a child] (LRL, sixteenth century).

Je ne suis plus un enfant, je ne me repaît pas d'une fraise [I am no longer a child, you can't tempt me with a strawberry] (LRL, seventeenth century).

Pleurer comme un enfant [To cry like a child] (Académie, 1694).

Badiner comme un enfant [To joke like a child] (Académie, 1694).

Of something serious it is said: "*Ce n'est pas un jeu d'enfant*" [It is not child's play] (Académie, 1694).

Faire l'enfant [Make like a child, i.e. joke, behave like children] (Oudin, seventeenth century).

Il ne faut pas faire l'enfant [Don't act like a child] (LRL, undated).

Many proverbs in circulation in the nineteenth and twentieth centuries show traces of the feelings of inferiority and disgrace inherent in being a child. In Béarn, around 1892, it was said of brash young people, "*qu'ha encoere lou creix au cul*" [he still has egg shell on his backside]. The equivalent in standard French was: "*Qui lui tordrait le nez, il en sortirait du lait*" [If you twisted his nose, milk would come out of it], or, as was said in Aube around 1912: "*On lui tordrait le nez qu'il en sortirait du lait*" [If you twisted his nose, milk would come out of it]. In the area around Troyes, to make fun of a child who wanted to act like a man, people said to him: "*Va dire à ta mère qu'elle te mouche*" [Go tell your mother to blow your nose]; and, to someone playing pranks: "*Les enfants s'amusent, les nourrices ont bon temps*" [While the children play, the nurses enjoy themselves].

Though these proverbs, collected in the twentieth century, are traces from the past, we do know that childishness and infantile behaviour are still insulting ideas, despite the greater importance of youth today. Our society's much-vaunted egalitarianism, in contrast to ancient society, which preferred to be hierarchical, has not rid our vocabulary of the insult in words such as "child", "childish", "infantile", "infantilism", "puerile" and "puerility". Quite the contrary: the idea of being an adult has never been so strong. The marked — if not total — disappearance of social distinctions has made the distinction between child and adult even more obvious and fundamental.

However, this more marked distinction is accompanied by a certain increase in importance. Being weaker, more fragile and less "reasonable" than adults, children, like women and old people, have the right to special consideration and this is an important feature of what we call civilisation. Those who slaughter their enemy's women and children or take shelter behind their own are called "barbarians". Admittedly children do not have the right to seats in the Paris Métro as do women, old people and invalids; but in the stampede of moments of panic, disciplined groups apply the maxim: "Women and children first", which excludes old people. The history behind these privileges for the weaker members of society — who, individually, may be stronger than some unprivileged adult males — has yet to be written. However a child's life has obviously long been considered of little worth — in a similar way to that in which we consider the life of an embryo of little worth; proverbs confirm this as much as secular and religious literature.[16]

What value then does a child have in our eyes? Innocence is the value most often mentioned in our culture. But how long has this been so?

The expression: *"Innocent comme l'enfant qui vient de naître"* [Innocent as a new-born babe], which is one of the sayings from Aube in 1912, is found among the ancient proverbs published by Le Roux de Lincy, who found it in the 1835 edition of the *Dictionnaire de l'Académie*. Yet it was mentioned as early as the first edition, in 1694: "There is a proverb used, when one wants to assert that one is not guilty of something of which one has been accused *'on est aussi innocent que l'enfant qui vient de naître'"* [one is as innocent as a new-born babe] Obviously this expression goes back a long way.

But is this really childlike innocence in the sense in which we understand it? Purity of heart, incapacity to commit evil deeds and naïvety are assumed as much in two and three year-olds, indeed in older children, as in the new-born which makes us cherish childhood. This is the opposite of what was formerly called "malice", i.e. the desire and the will to do evil. It seems to me that by referring to the innocence of the new-born child, the traditional expression means something else: the fact that it is physically impossible for a new-born to have sinned. But, as for the rest, all Christians at that time accepted that children, like adults and perhaps even more so, tended towards evil because of the existence of original sin. It was the eighteenth century philosophers, Rousseau in particular, who created the myth of childlike innocence in order to combat the traditional idea. In this day and age we seem both to believe and to disbelieve this myth.

For some time, however, children had been considered less guilty than adults in committing the same offence, or indeed completely innocent in the eyes of the Church if they had not yet reached the age of reason. This attenuated responsibility on the part of the child is noticeable from the early Middle Ages. There is a Basque proverb translated into French in the seventeenth century which apparently refers to this: *"La cicatrice receuë en l'enfance s'efface pour le temps de la jeunesse"* [The scar received in childhood disappears as one gets older], in other words, offences committed in childhood are not considered in adulthood. But the fact of not being held culpable increased the standing of children no more than it did that of animals, since in both cases the belief was based on the absence of reason.

From the sixteenth century to today, several proverbs have alluded to this lack of reason in children. Here are two which suggest it by association of ideas:

> *Enfans et sots sont devins* [Children and idiots are prophets] (LRL, sixteenth century).

> *Les enfants et les fous disent la vérité* [Children and fools tell the truth] (Alsace, 1966).

Children's sincerity, alluded to in the second adage, is an essential component of their naïvety and innocence. But does the proverb aim to glorify it or to teach adults prudence? It could be either. The other proverb, typical of an earlier mentality, is not concerned with childish innocence and it does not moralise. Yet it unquestionably introduces a "virtue" of childhood — reading the future — a virtue apparently reserved for those incapable of correctly reading the present.

Philippe Ariès has claimed[17] that formerly childhood was less distinct than today, was less important and that it was seen as an unfortunate period that man had to go through in order to reach adulthood. He has claimed also that, as a result, less effort was made then than today to keep children as children for longer. These ideas hardly seem to be confirmed by comparing ancient and recent proverbs.

Those collected in the twentieth century emphasise even more explicitly than earlier proverbs did children's lack of reason, wisdom and virtue. For example, by way of excusing youthful indiscretions, it was said in Aube around 1932: *"On ne peut être jeune et sage"* [One cannot be both young and wise], or: *"Il faut bien que jeunesse se passe"* [Youth must have its fling], or: *"C'est jeune et ça ne sait pas."* [When you're young, you just don't know]. In a recent Alsatian collection there is a more excessively pessimistic proverb, showing neither humour nor a feeling of complicity: *"Jeunesse n'a pas de vertus"* [Youth has no virtues]. Already around 1892 hostility towards young people was marked in the proverb from Béarn: "*Qui a filles et garçons ne parle de coquines ni de larrons*" [He who has sons and daughters does not speak of strumpets or thieves], the equivalent of the ancient French proverb: "*Cil qui d'autruy parler voudra, regarde soi, il se taira*" [If people who like to talk about others would look at themselves, they would keep quiet]. The idea that the full human status of being an adult can only be attained in stages is clearly expressed in two nineteenth century proverbs from the Alps:

> *A quinze ans on est grand; à vingt ans on a sens; à trente ou quarante on a du bien; sinon jamais on n'a rien* [At fifteen you are big; at twenty you are sensible; at thirty or forty you are wealthy; if not, you will never have anything] (Champsaur and Gapençais, 1885).

> *Qui à vingt ans ne sait, à trente n'a, à quarante n'a ni ne sait* [If at twenty you know nothing and at thirty have nothing, at forty, you'll neither know nor have anything] (Hautes-Alpes, 1845).

Even before the nineteenth century, popular wisdom warned those who missed out stages: "*Cet enfant ne vivra pas, il a trop d'esprit*" [That child won't live, he has too much spirit]. This dictum, quoted by Le Roux de Lincy with no indication as to its origin, had already been mentioned by Rétif de La Bretonne whose parents are said to have used it with respect to him before the mid-eighteenth century.

I have pointed out the contradictions between these proverbs and Philippe Ariès' theses because I expected them rather to confirm them. But his theses are backed up by too much documentation not to be able to resist such a weak attack. It also happens that proverbs show the reaction of adult males against moral and ideological changes imposed on them from above and with which they are not happy. For example, anti-feminist proverbs are markedly more numerous among those collected by Quitard around 1861 than among the ancient proverbs published by Le Roux de Lincy. Undoubtedly this is because men were losing the right to beat their wives. At the end of the Middle Ages, their right to do so had been recognised in all regions of France and all social milieux.[18] In the same way, proverbs after the seventeenth century give a more pessimistic view of children than before, perhaps as a reaction by traditionalist adults against the increased importance of childhood and against the increased duties society expected them to carry out for their children.

In addition, it is difficult to know exactly what meaning those who use them give to sayings; and sometimes it is a subtle shift in meaning which best shows our change of attitudes. When someone says nowadays: "*Il n'y a plus d'enfants*" [They are never children nowadays], it seems to me — but each must judge for himself — that it is said with a sort of indignation tinged with humour or complacency, because a child says or does things which he "ought not" to say or do, in the sense that his actions belie our idea of "childlike innocence". In the seventeenth century, according to the first edition of the *Dictionnaire of the Académie*, "When one sees a child who has reason and spirit at an early age, one says 'They are never children nowadays'. Was it said ironically? The *Académie* does not tell us. But if so, the adage used to be a way of showing admiration whereas today — if I am correct — it expresses indignation. Thus, the same saying which indirectly shows our desire to keep children innocent — and submissive to adults? — was formerly used to show regret that the child ordinarily was only a human being without reason.

CHILDREN'S UPBRINGING

For a long time, children have also been defined as beings needing to be brought up correctly:

> *Ce que Hansel n'apprend pas, Hans ne l'apprendra plus* [What John doesn't teach, little Johnny will never learn] (Alsace, 1966).

> *Enseigner convient aux enfans ce qu'est de faire quand seront grands* [The purpose of teaching children is to show them how to behave when they're grown up] (LRL, sixteenth century).

Undoubtedly the following ambiguous but perhaps still significant dictum must be cited in this connection: "*L'enfant de cent ans qui a perdu son temps*" [The hundred-year-old child who has wasted his time]. It is surprisingly modern both in the value it attaches to time and in the value it attaches to adulthood.

Yet is childhood the only age at which one can be taught? Today everyone knows the proverb: "*On apprend à tout âge*" [You're never too old to learn], which refutes this idea. If it is indeed a recent proverb, as I believe — so far I have only found it in the collection of adages from Aube published in 1932 — we cannot draw the conclusion that a transformation in favour of permanent education took place, noticeable in the attitudes which prevailed between the two wars. On the contrary, I consider it to be one of those paradoxical proverbs which

indicate support for the opposite idea to the one which they state. The
fact that this saying was not in current use in the Middle Ages is no
doubt because the presence of adults in schools was less shocking then
than in 1932.

Moreover, we must try to discover whether men were formerly as
conscious as we are of the importance of education and upbringing.
We know the value they placed on birth, which is shown by many
proverbs, including this one, relating to bastards: "*S'ils font le bien c'est
d'aventure. S'ils font le mal c'est de nature*" [If they do good, it is by
chance. If they do evil, it is their nature] (G. Bouchet, sixteenth
century). That does not mean to say that they underestimated the
importance of physical and spiritual "nourishment", particularly in
the case of infants. Indeed, nursing was seen as the continuation of
gestation, the mother's milk was considered to be blood, comparable
to that which the embryo fed on in the womb, though bleached white
by the breasts' "special ability to turn it into milk". Was this what was
meant in the expression: "*Bon sang ne saurait mentir*" [Good blood
would never lie]? We cannot be sure, as there appears to be much
inconsistency in ideas in this area at that time. Be that as it may, the
infant was thought to absorb its wet nurse's "humours" and character
traits, together with her milk. "Is it not said", wrote Guillaume
Bouchet, "of a cruel man that: '*Il a esté alaicté d'une lionne*' [He was
nursed by a lioness]?" Once it had been weaned, a child was not
supposed to be fed exactly like an adult: wine in particular was
forbidden, as shown in the proverb: "*Soleil qui luisarne au matin, femme
qui parle latin et enfant nourri de vin ne viennent point à bonne fin*"
[Sunshine in the morning, a woman who speaks Latin and a child who
drinks wine do not come to a good end] (Cotgrave, 1673). As for
spiritual "nourishment" — which we call upbringing — it seemed
equally as critical for a child's future:

> *Fille telle comme elle est eslevée, et estoupe comme elle est filé* [A girl is as she
> is raised and tow is as it is spun] (LRL, sixteenth century).

> *Nourriture passe nature* [Upbringing transcends heredity] (Champsaur
> and Gapençais, 1885).

> *Qui est avec les chiens apprend à aboyer* [He who runs with the dogs learns
> to bark] (Béarn, 1892), equivalent of the French proverb: *On apprend à
> hurler avec les loups* [It is with the wolves that one learns to howl].

Thus popular wisdom has always required that parents watch over their children's education and upbringing:

> *Qui élève des enfants en a de la joie* [He who raises children gets joy from it] (Catalonia, 1969).

> *Soigner les enfants, métier de sage* [Taking care of children is the occupation of a wise man] (Provence, 1965).

> *En le soignant quand il est tout petit, le chêne devient grand* [By taking care of it when it is very small, the oak tree becomes tall] (Béarn, 1892).

> *Faut nourrir les enfans cette année et différer à carder les laines jusques à l'autre* [The children must be fed this year and the carding of the wool put off until another], i.e. the children's upbringing must take precedence over everything, explains this Basque proverb's translator in the seventeenth century.

> *Enseigner convient aux enfans ce qu'est de faire quand seront grands* [The purpose of teaching children is to show them how to behave when they're grown] (LRL, sixteenth century).

> *Bien labeure qui chastoie son enfant* [Good work it is to chastise one's child] (LRL, thirteenth century).

Le Roux de Lincy translates the above proverb as meaning "*bien travaille qui élève son enfant*" [He works well who brings up his child] and explains that, in old French, "*chastier*" [to chastise] did not mean "to punish, to correct", but "to bring up, to instruct, to indoctrinate". As proof, he cites the thirteenth century poem entitled "*le Castoiement d'un Père à son fils*" [A Father's Chastisement of His Son] and which is nothing more than a series of precepts with examples to support them. Le Roux de Lincy adds that the saying "*Qui aime bien chastie bien*" [He who loves well, chastises well] is used in the same way. Myself, I certainly accept the ancient correspondence between "*chastier*" and "*éduquer*" [to bring up], but stress also the etymology of the word, from the Latin *castigare*, i.e. to make chaste. Moreover, almost all proverbs referring to children's upbringing are explicit about very strict training:

> *Qui bien ayme, bien chastie* [He who loves well, chastises well] (Lagniet, 1657).

> *Chastie ton enfant pendant son bas-âge afin qu'il ne vienne à se perdre et devenir misérable* [Chastise your child during his early years so that he does not

lose his way and become miserable] (Basque country, seventeenth century).

L'arbre est devenu tortu pour n'avoir pas été redressé lorsque ce n'estoit qu'un sion [The tree has become twisted because it was not straightened when only a sapling] (Basque country, seventeenth century).

Qui bien ama, bien corrigea [He who loved well, punished well] (Champsaur and Gapençais, 1885).

Plus on aime l'enfant, plus on le châtie [The more one loves a child, the more one chastises it] (Alsace, 1966).

L'enfant bien dressé, l'homme bien éduqué [A well-trained child is a well-brought-up man] (Alsace, 1966).

Enfant échaudé craint le feu [Once bitten, twice shy, literally a burned child fears fire] (Alsace, 1966).

Il faut ployer l'arbre pendant qu'il est jeune [A tree must be bent while it is young] (Alsace, 1966).

Given the longevity of such expressions, has nothing changed in this field? The verb "*châtier*", even if it has always had the meaning of "to punish", "to correct", "to repress", is no longer confused with "*éduquer*", which has increased in usage. This has happened to such an extent that the traditional proverb: "*Qui aime bien châtie bien*", which has always been paradoxical, is even more paradoxical today than it was. Moreover, a double translation — from French to Alsatian and from Alsatian to French — results in it bordering on nonsense, the final Alsatian version being: "*Plus on aime l'enfant, plus on le châtie*" [The more one loves a child, the more one chastises it]. To carry the paradox to this point is to stick to the letter of the saying and not to understand its spirit. Indeed, it could only be accepted in a society convinced that a child, by being born, carried a tendency for evil, which had to be repressed for its good in this world and in the next. There is also the image of straightening the sapling so that the tree may be upright. It is striking to note that in the twentieth century, using the same elements, a completely different image has been given: "*Il faut ployer l'arbre pendant qu'il est jeune*" [A tree must be bent while it is young]. It appears to no longer be for the child's good that it is corrected, but in order to break his will, making him submissive to his parents and capable of making his way in society when grown up. In short, the ancient proverbs which developed the theme of strict training were no more paradoxical than the Christianity of the time, accepted in theory by society as a whole. In the twentieth century, on the other hand, no longer based on Christianity and radically opposed to the new tendencies of "enlightened" pedagogy, proverbs spring out of a traditionalism which expresses parents' will for power, as their authority is disintegrating. Moreover, I no longer find proverbs, in recent collections, which warn against the consequences of indulgence, whereas in the past they were numerous:

> *Enfant trop caressé, mal appris et pis réglé* [A child who is cuddled too much is badly taught and even harder to control] (LRL, undated). .

> *Un enfant eslevé tendrement vient souvent à mourir misérablement* [A child raised tenderly often dies miserably] (Basque country, seventeenth century).

> *Un enfant nourri trop délicatement est fayneant quand il est devenu grand* [A child fed too delicately is idle when he grows up] (Basque country, seventeenth century).

> *L'arbre est devenu tortu pour n'avoir pas esté redressé lorsque ce n'estoit qu'un sion* [The tree has become twisted because it was not straightened when only a sapling] (Basque country, seventeenth century).

> *L'enfant gasté: c'est celui que la mère caresse le plus* [A spoiled child is one whose mother cuddles him most] (Oudin, seventeenth century).

The mother was considered the most indulgent member of the family. Basque proverbs constantly contrasted her softness with a stepmother's harshness, as in: "*celuy qui n'a pas voulu obéir à sa mère obéira [par force] à sa marastre*" [he who did not want to obey his mother will obey his stepmother [by force]]. But this softness was often excessive, like that of the monkey mother who suffocates its young by holding it too tightly, which was regularly quoted by seventeenth century ecclesiastic writers: "*Une mère qui a trop de tendresse pour ses enfans les fait teigneux*" [A mother who has too much affection for her children makes them loathsome], it was commonly said in the Basque country. Thus mothers' methods for raising children were systematically distrusted, particularly for young boys, whose mothers were not allowed to keep them near them after their very youngest years. At the age of seven at the latest, boys were handed over to a man — their father or a schoolmaster — only a man being considered capable of the necessary strictness: "*Aux hommes on baille des femmes, et aux enfants des verges fermes*" [Men are given women, and children firm rods]

(LRL, sixteenth century). This proverb also suggests that all sexual
activity was forbidden until adulthood, if not until marriage.[19]

As for girls, whose mothers were to oversee their upbringing until
the age at which they left home to get married or to work elsewhere
as a servant, their nature was thought to suffer as a result:

> *Femme trop piteuse rend sa fille teigneuse* [A woman who is too indulgent
> makes her daughter loathsome] (LRL, sixteenth century).

> *De mère piteuse, fille teigneuse* [An indulgent mother makes for a loathsome
> daughter] (LRL, undated).

> *Mère vertueuse fait sa fille paresseuse* [A virtuous mother makes her daugh-
> ter lazy] (Champsaur and Gapençais, 1885).

The last proverb, which perhaps stems from the other two, seems
to have missed the lesson: it becomes paradoxical and is similar to
those which set children against their parents, such as "*A père avare,
fils prodigue*" [A spendthrift son for a miserly father]. This shift from
one to the other might be indicative of the weakening of the ideal of
severity in upbringing.

Indeed, did this ideal exist in all classes of society from the beginning of French culture? There are several reasons to think not. Firstly,
there is the expression, in common usage in the seventeenth century:
"*Je vous traitteray en enfant de bonne maison*" [I will treat you like a child
from a good home], i.e. "strictly, with harshness" as Oudin explains.
If by "good homes" are meant rich, old and powerful families, as we
can assume, this saying suggests that they were the first to give their
children a strict upbringing; and the disappearance of the saying after
the seventeenth century might indicate that this ideal spread into the
other classes of society or indeed that the social elite were the first to
abandon it.

It should also be noted that, among the old proverbs published by
Le Roux de Lincy, almost all of those which preached affection
towards children were dated before the sixteenth century:

> *Enfant haï ne loera jà bel* [A hated child is never considered handsome]
> (undated).

> *Et j'ay bien oy dire, XIII ans a accomplis que d'un enfant haï n'a beau jeu ne
> beau ris* [And I have heard it said, a child who has been hated for thirteen
> years neither plays nor laughs happily] (LRL, fourteenth century).

> *Enfant haï est toujours triste* [A hated child is always sad] (undated).

Enfant aime moult qui beau l'appelle [A child dearly loves he who calls him handsome] (fifteenth century).

Could not the orders for severity have become popular at the time of the Protestant and Catholic Reformations, and for the reasons I have mentioned? The proverbs give us only weak indications of this, but it is not implausible and it coincides with the theses developed by Philippe Ariès from a greater selection of documents.

BOOKS AND COLLECTIONS OF ADAGES QUOTED

Proverbs Collected Before the Nineteenth Century

Le Roux de Lincy, *Le Livre des proverbes français*, 2nd edition, Paris, 1859; in particular vol. I, pp. 215–18. For many of these proverbs, the author indicates the collection or literary work from which they are taken, which allows them to be dated. For others, on the other hand, he gives neither date nor reference, without explaining why. Some of these undated proverbs are nonetheless very old.

Bouchet (Guillaume), *Les Serées*, 1st edition in the sixteenth century; 2nd edition, Paris, 1873, 6 vol.

Voltoire, *Anciens Proverbes basques et gascons*, collected by Voltoire and brought up to date by G. Brunet, Bayonne, 1873, 29 pp. These proverbs are taken from 616 Gascon "*moutets*" published by Voltoire in his *Marchand traictant des propriétez et particularitez du commerce*, Toulouse, 1607. A critique of this book can be found in *Revue des langues romanes*, vol. VI, July/December 1874, pp. 296–309 (in Gascon, no translation).

Oudin, *Curiositez françaises...avec une infinité de proverbes*, Paris, 1640.

Oihenart (Arnauld), *Proverbes basques*, collected and translated (in the seventeenth century) by Arnauld Oihenart; 2nd edition by G. Brunet, Bordeaux, 1847 (bilingual French/Basque).

Lagniet (Jacques), *Recueil des plus illustres proverbes*, Paris, 1657 (illustrated French proverbs).

Cotgrave, *A Dictionarie of the French and English Tongues*, 1st edition, 1611; 2nd edition 1673. See article *ENFANT*.

Dictionnaire de l'Académie française, 1st edition, Paris, 1694; 2nd edition, Amsterdam 1695; 3rd edition, Paris, 1740; 4th edition, Paris, 1762; 5th edition, Paris, 1799; 6th edition, Paris, approximately 1835.

Proverbs Collected in the Nineteenth and Twentieth Centuries

B. Chaix, *Préoccupations statistiques...du département des Hautes-Alpes*, Grenoble, 1845, pp. 340–7 (proverbs in patois without translation).

J.A. Chabrand and A. de Rochas d'Aiglun, *Patois des Alpes cottiennes (Briançonnais et vallées vaudoises)*, Grenoble, 1877, 228 pp. (bilingual French/patois).

F. Allemand, "Proverbes alpins spécialement recueillis dans le Champsaur et le Gapençais", *Bulletin de la Société d'études des Hautes-Alpes*, vol. III, 1884, pp. 369–80; vol. IV, 1885, pp. 219–24 (patois).

G. Guichard, "Uno pugno de prouverbes douphineus e de coumparaisous des Trieves", *Bulletin de l'Académie delphinale*, vol. II, 1887–1888, pp. 355–97 (patois).

Blade (Jean-François), *Proverbes et Devinettes populaires recueillis dans l'Armagnac et l'Agenais*, Paris, Champion, 1879, 236 pp. (bilingual French/patois).

V. Lespy, *Dictons et Proverbes du Béarn. Paroémologie comparée*, expanded 2nd edition, Pau, 1892, XVI-285 pp. (bilingual French/patois).

C. Dauge, *Le Mariage et la Famille en Gascogne d'après les proverbes et les chansons*, Paris and Bordeaux, 1916, 294 pp. (bilingual French/Gascon).

Morin (Louis), *Proverbes et Dictons recueillis dans le département de l'Aube*, Troyes, 3 vol., 1904, 1912, 1932 (French).

Mauron (Marie), *Dictons d'oc et Proverbes de Provence*, Forcalquier, 1965, 493 pp. (bilingual French/Provençal).

Illberg, *Proverbes, Dictons et Poèsies d'Alsace*, Forcalquier, 1966, 367 pp. (bilingual French/Alsatian).

Guiter (Henri), *Proverbes et Dictons catalans*, Forcalquier, 1969, 637 pp. (bilingual French/Catalan).

Chapter 12

The Young Woman in Ancient French Proverbs

There have probably been happy and unhappy young women in most societies — or moments of joy and moments of unhappiness for most individuals. But historians, like other social scientists, are not yet able to talk seriously of happiness and unhappiness, which are too subjective and too ephemeral. It is also difficult to ascertain how many determined and clever young women managed to shape their lives as they had decided and how many, on the other hand, allowed themselves to be guided entirely by the will of others. Leaving aside these unanswerable questions, and others which have been studied too much recently,[1] I will devote this short chapter to ancient society's attitude towards young women, i.e. to its image of the ideal, well-brought-up young woman. To what extent has this image changed? Each reader must decide for himself or herself.

I will not be looking for this image in educational treatises — for they were read by only a very small minority of the population — but rather in that precept of popular wisdom, the proverb.[2]

My first comment is that proverbs about young women were less plentiful than those about women in general: only thirty-three of the former in Le Roux de Lincy's (LRL) collection of ancient French proverbs, compared to one hundred and fifty-seven of the latter. The term "woman" and not "young women" is used to represent the female half of humanity, in the same way as the term "man" alone is used to represent the human race. Furthermore, young girls were considered only children, just as adolescent girls were mentioned only in connection with their immaturity. When they were referred to in

231

proverbs as "young women", it was scarcely ever with reference to any subject other than their marriage or their honour.

FORTUNE GOES WHEN A DAUGHTER IS BORN

In the seventeenth century the Basques had a saying "*De deux soeurs la famille est trop chargée*" [A family with two daughters is too heavily burdened]. Gascon peasants were still expressing the same sentiment towards the end of the nineteenth century:

> *Une fille: bonne fille; deux filles: assez de filles; trois filles: trop de filles.* [One daughter: a good daughter; two daughters: enough daughters; three daughters: too many daughters.]

> *N'ayez pas trop de filles ni trop de vignes.* [Have neither too many daughters nor too many vines.]

> *Mieux vaut un bon tenon que cent mortaises.* [Better one good tenon than a hundred mortises, i.e. one son than a hundred daughters.]

This attitude was largely due to the fact that a son represented a greater working capacity than a daughter. Consequently a girl was particularly valuable in terms of the son-in-law that she was able to bring her father. According to one saying common in the seventeenth and eighteenth centuries, families hoped to gain "*d'une fille deux gendres*" [two sons-in-law from each daughter]. Yet a son-in-law could never be as valuable as a son: "*Qui n'a que des filles pour des gendres sera à toute heure en grand esclandre*" [He who has only daughters to give him sons-in-law will at all times be in great confusion]. (LRL)

In the usual situation, in which one had both sons and daughters, one of the sons was designated to remain in the parents' house and to marry there, whereas the daughters were fated to make their lives elsewhere: "*La fille n'est que pour enrichir les maisons étranges*" [A daughter is only for gracing another's house] (LRL). She graced it not only by her presence, her fertility and her work, but also by the dowry she brought when she married. And, of course, she impoverished her father's house accordingly: "*Qui a des filles à marier, luy faut de l'argent à planté*" [He who has daughters to marry off needs money aplenty] (LRL).

Parents were conscious of this right from their children's births, as shown by a Provençal proverb still in circulation well into the twentieth century: "*Le bien vient quand le garçon naît, le bien s'en va quand naît la fille*" [Fortune comes when a boy is born, fortune goes when a girl is born].

This is the second reason for the preference shown for boys in many families. Thus, Pierre Bourdieu[3], who studied peasants from the Béarn from the beginning of the twentieth century, found the following: "The T. family had five younger daughters. The parents gave the eldest son preferential treatment: they gave him the good piece of salt pork and everything else...For the younger sisters, no meat, nothing." On the other hand, the eldest son was expected to marry with the best interests of the family in mind and not just to follow his own inclinations: he had to "bring in" a large dowry which would provide dowries for his sisters. It was this which made the T.'s eldest son unhappy, as it did many other heirs.

In order to discourage young men from marrying for love alone, numerous proverbs existed to warn them against young women's looks:

> *La belle est d'ordinaire fainéante* [A beautiful woman is usually bone idle] (Basque, seventeenth century).

> *Femme fort belle, rude et rebelle* [A very beautiful woman is rough and rebellious] (sixteenth century).

> *Belle femme, mauvaise tête; bonne mule, mauvaise bête* [A beautiful woman, a bad disposition; a good mule, a bad beast] (sixteenth century).

Obviously then, a beautiful woman was more likely to be married off early. Moreover, this is stated explicitly in some proverbs:

> *Belle fille et méchante robe trouvent toujours qui les accroche* [A beautiful young woman and indifferent dress will always find someone to take them in] (eighteenth century).

> *Un bon visage est toujours une bonne dot* [An attractive face is always an attractive dowry] (Catalonia, twentieth century).

It would not have been necessary to say, in the fifteenth century: "*Autant se prise beau varlet que belle fille*" [A handsome bachelor is as valuable as a beautiful young woman], if, on the contrary, beauty had not generally been more highly valued in young women than men. Young women played on their beauty just as much as on their dowries in order to get married.

In order to succeed in making a good marriage, a young woman who was beautiful and rich needed one more attribute: a good reputation. *"Bonne renommée vaut mieux que ceinture dorée"* [A good name is worth more than a golden sash], has been said since the Middle Ages in all parts of France. It was difficult for a father to conserve his wealth, show off his daughter's beauty by allowing young men to court her and preserve her reputation at one and the same time.

Need or greed could force him to postpone his daughters' marriages; but waiting too long risked tarnishing their reputations. This would make marrying them off more difficult or more expensive and also besmirch the family's honour. Proverbs have stressed this for centuries:

Il ne faut point faire grenier de filles [Don't keep your daughters in the attic] (LRL).

Filles sottes à marier sont bien pénibles à garder [Daughters who are difficult to marry off are difficult to take care of] (LRL).

Filles et verriers sont toujours en danger [Daughters and glassware are always in danger] (sixteenth century).

Les filles et les pommes sont une même chose [Daughters are like apples] (if left too long they spoil) (LRL).

Pomme un peu mûre doit être cueillie; fille grandette doit être mariée [An almost ripe apple must be picked; an almost grown woman must be married] (Béarn, 1892).

Quand la fille est mûre pour être mariée, la garde n'en est pas assurée [When a daughter is ripe for marriage, she is difficult to keep] (Basque, seventeenth century).

Filles et vignes sont difficiles à garder; il y a toujours quelqu'un qui passe et qui voudrait en tâter [Daughters and vines are difficult to keep; there is always a passer-by who would like to sample them] (Provence, 1913).

Jeune fille de seize ans, enlève-la à la critique [A young woman of sixteen should be kept away from possible criticism] (Gascony, 1916).

Fille mariée, fille sauvée [A daughter married is a daughter saved] (Gascony, 1916).

In order to protect their virtue, it was necessary to watch over daughters constantly: *"Qui a des filles est toujours berger"* [He who has daughters is always a shepherd] (LRL). In order to make life easier, there was a tendency to shut them away, in a convent if they came of a good family, or at home:

> *Fille qui trotte et géline qui vole, de légier sont adirées* [A daughter who roams and a hen which flies, both are easily taken] (fifteenth century).

> *Fille trop vue ni robe trop vêtue rarement chère tenue* [A young woman who is too often seen and a dress which is too elaborate are rarely highly prized] (sixteenth century).

Even then it was important that daughters did not take the first opportunity to escape: mothers were responsible for the upbringing which accompanied their confinement or surveillance.

> *Fille telle comme elle est élevée, et étoupe comme elle est filée* [A daughter is as she is raised, and tow is as it is spun] (sixteenth century).

> *Au train de la mère, la fille* [A daughter will follow her mother's example] (sixteenth century).

This upbringing had to be strict:

> *De mère piteuse, filles teigneuses* [An indulgent mother produces loathsome daughters] (LRL).

> *Femme trop piteuse rend sa fille teigneuse* [A woman who is too indulgent makes her daughter loathsome] (sixteenth century).

> *Fille sans crainte ne vaut rien* [A fearless daughter is worthless] (sixteenth century).

The daughter had also to learn the modesty becoming of her sex: "*Fille aymant silence a grand science*" [The daughter who likes being silent has a great skill] (LRL). In addition, she had to be given work to do, which had the triple advantage of making her presence at home profitable, teaching her her future station as housewife and not allowing her leisure time in which to get into trouble:

> *Fille oisive, à mal pensive; fille trop en rue, tôt perdue* [An idle daughter thinks of evil; a daughter too often in the street is soon lost] (sixteenth century).

> *Fille qui au matin se lève son affaire mieux achève* [A daughter who gets up in the morning meets with a better end] (fifteenth century).

> *Fille qui trop se mire peu file* [A daughter who looks at herself in the mirror too much spins little] (sixteenth century).

Fille fenestrière ou trottière rarement bonne ménagère [A daughter who spends all her time sitting at the window or roaming is rarely a good housewife] (sixteenth century).

The constant association of application and skill with modesty and, on the other hand, coquetry with immodesty and laziness is striking. There must certainly have been, as there are today, vigorous and active young women who were tireless workers and good housewives but also intrepid and headstrong, flirtatious and quick to satisfy their desires: psychological probability suggests it and through historical records or literature we catch glimpses of this type of young woman in all milieux, from Brantôme's "*dames galantes*" to the female servants in Molière's comedies. But they are not found in proverbs. Today, we are still fascinated by the conflict between Martha the housewife, and Mary Magdalene the flirtatious and idle courtesan, loved by men...and by Christ himself.

IV. THE SEX LIVES OF SINGLE PEOPLE

"Late Marriages and Sex Lives", published in Annales ESC (November/December 1972), is my reply to an article by André Burguière which appeared in the previous issue of the same journal. It was my first publication on the subject and was followed by the book les Amours paysannes ("Archives" collection, 1975), in which I enlarged upon my criticism of a purely statistical approach to the sex lives of single people.

"Repression and Change in the Sex Lives of Young People" was first presented in the form of lectures at several American universities in 1977, and then published in English in the Journal of Family History (vol. 2, no. 3, Autumn 1977). An abridged French version was presented at various conferences and published in the journal Communication. The longer version given here was previously unpublished.

This chapter would not be complete without considering the very impressive statistical research on illegitimacy undertaken in England by the Cambridge Group for the History of Population and Social Structure. I therefore present a critique, entitled "Family Life and Illicit Love in England", which appeared in History and Theory, of a collection of articles by Peter Laslett, director of the Cambridge Group: Family Life and Illicit Love in Earlier Generations (Cambridge University Press, 1977).

Chapter 13

Late Marriages and Sex Lives

Discussions and Hypotheses for Research

Not everyone seems to have been convinced by the article I wrote in 1969, entitled "Contraception, Marriage and Sexual Relations in the Christian West",[1] to judge by the references made to it by André Burguière and Jacques Depauw in the previous issue of *Annales*.[2] But to which parts of the article are they referring? To the underlying assertions, which appear to me to be firmly established, or to the suggestions and ideas for further research which I proposed by way of conclusion?

I believe that I have satisfactorily demonstrated three points. Firstly, that two archetypal patterns of sexual behaviour existed in the prevailing ideology in western Europe: on the one hand marital behaviour, the purpose of which was procreation, and which, with some reservations,[3] was accepted by the Church; on the other hand, a pattern of behaviour characterised by passion and the pursuit of pleasure. This second pattern of behaviour, which a large part of profane literature took as its theme and glorified, was wrong in the eyes of the Church, even and especially when it was present within marriage. Logically, all sterile intercourse was part of the latter pattern of behaviour, according to all or almost all of the writers who referred to it from the sixth to the eighteenth century.

Secondly, I believe I have demonstrated that the combining of these two patterns of behaviour scandalized not only ecclesiastic writers but also those secular writers who seemed to be the least devout, although, from the eighteenth to the twentieth century, this combination became accepted first among laymen, then among clerics. I did nothing but suggest the sequence of this transformation.

Finally, I maintained that the theological concept of a "sin against nature" gives a very bad description of the actual moral status of the different sexual practices which it encompasses. Whereas at the level of doctrine the "sins against nature" are considered to be the worst of the sexual sins, in reality, practices such as masturbation or *coitus interruptus* are much better tolerated than incest or adultery, or even, for that matter, fornication. This premise is open to discussion, but I am ready to support it with new evidence, as and when required to do so.

By means of these three premises, I wanted to show that historians had been in too much of a hurry to believe in the chastity of single people in the West in the seventeenth and eighteenth centuries. For such an opinion was based, explicitly or not, on the idea that any extramarital activity at that time had to be fertile; on the idea that all sterile practices were condemned as strictly by society as they were in theological discourse; that they were as infrequent outside of marriage as within marriage. This did not take into account the reasoning behind the two patterns of behaviour.

But to criticise one thesis is not to support the opposite. It would be ridiculous of me to claim that, because they accepted the idea of the two patterns of behaviour to the point of being scandalized when they were confused, the clerics and nobles of the sixteenth century never produced bastards. For well we know that both produced them, and that they were sometimes even happy to do so. However, we know too that certain members of the nobility — particularly certain ladies — practised *coitus interruptus* outside of marriage even though it would have seemed peculiar to them to have practised it within marriage; and that certain clerics provided their mistresses with abortive or sterilising drugs. So far, for these particular milieux, we have not succeeded in seriously assessing the proportion of sterile extramarital practices in relation to fertile ones.

As for the popular milieux, in which I did not even know if the idea of two patterns of behaviour held true, I was very careful to assert that they practised *coitus interruptus* outside of marriage and not within marriage. I contented myself with calling for research to be done on their ideology and their customs. From the very beginning of the article I maintained that one could not prejudge what they accepted and understood of the prevailing ideology.

It is true that after establishing some facts and criticising some theories, I suggested over-confidently what could only be hypotheses for research. Without providing reliable proof, I said that I could not believe — which I still cannot — that the majority of young people in the seventeenth and eighteenth centuries remained celibate for ten or fifteen years after puberty without engaging in any sexual activity. I suggested that they turned to masturbation or other sterile practices. Therefore, it is in no way surprising that these beliefs and hypotheses for research did not generate great enthusiasm; and if they had only been the butt of limited and soundly supported criticisms such as those of Jacques Depauw, I would have waited until I had finished the research I have begun on the registration of pregnancies before replying. However, André Burguière went much too far, not only by appearing to reject entirely the ideas that I had expressed in 1969, but by offering in return a comprehensive theory which seems to me to be unacceptable. As he kindly invited me to reply to his criticisms, I wished first to distinguish the established facts from those in my 1969 article which were hypothetical; and I shall now take the risk of prematurely putting forward my thoughts on the behaviour of young single people in the seventeenth and eighteenth centuries.

I do not know whether Burguière is correct in establishing the six-teenth century as the beginning of the trend towards increasing age at marriage, but it does not seem implausible. In any case, it seems essential to both of us to stress the importance and the originality of this phenomenon, characteristic of Western Europe in modern times. There were certainly considerable demographic and economic conse-quences — although those suggested by J. Hajnal[4] and André Bur-guière remain very hypothetical — and it is probable that it also had an effect on people's sex lives. Our opinions differ as to the conse-quences of this trend.

André Burguière — like a number of other researchers — believes that he can conclude from seventeenth and eighteenth century statis-tics on illegitimate births that the great majority of single people of that time were completely chaste. And, looking to provide from this chastity a theory which conforms to the ideas of our Freudian era, he assumes that they achieved this chastity by sublimating their libido. In common with Emmanuel Le Roy Ladurie, he appears to think that, in certain cases, it would have given rise to neuroses; but in general, the libido would have been devoted, without noticeable damage, to religious fervour and — if I have correctly understood the idea which he shares with J. Hajnal — in a sort of desire for economic power which is characteristic of our capitalist society.

I admit that I find it difficult to imagine how, in the past, 95% of the young peasants managed this sublimation which Freud speaks of in connection with several nineteenth and twentieth century intellectuals and artists. Neither do I understand how, after using sublimation — or neurosis — as a solution for ten or fifteen years, those young men found in themselves the resources of sexual energy which gave them the desire to marry and to give their wives many children. It is particularly difficult to comprehend as, by rejecting my theory of the two patterns of behaviour, it is implicitly assumed that they married for love, as we do today.

I do not see from which of Freud's writings one can draw such a theory of sublimation. On the contrary, I find in one of his 1908 articles:[5] "Our third stage of civilisation[6] demands of individuals of both sexes that they shall practise abstinence until they are married and that all who do not contract a legal marriage shall remain abstinent throughout their lives. The position, agreeable to all the authorities, that sexual abstinence is not harmful and not difficult to maintain, has also been widely supported by the medical profession. It may be asserted, however, that the task of mastering such a powerful impulse as that of the sexual instinct by any other means than satisfying it is one which can call for the whole of a man's forces. *Mastering it by sublimation*, by deflecting instinctive sexual forces away from their sexual aim to higher cultural aims, *can be achieved by a minority and then only intermittently, and least easily during the period of ardent and vigorous youth*. Most of the rest become neurotic or are harmed in one way or another. Experience shows that the majority of the people who make up our society are constitutionally unfit to face the task of abstinence."

I do not cite this text as proof of how impossible it might have been for 95% of French peasants to be truly chaste, but because, if this chastity were proved, it would call back into question many of the fundamental ideas upon which our twentieth century is based.

But is this chastity proved by the statistics which we have for the seventeenth and eighteenth centuries? Given the current state of research, it is this belief that I question. Chastity cannot easily be measured using statistics.

Until now we have been content to produce illegitimate birth rates, for such and such a locality, and to consider them as immediately revealing extramarital sexual behaviour: if the figure is low, the society is thought to have been chaste; if it is high, the society thought to have been "immoral"; if it increases over the years, immorality is thought to have gained ground. We find this excellent instrument provided for us by demographers so useful, that we no longer appreciate the distance separating a given illegitimate birth rate from the very varied sexual behaviour which may give rise to it. In reality, the proportion of illegitimate births tells us about one thing only: the comparatively great resistance offered by a society not so much to the growth of extramarital sexual behaviour as to extramarital births themselves.

In order to pass from one to the other with some plausibility, it would be necessary at least to do serious research on the manifestations of social condemnation and what provokes it. Does their environment really condemn all extramarital behaviour in men? How was this done? Is it condemned equally in men and women as Christian doctrine would have it in principle? Nothing is less certain. In numerous societies or social milieux, people tend to admire the man's sexual "prowess" and to condemn the woman's "abandon". Conversely, it should be noted that certain sterile practices such as homosexuality, indeed perhaps even masturbation[7], tend to be tolerated better in women than in men.

As for those women proved guilty of having sinned, how did society's condemnation manifest itself? Societies do exist in which family honour demands that, even in the absence of any illicit conception, a father must kill a daughter guilty of having lost her virginity before marriage. This does not seem to have been the case in France in the past. Is the young woman even excluded from her family and village from that moment onwards? Nothing in the current state of our knowledge leads us to believe this. This serious sanction seems only to be applied when the young woman has conceived and her pregnancy becomes visible. As for extramarital sexual activity, I would therefore tend to agree with Pierre Chaunu, who speaks of a "Cathar"[8] mentality.

Before concluding that they were chaste, let us reflect therefore on the possibilities that young people had to satisfy their sexual urges within the repressive system of the time.

I am reputed to have said that they practised *coitus interruptus* outside of marriage, then forgot it once married. I do not see the situation like that. I would gladly believe that, still ignorant of contraceptive practices, young men could neither use them, nor take advantage of them with young women of their age. As a result of this ignorance, not only were young men's relations with young women comparatively fertile, but also, and more importantly, such relations were considerably limited in number.[9] Just because a practice has been used by "primitive" peoples, it does not follow that any individual can easily rediscover it when he needs it: the patterns of human sexual activity are to a large extent cultural and as such require intellectual or practical initiation.

But a great many other means of achieving pleasure without making a child existed. Firstly, there was homosexuality, to which ancient penitentials constantly made allusion concerning adolescents.

It is true that sodomy was a very serious crime which the tribunals punished by burning at the stake. However, if cases of execution by fire are known up to the beginning of the eighteenth century, sodomites are also known who were notorious enough for their reputations to have reached us; and who were not, however, executed nor even harassed, because of the rank or patronage which they enjoyed. In particular, I would be surprised if homosexuality among adolescents was repressed in such a terrible manner.

During the early Middle Ages, penitentials alluded to it in very different terms to those used in referring to sodomy among adults: not only were the penances much lighter — and often lighter than for debauchery or heterosexual fornication[10] — but it is obvious that they are speaking of typically juvenile practices, which were to give way to other patterns of behaviour after marriage.

A certain number of synodal statutes and confessors' manuals after the early Middle Ages confirm this impression. The statutes of the diocese of Cambrai, produced between 1300 and 1310, do not reserve for the bishop absolution for sodomy committed by women of any age and young people under the age of twenty.[11] This can certainly be explained by the fact that their responsibility appears less than that of adults, but also perhaps because the bishop could not alone have absolved such a frequent sin.

We have more explicit evidence about this frequency. Gerson, for example, writes in his *Confessional* at the beginning of the fifteenth century: "The fourth sin against nature is men in company with each other, from behind or otherwise. Or women having relations with each other in detestable and horrible means which must neither be named nor written, or women with their husbands in unnatural positions, etc. I rely on the confessor's good intentions to inquire wisely and cautiously in such a way that he is not responsible for teaching them the way to this sin. *And young unmarried men and women must also be interrogated wisely and cautiously as I have said. For it*

is rare for them not to commit villainous and abominable sins once they are
old enough if they are not married young. And even within marriage
young people are guilty of many villainous excesses. I am ashamed
to speak so much of them for sins against nature are so horrible and
so abominable before God that several times he has taken vengeance
against them as we know from those five towns in the Bible which
were engulfed for the dreadfulness of this sin."[12]

We must not see the denunciation of the beginnings of our "Malthusian" practice in the conclusion of this text, but an observation confirming that of today's sexologists, i.e. that sexual habits begun during
adolescence are difficult to get rid of afterwards.

Gerson also reminds us of certain material conditions of life in the
past, likely to encourage the condemned practices: "Several confessors found [penitents] who throughout their youth had taken part in
confession every Easter without daring to confess the dissipation that
they had fallen into at the age of 9, 10, 11 or 12 years with their brothers
and sisters when they slept together in their youth. Therefore shepherds and shepherdesses, and the people who also watched over
animals in their youth are to be interrogated. For many sins are
committed at such an age".[13]

Did the conditions of daily life change much between the fifteenth
and the eighteenth century? One would need to carry out research
into whether the confession manuals from the seventeenth and eighteenth centuries give indications on this point which are similar to
Gerson's.

Philippe Ariès saw clearly how much Gerson's attitude already
foreshadowed that of seventeenth century educationalists. And certain of these educators' texts tell us in veiled terms of their obsessive
fear of homosexual relations between children. As an example, we
have that instruction to prefects of the Collège Henri-IV in La Flèche,
forbidding them to allow any pupil to enter another's bedroom under
the pretext of borrowing some object. And if, as an exception, they
believed it necessary to give such permission, the bedroom door or
the room's curtain was to remain open.[14] Even if such prudence had
reflected the good fathers' obsessions more than those of their pupils,
can one imagine that these pupils noticed these precautions without
harm?

The same concern existed in the parish schools attended by working-class children. In a manual for the masters,[15] when it comes to
talking of how to behave towards the children "who ask to go to the
communal necessities", mention is specifically made of the fact that:

"They must be forbidden from being in that place two at a time for reasons of great importance, about which I am silent because of the horror of the danger involved". Even if one admits that this prudence is not as strange as that of the Jesuits of La Flèche, the way of expressing it also indicates obsession.

Another major sin, bestiality, also punishable by death in theory, was undoubtedly not as insignificant in seventeenth and eighteenth century rural society as it is in urbanised Europe today. It must have also have been a pattern of behaviour more widespread among young single people, incidentally more often shepherds than labourers. (See Gerson's text, cited above).

In any case, I particularly wish to draw attention neither to homosexuality nor bestiality, but to the "solitary practices" which seem to me to have been much more widespread in our Christian civilisation. As Dr. Hesnard clearly saw it,[16] the situation is different in other civilisations which repress sexuality, such as Muslim civilisations. On such a subject, naturally, I cannot give direct and statistical proof as is given for heterosexual relations between single people. I am therefore going to draw conclusions from the teachings of contemporary sexology and those of confessors in the past.

Why are my opponents not interested in masturbation? Do they think that, since it is an "abnormal" practice, like homosexuality or bestiality, it must necessarily and in all societies, occur less frequently than fornication? In our society at any rate, sexologists seems to consider it as a statistically normal stage of sexual development. And if they call the persistence of these practices after puberty abnormal and dangerous, does that mean that it was not frequent? "Such a phenomenon", writes Dr. Hesnard, "is much more frequent than the elective isolated fixation to such and such a partial erotic tendency, for the simple reason that all sexual self-restraint which goes beyond a certain tolerance threshold — variable with each individual — reinforces auto-eroticism".[17]

Do they think on the other hand that it is such a banal activity and one of such little consequence that it is unnecessary to speak of it when attempting to assess men's chastity in the seventeenth century? Freud wrote as early as 1908: "In considering the question of abstinence, the distinction is not made nearly strictly enough between two forms of it — namely abstention from any sexual activity whatever and abstention from sexual intercourse with the opposite sex. Many people who boast of succeeding in being abstinent have only been able to do so with the help of masturbation and similar satisfactions which are linked with the auto-erotic sexual activities of early childhood."[18]

Are these diagnoses valid for French society in the past? I believe that patterns of behaviour considered to be "against nature" because of their inherent sterility, were less easy to repress than fornication. They were therefore more widespread in a society which repressed illegitimate births more strongly than twentieth century society and which was even less prepared to encourage people to marry young. This reasoning is particularly valid for the "solitary practices" which are easily undertaken without a witness and whenever the feeling comes upon you. Moreover, if, by any chance, one was discovered, the sanctions were much less strict than for sodomy or bestiality.

To my knowledge, masturbation was never legally considered an offence, in a society where it certainly existed, as theologians and confessors attested. What is their attitude towards it? I have already pointed out that the penitentials of the early Middle Ages generally considered it a markedly less serious sin than fornication,[19] and I am prepared to provide further proof.

With the theological renaissance of the twelfth and thirteenth centuries, strictness increases, at least theoretically, since theologians consider it as one of the ways of sinning against nature and make sins against nature the worst of the sexual sins.[20] But did this strictness also exist in the confessional? I have claimed,[21] basing my claim on the synodal statutes of Cambrai, that generally this was not the case at the beginning of the fourteenth century. This conclusion is open to discussion, and I would like to qualify it here. For it appears that, during the fourteenth and fifteenth centuries, an effort was made to treat this practice more strictly and to give it the status which it had in theological literature in penitential sanctions.

In his *Doctrinal de sapience*, written in 1388,[22] Guy de Roye, Archbishop of Sens, wrote: "...the first [example of a sin against nature] is when a man or woman, alone and knowingly, while watchful, enters the mire of sin, *which simple priests cannot absolve*: for because of the gravity of the sin the sinner is handed over to Bishops or to their lieutenants or Penitentiaries".

Soon afterwards, John Gerson — who felt it necessary to devote an entire book to diurnal "pollution" — writes in his *Confessional*: "It is a sin against nature more serious than to have been in the company of a woman or a woman with a man and is reserved for the prelate".[23] Thus, I was perhaps wrong, in my previous article, to consider the 1387 synodal statutes of the diocese of Nantes exceptionally strict on this point; and perhaps to have thought that only sodomy was meant in expressions such as "*de vitio contra naturam enormi*" [monstrous sin against nature] (Albi, 1553), "the sin against nature" (Paris, about 1580), or "*nefandum scelus contra naturam*" (Rheims, 1621), [the detestable crime against nature] (Rheims, 1677). A more complete and careful survey remains to be done, for the presence or absence of the sin of *mollities*, in the list of cases reserved for the bishop, would provide a solid indication of its frequency: its lasting presence would indicate that the case presents itself rarely enough that the bishop could actually absolve it in person; its absence would prove that because of its frequency it is impossible, in practice, to give to this sin the status which theologians assign to it in theory. In the absence of such research, I retain only, from the evidence of Gerson and Guy de Roye, that in the fourteenth and fifteenth centuries the Church makes an effort to eliminate this serious vice or to reduce its frequency.

To read parts of the same Gerson's texts, moreover, one wonders whether making people feel even more guilty about sin was in fact a good method: was not the result that people no longer dared to admit to it in confession? "...If the confessor was not skilful and circumspect when interrogating on sins of this sort", writes Gerson, "*it is only rarely and with difficulty that he would be able to obtain the confession of such vices* from the mouth of those who are infected by them...That is why, after several friendly and affable sentences — and not severe ones — on other matters or vices, the confessor must gradually come obliquely to enquiries on this sort of sin".[24]

The remainder of this advice also gives us information on the frequency of masturbation and about those who engaged in it: "...If he does not want to reply, then ask him frankly: 'Friend, do you stroke or rub your penis *like children habitually do*?' If he says only that he has never held it like that nor stroked it, one can progress no further, *except to admire him and say that it is hard to believe*, exhorting him to think of his salvation because he is in the presence of God and that it is very serious to lie in confession, and other similar things. But if he says that he has held it and stroked it, [say to him]: 'Friend, I believe you, but for how long? For an hour, or half an hour? Until your penis was no longer erect?' And let that be said as though the confessor did not consider that to be unusual or wicked. If he confesses that he has done so, then it must be pointed out to him that he has committed the sin of mollities, even if, due to his age, no pollution has resulted from it — for there [in pollution] is found the culmination of seductive delight — and that he is more likely to have lost his virginity, at least his soul's virginity in this way than if he had had intercourse with women as he might at his age...These things being said, he must then scold him vehemently and pronounce his atrocious vice, and advise him to confess the others boldly because that one is the worst..."

"That same master[25] then advised submitting older men and women to the same interrogation — with a small number of changes — because, through experience, he had found that many adults have been tainted by such a vice, and had never before confessed it: some out of modesty at first, then by forgetfulness; the others due to modesty which is still so strong that they say they intended never to confess...In truth, he has known many who excused themselves by claiming ignorance, saying that they had never heard or [never] known that such touching, which was not a desire to know women carnally, was a sin".[26]

This long text, which I have had to abridge considerably, is not the product of a bookish culture, nor of the personal obsessions of its writer alone, but of very remarkable observation of reality, whether one owes this to Gerson himself or to the the Parisian master of theology to whom he refers. If need be, I can offer as proof the fact that on several points Gerson again finds himself in agreement with today's sexologists who describe masturbators' general behaviour. Firstly, there is a very strong sense of having sinned which prevents most of them from admitting to it during confession. Undoubtedly this holds true for the majority. Sexologists confirm that "solitary practices" are generally closely linked with timidity towards women, to respect for established morality and that they are reinforced in those who have this sense of having sinned.

It is true that in this text we see adults who have long ago renounced solitary practices and who remain so little affected by them that they have forgotten them. But it is probable that those who are still ashamed are still practising them. Finally, there are those who appear not to be conscious of their sin. The speech directed to them by Gerson at the beginning of the fifteenth century recalls the implicit convictions of the penitential writers of the early Middle Ages: for those people, what a Christian must avoid above all, is relations with women; masturbation is only a venial weakness; indeed a paramedical practice aimed at preventing the suppression of sexual desire. Is it so different from the behaviour of those saints, mentioned in legends, who throw themselves into the snow in order to cool their ardour? From a modern point of view, one could conclude that those masturbators do not have fantasies: they indulge in narcissistic behaviour as Freud and his disciples describe it. Hence their clear conscience.

Finally, the last comparison between Gerson and sexologists: Gerson's accusation that prolonged masturbation encourages other abnormal patterns of behaviour: "And he who makes a habit of it and who persists in doing so, the devil will make him stumble into several other villainous and terrible sins which no one should name or write".[27]

From the beginning of the fifteenth to the end of the eighteenth century, confessors do not appear to have decreased the attention paid to masturbation. I see signs even of increased obsessive fear in the fact that words which originally signified other things were used to refer to this vice: from the thirteenth century, it seems, it is called *mollities*, whereas in antiquity this word seems to have referred to passive homosexuality; from the sixteenth century onwards, they begin to liken masturbation to Onan's sin. This is shown by Benedicti, among others, in 1585: "Whosoever procures voluntary pollution outside of marriage, which the Theologians call '*mollities*', he sins against the natural order...Therefore it is one of the cases reserved for the superiors, in several orders depending upon what is contained in the latter's statutes... *Because of this sin, Her and Onan, Juda's two children...were killed by a spirit*".[28] It is, of course, a matter of finding in the sacred texts the greatest possible number of condemnations of a practice undoubtedly more frequent then than in the time of the Hebrews or of St Paul.[29]

As for those who engage in these practices, Benedicti, after briefly mentioning monks of various orders, who had to confess to their superiors, Benedicti speaks more explicitly of the laymen: "And yet there are those who are so addicted to the filth of this sin — *as is most often the case among the youth of either sex* — that the men do not want to marry, nor the women to take a husband, when by this means they satisfy their immodest appetites over many years, or indeed, alas, until the tomb..."[30] Once again, then, we find confirmation that these practices are very common among the youth of both sexes. Should we stress that we are talking here of youth and not of childhood? I would tend to do so despite the imprecision of the words "child", "adolescent" and "youth", to which Philippe Ariès has already drawn our attention. Should it be understood that those stubborn people who do not wish to marry are youths and deduce from that that "youth" be located somewhere between puberty and the age at marriage? I am willing to accept that; but it remains open for discussion.

In any case, we are now referring to laymen and no longer to monks. And Benedicti describes more explicitly than Gerson those people so involved in auto-eroticism that they refuse to marry. That implies, it seems to me, that such sinners were common rather than the exception. Perhaps we should make a small place for this kind of behaviour beside the social and economic reasons for remaining celibate at that time. We should note that at the end of the sixteenth century, Benedicti speaks of persistent masturbators in the same way as John Bromyard in the fourteenth century spoke of fornicators.[31] Is this indicative of a change in the sexual practices of single people?

One may also wonder whether the impotence caused by sorcery, which was widely talked about at the time, was not caused by prolonged auto-eroticism rather than by the wizards who were believed to be responsible and who indeed prided themselves on it. For Benedicti, those who refused to marry proved their obstinacy in sin, for God made marriage the remedy for all forms of incontinence. But for those of us who believe we see the logic of auto-erotic behaviour, those who are unable to consummate their marriage are perhaps not so very different from those who refuse to take a wife.

Another difference of opinion between our contemporary sexologists and the confessors of the past appears in the system of penitential repression indicated by Benedicti: "And one is well advised to confess the circumstances. For example if someone committing this sin thinks he is dealing with or desiring a married women, aside from the sin of *mollities*, it is adultery; if he desires a virgin, it is debauchery; if he desires a female relative, it is incest; if he desires a nun, it is sacrilege; if he desires a man, it is sodomy; similarly a woman in the place of man".[32]

Just as the extent of auto-eroticism is principally due to marrying late and to the repressing of extramarital heterosexual activities, such a penitential system, which tries to repress fantasies, should logically encourage the development of veritable narcissism among masturbators, hence their disgust with marriage. The repression undoubtedly had little effect.

In the seventeenth century, the situation is no better. In 1628, in his French version of Cardinal Toledo's *Somme*, M. A. Goffar writes: "It is a very grave sin and one which is against nature: it is not permitted either for health or for life, nor for whatever purpose. Therefore those Doctors who advise this act on health grounds sin grievously, and those who obey them are not exempt from mortal sin. *This sin is abandoned with great difficulty, particularly as the temptation is ever-pre-*

sent: therefore it is so common that I believe that the majority of the damned are tainted with this vice. I think that there is no other effective remedy but to confess often to the same Confessor, and to do so if possible three times a week: this Sacrament being a particularly appropriate curb on this sin, and whosoever does not use it, let him expect no change, except by special grace or a miracle of God".[33]

Despite the Jesuit principle of frequent confession, which appears here, it seems clear to me that they must have abandoned the reserving of this sin for the bishop: every confessor must have had to help each of his penitents almost daily in the fight against such a formidable and widespread evil.

The Jansenists are no less conscious of the danger and of the necessity to fight the craving at all times. In a letter to M. de Sacy on the subject of the education of the Prince of Conti's children, Lancelot writes that, in order to protect them from attacks of the devil, they had "an angel always visible beside them, by day or by night, in the bedroom or at church, at their play or during visits, and even *during the most private activities*".[34] I do not know whether, by this means, the citadel of their virginity was to be successfully defended up to the end, nor what the subsequent sexual development of these princes was. But I will make two comments on this text. Not all young people could have been watched over as well as those two. On the other hand, however, this degree of supervision was the logical outcome of seventeenth century Catholic education: Jansenists and Jesuits, in the confessional or colleges, as well as in the princes' home, could imagine only continuous supervision of the young as a way of preserving young souls from fatal temptation. I am not aware of any text which documents the success of this strategy.

The religious fervour of a great number of seventeenth century men and women is indisputable. And I do not doubt that a certain number of them were able, by means of their fervour, to sublimate their libido and convert their urges with a certain degree of success. But what about the others, who made up the great majority?

I would perhaps be attracted to the theory of widespread sublimation if I had proof, or a feeling that, for the majority of the population, the seventeenth century was a century of other than erotic passion. But who will claim that the sixteenth century was less passionate? What characterises the seventeenth century in France in relation to the sixteenth is the work of education, of civilising the elite and the masses. Intellectual and religious education certainly had its part to play, but moral education was of the greatest significance. Seventeenth century morality, and sexual morality in particular, remains, despite Salesian efforts, dominated by the idea of sin. It is a continual struggle against temptation; a defensive struggle — defending childish innocence of which they were becoming increasingly conscious — in which, only the enemy can be victorious. Defending the free arbiter or the inability of man to save himself, are only two contradictory ways of placing sin at the centre of religious life. It is true that genuine sublimation is found among mystics at the beginning of the century. But when mysticism turns to quietism, is that not a third way of taking up a position in relation to sin? Thus all the religious quarrels of the seventeenth century are dominated by the question of sin.

In the absence of detailed studies, it is difficult to know to what extent the sense of sin existed among working class people. Sometimes, missionaries are dismayed not to find it; sometimes, it seems to me that the sense of taboo dominates popular morality. In any case, it is the orthodox morality of the times which the Church tried to spread among working-class people, more so than in past centuries. A moral code which was able to cause the decrease of incest, adultery, fornication, rape, even juvenile homosexuality — all this has yet to be researched — but a moral code which could not root out "solitary practices" where they were established. I am even inclined to believe that repressing the other, more visible forms of pre-marital sexual activity must have spread auto-eroticism in social milieux where it would not, hitherto, have been widespread.

Finally, when the development of Jansenist moralism is stressed as a means of proving and explaining sexual abstinence in the seventeenth and eighteenth centuries, it seems to me that, on the contrary, it substantiates my thesis of widespread "solitary practices". Jansenism, as a religious attitude characterised by the obsessive fear of sin, cannot be understood without experience of sin. Which sin is more immediately taken to be one than the sin we are speaking of? What kind of sex life develops more the fear of the Father?

One could object that the massive diffusion of solitary and homosexual practices to which I allude might have had more marked effects than we notice on the subsequent sex lives of French people in the seventeenth century. I refused to accept that after fifteen years of perfect sublimation and converting of the sexual urges, one could still find the necessary sexual energy to marry and reproduce. After fifteen years of masturbation or homosexuality, one may ask, would that have been easier? Indeed today's sexologists confirm that auto-eroticism fosters timidity towards the opposite sex; that it creates a feeling of guilt and an inferiority complex which make amorous conquest difficult. Moreover, they maintain that a too lengthy auto-erotic fixation, even if it does not imply truly narcissistic behaviour, encourages premature ejaculation, makes conjugal relations disappointing, and runs the risk of leading to a return to juvenile practices after a short period of marriage. How then to reconcile the hypothesis of widespread habits "against nature" with the observation that the vast majority of men of that time got married and had many children?

Obviously the sex life of a society forms an integrated whole: one cannot study extramarital behaviour without paying attention to its repercussions on conjugal relations. I will reply, however, in two ways to the objection made: firstly, by trying to see if the practices "against nature" which I suggest were widespread during youth, can be reconciled with what we know of marriage in western Christian society; then, by looking to find out whether heterosexual activity prior to marriage is as rare as is generally accepted.

First and foremost, did marriage in the past necessitate as it does today, amorous conquest? I know very well that literature portrays a certain number of amorous adventures which end in marriage. But does that make it the rule? I do not think so. The main function of profane literature is to speak of adventures and of love, and it may be tempted to give the love adventure "a happy ending", to immortalise it in marriage rather than in death. This is a reflection more of the problems of literature than the reality of marriage, up until the eighteenth century. I believe I have, in my previous article, showed sufficiently to what extent, among ecclesiastic or lay moralists, and in erotic literature itself, amorous and marital patterns of behaviour were perceived as separate; and I could cite still more texts in support of this idea.

No doubt I will be told that this distinction, even assuming that it holds true for the nobility and part of the middle class, does not hold true for the working classes; that the working classes married according to the dictates of their hearts. And indeed, I do believe that, in poor families, young people were more involved in the choice of a partner. That does not however mean — despite what Marivaux says — that they chose a wife according to the same criteria and using the same processes as when they were looking for a mistress. Both the trials involving the breaking of marriage promises and the rates of pre-marital pregnancy — which we will speak of later — would be worth studying from this perspective, but particularly in the seventeenth century they would no doubt prove to be the exception rather than the rule. It is true that no historian has yet studied this question in detail; but, given the current state of research, it seems to me that in general the reality of marriage among working class people is very different to a love story.

We ought not to believe that the contrast between these two archetypal patterns of behaviour, which I described in my previous article, is the invention of Christian theologians and, as such, could only have influenced the most cultured classes of society. Theologians found this vision of love and marriage ready-made in Graeco-Roman culture. Not only among the Stoics, as Noonan, would have us believe,[35] but deeply rooted in normal practice, just as Marcel Detienne has recently reminded us in an already famous small volume.[36] Nor does it appear that the antinomy between marriage and amorous passion is characteristic of western or Indo-European culture: the ethnologist Luc Thoré discovered it in Africa, among the Wolofs and the Tukulors, as well as among various other, non-Senegalese, peoples.[37] Based on this discovery, he developed a general theory of conjugal relations in the three types of society known to man: despite all other contradictory behaviour, traditional societies, be they matrilineal or patrilineal, prohibit spiritual and emotional intimacy between husband and wife just as they forbid sexual relations between relatives; both these prohibitions being necessary for social cohesion. Today's urban and industrial society might therefore be said to be at variance with all traditional societies by encouraging the establishing of marital intimacy and real verbal communication between spouses. But, by throwing an individual into the arms of a stranger, our society greatly emphasises "the rupture with the childish and reassuring world of maternal proximity". The "matrimonial adventure" would therefore include more risks than in other societies, and a much greater proportion of failures. Hence the importance of aptitude to married life, whereas marriage in traditional societies, being less demanding, could adapt to lesser receptiveness.

Moreover, no matter what might be the value of this general theory of conjugal relations, Pierre Bourdieu has clearly shown how, until about 1914, the old type of marriage existed in certain parts of France.[38] Among the peasants of the Béarn, he stressed the importance of economic factors within the marriage system; families' mediation in marriage, and the restriction of the freedom of choice, corresponding to the segregation of the sexes.[39]

It remains to be proved that what can be observed among the peasants of the Béarn today, existed in most parts of France in the seventeenth and eighteenth centuries. But, given the current state of research, and taking into account the similarities between this system of marriage and the one presented to us by ecclesiastic writers from the sixth to the eighteenth century, and with what we know of noble and middle class marriages in the seventeenth and eighteenth centuries, it is reasonable to make this assumption. It remains the task of those who believe that marrying for love was the rule in the countryside at that time to begin to provide proof of it.

Until we receive proof to the contrary then, let us accept that timidity, which was in theory characteristic of auto-erotic behaviour, did not prevent young people from getting married. But, once they were married, how did they adapt to married life?

I suggest first that the warnings of today's sexologists against the harm done by the prolonged practice of masturbation concerns perhaps only borderline cases, and that in general a certain amount of adaptation to married life is possible. In assuming solitary practices to be widespread, I did not mean to say that narcissistic behaviour was itself very widespread. Several comments made by confessors indicate that in general, it was only a practice to mark time and was not a substitute for the desire for heterosexual intercourse. The majority of confessors try to discover the masturbator's fantasies and believe them to be mostly heterosexual. The category of masturbators mentioned by Gerson, who "had no wish to know women carnally" appears to me to be the exception, excluding the clergy. The same is true for those who, according to Benedicti, have no inclination for marriage. Moreover, in the advanced stages of auto-erotic behaviour, ejaculation takes place extremely quickly: that is not what Gerson assumes, when he speaks of half an hour or an hour. It follows therefore that, generally, masturbation perhaps lessened one's talents for amorous conquest and marital pleasure, but did not eliminate the desire to have intercourse with members of the opposite sex. We can even surmise that it maintained and sharpened it to a certain extent, as studies of the sexuality of Second World War prisoners have shown. Moreover, to the best of my knowledge, nobody claims that masturbators, even the most persistent ones, were never fathers of large families.[40] The issue is to find out to what extent they were capable of finding sexual contentment in marriage.

The few indicators which are to be found on this point do not contradict the hypothesis of a lengthy fixation on auto-eroticism before marriage, but, on the contrary, rather confirm it. Firstly, is it a coincidence that impotence caused by sorcery appears to become more common as the Catholic Reformation begins? Mme M. Caumette has shown, in an as yet unpublished dissertation,[41] that ceremonies against conjugal impotence only appear in rituals between 1616 and 1760. Historians, inquisitors, wizards and their victims are convinced that it is an aspect of an epidemic of witchcraft from the end of the sixteenth to the beginning of the seventeenth century. But why could it not also be related to the increased repression of juvenile sexuality? Obviously that would provide evidence in support of a certain amount of abstinence more than in support of a spread of masturbation or of homosexuality.

The point must be made that, although solitary pre-marital practices cannot be held responsible for the contradiction between marriage and sexual passion, they are, however, in keeping with it. Marriages may not be arranged for love, but they certainly are arranged for the very deep social reasons analysed by Marcel Detienne and Luc Thoré in a very general way and without specific reference to Christianity. But young French men's solitary practices, to the extent to which they could lead them to being disappointed in conjugal relations — as sexologists claim — could thus reinforce this feeling of contradiction and give concrete proof of it.

Finally and most importantly, when one manages to infiltrate the secrets of the marital bed, with the help of seventeenth century theologians and casuists, one is struck by the high rate of auto-eroticism which is found there. Mme A.C. Kliszowski shows it clearly.[42] "All the theologians of the time", she writes in the conclusion of her study, "allow women to arouse themselves by caresses before intercourse — *se excitare tactibus* — and a great majority of them also authorise her to do the same after the penis is withdrawn, if she has not yet achieved orgasm. What an astonishing introduction to solitary pleasures, with the blessing of the religious authorities! Thus, we get the impression that each of the partners must accomplish his procreative *duty*, with scarcely a thought for how his or her partner feels".

After what we have seen of pre-marital sexuality, I question the idea that partners could have been "initiated" into solitary practices in this way. But as for the rest, this conclusion, based on many texts,[43] seems very interesting to me. Theologians are led to ask this question because they base marriage on procreation, and to the extent to which they accept the Galenic theory of the double seed. They are forced to retain at least part of this theory, despite their acceptance of Aristotle, to the extent to which they cannot accept that sexual pleasure exists without the emitting of the seed necessary or useful for procreation without destroying their vision of sexuality. That is obvious. But, no matter what their understanding of the biological phenomenon of reproduction may have been, it is also obvious that, if they had shared our ideal of marital intercourse, they would not have been able to phrase the question in such terms and still less answer it as they did.

That does not mean that couples at that time could not themselves discover marital intercourse as we today hope to practise it. It does, however, mean that nothing in the prevailing ideological structures of the time inclined them to do so, and that the marital behaviour offered to them in no way forced them to break off the sexual training given them by their solitary practices before marriage. Conversely, one could say that Christianity fostered solitary practices not only by repressing all other, less private, forms of pre-marital sexual activity, but also by the strictly genital vision of sexual relations within marriage that it upheld.

A second reply to the objection expressed above: I do not believe that extramarital heterosexual relations were as rare as is generally believed. I have three reasons for this belief: firstly, that would mean ignoring adultery; secondly, the rate of pre-marital conception must be taken into consideration with more determination and thought than is ordinarily done; finally, not enough thought is given to the frequency of extramarital relations which illegitimate births may indicate.

If one could then assume that a not insignificant proportion of young single people had sexual relations, albeit occasionally, that would reinforce the idea already proposed that relatively long-lasting solitary or homosexual practices did not lead to the structuring of integrally narcissistic or homosexual behaviour. Or, to look at it the other way around, if pre-marital practices do not destroy the desire for intercourse with the opposite sex but to a certain extent foster or deepen it, there must logically have been more heterosexual pre-marital relations than has been accepted up to now.

For a start, why assume that the men of that time — who in this case are more important to us than the women — had sexual relations with young women or widows rather than with married women? I will cite, not as proof but as an argument of good sense, taking into account the conditions of the time, a well-known passage from the seventh discourse of *Dames galantes* where Brantôme says: "There can be absolutely no doubt that anyone who wants to quickly enjoy sexual pleasure must turn to married women, without taking a great deal of time and trouble; this is even more true since — as Boccace says — the more one fans a fire, the more it rages. So it is with a married woman, who gets so aroused by her husband that, he being unable to extinguish the fire he creates in his wife, she must look for it elsewhere or be burnt alive." A young woman, on the other hand, "fears this first assault on her virginity, for it is sometimes more trying and painful than gentle and pleasant." A second argument: "All women and young women are prevented from doing it very often by their fear of causing their belly to swell up without eating beans, which married women are not afraid of: for if they swell up, it is the poor husband who has done it and who bears all the responsibility".[44]

It is certainly difficult to arrive at definite conclusions in this area. But there again, we are reaching conclusions before having begun to study the question.[45] The few documents that I am familiar with — aside from the texts of theologians, casuists and confessors — lead us to believe that adultery was strictly punished.[46] But to what extent was this strictness felt by contemporaries and did it prevent women from deceiving their husbands? Whole groups are seen complaining insistently about the profusion of adultery, which they attribute to the leniency of the punishments.[47] It is therefore necessary for the research to go further: to become interested in the charivaris and other more or less spontaneous manifestations of the population's condemnation, in trials, sentences, testimony, etc. Documenting such sources would allow us to perceive, behind individuals' and social groups' attitudes, how much adultery there really was among the people. It would be particularly useful to research what type of relationship was generally pursued and suppressed: long-term relationships, implying the involvement of both the heart and the senses; or brief sensual relationships, which occurred on the spur of the moment? Can we believe that the most suppressed type of relationship was in reality the most frequent?

For if, as I claim with P. Bourdieu, the contracting of a marriage was rarely an affair of the heart; if, as several of the confessors quoted and literary passages mentioned in my previous article say,[48] a significant number of young women began masturbating before marriage; if, even without reaching the extreme practices revealed by A.C. Kliszowski, marital relations often remained more genital than fully sexual in the Freudian sense of the word; then we can expect that a not insignificant number of married women had brief and furtive liaisons, involving only their sensuality; and if relationships of this type are only by chance found in adultery trials, we would have the right to think that for the most part they escaped legal or social repression, either because they mattered less — and were in short less scandalous — than a real affair in which the "whole" woman was involved; or because they were more difficult to discover. Moreover, it is not impossible that a typology of the facts of fornication, like that which we will mention briefly in a moment, might also help us to develop an idea of the respective importance of these types of adultery.

In the absence of such research, I see no reason for ignoring adultery or for considering it less frequent than fornication when trying to assess the importance of illicit relations.

It must be pointed out immediately that fornication itself can be assessed by both illegitimate births and pre-marital conception. Because of the distinction that is usually made between sexual liaisons ending in one or the other we hesitate to use the rates of pre-marital conception. One wonders whether they might not indicate, for certain regions of France, archaic habits rather than libertinage, as P. Laslett showed us in the county of Leicester.[49] Given the current state of our knowledge, it is an exaggerated scruple[50] which therefore tends to make us greatly under-estimate the frequency of extramarital relationships.

Summarising the distinction between illegitimate births and pre-marital conception, P. Chaunu defines the latter as indicative of engaged couples' freedom, and the former as the master's rights over his servant. At a certain level of analysis, this distinction is useful. But let us not be fooled by it: the same type of sexual relation may very easily lead either to an illegitimate birth or to pre-marital conception. The registrations of pregnancies show us that — in towns at least — many illegitimate births result from relations between men and women of the same social background, relations which might have led to marriage. The series of trials for breaking marriage promises — for example those from Carcassonne which Mme M.-C. Phan has recently studied[51] — teaches us a great deal about this type of case.

On the other hand, pre-marital conception could not result exclusively from relations between recently-married couples. When a young man of quality deflowered or impregnated a young working class woman, confessors demanded that he rectify his offence by providing a dowry and marrying off the young woman. I suppose then that some of these seduced young women manage to get married before the birth and that they should also be added to our statistics on pre-marital conception. Moreover, nothing guarantees us that the seducer was always young and that it may not have been a master-servant relationship, i.e. the kind which, generally, leads to an illegitimate birth. Let us assume that the number of such liaisons was negligible. The fact remains that an illegitimate conception might be due to liaisons of a very different nature.

Some such pregnancies were the result of the freedom allowed to engaged couples, which might either be a lingering old tradition, such as the customs found in Leicester, or a modern practice. Others, on the contrary, may have preceded the engagement, which would then have been the result and not the cause. They would, in that case, be entirely similar to those relations which in different circumstances may lead to illegitimate births. If one tried, it would not be very difficult to distinguish one from the other. For, in many parishes, the parish priests indicate the date of engagement and it would be easy to find out whether conception was before or after. Pierre Chaunu, who is interested in the question of engagements, seems to think that, even when the parish priest recorded it at the time of the first marriage banns, engagement in fact lasted much longer. For the time being, I am in no way convinced that this was the rule. And, given the current state of our research, it seems legitimate to me to consider those conceptions leading to births in the first months of marriage as having preceded the engagement.

Let us take the example of Tamerville, where a particularly precise study has been done.[52] In 1624–1690, 9% pre-marital conceptions are found there; in 1691–1740, 11.3% are found; and in 1741–1790, 20%. In these statistics, Philippe Wiel does not count births occurring in the eighth month of marriage, which he may be right in doing, but let us note that he runs the risk of underestimating the frequency of these conceptions rather than of overestimating them. What I find particularly striking in the very detailed table which he gives us, is the small number of births which occurred in the fourth and fifth months of marriage. It seems to me therefore that one can detect here the two types of pre-marital conception which I suggested: in the first months, those which no doubt preceded the engagement; in the later months, those which no doubt followed it; between the two, almost nothing. I note too that it is the increase in the first kind which leads to the overall increase in pre-marital conceptions: in the first three months of marriage, there are 3.1% of births in 1624–1690; 8.49% in 1691–1740;

and 13.35% in 1741–1790. In contrast, births occurring in the seventh and eighth months of marriage decrease or show little change since they go from 9.8% to 5.24% and 6.3%. One can therefore assume that it is indeed the increase in intercourse prior to engagement, thus traditionally illegitimate intercourse, which explains the overall increase in pre-marital conception.

What exactly were these relations prior to engagement? It is generally believed that those who later married were first lovers who went around together faithfully, even before their families made the decision to marry them. It could also be thought that for a long time the families had been in agreement to become united by marriage and that, when the young people could no longer resist the attractions of sexual intercourse, they considered it normal or useful that they "initiated" each other. In any case, it would have been an exclusive and steady relationship. All these assumptions are not ordinarily made so explicitly. But the conclusions drawn from the examining of pre-marital conception rates prove that they were implicitly made. To assume that is to elaborate a novel which conforms to our mythology, to today's vision of love and marriage, but which nothing proves corresponds to actual seventeenth or even eighteenth century behaviour. It is entirely possible that a certain number of conceptions were the result of brief sexual encounters, which were not exclusive, born of a chance meeting in an appropriate location, at an age when sexual urges become too demanding. It is even probable that many of these first sexual encounters bordered on rape: stereotypes of the time, if not of nature, demand it.[53]

Even steady relationships, particularly with young women under twenty years of age, are not always fertile, as shown by fertility statistics for women between fifteen and twenty. Even in this case, therefore, it must be acknowledged that, by using pre-marital conception rates, we systematically underestimate the number of young people who had sexual relations before marriage. We underestimate it even more if, as I believe is probable, a large number of pre-marital conceptions resulted from brief encounters and not steady relationships. To be sure, I cannot for the moment conceive of a way of establishing, based on the number of pre-marital conceptions, the real proportion of young people having had sexual relations. But we must be very conscious that in any case we underestimate this proportion, and no doubt considerably.

Thanks to the registration of pregnancies, illegitimate births, on the other hand, provide us with a basis for roughly calculating the frequency of the type of relations from which they result. Take for example the registrations of pregnancies for Grenoble, studied by Misses Sapin and Sylvoz.[54] For the period 1680–1735, 864 of them allow a typological analysis; and only 322 for the period 1736–1790. The two researchers distinguished three types of physical relations: those where there is one sole encounter, which is often a rape; those where relations were few in number; and finally those which were "ongoing and steady" over a period of months or years. During the first period, 137 pregnancies would fall into the first category, i.e. 15.9% of analysable liaisons; 604 would fall into the second category, which represents 70.2%; and 119 into the third category, i.e. 13.8%. During the period 1735–1790, this division changed greatly, to judge by the 322 analysable registrations: there are only 12.7% pregnancies of the first category; more than 36.5% of the second; whereas there are now 50.5% of the third. This qualitative change in sexual reality is alone more historically important than the increase in the illegitimate birth rate which so fascinates demographer historians. But there is more.

Let us assume, since we are only illustrating an approach, that the registrations tell us exactly what happened; let us also accept, provisionally, the table proposed by J. Bourgeois-Pichat of the probability of conception according to the frequency of sexual relations.[55] One encounter would have 8 chances in 100 of being fertile. That means that 137 liaisons of this kind leading to pregnancy can be considered as the known part of a much greater collection of similar liaisons. Overall, this can be assessed as: $(137 \times 100) \div 8 = 1{,}713$ rapes or other liaisons involving one encounter.

With respect to the other types, establishing the number of actual liaisons having led to the pregnancies which we know of is less easy, due to lack of information about the exact frequency of the relations and the length of the affair. It seems however that, if we were to use the same hypotheses as in the preceding case, it would be necessary to multiply liaisons of the second type by a modest coefficient, 2 or 3 for example, and not to multiply at all the known liaisons of the third type, in order to calculate the actual number of liaisons. At the end of such a calculation, we would come to the conclusions that the 864 liaisons having led to an analysable registered pregnancy represent the known part of 3,644 sexual liaisons, which can be broken down into 47% of the first type (15.9% of the pregnancies), 49% of the second type (70.2% of the pregnancies) and 4% of the third type (13.8% of the pregnancies).

In fact, the table put forward by J. Bourgeois-Pichat does not agree with the data from Grenoble.[56] If, for example, we were to consider as "steady and continuous relations" a relationship involving intercourse ten times per month — which is far from being a maximum given the ages of those involved and taking into account that these are illegitimate and not conjugal relations — conception should have taken place within 2 months on average. Yet relations last for months or years before conception. And even if we were to make the improbable hypothesis that by "steady and continuous relationships", we must include those where the lovers meet only twice per month, conception should have taken place after 7 months, which again seems to be below the data from Grenoble.

Since there is no reason to believe that women having had relationships of the third type were naturally less fertile than those who engaged in the first and second type — for the typology is based on frequency and not on the length of relationships — we must accept at least one of the following two explanations: either the probability table used greatly overestimates the chances of conception, and hence the number of liaisons of the first and second types would be even higher than we calculated; or else fertility is not natural in relationships of the third type. In fact, it is very probable that we must accept both.

It is possible that the presence of a military garrison in Grenoble makes it a slightly abnormal case in relation to the rest of France. But if one were to find a typological division of sexual liaisons similar to that of Grenoble in other regions of France — with this great minority of pregnancies after rape or a single encounter — that would force us to qualitatively and quantitatively modify our vision of French sexuality in the seventeenth and the first half of the eighteenth centuries. Although there were men who "specialised" in rape — even though it is possible that such behaviour might have been less unusual then than today — that would lead us to imagine a greater number of individuals having had, in one way or another, extramarital sexual relations.

Moreover, if this very marked decrease in pregnancies resulting from the first and second types of sexual relations and this considerable increase in the third, were to be found in places other than Grenoble, that could to a large extent explain the increase in the illegitimate birth rates during the eighteenth century. For, without contraception, the evolution of the typological division in Grenoble must imply a markedly higher number of illegitimate births for the same number of amorous liaisons at the end of the century than at the beginning.

Paradoxically, it is the converse which we find in Grenoble, through our collection of registrations of pregnancies. If the parish registers were to confirm this decline in illegitimate births,[57] we would have to conclude that either the number of sexual liaisons diminished — which would be surprising or that contraception was introduced into those steady long-term relationships which became in the majority.

The Grenoble registrations of pregnancies thus lead us to believe that, when one bases reasoning on the illegitimate birth rate, one ordinarily greatly underestimates the number of liaisons from which it results. There are two reasons for this, of differing importance according to the periods: on the one hand, the brief nature of the liaisons and the very limited number of sexual acts to which they gave rise (and that seems especially true for the seventeenth century and the first half of the eighteenth); and on the other hand, contraception. The latter seems to become customary in steady if not long-term affairs; or, at least, we have reason to believe that it existed in affairs of this nature. The number of these affairs seems to increase during the eighteenth century, and not only in Grenoble.[58]

One could cite many other reasons why the proportion of people who engaged in extramarital relations is underestimated. Firstly, the fact, already stressed by Peter Laslett,[59] that rural illegitimate birth rates are considered independently of the urban rates, while pregnant young women seem to have often been chased from their villages and to have given birth in a town. It is true that studying the registrations of pregnancies, while confirming the phenomenon, shows it to be less widespread than one might have thought. But this study has only begun, and it is still possible that Paris was a city where pregnant young women took refuge.

Secondly, it is well known that prostitutes existed in France who had numerous brief sexual encounters and who also had access to contraceptive methods. Jacques Solé[60] and Jacques Depauw have begun to tell us about these prostitutes. But there again, more research is needed. Of what significance is prostitution? What are the different types of prostitutes? How are they divided between town and country? How important and of what sociological composition are their clientele? I have trouble understanding how one can toss out claims concerning extramarital sex life in France under the Ancien Régime in the absence of the studies which would answer these questions.

For my part, I did not intend to specifically define extramarital sex lives of the times. Nor did I want to deny that western civilisation strongly repressed sexuality. Certain literary texts might cause us to doubt that, but the illegitimate birth rates confirm it, in any case for French country life in the seventeenth and the first half of the eighteenth century. However, that does not mean that the men of that time were particularly chaste. As in my previous article, I wanted to show how unreasonable it would be to believe that, and I tried to suggest more probable and more fruitful hypotheses for research. I hope that I have also shown the risks of excessive caution. Those historians who refuse to go beyond their figures inexorably lead those who are trying to develop a concrete picture of men's lives — a natural enough desire — to adopt an erroneous vision of the past.

Chapter 14

Repression and Change in the Sex Lives of Young People

By a slight over-simplification one may say that there exist two fundamentally contradictory views of the evolution of our sexuality. Whatever value they attach to the process, some believe that an "eroticization" of Western behaviour has been occurring over several centuries. Others, on the other hand, think that at least until the beginning of the twentieth century, our sexual drives have been subjected to increasingly effective repression. The first idea, several centuries old, is now the assumption of quantitative historians; the other, which goes back to Freud and Engels, has received the support of many great cultural historians — Huizinga, Lucien Febvre, Norbert Elias, Philippe Ariès, etc. — and of numerous specialists in other human sciences. I find it surprising that two such contradictory ideas have been able to coexist for such a long time without really coming into conflict.

In this article, I do not claim to impartially examine everything which can be said in favour of either of these historical perspectives, nor to conclude that one is true and the other false. On the contrary, I believe that what has occurred has been both a certain intensification of repression and a certain eroticization. I shall try to make this clear with respect to juvenile sexual activity, and with reference not only to the period 1750–1850 — the period focused on by many historians and demographers — but also to the centuries between the end of classical antiquity and the beginning of the twentieth century.

Obviously, over so long a period, I am in no position to construct a

267

rigorous proof, and I am fully aware of the hypothetical nature of my conclusions.

I do believe, however, that French demographic historians have not taken sufficient notice of the hypothesis that sexual repression intensified throughout the early modern period; that they have too readily believed that it was demolished by their statistical data; and that it is therefore useful to explain what makes the hypothesis plausible. This seems particularly important to me at a time when both the French translation of the American historian Edward Shorter's book and Michel Foucault's *Histoire de la sexualité*[1] are being published. The latter writer, having emphasised so strongly the rise of repression in other fields since the sixteenth and seventeenth centuries, has quixotically come out against the notion of progressively increasing repression of sexuality and has himself adopted eroticization as his theme.

THE TIME OF GREATEST SEXUAL REPRESSION

Comparatively speaking, the sex lives of Western youth in the seventeenth, eighteenth and nineteenth centuries seem to have been dependent on two facts. On the one hand, as far as ethics is concerned, there is the fact that sexual activity was only considered acceptable within marriage. Continence outside of marriage was demanded more strictly of women, but was also expected of men. It is this which makes Western sexual morality, born of Christianity, original.

On the other hand, as far as demography is concerned, it has been statistically proven that the peoples of Western Europe used to — and still do — marry later than most other peoples in the world, and that as a result the proportion of single people of marriageable age was higher in the West than almost anywhere else. Thus, in about 1900, between 25% and 59% of Western women in the 25–29 age group were unmarried, whereas in Eastern Europe, only between 2% and 15% were unmarried, and in other countries between 1% and 13% were unmarried.[2] In the seventeenth and eighteenth centuries, the contrast would have been even more striking as we know that in France and England, at least, marriage took place later then than at the end of the nineteenth century.

It was the coinciding of this moral principle and demographic fact which created the situation in which the sexual urges of Western

European youth were more heavily repressed between the seventeenth and nineteenth centuries than in any other time or place.

The pattern of marrying late is not a consequence of Christianity, since it did not exist in the Christian countries of Eastern European. Furthermore, canon law allowed people to get married when they reached the age of puberty, i.e. at fourteen for boys and twelve for girls. That was the legal age for marriage in ancient Roman law, which remained unchanged, and even that was interpreted liberally by the canonists: "What age is prescribed? At least eleven and a half for a girl and thirteen and a half for a boy: before this age any marriage contracted is invalid, unless aptitude and inclination replace age, as the law states. For example, if a boy of ten years of age has such discretion and such a constitution that he can ejaculate or can deflower a virgin, there is no doubt that he may contract a marriage...The same can be said of a girl, for whom marriage is valid from the time she can tolerate a man's company".[3]

Such attitudes are quite logical, since, in Christian doctrine, marriage is the remedy against fornication given to man. Moreover, until the eighteenth century, priests used to lecture parents and even teachers on this subject: "Have you not neglected to get your children established in life, despite being able to do so? Have you not caused them to give in to debauchery by failing to get them established?" asked Antoine Blanchard, in the eighteenth century.[4] Benedicti, in the sixteenth century, wrote that "those people sin who prevent their menservants and womenservants from marrying when the time is right, though they know that otherwise the servants run the risk of taking the wrong course of action. Mortal Sin".[5]

However, there was a change in the ecclesiastical prescriptions on this point. In the sixteenth, seventeenth and eighteenth centuries, no age was ever specified beyond which it was not recommended that young people remain unmarried. This point is even more significant since at this time — as many statistics prove — young men and women got married an average of about ten years after the age of puberty. In other words, for about ten years young people experienced sexual desires which they did not have the right to satisfy, and moralists did not specifically tell parents that they were guilty of laying their children's virtue open to such a long and strong temptation.

Yet they had said so during the Middle Ages. At the beginning of the fifteenth century, Jean Gerson wrote concerning adolescents:

"Very rare are they who, from the time they come of age, do not commit villainous and abominable sins, if they do not marry young".[6] And in the barbarous times of the early Middle Ages, a Roman synod had decided: "Sons, when they reach the age of puberty, must be forced to take a wife or to choose ecclesiastical continence; as for daughters of the same age, their fathers will choose chastity or marriage for them."[7]

This change in ecclesiastic prescriptions is first and foremost a reflection of changing attitudes towards juvenile sexuality. In the early Middle Ages, the Church commanded parents to marry their children when they reached the age of puberty because it considered it very difficult, if not impossible, to prevent young people from engaging in sexual activity, at least outside of the monasteries. This belief is clearly shown in the instructions given to confessors: with certain exceptions, they were forbidden to give the sacrament of penance to young people, because every penitent was expected to be continent for a period of years and young people were considered incapable of this.[8]

In theory, I agree with Edward Shorter in thinking that sexual desire is not exactly the same in all societies and at all times. But I cannot accept that young people in early Western society had no desires whatsoever. Their desires may have been different from those nowadays; but there can be no doubt that they existed and were strong. Between the early Middle Ages and the nineteenth century, it is less the strength of their desires which changed, but more society's attitudes towards them. In the early Middle Ages the Church considered youth to be an age during which desire is uncontrollable; in the seventeenth, eighteenth and nineteenth centuries, on the other hand, youth was considered as the age during which desire ought to be repressed. One last comparison will make this clear: in the fourth century, St Ambroise exhorted married people to "renounce the acts of youth once they are sure of having descendants".[9] In contrast, at the end of the eighteenth century, when Malthus was preaching in support of birth control, he chose to exhort young people and not adults to remain continent.

Yet in theory Malthus, St Ambroise, eighteenth century Catholic moralists and those from the early Middle Ages had the same sexual code of ethics, i.e. a Christian code of ethics. The radical change in their attitudes towards juvenile sexuality is unconscious and must be considered in relation to other complex transformations — economic, social, demographic, cultural, etc. — which I shall attempt to analyse in the remainder of this chapter.

Because of a lack of statistical data, we cannot be sure that towards the end of antiquity and the beginning of the Middle Ages marriage at puberty was in fact the rule in Western Europe as it was in most other regions of·the world. But the statistics which we do have show that, from the end of the Middle Ages to the Industrial Revolution — i.e. at the time when moralists were becoming increasingly vague as to the appropriate age at which children should marry — the average age of young women at their first marriage rose slightly and consistently everywhere. In fifteenth century France, the age at first marriage was perhaps not as low as in Italy, where depending on the region, young women usually got married at the age of sixteen, seventeen or eighteen. But in Dijon, the average age at marriage is believed to have risen from twenty in the second half of the fifteenth century to twenty-one in the first half of the sixteenth.[10] Although there were significant differences between one area and another, it seems that, in French towns and villages, the age at marriage rose from an average of twenty in the sixteenth century to twenty-four or twenty-five in the eighteenth.

I presume that the main reason for this increase in the age at marriage of young women was the increasing difficulty for young people to get themselves established — and for fathers to provide dowries for their daughters — this being a result of the increasing population, the relative drop in wages, the dividing up of peasants' property and proletarianization. But, no matter what the reasons may have been, the result of the increase in the age at marriage is clear: young women were forced to remain continent approximately five years longer in the eighteenth century than in the fifteenth.

The fate of young unmarried men, in this respect, was markedly different: in towns at least the increase in their average age at marriage was not as great because men already got married at about twenty-five at the end of the Middle Ages. But medieval society did not repress their sexual urges as strictly as society in the sixteenth to nineteenth centuries. Jacques Rossiaud has shown this recently with reference to towns in south-eastern France, and his conclusions — which I shall now summarise — are no doubt valid for urban society in most regions of Western and central Europe.[11]

PROSTITUTION AND RAPE IN TOWNS IN THE LATE MIDDLE AGES

In early French society, marriage and property ownership were closely linked: in order to marry, one had to have property and, in turn, one had to had a wife when one was economically independent. For this reason the verb "*s'établir*" [literally "to establish oneself" or "to settle"] meant in old French both to become economically independent and to get married.

In towns, most young men worked as servants, apprentices or journeymen and, except for some of the latter, their financial situation forced them to remain celibate. Within the society, these bachelors, who possessed nothing[12], were in conflict with married men, who monopolised not only economic, social and political power, but also sexual power, since they prohibited anyone from making approaches to their wives, daughters and female servants. These monopolies were however constantly being threatened — by strikes, riots, rapes — and, as, unlike the beggars who were periodically expelled from towns, these bachelors were absolutely essential to the work force, married men had to make concessions to them. Sexually, they could only protect the virtue of their wives, daughters and female servants by making a sufficient number of prostitutes available for the bachelors.

In fifteenth century France, all towns seem to have had municipal brothels, often built with public funds, always administered or organised by the town council, and in theory reserved for bachelors alone. The cost of a visit to these brothels was very low: approximately one eighth to one tenth of a journeyman's average daily wages. Thus bachelors, kept apart from "honest" women and young unmarried women, could still satisfy their sexual desires with "public" or "common" young women.

In spite of this, rape was frequent and followed a very distinct pattern. Eighty per cent of the rapes which we know about were gang rapes and usually quite public events. With some variations, the pattern was basically always the same: they sought out the victim at her home at night; they kicked up a hullabaloo beneath her windows, by calling her and shouting out that she was a harlot; then, as she said nothing, they broke down the door, grabbed her, dragged her outside, then hit and raped her — each in turn, which sometimes lasted all night — then they took her back home and often tried to make her accept money. Because of the noise, the neighbours knew what was happening; they would listen and watch through the chinks in their shutters, but four times out of five, they remained silent and did nothing.

Yet only in 10% of such cases did the rapists have previous criminal convictions. In general, they were young bachelors between eighteen and twenty-four years of age who had never been brought before the law: servants, apprentices, journeymen, shop assistants, clerks, sons of artisans and merchants. After estimating that at least one in every two men in Dijon had taken part in a rape at least once in his life, Rossiaud wonders whether rape was not a kind of rite of passage from adolescence to adulthood. Undoubtedly it was a rite of passage for those women who were their victims, if for no one else.

The victims were usually poor women, servants, newcomers to the town or women suspected of having had sexual relations outside of marriage with one or several men. Rightly or wrongly, they were all considered by their rapists as being women of low morals. Be that as it may, gang rape and public rape caused them to fall from the category of honest women to which they claimed to belong to that of "public and common" young women, i.e. from the category protected by married men to that which was abandoned to bachelors.

Such were the dangers to young women in towns in the late Middle Ages once they reached puberty, and this may be one of the reasons why they were married at an early age. But for young unmarried men, youth and celibacy were not so oppressive. It was a time of friendships between men in the guilds and the *"abbayes joyeuses"**, a time of lack of responsibilities and sexual freedom. After the sixteenth century, these privileges of masculinity were, to a large extent, eliminated by the civil authorities and sometimes the ecclesiastical ones. The municipal brothels were all closed between 1520 and 1570; public rape seems to have disappeared over the course of the century; and the rowdiness of the *"abbayes joyeuses"* was increasingly forbidden in the seventeenth and eighteenth centuries.[13]

In the country, there were also prostitutes and rapes, as shown by the documents in the appendix. But as far as I know, there were no public brothels and it seems to me that commerce with prostitutes was not as common among young peasants as among young city-dwellers. As for young unmarried women, they seem to have had more freedom in the country than in cities to go around with young bachelors from their villages and to obtain a certain amount of sexual

---

* the name given to the traditional meetings of the marriageable young people of a town or village.

pleasure from this without running too much risk of losing their honour in so doing.

PRE-MARITAL COURTSHIP IN THE COUNTRY AND ITS BANNING

In an old song from the Montbéliard region of France, a peasant said to the young man who was asking to marry his daughter:

> *Ma fille est encore trop jeunette*
> *Encore trop jeunette d'un an*
> *Faites l'amour en attendant.*[14]

> [My daughter is still too young
> Still a year too young
> Make love to her while you wait.]

Granted, "make love to her" did not have the same meaning then as now. Here, it was used to mean "court her". However, when courting, many things were permitted which, for both the young unmarried woman and the man, could mitigate the privation of celibacy. I hope I shall be forgiven for going into this subject in some detail: the evidence we have is ambiguous and Edward Shorter, who is familiar with some of it, interprets it differently to myself.

The most explicit evidence is to be found in Dr. Baudouin's book concerning the *"maraîchinage vendéen"*, a courtship custom which remained in existence at the beginning of the twentieth century in several villages in the Vendée. In these villages, young men and women, from the age of fifteen to their marriage, were allowed to openly "French kiss" and, less openly, to give each other pleasure by mutual masturbation.[15] In Shorter's opinion, such freedom was new and indicated a modernisation of behaviour, similar to petting among young middle class people in the second third of the twentieth century. He stresses the fact that no one has proven that *"maraîchinage"* existed before the beginning of this century.[16] I am going to present several facts which convince me that, on the contrary, such petting among young peasants in the Vendée was the last vestige of an ancient custom.

First and foremost, its antiquity has been shown to us by both Dr Baudouin around 1900 and by a priest from the Vendée who wrote around 1880. This is worth noting, for nineteenth century priests and folklorists rather tended to associate virtues with tradition, and vices — particularly sexual ones — with modernisation and dechristianization. In this case, on the contrary, the curé, who deplores "*maraîchinage*", considers it to be a custom which has been in existence for centuries among peasants who were otherwise known to be faithful to the Church.

Secondly — as Shorter well knows — nothing similar existed yet among the young bourgeoisie at the time when Dr. Baudouin was describing the "*maraîchinage vendéen*". It seems unbelievable to me that modernisation, whether in the sexual field or any other, could make its effects felt among the most traditional peasants well before showing up in the customs of the bourgeois and working classes.

Thirdly, "*maraîchinage*" was not as peculiar to the villages of the Marais de Monts as Baudouin first believed. Very similar customs have been reported in the *département* of Deux-Sèvres and even in the Bocage Vendéen, which Baudouin had systematically contrasted with the Marais.[17] It is true that there, the traditional "*migaillage*"* had begun to change as early as the beginning of the twentieth century.

Fourthly, we have older, albeit less detailed, evidence of similar customs in several other regions. In 1877, a medical pamphlet against masturbation in women described the petting among young people in the Pas-de-Calais as follows: "At a wedding between country folk of the lower classes, the wedding guests, young unmarried men and women, retire two by two into a room, four, five or six couples in all and there, after some gibes in rather poor taste, they find themselves deftly plunged into the dark. Then the young men take their companions onto their laps and the young women, who would not for all the world give themselves to their lovers, allow themselves to be fondled and enjoy it greatly, their modesty being thus rather pliant".[18]

In the first decades of the nineteenth century we have no such precise descriptions of the manner in which peasants caressed when "making love". As far as I am concerned, this does not mean that they gained no sexual pleasure from it, but rather that the observers of the time — and their readers — were less interested in such details. For one thing is sure: these bourgeois observers were shocked by the amount of freedom which the peasants allows their daughters in their courting; and they were surprised that such freedom did not result in

---

*   The "*migaille*" was the name for a kind of bottomless pocket at the waist of a skirt. Dr Boismoreau described a practice in the Bocage Vendéen by which a young man slipped his hand through the "*migaille*" and masturbated a young woman, which Boismoreau called "*migaillage*".

a greater number of illegitimate births. "Young men's courting, which is perhaps not sufficiently restricted, does not however present as many regrets as in all the regions for which we have looked at the rates of illegitimate births", said an observer of the mountain people of the Hautes-Alpes.[19] Similar comments are made of the Côtes-du-Nord: "In lower Brittany, as in England, the young unmarried women enjoy great freedom. They run about night and day with the young men, without any long-term harm seeming to have come out of it". No doubt this means that, like the *"migailleurs"* of the Bocage vendéen, they showed their love "by looking tenderly at each other and by putting their hands in each other's 'pockets'."[20] More strict comments were made concerning the department of Haute-Loire: "As for morals, it is unfortunately true to say that one could look in vain to find that simplicity and innocence formerly regarded as the prerogatives of mountain people and the happy compensation for the social skills they lacked. Debauchery is barely concealed and even vices unknown in the cities may be found."[21]

Moreover, we have pre-nineteenth century evidence which is sometimes very explicit concerning the freedom of traditional courting: for example concerning the nocturnal visits in the county of Montbéliard in the eighteenth century[22]; concerning courting in the *"escraignes"** in Champagne in the seventeenth century or those in Burgundy in the fifteenth and sixteenth centuries[23]; or again concerning *"albergement"* in Savoy at the beginning of the seventeenth century. "On Saturdays and feast days, which Christians usually devote to rest and God's service, the young peasants usually stay up until late at night in the company of marriageable young women and, under the pretext that their homes are far away, they ask for hospitality and seek to share the young women's beds, which is commonly called *"alberger"*. The women, after having come to an agreement that their chastity will be protected, and not meeting any opposition from their parents, do not refuse them: they foolishly trust in the the young men's loyalty, alone in the same bed, having however not removed their chemises. Despite the ineffective protection offered by the chemises, it often happens that sexual passion breaks down this ridiculous pact and the door of virginity, and that those who shortly before were virgins become

---

*   *"Escraignes"* were igloo-shaped buildings in Burgundy and Champagne which were made from lumps of earth or sod. During the winter, young unmarried women used to spend the evenings in these *"escraignes"*, sewing, chatting, etc. As a result, young unmarried men used to frequent the *"escraignes"*, in order to court them.

women. What else can be expected of a night-time encounter between lovers, completely alone in this way?"[24]

All these customs involved young people who were not yet engaged. One can assume that, in general, sexual freedom was even greater after young people became engaged than before, and it is even known that in some regions, like Corsica or the Basque country, the engaged couple lived together like man and wife well before their union was blessed by the Church. All such traditional freedoms, whether before or after engagement, were repressed and finally disappeared.[25]

After the Council of Trent, the Church mounted a campaign against engaged couples living together and the episcopal ordinances allow us to establish the date when it was forbidden in each diocese. For example, in the dioceses of Bayonne and Alet, in the Pyrenees, where it was the tradition for engaged couples to cohabit, cohabitation before marriage became grounds for excommunication after 1640. We know the result of this repression to a certain extent: in the Basque village of Urrugne, near Bayonne, only 14% of pregnancies took place before marriage between 1671 and 1730; in Bilhères-d'Ossau, a village in the Béarn, 13% of pregnancies were pre-marital in 1740–1779, then 8% in 1780–1819 and only 3% in 1820–1859.[26]

As for courting before engagement, we know that, in Savoy, "*albergement*" became grounds for excommunication after 1609 and that by 1819, except in one village, it was no longer practised. It even seems to have totally disappeared by 1820.[27] Meeting in the "*escraignes*", traditional in both Champagne and Burgundy, became grounds for excommunication in the diocese of Troyes in 1680. After 1686, according to the bishop, such encounters were already rare; and it seems that they did not reappear in the eighteenth century, at least not in their original form.[28]

It was not only the Catholic Church which was repressive in this way and indeed repression continued into the eighteenth and nineteenth centuries. In the Protestant county of Montbéliard, nocturnal visiting was not tackled until 1772 and even then not so much by the religious authorities as by the civil authorities. It is true that they survived — perhaps saved by the French Revolution — until the last decades of the nineteenth century, as they survived in most of the Protestant countries of the Old and New Worlds. As for the "*maraîchinage vendéen*", I have not found any ecclesiastical passages from before 1880 which denounce it, which is perhaps why the custom was still very much alive at the beginning of the twentieth century. Be that as it may, in this region repression was carried out by the mayors of the Third Republic,[29] and such repression seems to have prevailed over the traditional customs, which have today disappeared.

Thus, in these regions at least, it is obvious that, between the seventeenth and twentieth centuries, young unmarried men and women had had great freedom in courtship according to ancient custom, which they then lost. But how did they traditionally make use of such freedom? This is one of the points upon which I disagree with Shorter. Like Wikman in Finland, who was the great historian of nocturnal courting in Europe, Shorter believes that young people gained no sexual pleasure from these encounters.[30] In any case, for any given age, those who defended traditional customs declared the chastity of such acts. For an example, see what Noël Du Fail wrote in the sixteenth century: "In Germany...young unmarried men and women slept together without any hint of scandal, and their parents, asked about these liberties, reply: '*Caste dormiunt* [they sleep chastely], it is a game with no villainy, and some very good and happy marriages are produced and begun in this way.'" The Frenchman Eutrapel, however, had a different opinion after this period: "Eutrapel who was remarkably scrupulous and did not easily form a good opinion of this close courtship, even concerning Germans today, who having degenerated and lost their original rustic naïvety have become so like the French, the Spanish and the Italians, said that there was no great safety in such approaches: that nature was far too mischievous and that it was putting fire much too near the tinder..."[31] In any period we can find people who did not believe that men could remain chaste when in bed with the woman they loved. For example, there was Noël Du Fail in the sixteenth century, the Archbishop of Tarentaise in the seventeenth and the Duke of Wurtemberg in the eighteenth. These opponents of the traditional customs claimed that such freedom was the cause of countless pre-marital pregnancies and illegitimate births.

To tell the truth, their vision of things does not seem more justifiable to me than that of those who defended the traditional customs. In my opinion, human nature, which they mention, is very reliant on the culture. In some societies, the fact of being alone with a young — or not so young — woman is a sexual stimulus which drives any man to try to have intercourse with her, even more so when the man and woman are in the same bed. Yet — even though "to sleep with someone" does have the same meaning in both French and English — peasants formerly slept with their entire families and yet incest was not common among them, despite what has been said by Bishops of the Counter-Reformation and many historians. Often they even slept with their servants, both male and female, and with guests, which again did not usually have sexual implications. On this point, I am in agreement with Shorter.

But the lovers in question were not in bed with the parents of the young women they were courting: they were in a lovers' bed, either alone with their loved one (in Savoy and in the county of Montbéliard) or near other pairs of lovers (in the Vendée). They were not there in order to sleep but rather to "make love". I do not believe that in peasant culture, they "made love" spiritually or platonically. All the descriptions which we have of rustic lovers show them smacking each other, twisting their fingers or hands, or closely intertwined. This is perhaps symbolic language, but physical, not verbal. Thus we can assume that, at night and in the intimacy of their beds, their dealings were no less physical and that they gained some amount of sexual pleasure from the rubbing of their bodies or playing with their hands and mouths. Only one thing was strictly forbidden: intercourse.

Why did young people in the Vendée or in Deux-Sèvres systematically get together with other couples to engage in *"maraîchinage"*? Evidently it was in order to prevent some from getting carried away and going beyond behaviour which was customarily allowed. In Savoy, before going to bed with the young woman who he was courting, the young man had to swear to respect her virginity. In Scotland, there was a symbolic tying together of the woman's legs; in Scandinavia, Wikman describes other means of avoiding the risk of intercourse, and no doubt there were similar patterns in the county of Montbéliard, since an eighteenth century observer noted that it was "rare for such familiarities to have a result which would damage the woman's reputation".[32] Intercourse was forbidden by tradition everywhere — at least before the couple was engaged — and it seems as though traditional means were in place everywhere in order to respect this taboo. But, although this taboo was respected by almost all couples, tradition also provided them with a pattern of sexual behaviour which was *absque coitu* [without intercourse], which allowed them to satisfy their urges sufficiently. Moreover, the effectiveness of this model can be statistically measured: in the Vendée in the 1830's, where traditional customs survived more than elsewhere in France, the rate of illegitimate births was lower — much lower — than in any other *département* in France.[33]

THE CHALLENGE OF STATISTICS

Demographers have established that illegitimate births and pre-marital pregnancies increased greatly both in the country and in towns between 1750 and 1850, and most see this as incontrovertible proof of the eroticization of behaviour. However, this view of the situation is much less obvious when one considers the repression carried out for centuries. Thus far in this article, I have only shown one part of how this was shown, with particular reference to young people's sexuality. There were many other, less specific examples, such as the suppression of concubinage,[34] the banning of "impure" words and images, etc. Thus it is advisable to look for a change in the pattern of juvenile sexual behaviour which takes into account both the statistics and all the evidence of repression.

Let us first emphasise that in the eighteenth and nineteenth centuries, as in previous centuries, no unmarried woman became a mother by choice: every unmarried mother would have preferred to have sexual relations and children within a legitimate marriage. The increase in the rate of illegitimate births at that time could therefore not have been a sign of women's sexual liberation; rather it indicates the greater difficulty which they faced in marrying the men with whom they had sexual intercourse. It seems to me that this is why the illegitimate birth rate rose first among women of the lower classes. It did not indicate that were more "liberated".

As in previous centuries, the difficulty in getting married could have resulted from an increase in population in a traditional economy. For example, we know that the celibacy rate and the age at first marriage rose in the eighteenth century in small towns such as Thoissey (Ain) or Boulay (Moselle), in villages in the county of Arthies (Val-d'Oise), or in Isbergues (Pas-de-Calais), all of which were little affected by industrialisation.[35] In those places where, on the contrary, the age at marriage dropped — for example in Sainghin-en-Mélantois (Nord) or in Cortaillod (in the canton of Neuchâtel), this might be as a result of industrialisation. A comparison of the last two villages shows however that economic explanations alone are not enough: in Sainghin, the illegitimacy rate rose from 0.6% before 1789 to 5.7% after 1810, whereas in Cortaillod it remained around 1%, with only the rate of pre-marital pregnancies increasing.[36]

In France, the increase in illegitimacy rates might to a certain extent result from women being rendered legally defenceless against their seducers. Before the Council of Trent, when a young man had

promised a young woman that he would marry her, sexual intercourse between them validated the marriage, and it was enough that
the woman was able to prove that the promise had been made for the
Church to consecrate their union. After the Council, this became
impossible in a Catholic country, although it survived in Protestant
countries, as in the canton of Neuchâtel for example. In the seventeenth century, however, when the seduced woman was under
twenty-five years of age, her parents could apply pressure on her
seducer by threatening to bring charges of abduction and seduction
against him. As this crime was punishable by death, the seducer often
preferred to marry the woman. But the Church's opposition to forced
marriages and the State's opposition to unequal marriages combined
to take this possibility away from parents after 1730. Under these
circumstances, it is hardly surprising that an increasing number of
women were unable to marry the men who had given them a child.

Traditionally, when he did not marry the woman whom he had
made pregnant, the seducer had to at least pay the costs of childbirth
and child-rearing That was demanded of him as soon as the woman
had lodged a complaint against him, even though it meant paying
him back if it turned out that she had accused him incorrectly. This
procedure, which annoyed liberal jurists, was ended in the eighteenth
century. After that time, before she could receive anything, the
woman had to provide proof of her accusations, which was often
difficult and always took a long time. The final step was that, after the
Revolution, the Civil Code forbade any search for the father of an
illegitimate child. Thus, unmarried mothers were considered to be the
only ones responsible for their children's conception and had to bear
the financial consequences themselves, despite the fact that most of
them had no resources. This shift to the right — one of the obvious
consequences of which was the increase in the number of children
abandoned in the eighteenth and nineteenth centuries — may have
also encouraged men to seduce women after promising to marry them
and then to abandon them.

Other laws may also have contributed to the increase in pre-marital
pregnancies. Like Shorter, I have for a long time seen this increase as
merely a manifestation of the trend towards marrying for love.[37] But
it could also be explained along almost opposite lines: in the same way
as the popular revolts of the seventeenth century bear witness to the
reinforcing of royal absolutism against which the revolts only offered
resistance, so pre-marital pregnancies might have been young people's final weapon against their parents' growing tyranny. The Coun-

cil of Trent's decree concerning the reformation of marriage on the one hand, the royal laws against clandestine marriages and against abduction and seduction on the other hand, did in fact take away from them any other ways of marrying their loved ones against their parents' wishes. It seems that the increase of pre-marital pregnancies began in the seventeenth century, in the middle of a period of repression; and furthermore we know that some women at least did not hesitate to get pregnant by the men who they wanted to marry, in order to force their parents' hand.[38] More research needs to be done in order to discover whether such behaviour was the exception or whether it was frequent enough to explain at least in part the increase in pre-marital pregnancies — and, of course, the increase in illegitimate births, for parents did not always allow their hand to be forced, and lovers were not always faithful.[39]

Aside from these legal changes, I distinguish four factors, of varying importance, which could explain the increase both in the number of illegitimate births and in pre-marital pregnancies. The first is the rise in age at marriage and the increase in the proportion of bachelors, which I have already mentioned. Indeed, it is obvious that — all else being equal — the greater the number of bachelors in a group of women of marriageable age, the greater the risk of illegitimate pregnancy.

The second is the abolition of the freedom of traditional courting customs. Undoubtedly this forced the more obedient to repress their sexual urges or to satisfy them on their own. But not all young unmarried people resigned themselves to this. Those young men and women who persisted in having sexual relations could only do so in secret. Because they no longer had the traditional supervision of the young people of the village and because they had lost the non-coital pattern of making love, they were more likely to have intercourse than in the past and thus more likely to conceive children outside of marriage.

This hypothesis is actually based on fact: it is striking to notice, on a map of illegitimate birth rates in France around 1830, that those departments in which traditional freedom survived were also those in which the number of illegitimate births was the lowest: the department of Hautes-Alpes was only sixty-eighth, and almost all the illegitimate births there were probably due to the garrison towns;[40] the *département* of Deux-Sèvres was seventy-fourth; Haute-Loire was seventy-nineth; Côtes-du-Nord eighty-third; and the Vendée eighty-sixth and last.[41] In the Bocage Vendéen, where, around 1900, young

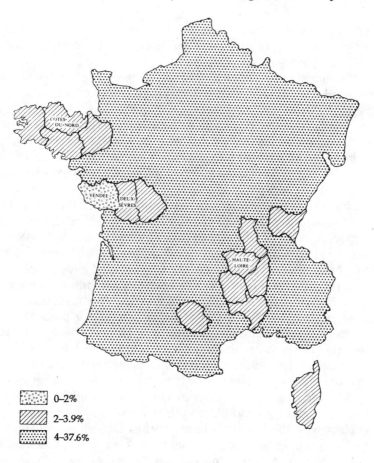

Illegitimate birth rates c. 1830 (Based on A. Hugo I, 77).

people only abandoned the traditional "*migaillage*" in order to substitute *coitus interruptus* in its place,[42] the illegitimate birth rate remained approximately stable,[43] and the marital fertility rate began to drop. At the same time, in those areas in which the traditional pre-marital practices were repressed before *coitus interruptus* became popular, the marital fertility rate remained high and pregnancies outside of marriage increased.

In towns, the closing of municipal brothels — whose purpose was to keep young unmarried men away from "honest" women — might have been a third factor in the increase in illegitimate birth rates, although it is difficult to judge the immediate effects of this, since we do not have illegitimacy rates for France in the sixteenth and the beginning of the seventeenth century.

The fourth factor seems to me to be the growing number of young unmarried women from the country who went to the towns looking for work. Poor, isolated and more used to "making love" than young women born in towns, they must have been easier to seduce. In fact, of the young unmarried women who registered their pregnancies in large towns in the eighteenth century — in Nantes, for example — the majority were young women from the country who were living and had become pregnant in towns.[44]

I have shown elsewhere how the number of pre-marital pregnancies began to increase in the country in the first half of the seventeenth century; and that, in the second half, the number of illegitimate births in towns began to increase, and the number of foundlings even more so.[45] Nonetheless, the effects of the four factors I have proposed can only fully be measured after 1750, when the moral pressure of the Catholic Reformation on towns and the country was slightly relaxed. It is only natural that there would be alternating phases of great repression and of relative relaxation of repression, which are logically connected, over the period of several centuries which I am examining. I am not attempting to deny this cycle. But I wished first and foremost to show that the repression which reached its peak between 1650 and 1750 had started as early as the sixteenth century, and that it continued into the eighteenth and nineteenth centuries. I will now attempt to explain why the relative relaxation after 1750 allowed illegitimate births and pre-marital pregnancies to reach a much higher level than before the Reformation. In my opinion, this is not because sexual urges were less repressed in the eighteenth and nineteenth centuries than in the fifteenth and sixteenth, but rather for the reasons which I have stated, and particularly because the ancient structures of people's sex lives had been destroyed.

THE INTERNALISATION OF DESIRE

Although the rise in pre-marital pregnancies and illegitimate births is, for demographers, the main indicator of the change in habits, this is not so for a historian of sexuality. For him, the most important point is that tolerated and acknowledged patterns of sexual behaviour were replaced by reprehensible and secret ones, perceived quite differently.

Yet, if we consider the whole of sexual activity among marriageable unmarried men and women — in the seventeenth, eighteenth, nineteenth and well into the twentieth century — clandestine intercourse probably played only a minor role. On the whole, no doubt, young people most often satisfied their sexual urges through practices which were even more secret and which were sometimes perceived as being even more reprehensible.

The emergence of the problem of "Onanism"[46] in eighteenth century medical writings obviously does not mean that the "solitary practices" were not indulged in before that time. From the early Middle Ages to the eighteenth century, ample proof of the existence of such practices is provided by confessors, and if doctors rarely spoke of it, that can be explained by the fact that they saw in it no danger to health.[47] Some, such as Fallopius in the sixteenth century, even recommended masturbation as a means of enlarging the penis.[48] But, after indicating my total disagreement with Shorter on these points, I must say why I believe, as he does, that such "solitary practices" gained ground over the centuries, and that this fact is significant in the formation of the medical myth of "Onanism".

During the early Middle Ages, solitary masturbation seems to have been for the most part a sin committed by clerics: the penitentials, which, concerning other sexual sins, always implicate laymen, scarcely speak of any but ecclesiastics concerning this sin. This ceases to be true at the beginning of the fourteenth century: see the list of cases reserved for the Bishop of Cambrai (*see*, pp. 105). At the end of the century, Gerson, in the special treatise which he devotes to this sin, testifies that it is frequent among adolescents, and that many adults can even be found who continue to masturbate.

At the same time, the attitudes of ecclesiastic authorities towards it changed. In principle it is one of the most serious of sexual sins because, as the theologians say, it is a "sin against nature". In practice, however, confessors seemed for a long time to consider it a lesser evil. The penitentials only administered several weeks of penance to masturbators, whereas those guilty of fornication with a woman received penances of one or several years. From the twelfth century to the last quarter of the fourteenth, moreover, masturbation is not listed among the "reserved cases" — those sins which the Bishop alone can absolve. It only appears on the list after 1388, as though the ecclesiastic authorities, observing that it was practised by people intending to marry — and no longer only by clerics committed to celibacy — decided to mount a campaign against this sin.

In fact, "pollution" of this kind could not long remain a reserved case if it was common among the people. This is probably why the lists of reserved cases from the sixteenth, seventeenth and eighteenth centuries do not mention it, while we find an increasing number of references to the frequency of this habit among adolescents of both sexes.[49] To the question "What now are the most common mortal sins?" a 1682 manual for confessors in the diocese of Châlon-sur-Saône replied: "Among young people they are dishonest thoughts, the sins of laxity and impurity", i.e. erotic thoughts and solitary masturbation. It was recommended that confessors systematically interrogate young unmarried women as well as men on this subject. Given that, from the Middle Ages onwards, the Church was conscious of the risk of teaching sins to those innocent of them, and that the command for prudence increased in the seventeenth and eighteenth centuries, such systematic questioning would only have been recommended if the sin was not uncommon.

As adolescents were increasingly prevented from satisfying their sexual desires in any other way, they turned more and more to masturbation. Those schools and colleges which had been founded in the sixteenth and seventeenth centuries as much in order to preserve adolescents' chastity as to educate them, acquired in the eighteenth century the reputation of being places of corruption where this "virus" was inevitably caught. Educators and confessors were able to impress abomination of the sin upon children, could forbid them all other sexual activities, through strict surveillance, but nothing could prevent nor cure the habit of the "solitary pleasure", even in the best-behaved children. Thus masturbation appeared to these doctors of the soul to be an incurable disease. This then was the backdrop against which the medical myth of "Onanism" began and grew.

An English moralist named Bekker seems to have been the first, around 1710, to combine medical arguments with the ethical arguments against masturbation. His book, entitled *Onania, or the Heinous sin of Self Pollution, and all its frightful consequences in both sexes considered with Spiritual and Physical Advice to those who have already injur'd themselves by this abominable Practise*, was very successful: twelve editions by 1727 and many others afterwards. Moreover, between one edition and the next, the book was expanded by new letters from repentant sinners who, in order to thank the writer and to contribute towards saving their fellow man, collected examples — each more horrible than the last — of the illnesses likely to afflict masturbators.[50] When the celebrated Dr. Tissot wrote the first of a long series of medical books on this subject in 1760, he only brought scientific caution to the myth which had been spontaneously created. This medical myth, produced and enlarged by repression, came to reinforce the repression even more. I doubt that it "cured" many adolescents of their "villainous habit", but it definitely increased their torment.

That is not all. Repression did not only force single people to satisfy their urges by practices which were secret and perceived with anxiety: it led them to take even more pleasure in erotic thoughts and in analysing their unsatisfied desires. This kind of "intellectual masturbation" increased our sensibilities — of which we are generally quite proud — but has also led us to structure our desires in solitude, which makes sexual harmony within a couple more difficult. I will give only a few examples of this historical process which can be called "eroticization" and which deserves to be studied in more depth.

Firstly, pornographic literature was born in modern times, and is very different from the amorous or bawdy stories of the Middle Ages and the Renaissance. Such literature of transgression shows, by its very existence and its status, the strengthening of sexual repression. And if one were to make a systematic analysis, it would no doubt allow us to specify the changes in erotic imagination.

On the other hand, one could show how the analysis of feelings has progressed by studying the vocabulary.[51] Thus, the words "*tendresse*" [in English "tenderness"] and "*sentiment*" seem to to be creations of the seventeenth century; and "*sentimental*" the creation of the second half of the eighteenth century. The word "*amour*", although it already existed in the fifteenth century, was often used then to signify something which one does rather than something which one feels. This usage soon only survived among peasants. New words and usage, concerning feelings, often appeared first in devout literature; in such a way that Christianity, which played an important role in the repressing of Western sexuality, appears also to have assisted in our sentimental education.

Obviously, there were many other factors which participated in this education: I am thinking particularly of the novel, that most intimate of literary genres — since poetry was, for thousands of years, intended to be heard rather than read. It is a genre which was only really born in modern times and only triumphed in the nineteenth century. I see in this triumph another manifestation of the advance of solitary reverie. Indeed, to a certain extent, our entire modern society — our sensibility and our passivity — seems to have arisen from sexual repression.

APPENDIX

SIXTEENTH CENTURY RAPES

The Rape of Jeanne Jacquet (1516)

Jeanne, daughter of the late Jean Jacquet...is about 20 years of age and lives with her mother who is remarried to Jean de Bergières. On the night of the feast of St Peter and St Paul (29 June), the defendant Henry Chevry, a cleric who lives in Villy-le-Maréchal, accompanied by Colas Houzelot from Ronceray, Jean Benoît from Saint-Jean-de-Bonneval, Claude Ruynel, and one Pierre, the servant of Martin Godey from Villy-le-Maréchal, came knocking on Jean de Bergières' door and on his neighbours'.

When one of the neighbours asked the visitors what they wanted, they answered: "Do not listen to any noise you might hear", and they knocked once more at Jean de Bergières' door. Everyone inside the house was in bed. The mother, upon hearing the noise, made her daughter get up and go to the attic. While this was happening, the companions were breaking down the door. Jean Benoît, Claude Ruynel and the servant entered the house and began looking for Jeanne. They looked in her bed, in the bread store, in the oven, and when they failed to find her, they went up to the attic where they discovered her. They forced her to come down, dragged her outside and took her to a garden where they raped her, one after the other. The defendant, who had not gone into Jean de Bergières' house, at first refused to emulate his accomplices' actions. "Come! Come! Boldly!", they cried to him. "Cover her eyes then", replied the defendant, "for she would easily recognise me". Pierre, Martin Godey's servant, covered Jeanne's face with his hand. Then the defendant drew near to her and raped her, but Jeanne did recognise him for she pushed aside the hand that Pierre was holding over her face and scratched him. Jeanne adds that the defendant and his accomplices beat her so hard when they were dragging her that ever since she has been unable to work and has had to leave the house in which she was a servant.

Jean Cototte, a wine grower whose house is next to Jean de Bergières' did hear a row around two in the morning, the sound of blows — but he could not say who or what was being hit — and Jean de Bergières' voice shouting "Jacquinot Cototte! Jehan Denisot! Help!" But he did not stir...

Jeannette, the wife of Jean Le Bigle, a wine grower whose house is a stone's throw away from Jean de Bergières', testifies that she was in bed with her husband when she heard Jean de Bergières crying: "Murder!

Neighbours, friends, help!" She got up and, looking between two boards, she saw three men she did not recognise running towards Jean de Bergières' house. Then she wanted to go outside, but one of the men came towards her and said: "Do not come out; we do not wish to do any harm; we want to catch a harlot." She closed her door and looking out again from between the boards, she saw the three men near Jean de Bergières' house. "By God's Death and Flesh", they were saying, "Open the door, harlot!"...

Claude Roslin, the mayor of Villy-le-Maréchal, testifies that two or three days after the feast of St Peter and St Paul, as the rumour was that the defendant and his accomplices had abducted Jeanne, he summoned several witnesses before him in order to begin proceedings on the case. Upon hearing this, the defendant and his accomplices left the region. Two or three weeks later, the defendant came back, sought out the witness, and came to an agreement with him.

Jean Fourny, a wine-grower who was the provost of Isle-Aumont at the time of the abduction, testifies that Jeanne's mother sought him out about a week after the feast of St Peter and St Paul and asked for justice to be done. He therefore held an investigation and showed the results to Maître Antoine Huyard, Lieutenant to the bailiff of Isle-Aumont, who, after having seen it, ordered the arrest of the defendant and his accomplices and entrusted him with carrying it out...[The provost goes to the defendant's home and finds him hiding in a haystack.] He climbed up the haystack with a ladder and plunged his spear into the hay, saying "Come out! Must you hide for having done such a thing?"...Henry Cheverny, upon finding himself summoned, asked the witness to let him go, and asked for the summons not to be pursued, saying that he preferred to give him something by way of compensation than to be summonsed. "Don't give me anything if you don't have to", the provost answered several times, "I ask nothing of you, except for this case". However, upon receiving 3 *sous* and 4 *deniers tournois* by way of compensation, he let him go. As for the Sergeant, he received 10 *deniers*.

It was the witness' successor as provost of Isle-Aumont who, after another investigation, had the defendant summonsed to appear in person before him and finally turned him over [to the *Officialité*] since he was a cleric.

A.D. Aube, Inventaire, series G, vol. II, p. 387.

The Rape of Perrette (1516)

Perrette sent her little boy to be nursed in the home of Jean Gauthier, a wine grower who lived in Barberey-aux-Moines. On the day of St Denis (9 October) she was in Barberey, having come to see her child.

In the evening, when Jean Gauthier was already in bed and his wife and Perrette were undressing in front of the fire in order to follow him to bed, they heard someone knocking at the door. Jean Gauthier's wife went to open it, and found Jean Conte and Jean Villain outside. They came into the house and asked to buy some larks. "My children", said Jean Gauthier, "I have no larks." Then one of them said: "Jehan Gauthier, you have two women, you don't need them both. Keep your own, we need this one." "You will not have her nor will you have me", answered Gauthier's wife. Finally they left, saying "Others will come before long."

Whereupon Gauthier's wife and Perrette climbed into the bed where Jean Gauthier and his manservant already were. An hour or two later, the defendants came back with several accomplices. They knocked at the door with great violence, and when nobody came to open it, they took it off its hinges. Once inside, they pulled Perrette out of bed, beat her, and dragged her outside, clad only in her chemise. They took her out to the fields like that, beating her with sticks until her skin was black and blue.

Once they were out in the field, they had her put on her petticoat which one of them had taken. Then Jean Conte and three or four of his accomplices raped her, and one of them knew her twice. Then they took her back to Jean Gauthier's house, and as they were leading her back, they said: "If we were to find out that you were going to make a complaint against us, we would cut your throat." Perrette, in fear of being killed or thrown into the river, replied that she would not complain. When they got back to the house, the defendants and their accomplices asked her once more: "By God's Death! Are you going to make a complaint against us?" and one of them wanted to give her money, but she refused to accept it.

As for Jean Gauthier, he claims...that when he saw his house invaded by the defendants and their accomplices, he went up to the attic to find his javelin, but could not locate it.

A.D. Aube, Inventaire, series G, vol. II, pp. 385–6.

Chapter 15

Family Life and Illicit Love in England
A Review of Peter Laslett's Book[*]

Whether they realise it or not, the social sciences need history. I am as convinced of this as Peter Laslett, Director of the Cambridge Group for the History of Population and Social Structure. As people facing the twenty-first century, we need to know "how far we differ from past people and how much we are the same". I would add that we need to understand how past social structures changed, over what time-scale, using what mechanisms and for what reasons. At the same time, it is essential to make social scientists aware of those components of present-day society which come to us from the past, are explained by the past — no matter what pretexts the present disguises them with — and which, to a certain extent, limit our future. Neither individuals nor societies can wipe the slate clean; and the fact that, like individuals, societies are often in a sorry state because of their histories, can only increase the interest which genuine historical sociology holds for us.

It must be said that currently the only serious collaboration is between historians and demographers, and it must be admitted that such collaboration is mostly due to the demographers' efforts. Indeed they themselves felt the need to delve into the past and, unlike most other social scientists with an interest in history, they knew how to

---

[*]   *Family Life and Illicit Love in Earlier Generations*, Cambridge and New York, Cambridge University Press, 1977.

get hold of ancient documents. In this task they were guided and supervised by Chartists and historians, but it was always the demographers who led the investigation, and in particular it was the demographers who perfected the methods used in historical demography. This field has not only extended the demographers' area of interest into the past, but enhanced the study of history, as shown by the sheer volume of French, English and American publications over the past twenty years. To go even further, because of the rigour of these methods, historical demography has changed the epistemological status of history. The Director of the Cambridge Group is one of those historians who understood this as early as the beginning of the 1960s. But rather than locking himself into the demographers' narrow problematics — as did many young historians, particularly in France — he immediately began to try to escape from it and to carry the rigorous methods out into the wider field of historical sociology.

His undertaking gained in importance because sociologists proved unable to establish as fruitful a partnership with historians as demographers had been able to develop. Primarily, this is because many sociologists are not interested in the past, not believing that studying it is relevant to understanding the present. Secondly, scorning the historian's esoteric and fastidious task of gathering and criticising documents, sociologists only make use of his conclusions without being able to assess either their reliability or their scope. Thus they find themselves in the paradoxical situation of being more certain about the past, of which we shall never have more than an incomplete and distorted image, than about the present, the complexity of which they are very familiar. Finally, it does happen that they themselves invent a largely mythical history of the phenomena which they are studying, based solely on their analysis of the present and the requirements of their theories. For an example of this, take the history of the family which sociologists had us believe for more than a century. As a result of the detailed work of the Cambridge Group, we are now convinced that the simple family unit, which sociologists believed to be characteristic of industrial societies, existed and indeed prevailed in north-western Europe several centuries before the Industrial Revolution. It even appears that, contrary to all expectations, the proportion of extended and multiple family households increased in England when industrialisation took place.

In fact, although historical demography was originated by demographers in collaboration with historians, the historical sociology which Peter Laslett gives us is the result of a demographer-historian who disagrees with the poorly thought out historical theories of traditional sociology. However, in the seven historical sociology essays which he has grouped together under the title *Family Life and Illicit Love in Earlier Generations*, confrontation with sociologists seems no longer to be an issue. Instead the introduction is aimed at historians: he tries to show how examining statistics from the past can help them to shed light on contemporary beliefs concerning the family.

The first, previously unpublished essay, "Characteristics of the Western Family Considered over Time", opens up new perspectives on the Western family pattern. According to the essay, it is distinguished not only by the predominance of the simple family unit — which may also be found in other regions of the world with completely different cultures — but by the existence of three other characteristics: the high average age at first pregnancy, the small average age gap between spouses and the high proportion of servants or households including servants. The ten tables of statistics in this first chapter support this theory by showing the absence of at least one of these characteristics in the southern, central and western parts of Europe, whereas all four are found in the north-western countries: England, the northern half of France, the Netherlands, Scandinavia and part of Germany. The only one of these characteristics which is at all doubtful — as the author acknowledges — is the existence of a large number of servants, since the percentage of servants in the province of Holland was only 5.9%. I would add that, in several villages in the northern half of France, there appear to have been even fewer,[1] and that the three figures given for France are not very significant since two of them concern towns. In this respect, England seems much more "Western" than the other countries. This is perhaps due on the one hand to the very unequal system of property ownership and the existence of very large farms, and on the other to the practice of "fostering", which surprised and shocked people from the Continent on their travels across the Channel. However we must not conclude too hastily that the model given is exclusively English: other phenomena such as industrialisation, despite being particularly English, have nonetheless been characteristic of the West as a whole. Moreover, there are many societies in the world in which there are no servants at all.

Laslett's theory would be particularly interesting if there was a logical relationship between the four characteristics considered. The fact that married children were not usually welcome in their parents' house — proven by the almost non-existence of multiple family households — made marriage more difficult and thus raised the average age at first pregnancy despite the not insignificant rate of illegitimate births. But this also calls into question the Western custom of only marrying a young woman if she had a dowry, the importance of which the Cambridge Group seems to me to underestimate. Moreover and conversely, because of the late age at first pregnancy, it was more likely that young people might marry after their parents' deaths, which inevitably limited the number of extended households. This also points out the relationship between the small age gap between spouses and the advanced age of young women at their first marriage, and therefore at their first pregnancy. Lastly, if parents were unable to provide their daughters with a dowry, they had to earn their dowry by working as servants for many years. That is particularly logical at a time when many heads of households had to work on other people's farms in order to provide for their families, as was the case in English society. Thus I regret that Peter Laslett has as yet given little thought to the relationship between the four characteristics of the Western familial pattern, the customs for the formation of couples and economic and social structures.

No doubt he deems such an analysis premature. Fearing to imitate so many sociologist who have championed their own theories at the cost of establishing facts, he wants first and foremost to define the extension of the "Western familial pattern" within time and space. If it had existed in the West before the dowry system began, or before the development of a landless peasant class, the explanations that I am suggesting would prove obsolete. The Cambridge Group researchers have the impression that this familial pattern existed in England as early as the Middle Ages, perhaps in antiquity.[2] I am in no way convinced of this, particularly since a certain number of facts suggest that in France it arose between the last centuries of the Middle Ages and the Industrial Revolution. Thus it could be the result of economic and social changes which laid the groundwork for the Industrial Revolution throughout the West. Be that as it may, I doubt that one can establish unquestionable facts in this area for antiquity and the early Middle Ages, and it would therefore seem judicious to me to begin immediately to explore the logic of the pattern.

The second essay, "Clayworth and Cogenhoe", is remarkable for the simplicity of the methods used, the effectiveness of the statistical analysis and for the wealth and originality of the conclusions. It is worth mentioning that the article of the same title published fifteen years ago, although greatly revised and extended for this book, possessed the same qualities. The Cambridge Group has been able to derive some very important information concerning English society in the seventeenth century from parish registers kept by the rectors of these two villages: the diversity of trades in the villages; the almost complete absence of the large complex households which sociologists had believed to be characteristic of the pre-industrial period; and the continuous turnover of a population which had been believed to be very sedentary. The turnover rate in Clayworth was 61.8% over a period of twelve years and in Cogenhoe, 52.2% over 10 years — or 39.6% and 36.1% if one only considers population migration and not births and deaths.

In place of the image of the peasant rooted to the soil for several generations, Peter Laslett has substituted that of farmers and labourers forced to change parish several times in the course of their short married lives; in place of the image of faithful old retainers working in the same household for their whole lives, he substitutes that of servants who are almost always young and who do not stay in one place. Laslett claims this to be true not only for England in the seventeenth century, but northern France in the eighteenth. Thus, in Longuenesse (Pas-de-Calais) — where the turnover rate was lower than in the two English villages — between 1778 and 1790, 51% of servants remained in the parish for only one year, 14% stayed for two, 8% for three, 6% for four, 4% for five, 10% for between six and twelve years and 7% for thirteen years and more (see Table 2.6 reprinted in the appendix, p. 306). The old faithful retainers did exist — in France at least — but they represented only a tiny minority, as these figures show.

However, I am not satisfied with this proof. In my opinion, the method of calculation chosen by Laslett and his colleague Emmanuel Todd greatly exaggerates the movement of servants. Let n_1 be the number of servants in Longuenesse in the 1778 census, n_2 their number in 1779, n_3 in 1780...n_13 in 1790. The author does not give us these figures, but by using Table 2.6 it is possible to estimate the total number N of servants in Longuenesse in the censuses from 1778 to 1790 and their average number n in an average year:

$$n = \frac{(78 \times 1) + (22 \times 2) + (13 \times 3) + (9 \times 4) + (6 \times 5) + \left(15 \times \dfrac{6 + 7 + 8 + 9 + 10 + 11 + 12}{7}\right) + (10 \times 13)}{13} = \frac{492}{13} = 37.8$$

In other words, there were thirty-seven or thirty-eight servants in Longuenesse on average, of which six (or 16%) remained only one year, whereas eleven (or 30%) stayed between two and five years, ten (or 27%) between six and twelve years and ten (or 26%) thirteen years or more. This is quite different from the image portrayed by Table 2.6! Although it is true that there were many individuals who did not stay in Longuenesse for more than a year, at any given time these "nomads" never represented more than a small minority of the servants in the village. The majority of the servants (54%) stayed in the village for at least six years, and more than a quarter (26%) stayed there as servants for thirteen years or more.

Such carelessness on the part of the author is an opportunity for me to make two points. Firstly, even in the best studies and even when authors are not trying to prove a pre-conceived idea, they may still give us an incorrect impression by the use of faultless statistics. Secondly, microstatistics — of which I am a great supporter — do however have several disadvantages. If instead of working with individual villages, the Cambridge Group researchers had studied migration patterns based on regional censuses, they would probably have found the same "nomadic" servants in several villages over the thirteen years in question. They would then have realised that such servants cannot be counted each time that they appear if servants who remained thirteen years in the same village are only counted once. My idea is obviously unrealistic given that annual censuses for entire regions do not exist and that problems of identification, already difficult within one parish, would become insurmountable within a region. My aim is only to point out one of the disadvantages of analyses carried out within individual parishes, no matter how many are done.

The greatest merit of the third essay, "Long-term Trends in Bastardy in England", is that it is based on the study of a large number of parishes — one hundred and sixty-five or even four hundred and four for some tables — which, if I am not mistaken, is a record number. In France, the extensive survey carried out by the Institut National d'Etudes Démographiques (INED), the first overall results of which were published in November 1975, has the disadvantage of only covering the period 1740–1829. Thus, as far as the number of bastards is concerned, it could only confirm and clarify what has been known since the eighteenth century, i.e. that their numbers increased continuously during the period. The Cambridge Group's study, on the other hand, covers more than four centuries — from the 1540s to the 1960s — and thus provides information on a period about which we previously knew nothing specific — or at least nothing before the publication of *The World We Have Lost* (1965), which itself contained statistics on illegitimacy based on a sample of fifteen parishes.

Since 1965, the statistical base of the study has been broadened significantly, which has provided interesting refinements to the first set of results, but does not change the general pattern of the statistics. They reveal a high level of bastardy in the sixteenth century reaching its peak in the 1600s; a low level in the seventeenth century with a marked drop in the 1650s; then regular and continuous growth from 1650 to 1820 approximately, with a high level in the years 1820–1850 exceeding that of the 1600s. This overall pattern is found in all regions of England, although the levels reached and the rates of change are strikingly different from one to the next (see graph p. 300). This pattern of illegitimacy in England is similar to that found in France and in other European countries — about which much less is known for the sixteenth and seventeenth centuries — with the European statistics being replicated at least half a century later. This is the most interesting point raised by the figures. It remains only to interpret and explain the variations.

The main issue is to find out to what extent they reveal men and women's tendency to have sexual relations outside of marriage. On this point, the author's caution contrasts sharply with many French historians' lack of the same. Indeed he stresses that they represent variations in the "illegitimacy ratio" which is a more ambiguous indicator than the "illegitimacy rate".[3] Certainly, the illegitimacy ratio is roughly proportional to the frequency of extramarital sexual relations, but also to the numbers of single women or widows of child-bearing age. In other words, it is inversely proportional to the marriage rate. Moreover, it is directly proportional to the almost impossible to measure fertility of extramarital relations, but inversely proportional to marital fertility. In principal, all else being equal, the illegitimacy ratio increases when the marital fertility rate drops, or when the age at marriage rises.

What is surprising in England is that the opposite seems to have occurred. Between 1640 and 1690, at a time when the illegitimacy ratio was at its lowest, the mean age of young women at their first marriage seems to have been at its highest and the marital fertility rate at its lowest. While the illegitimacy ratio increased, throughout the eighteenth century, and reached levels at the beginning of the nineteenth century which were much higher than those of the sixteenth century, female celibacy was decreasing — as shown by the drop in the average age at marriage — and the marital fertility rate was apparently rising. Lastly, from 1850 to 1940, there were again decreases in both illegitimate births and marital fertility. The conclusion which could be drawn from these parallel developments is that the trend in sexual relations outside of marriage varied more than the illegitimacy ratio. Another possibility is that the fertility of such relations varied in the same direction as those of marital relations, but much more so. This could suggest the following hypothesis: when lovers had recourse to contraceptive methods, married couples followed suit, albeit with less dedication. Peter Laslett, with due caution, prefers to stick to the facts. He contents himself with pointing out the parallels between the changes in the illegitimacy ratio and rate over four centuries.

But are these facts established beyond all doubt? Is it possible to speak of changes in age at marriage and in marital fertility in pre-industrial England with as much assurance as for variations in the illegitimacy ratio? I am not convinced that it is. In both cases, the author provides only one set of evidence, that of Colyton. I do know that he is also referring vaguely to the approximately fifteen villages for which the Cambridge Group has reconstituted families following Louis Henry's method. But as far as I know this difficult work has not yet yielded any publications, and no figures relating to these villages has been cited in this book. Thus the attentive reader is placed in the position of having to rely on the author — particularly insofar as fertility is concerned. This is even more disconcerting because in other respects this collection of essays is full of justifications and figures.

There is more. Tables 3.1 and 3.2 (see Appendix, pp. 307–309) provide us with the decadal ratios of baptisms to marriage, i.e. a rough picture of marital fertility, Table 3.1 giving figures for twenty-four selected parishes, and Table 3.2 for four hundred and four parishes. In both cases, the facts are identical: according to table 3.2, for example, when there were on average more than four children per marriage — between 1610 and 1709 — the illegitimacy ratio ranged between 0.94 and 2.61 (1.3 on average); when there were fewer than four children per marriage — from 1580 to 1609 and, with one exception, from 1710–1809 — then the illegitimacy ratio reached high levels: 3.04 on average between 1580 and 1609 and 3.7 between 1710 and 1809.

Was this only due to changes in the marriage rate? The question must be asked, for, on the one hand, it is usually accepted that the age at marriage rose in the seventeenth century and dropped in the eighteenth; on the other hand, the drop in the rate of demographic growth, very marked between 1650 and 1699, suggests a drop in fertility. Yet, as in all European countries, it is the mortality rate which seems to me to explain this demographic stagnation. Indeed, if we calculate the ratio of deaths to baptisms, this will give a rough indication of the mortality rate: between 1580 and 1639, it is always below 0.94 (0.82 on average); between 1640 and 1699, it is always above 0.98 (1.06 on average); between 1700 and 1809 — with the exception of the 1720s — it is below 0.86 (0.815 on average).

In the second half of the seventeenth century, more individuals from all age groups died than in previous or subsequent periods. The deaths of pregnant women inevitably lead to a drop in the fertility rate. In particular, the increase in the number of deaths during the first weeks of life — rarely noted in death registers — gives the impression of a drop in marital fertility, given that on average English children were baptised about a fortnight after their birth. Lastly, it seems that the period between birth and baptism increased during the seventh century — Wrigley showed this in Colyton — and that, obviously, adds to the false impression that the fertility rate dropped. Under these circumstances, the study of marital fertility in England in the pre-industrial period seems to me to be very difficult; I have not been convinced by Wrigley's conclusions on birth control in Colyton in the seventeenth century, and it is difficult for me, not yet having seen the result of his new studies of about fifteen parishes, to accept the ideas put forward in this book concerning the parallel changes in illegitimacy and marital fertility in England.

The curve showing illegitimate births given in this chapter is interesting in that it is based on the study of a greater number of parishes. Yet it is its macrostatistical nature which makes the attempted analysis deceiving, for we do not, for the moment, possess the necessary instruments for a strict statistical analysis. On a national level, assessment of rates of fertility, mortality, marriage or celibacy remain too approximate. Specific data on these factors exist for some parishes only, indeed for one alone in the case of the fertility rate. It is deceptive to establish a correlation between the fluctuations in the fertility rate of one parish and those of the illegitimacy rate in the country as a

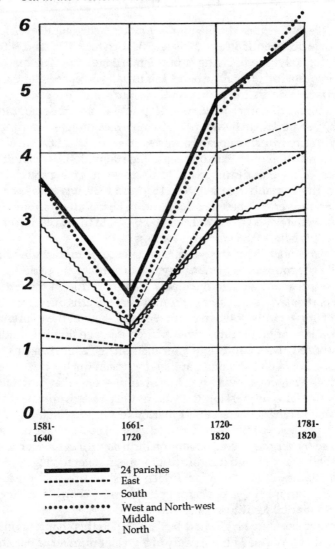

1581- 1640	1661- 1720	1720- 1820	1781- 1820

━━━━━━━ 24 parishes
- - - - - - - East
– – – – – – South
•••••••••• West and North-west
────── Middle
∿∿∿∿∿ North

Illegitimacy ratios in five regions of England.

whole, for the illegitimate birth curve given is nothing but the result of very diverse parish curves, many of which have very different shapes, particularly that of Colyton.[4] Thus, in my opinion, the author ought to have made more of an effort to point out the very hypothetical nature of his interpretations, or to point out to us specifically which new figures in the second edition of this work could corroborate them.

"Long-term Trends in Bastardy in England" offers us more than this significant illegitimacy curve covering four centuries. Even though he sometimes appears to be too obsessed by statistics, Peter Laslett clearly feels that, behind the abstraction of the illegitimacy ratio, there are women and men who had sexual relations in various circumstances which it is important to note, for that is what historical reality consists of. In France, it is possible to find out more about these women because of the thousands — perhaps hundreds of thousands — of declarations which they made to royal, municipal or seigniorial officers. In England, where this source does not seem to have existed, historians must patiently examine family records reconstituted from parish registers. The research is thus more difficult, but may eventually lead to a more accurate image of illegitimacy in rural areas. Indeed, because unwed mothers tended not to leave their villages in order to give birth in a large town, as was the case in France, it is possible to study these young women in their own social surroundings; to find out what they did after giving birth to bastards; to find out whether their propensity for illegitimate pregnancies continued or not, and why; whether they had inherited it from their ancestors and whether they themselves passed it on to their descendants. His treatment of these questions can be found in the final pages of the first version of this study.

In this version, the author gives us the proportion of women in three villages who had more than one illegitimate child: this proportion tends to increase or decrease at the same time as the illegitimacy ratio, but to a much greater extent. Does this indicate that it was easier to separate unmarried couples or to chase "women of low moral standards" from the village than it was to persuade single women and widows to refrain from intercourse and to keep themselves away from the not always desired temptation of the males of the village? This is what seems to have to have happened in France at the time of the Catholic Reformation. However, we must not forget that, when examining these tables of figures, those young women who only had one illegitimate child in the village in question could have had others elsewhere: why would they not have moved around as much as those servants and heads of families in the studies of Clayworth and Cogenhoe? Perhaps they were more migrant in some time periods than in others.

Be that as it may, the Cambridge Group researchers are clearly introducing yet another research style which it would be worth applying in other countries, even in those, such as France, which do already possess valuable records of declarations of pregnancies.

"All historians", writes Peter Laslett, "deal in societies to some extent, even if their chosen subjects are individuals or states of mind, and therefore all historians deal in quantities. The important distinction...is between quantification which is implicit and quantification which is explicit." This is a valid point to make. But it must not be concluded from this that one good approach to questions of historical sociology exists — i.e. the statistical approach — and that several bad approaches exist, namely, the "humanist" approaches. Nor must it be concluded that good documents exist which statisticians can make use of, while leaving bad documents for traditional historians. In fact the types of documents which can be used for statistical studies are innumerable, which of course does not exclude other ways of using the same documents. Even though he denies it in his introduction, when reading *Family Life and Illicit Love in Earlier Generations*, the reader too often gains the impression that the author is only interested in statistical approaches and that he is only familiar with one type of document, the parish register. The following essays, "Parental Deprivation in the Past", "The History of Aging and the Aged", "Age at Sexual Maturity in Europe since the Middle Ages", "Household and Family on the Slave Plantation of the USA", are all based on such registers. Together with those which we have already mentioned, that makes six of the seven chapters in the books which are based on this type of document. Other possible sources do however exist, some of which may be more appropriate for the questions asked. I will examine just two examples.

We have seen that English censuses from the seventeenth and eighteenth centuries cannot tell us how many children of a given age were motherless or fatherless. In the first place this is because most censuses did not give the ages of the people listed. This handicap leads the author to adopt the solution of comparing eighteen-year-old Americans to English single people from the seventeenth to eighteenth centuries as a whole, which is difficult to accept given that the average age at marriage was nearer to thirty than to eighteen! Moreover, a large proportion of such single people were servants and no census tells us whether or not they had lost their parents.

However, some documents do exist which should enable us to rigorously compare the proportion of motherless or fatherless children in pre-industrial England and in America today: these are the family records which demographers reconstitute from parish registers, following Louis Henry's method. These records indicate the date of birth of each child in a family and the date of his parents' deaths. Thus, they enable us to easily calculate the age of each child at his mother's or father's death when he outlived them. I do know that, upon reaching adolescence, the child often left his village — particularly in England — which means that, having no record of his death or marriage, we do not in fact know if he outlived his parents. All demographic research, however, — for example that relating to illegitimacy or to fertility — has to overcome difficulties caused by geographic mobility. Even so, the conclusions tend not to be as unsatisfactory as those of this fourth chapter.

To an even greater extent I question Peter Laslett's use of a Serbian census from 1733, in chapter 6 of his book, in which he is looking at age at sexual maturity in Europe. Even the principles upon which he bases his method seem questionable to me.

For example, after calculating that on average young women in Belgrade got married between their fifteenth and sixteenth birthdays, he asserts (p. 225): "These young wives must have been sexually mature if the Christian rules on the point were being observed." Yet the concept of sexual maturity and Christianity's rules concerning it are more ambiguous than he implies. Canon law allowed girls to get married at the age of twelve — and boys at fourteen — and I do not believe that the onset of the first menstrual cycle was the criteria for legal marriageability.[5] Canonists even allowed girls and boys to get married at a younger age when "malice compensated for age". "For example", writes Benedicti, "if a ten-year-old boy is able to ejaculate or 'deflower' a virgin, there is no doubt that he may contract a marriage...The same can be said of a girl, for whom marriage is valid *from the time she can tolerate a man's company.*"[6] Granted, for theologians, procreation was the main purpose of marriage. But it is not the only one, and never in the Christian tradition was the validity of a marriage dependent on the couple's fertility: couples were only expected to be able to consummate their marriage. No question was asked as to the quality of the man's sperm and even less as to the woman's ability to conceive.

The concept of sexual maturity is used somewhat loosely, it seems to me, as it is usually used to mean several very distinct things: legal marriageability; physiological puberty, which is a much less precise concept since it is linked to various phenomena such as the appearance of hair in the pubic region, the gradual growth of both breasts and hips, and the beginning of menstruation; and lastly the age of fertility. In the past, doctors' behaviour encouraged this confusion of meaning, which meant that the consistency of the Christian doctrine of marriage was never called into question. According to Laurent Joubert, a French doctor in the sixteenth century, a woman menstruated for the first time "at the age of twelve, which is the end of her puberty", and after that time, she was able to reproduce. However, he does know that a young woman, even after puberty, may be "incapable of conceiving...if she is not able to menstruate". Thus he makes a distinction between puberty and the beginning of menstruation. He knows too that it is not automatic "that any woman who menstruates conceives, for there are other conditions necessary for conception and generation". Conversely, he claims that a woman can conceive before menstruating for the first time. It is even possible that a woman "being always pregnant or nursing or in childbed",[7] may have a long and fertile married life without ever menstruating. In support of his reasoning, he quotes the example of a "woman from Toulouse" who "had eighteen children...without ever having any discharge of blood other than that involved in giving birth".[8] Just as the confusion between the age of legal marriageability, of puberty, of first menstruation and of fertility, generally determined, reinforced the Church's doctrine, so the insistence on these accidental conflicts justified those parents who married off their daughters who were immature or even below the age of puberty. But it would never have occurred to scholars of that time to find out whether *on average* the age at first menstruation really was twelve and whether *on average* young women who had reached puberty really were fertile. When we ask ourselves these questions, we are free from the social and religious problems posed by early marriages and we should free ourselves completely from traditional prejudices.

Moreover, demographers have noted for a long time that the fertility rate of married women between the ages of fifteen and twenty or even between twenty and twenty-five was lower than that of women aged between twenty-five and twenty-nine. It is probable that most of these still immature women nonetheless menstruated regularly and that they had normal sexual relations. Their immaturity was only evident in that they did not produce fertile ova, or that they produced significantly fewer than mature women. If this is the sexual maturity Peter Laslett has in mind, then demographic statistics are available as early as the seventeenth century, and they are numerous in France and in other western European countries. They indicate, it seems to me, that in the eighteenth and nineteenth centuries, there was a drop in the age at which women were able to reproduce. Indeed, just as Shorter pointed out in order to make a different point, the fertility rate of married women between fifteen and twenty and between twenty and twenty-four years of age tended to rise in several European countries and even in France while the introduction of contraception lowered the fertility rate of older women.[9]

If, on the other hand, the definition of maturity in question is the appearance of the first menstrual period, then demographic statistics do not directly give us the desired figures. We must use indirect evidence, the most useful of which is that provided by doctors. They indicate that in the eighteenth century and in the first half of the nineteenth, menstruation began at a much later age than nowadays. For example, an eighteenth century observer claims that in Sologne "women do not menstruate regularly before the age of eighteen or twenty".[10] In 1846, a doctor writes that in the valley of Oisan, in the Alps, "children of both sexes grow rapidly and reach puberty early. The sign which indicates this among young women usually begins at the age of sixteen or eighteen."[11] All such evidence, which is abundant, can be made into one or several statistical series. Edward Shorter, who has collected more than a hundred examples of such evidence, has divided them into two series: impressionistic observations, with which we must be content for the eighteenth century, yet which it is interesting to carry on until the end of the nineteenth, and clinical surveys which do not exist for France before the first half of the nineteenth century. The "impressionistic observations" give on average ages which are slightly higher than the "clinical surveys". Yet the difference is slight — between two and five months — and the two series both indicate a continuous drop in the age at first menstruation: from 15.9 years in the second half of the eighteenth century, the figures show a drop to 13.5 in the second half of the twentieth.[12]

Putting such documents into series obviously poses problems of various kinds and first and foremost problems of homogeneity. If women from Sologne menstruated at between eighteenth and twenty years of age, that was, we are told, a late age for France at that time. According to the doctor in Oisan, on the contrary, sixteen to eighteen years of age was an early age in 1846. Thus we must ensure that, within any one series, there are as many late ages, as many early ages and as many normal ages for each period considered. If not, we must make the necessary adjustments.

Similarly, we must also be aware of observers' prejudices. The one from Sologne maybe had prejudices against that accursed land, and the small size of its inhabitants was perhaps associated, in his mind, with a delay in sexual maturity. On the other hand, the doctor from Oisan does not hide his prejudice in favour of the mountain people's active lives. Thus, the sexual precociousness which he attributes to the young mountain women might be open to question. This is even more true in that the end of his evidence leads us to doubt it: "Among the latter women in the coldest areas this bodily function sometimes stops for the six months of the winter season, without such amenorrhoea causing any health problems."

Thus, all such evidence is not of equal significance and must not be confused. It must all be carefully examined, criticised, compared with other evidence and compared too with fertility statistics on women who married young. Such work demands a mind of great sensitivity and mathematical ability. I do not see any other way of writing the history of the age of puberty.

The confrontation between "humanist historians" and statisticians, which seems to be particularly animated in the United States, and in which Peter Laslett has become involved in writing this book, is in my opinion incorrect. One cannot be a good historic sociologist without fulfilling both roles at one and the same time.

Appendix

Table 2.6 Servants in Longuenesse, 1778-90: years of residence

78 or 51%	stayed for one year, that is, appeared in 1 list
22 or 14%	stayed for two years, that is, appeared in 2 lists
13 or 8%	stayed for three years, that is, appeared in 3 lists
9 or 6%	stayed for four years, that is, appeared in 4 lists
6 or 4%	stayed for five years, that is, appeared in 5 lists
15 or 10%	stayed for from six to twelve years, that is, appeared in 6 to 12 lists
10 or 7%	stayed for thirteen years or more, that is appeared in all 13 lists
153	

Table 3.2 Decadal ratios and indexes

Date	Ratio of baptisms to marriages (404 parishes)	Index of increase/decrease (404 parishes)	Bastardy ratio (98 parishes)
1580s	3.69	27.26	2.84
1590s	3.68	13.34	3.08
1600s	3.93	28.92	3.20
1610s	4.04	17.35	2.61
1620s	4.41	18.63	2.54
1630s	4.35	14.02	2.06
1640s	5.62	17.12	1.70
1650s	4.24	6.89	0.94
1660s	4.86	5.19	1.48
1670s	4.84	4.31	1.30
1680s	4.57	-0.07	1.52
1690s	4.80	8.99	1.82
1700s	4.26	16.00	1.80
1710s	3.94	10.70	2.12
1720s	3.82	-3.49	2.24
1730s	3.89	16.23	2.69
1740s	4.06	11.23	2.85
1750s	3.77	20.42	3.35
1760s	3.39	15.80	4.17
1770s	3.63	24.19	4.45
1780s	3.63	22.74	5.00
1790s	3.75	28.18	5.07
1800s	3.66	32.96	5.32
Mean of ratios 4.12		Mean of ratios 2.79	

Table 3.1 Detailed registration figures, ratios and indicators for master sample of 24 selected parishes, by decade, 1581–1810

Decade	Baptisms	Burials	Marriages	Ratio of baptisms to marriages
1580s[b]	[7,535]	[6,302]	[2,050]	[3.7]
1590s[b]	[8,162]	[7,644]	[2,211]	[3.7]
1600s	9,224	6868	2337	3.9
1610s	9660	7585	2223	4.3
1620s	9607	8047	2060	4.7
1630s	10012	7997	2043	4.9
1640s	[8712]	[8520]	1356	[6.4]
1650s	6981	7414	1790	3.9
1660s	7995	8234	1842	4.3
1670s	7805	8893	1766	4.4
1680s	7905	8951	1613	4.9
1690s	8469	8732	1823	4.6
1700s	9194	7876	2336	3.9
1710s	9247	7476	2499	3.7
1720s	9858	10236	2603	3.8
1730s	11157	8654	2963	3.8
1740s	11002	9141	3024	3.6
1750s	11727	9240	3419	3.4
1760s	12242	10574	4011	3.1
1770s	13508	10626	4371	3.1
1780s	14619	11516	4899	3.0
1790s	15400	12636	5012	3.1
1880s	16217	11357	6128	2.6
Total				
1581-1810	[236—238]	[204—519]	[64—379]	3.8

Square brackets surround figures which have had to be slightly amended to allow for periods of interrupted registration.

Index of increase or decrease^a (%)	Bastards				Overall bastardy ratio (%)
	Named	Inferred	Inflation coefficient	Total	
16.36	249	29	112	278	[3.7]
6.35	326	37	111	363	[4.6]
25.54	381	28	107	409	4.4
21.48	324	26	108	350	3.6
17.28	278	21	108	299	3.1
20.12	232	19	108	251	2.5
2.20	151	16	111	167	[1.9]
-6.20	31	7	123	38	0.5
-2.99	120	6	105	126	1.6
-13.94	118	6	105	124	1.6
-13.23	133	12	109	145	1.8
-3.10	157	4	103	161	1.9
20.86	175	10	106	185	2.0
19.	15	166	22	113	188
-3.83	241	20	108	261	2.6
22.43	300	31	110	331	3.0
16.91	363	39	111	402	3.7
21.20	364	56	115	420	3.6
13.62	500	76	115	576	4.7
21.33	567	147	126	714	5.3
21.22	655	141	121	796	5.4
17.95	791	143	118	934	6.1
29.97	867	153	118	1020	6.3
	7488	1049		8538	3.6

^a Difference between baptisms and burials in each decade expressed as a percentage of baptisms in that decade. Where burials exceed baptisms index has a minus sign.

^b 23 parishes only.

Notes and References

CHAPTER 1

1. For example, S. Ambroise, *Traité sur l'Evangile de Luc*, I, 43–45: "Young people whose fear of God calms and restrains their hearts often give up childhood deeds once they have children of their own".
2. *Les Amours paysannes*, Paris, Gallimard, "Archives" collection, 1975, pp. 198–9.
3. For example, E. Shorter, *The Making of the Modern Family*, London, Collins, 1976; E. Badinter, *L'Amour en plus. Histoire de l'amour maternel, XVII*^e*-XX*^e *siècles*, Paris, Flammarion, 1980.
4. One must be obsessed or understand nothing of Christianity's severity in the seventeenth century to believe that her spiritual advisor was reproaching the marchioness for being sexually attracted to her daughter.
5. Isaac's birth was one of God's miracles, his mother being of an age to no longer be able to reproduce naturally.
6. J.-L. Flandrin, *Families*, translated by Richard Southern, Cambridge University Press, 1979, pp. 133–9 and 174–9.
7. I am thinking in particular of P. Ariès' book, *L'Homme devant la mort*, Paris, Seuil, 1977.
8. In particular, J. Depauw, "Amour illégitime et société à Nantes au XVIIIe siècle", *Annales ESC*, July/October 1972, p. 1182; and especially A. Burguière, "De Malthus à Max Weber: le mariage tardif et l'esprit d'entreprise", ibid., pp. 1130–2 and 1137.
9. P. Laslett maintains that in England young women always got married as late as they did in the seventeenth century, a fact of which I am not at all convinced. On the other hand, the age at marriage did drop after the beginning of the eighteenth century in the country which spawned the Industrial Revolution.

CHAPTER 2

1. *Excellente apologie et défense de Lysias orateur sur le meurtre d'Eratostène surpris en adultère: où est traictée et comprinse toute la matière des adultères insérée dans le droit civil. Traduicte de grec en françois par noble Jacques des Comtes de Vintemille Rhodien Conseiller du Roy au Parlement de Bourgogne seand à Dijon, et commenté par M. Philibert Bugnyon, docteur es Droictz...* (Lyons, B. Rigaud, 1576; Bibliothèque Nationale, Paris, X 16 796).
2. *La Tour aux divorces.*
3. In the sixteenth century, there is only one title: *Responsio Bartholomaei La Tomi ad*

Epistolam quandam Martini Buceri de Disputatione Eucharistiae et Invocatione Divorum et de Coelibatu Sacerdotum... (Lyons, G. and M. Beringer, 1544).

In 1961, there are two titles: *le Célibat des prêtres* and *Célibat et Sacerdoce*. It is worth noting that in both cases the words appears in the same context: the problem of celibacy in the priesthood. Is this simply a coincidence? Is it in fact continuity over a period of more than four centuries? Or is the old problem currently re-emerging? Obviously, this question cannot be answered on the basis of these two surveys.

4. Cf. Appendix I, p. 33–34
5. Cf. Appendix I, p. 33–34
6. Cf. especially:

Livre des lamentations de mariage et de bigamie, composé en latin par maistre Mahieu de Gand et translaté en poésie françoise par Maistre Jehan Lefevre (Lyons, O. Arnoullet, undated).

Les Quinze Joies de mariage (numerous editions).

Les Ténèbres de mariage. Cy Ensuyt en brief langaige les ténèbres de mariage lesquelles furent sans mentir composées par un vray martir lequel fut dix ans en servage, comme appartient en mariage (Lyons, Mme B. Chaussard, 1546; Chantilly, Condé Museum).

De l'heur et malheur de mariage: ensemble les loix connubiales de Plutarque, traduictes en françois par Jean de Marconville... reveu et augmenté. Mariage est honorable entre tous, et le lict sans macule, Hebr. 13 (Lyons, B. Rigaud, 1583; Aix, Méjanes, G. 66 87). Numerous other editions.

...L'Enfer des Escoliers, des Mal Mariez, des Putains et Ruffians, des Soldats et Capitaines poltrons, des piètres Docteurs, des Usuriers, des Poëtes et compositeurs ignorans. Tirez des oeuvres de Doni Florentin, par Gabriel Chappuys Tourangeau (Lyons, B. Honorat, 1578; British Museum, 12 316.e. 21). (Other editions in Lyons in 1580 and 1583.)

Le Temps passé de Claude Mermet de Sainct Rambert en Savoye. Contenant...la consolation des mal mariez. De nouveau augmenté de la lamentation de la vieille remariée, de l'advis de mariage et autres poèmes sentencieux et récréatifs. Reveu et corrigé par l'autheur mesme (Lyons, Bouquet Basile, 1585; Bibliothèque Nationale, Paris, Rés. Ye. 1641).

Le Doctrinal des nouveaux mariez (Lyons, P. Mareschal, undated; Bibliothèque Nationale, Paris, Rés. Ye. 336), etc.

7. In these tales of chivalry, the word "*mariage*" is found ten times and "*épouser*" twelve times. For example: *Le quatrième Livre d'Amadis de Gaule, auquel on peut voir quelle issue eut la guerre entreprise par le Roy Lisnart contre Amadis. Et les mariages et aliances qui depuis en avindrent, au contentement de maints amoureux et de leurs amyes* (Lyons, B. Rigaud, 1574; Bibliothèque Nationale, Paris, Rés. Y². 1341. Lyons, B. Rigaud, 1575; at the library of the Château de Terre-basse).

Le Troisiesme Livre de Primaléon de Grèce...Auquel les faicts heroyques, mariages et merveilleuses amours d'iceluy sont tant bien deduites... (Lyons, J. Beraud, 1579; Bibliothèque Nationale, Paris, Y². 14 39. Lyons, B. Rigaud, 1587; at the library of the Château de Terre-basse).

...Propos amoureux contenans les discours des amours et mariage du seigneur Clitophant et damoiselle Leucippe... (Lyons, 1556, 1572 and 1577).

8. The word "*mariage*" is found nine times, "*noces*" five times, "*épousailles*" twice and "*fiançailles*" once, in occasional works similar to the following: *Discours de la magnifique réception et triomphante entrée de la Grande Duchesse de Toscane en la ville de Florence avec les cérémonies de son couronnement et espousailles...* (Lyons, B. Rigaud, 1558; Lyons Municipal Library, 314 522).

9. *B. Brissonii I.C. et suprema Pariensis Curia Advocati, de Ritu Nuptiarum liber singularis...* (Lyons, Ph. Gaultier, also known as Rouillé, 1564; Bibliothèque Nationale, Paris, F. 5447.)

10. *L'Amour, sacrement de mariage des fils de Dieu.*

11. *Amour et Mariage* is a literary essay, *Sexualité et Fidélité dans le mariage*, a philosophical essay; and *Amour, Mariage et Bonheur*, a study of sexology.
    It might seem that "*bonheur*" is not a novelty in the context of marriage. Indeed, "*l'heur et malheur de mariage*" is found several times in the sixteenth century. But there is a considerable change in meaning between "*heur*" and "*bonheur*". In the sixteenth century, "*heur*" particularly included the idea of good luck or good fortune, just as in the French word "*heureux*" [happy]. "*Heur*" referred only to an event, whereas "*bonheur*" today includes the idea of absolute bliss, which sixteenth century man imagined almost exclusively in the next world.
12. Cf. Appendix I, p. 33–34
13. For example in this title: *Les Sept Saiges de Romme...et aussi comment la femme de l'empereur ala de vie à trespas. Et aussi comment il se remaria à la fille du roy de Castille...et comment elle sceut que l'empereur avoit ung fils lequel il avoit commis à sept maistres pour le nourrir et apprendre pour estre empereur aprés sa mort, dont elle fut fort courroucée et comment elle se dessira le visaige et accusa le fils de l'empereur et dist qu'il la vouloit violer affin que l'empereur le fist mourir affin que se elle pouvoit avoir un filz qu'il fut empereur aprés le dexes de l'empereur...*(Lyons, O. Arnoullet, undated).
14. *La publicité c'est le viol*, and *Terre violée*.
15. Cf. Appendix I, p. 33–34
16. *Sensuyt un beau mystère de Nostre Dame à la louange de sa très digne nativité, d'une jeune fille laquelle se voulut habandonner à péché pour nourrir son père et sa mère en leur extrême pauvreté et est à dix-huit personnages dont les noms sensuyvent cy-après...* (Lyons, O. Arnoullet, 1543).
17. In the 1551 edition of l'*Histoire d'Aurelio et Isabelle*, someone wrote: "*...qui baille le plus d'occasion de pécher, l'homme à la femme ou la femme à l'homme*", instead of writing "*qui baille le plus d'occasion d'aimer*", as in the 1555, 1574 and 1582 editions.
18. *Les Eaux du péché, l'Image du péché, le Péché contre la chair, le Péché d'Adam et le Péché du monde*, vol. I, *la Fille pauvre*.
19. *D.N. Bermondi choveronii caesarei, Pontificijsque Iuris Doctoris praestantissimi...titulum de publicis concubinariis commentarij non minus docti quam percommodi, his ad quos adulteriorum et stuprorum (quae sunt nephanda scaelera) pertinet animadversio...* (Lyons, Senneton frères, 1550; Grenoble, F. 11 079).
20. *La Morphologie des homosexuels et le Terrain organique de l'homosexualité*, and *le Sentiment de la faute chez l'homosexuel*.
21. In the following title, the use of the plural form indicates that the reference is indeed to actual rapes: *Discours des trahisons et desloyautés des politiques de Paris qui avaient vendu ladicte ville à Henry de Bourbon chef des hérétiques de France...Avec le discours des cruautés, violemens, et sacrilèges qu'il a commis es faubourgs de Sainct Germain, Sainct Jacques et Sainct Marceau...*
22. Cf. Appendix I, p. 33–34
23. *De generatione et partu hominis, libri duo: authore Dominico Terelio, Medico Lucensi* (Lyons, Marsilii, 1578; Amiens, Médecine, no. 604).
    However, in another book, which does deal with human reproduction, it does not appear on the title page: *Liber phisionomiae Magistri Michaelis scoti.* At the end: *Michaelis scoti de procreatione et hominis physionomiae opus feliciter finit* (Lyons, Guill, Balsarin, undated; Bordeaux). Nonetheless, I do not believe that this was done out of a sense of decency.
24. At least one example of reproduction as a theme inspired by literature is found in R. Bretonnayau's book: *la Génération de l'homme et le Temple de l'âme, avec les autres oeuvres extraites de l'Esculape de René Bretonnayau...* (Paris, A. l'Angelier, 1583; Bibliothèque Nationale, Paris, Ye. 21 49). Since this book was not to our knowledge published in Lyons, we have not counted it in our survey.
25. Three copies of this book exist, one at the Lyons Library, one in Zurich and the third at the British Museum.

26. It is found in the following book: *Plusieurs Gentillesses pour faire en toutes bonnes compagnies et aussi plusieurs bonnes et utiles receptes esprouvées par Symon de Millau* (sic) (Lyons, Fr. and B. Chaussard, 1556; Arsenal, sc. et arts, 69 90).

    The following table of contents is found on the back of the title page: *Sensuyt plusieurs bonnes receptes de Maistres Symon de Millan parmi lesquelles: Pour faire que ung homme débilité par froideur puisse habiter...*

27. *Moralité nouvelle d'un Empereur qui tua son neveu qui avoit pris une fille à force. Et comment ledict Empereur estant sur son liet de mort la saincte Hostie luy fut apportée miraculeusement...* (Lyons, Mme B. Chaussard, 1544; British Museum, C. 20. e. 13 [53]).

28. *Un baiser dans la nuit* (novel), *Une rose et trois baisers* (novel), *la Belle Saison ou Embrassez qui vous voulez, Caresses!* (novel), *Flirt* (poetry), *Métaphysiques du strip-tease, Strip-tease party* (novel).

29. *Sadisme et Libertinage; la Femme cruelle...le masochisme dans l'histoire et les traditions; Amour, Erotisme et Cinéma; l'Erotisme au cinéma; Histoire de l'érotisme; les Sociétés secrètes érotiques; l'Erotomanie préschizophrénique; De la nymphomanie de la vache; Précis de sexologie.* For "homosexualité", cf. note 20; for "sexualité", cf. the notes which follow.

30. *Recherches sur la morphogénèse et la sexualité d'Hydractinia echinata.*

31. *La Sexualité.*

32. *Sexualité et Capitalisme.*

33. *Sexualité et Fidélité dans le mariage.*

34. Cf. Appendix II, p. 34–35

35. This can be seen by titles such as the following: *la Reine folle d'amour, la Révolution par l'amour, Amours 1900, Roma Amor.* One different book must however be added: *l'Amour en Grèce.*

36. The prevalence of these ideas and of their content, outside the context of popularised medicine, still needs to be researched.

37. The sentimental aspect of the phenomenon dealt with in these books could be questioned. Despite several different meanings of the word *"amour"* in certain books, at quite a low level, intellectually speaking, it does seem however that in the medical approach the word is defined as opposed to sexual instinct as much as by its participation in sexuality. This can be shown by the titles themselves: *Amour, Mariage, Bonheur; Amour, Ménage et Enfants; la Conduite de l'amour; la Vie sexuelle, de l'instinct à l'amour.*

38. *Le Grand Blason de faulses amours*, by Guillaume Alexis, was published at least five times in Lyons: 1497, 1506, 1512, 1529, 1538. *Le Loyer de folles amours* (Lyons, O. Arnoullet, 1538; Bibliothèque Nationale, Paris, Rés. Ye. 1289). *La Fauceté et Trayson et les Tours de ceux qui suivent le train d'amours* (Lyons, O. Arnoullet, undated; Grenoble, bel. let. 16 030, missing). *L'Amand desconforté...avec plusieurs préceptes et documents contre l'amour* was published at least three times in Lyons by Mme B. Chaussard. *La Deiphire de M. Leon Baptiste Albert qui enseigne d'éviter l'amour mal commencée* appeared with the four editions of *l'Histoire d'Aurelio et Isabelle. Chant Antérotique sur une vision d'Amour et Prudence par Jean Sevestre parisien*, etc.

39. *La Nef des dames vertueuses composée par maistre Symphorien Champier...Quatre livres...Et le quart est le livre de vraie amour* (Lyons, J. Arnoullet, 1503; Bibliothèque Nationale, Paris, Vélins, 1903).

    Dialogue très élégant intitulé le Peregrin traictant de l'honneste et pudique amour concilié par pure et sincere vertu, traduict de vulgaire italien en langue françoise par maistre François Dassy..., was published at least four times in Lyons: 1520, 1528, 1529, 1533.

40. *Contre l'amour* and *Prenez garde à l'amour*, to which can be added Ovid's book: *les Remèdes à l'amour.* Only two titles try to distinguish between kinds of love: *le Double Visage de l'amour*, and *le Grand Amour.*

41. For example, *l'Histoire et Ancienne Chronique de Gérard d'Euphrate, Duc de Bourgogne,*

traitant pour la plus part son origine, jeunesse, amours, et chevaleureux faits d'armes... (Lyons, B. Rigaud, 1580; British Museum, 245. d. 41).

When the two actors are well-known, the singular is sometimes used (which occurs four times) as in: *Luc Apulée de l'asne Doré. Plus y a sus les 4, 5, 6, livres traitans de l'amour de Cupido et de Psiches...* (Lyons, J. Temporal, 1553; Lyons Municipal Library, 801 453).

But the plural form is used more often (14 times): *Histoire éthiopique d'Héliodore...Traitant des loyales et pudiques amours de Theagene Thessalien, et Chariclea Ethiopienne...* (Lyons, Catherin Fontanel, 1559; Besançon, Bel. let., no. 41 13).

42. At the beginning of the century, the tendency was for collections of individuals: *Lhospital damours, les Demandes damours, la Conqueste du chateau damours, la Fontaine damours, le Sophologue damours, les Deux Soeurs disputant damours,* etc. After 1540, the trend is rather for *"amour"* in the singular: *le Pourquoy d'amour* (1537), *la Fontaine d'amour* (1545), *le Tuteur d'amour* (1547), etc.

It is possible that the "s", rather than indicating the plural form, was left over from a medieval grammatical case system. No matter what its origin, it appears that contemporaries saw it as a plural form, since the French title *les Arrets damours* is the equivalent of the Latin *Arresta amorum*.

43. Naturally, this is not so. But an entire study needs to be devoted to the variations in usage of the singular and the plural in the sixteenth century, looking at categories other than titles.

44. Concerning profane love in the Lyons titles, one can categorise seventy-seven examples as being existential and seventy-nine as referring to the essence of love. In the 1961 titles, on the other hand, universal love occurs eighty-three times and individual love affairs twenty-six times.

45. There are fifty-two examples of *"amour"*, *"d'amour"* and *"en amour"*, compared to twenty-seven of *"l'amour"*, *"de l'amour"* and *"en l'amour"*.

46. *Les six livres de Mario Equicola d'Alveto. De la nature d'Amour, tant humain que divin, et de toute les différences d'iceluy...* (Lyons, Jean Veyrat, 1597; British Museum, 524, b.9; ibid., 1598; Mazarine, 27 948).

47. Strictly speaking, neither the heart nor the soul appear in the titles which refer to love, but clearly such love can be perceived.

48. In several sixteenth century titles, love appears as a state, with its own dynamism, and which defines the framework for lovers' behaviour: *Conformité de l'amour au navigaige* (1548), *...tant de l'amour que de la guerre...* (1580, 1581, 1586, 1588), *...demandes que les amoureux font en l'amour* (1592), etc. In *l'Astrée*, at the beginning of the seventeenth century, love is the framework which defines lovers' *"amitié"* or *"affection"*.

49. The following books have female authors: *L'amour brisa le sortilège, l'Amour du bout du monde, Amour peux-tu revenir, Amour réponds-moi, L'amour s'en va, L'amour viendra peut-être, Au nom de l'amour, l'Autre Amour, le Chemin de l'amour, la Montée vers l'amour, Pardon mon amour, Par amour, Plus loin que l'amour, Qui es-tu mon amour, la Reine folle d'amour, la Révolution par l'amour, Un amour maladroit, Un grand amour, Un long amour*. It is often possible to recognise books written by men by their titles. But other men also make love the supreme value: *l'Amour et la Mort, l'Amour et le Divin, l'Amour fou, le Grand Amour*.

50. It appeared in two religious books and two books relating to secular love affairs. Three editions of one of these books, *l'Histoire d'Aurelio et d'Isabelle*, contain the verb *"aimer"*.

51. Book titles make it very difficult for us to distinguish between religious works such as *Aimer, Savoir aimer, la Grande Joie d'aimer, Dis-moi si tu m'aimes*, and books dealing with profane love such as *Aimer c'est persévérer, Je suis faible et tu m'aimes, Pourvu qu'il m'aime, le Temps d'aimer* and *Vienne le temps d'aimer*.

52. *Les bêtes que j'aime, L'Espagne que j'aime, Toutes ces pêches que nous aimons, Aimez-vous*

les oiseaux?, etc. It is difficult to distinguish these books from those in which *"aimer"* means "to love" rather than "to like", such as *Le fantôme que j'aimais, Aimez-vous les femmes?*, etc.

53. *Cy finist l'histoire du trés vaillant chevalier Paris et de la belle Vienne lesquels pour loyaument aimer souffrient moult dadversité avant qu'ils peussent jouir de leurs amours* (Lyons, 1520 and 1554).

    Deux Chansons nouvelles...L'autre d'un Oublieux donnant un escu pistolet a une Dame pour jouir de ses amours (Lyons, 1571).

    Histoire admirable d'Arnaud Tilve, lequel emprunta faussement le nom de Martin Guerre afin de jouir de sa femme (Lyons, B. Rigaud, 1580).

    Le Blason des dames suyvant le train damours, C'est assavoir le jouissant et le Tanne contredisant l'un contre l'autre. Composé de nouveau par maistre Nicole desire aultrement dit le Convoyte...(Lyons, P. de Ste Lucie, also known as le Prince, around 1535).

54. At the end of the article dealing with the verb *"sentir"*, Nicot's *Trésor de la langue françoise* gives:

    Sentement, sensus, Ordoratus, Odoratio, Olfactus.

    Avec grand sentement et flairement, Sagaciter.

    Qui n'a point de sentement, Insensile

    Mes sentements (Pasquier), Sensus mei.

55. *La Fontaine de vie de laquelle ressourdent trés doulces consolations singulièrement nécessaires aux coeurs affligez* (Lyons, J. de Tournes, 1543; Bibliothèque des jésuites, Lyons). *Les Allumettes du feu divin pour faire ardre les coeurs humains en lamour de Dieu... Aucteur F. Pierre Doré docteur en théologie* (Lyons, P. de Ste Lucie also known as le Prince, undated; Avignon, Calvet Museum, 1927).

56. *La Plaisante et Amoureuse Histoire du chevalier Doré et de la pucelle surnommée Cueur d'Acier* (Lyons, B. Rigaud, 1570 and 1577).

57. *Aretefila Dialogo Nel quale da una parte sono quelle ragioni allegate, lequali affermano, lo amore di corporal bellezza potere encora per la via dell'udire pervenire al cuore...* (Lyons, G. Rouillé, 1560; Grenoble, F. 61 68. Lyons, G. Rouillé, 1562; Bibliothèque Nationale, Paris, Z. 31 46).

58. *Beaucoup d'appelés, un seul coeur* or *Coeur à coeur avec Jésus* are titles of religious works; *le Chemin du coeur* and *Coeurs à nu* are titles of secular works. A title such as *Le coeur est un mendiant* shows that the heart, formerly seen as the seat of courage, has become the seat of an entirely passive emotion.

59. The word *"volupté"* is found in two titles from Lyons, the first of which unequivocally condemns it and the second presenting it as permissable only when not in association with love. *Clytemnestre, tragédie de Pierre Matthieu...De la vengeance des injures perdurables...et des malheureuses fins de la volupté* (Lyons, B. Rigaud, 1589; British Museum, 840, a. 9 [8]).

    Platine en françois...qui traite de honneste volupté et de toutes viandes et chose que lomme menge... (Lyons, 1505, 1528, 1546, 1548, 1571, 1588).

60. *Opera Vergiliana...De Venere et Vino...* (Lyons, 1517, 1528 and two undated editions). *Juvenalis familiare commentum...Decima rerumque libido notantur...* (Lyons, Gueynard also known as Et. Pinet, 1511; Albi, 194).

61. Cf. Marzio Galeotti's monograph which has already been mentioned: *...maris aut foeminae in coïtu sit major voluptas.*

62. Platine's book, *De honnesta voluptate*, seems to refer to both wordly and religious problems. It is know that Bart. de Sacchi, also known as Platina, Cardinal Bessarion's protégé, was a member of the college of abridgers in Rome, and was librarian at the Vatican when he died.

63. *Lamentation et Complainte d'un prince d'Albanie à l'encontre d'Amour et sa Dame*

contenant en soit la parfaite amitié, de deux vrays amans (Lyons, J. Saugrain, 1959; according to Du Verdier, II, 646).

Amitié bannie du monde... traduit en vers François Par Jean Figon de Montélimar en Dauphiné (Lyons, G. Cotier, 1559; Arsenal, bel. let. 23 54. Res).

The same work appeard in 1589 in an *Anthologie ou Recueil des plus beaux épigrammes grecs*, with the title: *l'Amitié exillée*, by Cyre Theodore Prodome, collected by Pierre Tamisier.

Perhaps the most important example is: *Notable Discours en forme de dialogue touchant la vraye et parfaite amitié, ouvrage dans lequel les dames sont deument informées du moyen qu'il faut tenir pour bien et honnestement se gouverner en amour* (Lyons, B. Rigaud, 1577 and 1583). This book is François d'Amboise's translation of Alex. Piccolomini's *Dialogo della bella creanze*.

64. The adjectives *"honneste"* and *"pudique"* are still found in titles, but are no longer found together, as in the first half of the century.

65. For example in *Astrée*: "This shepherd was Céladon's brother and Heaven had joined them with a *bond of friendship* which was stronger than that of kinship; on the other hand there were Astrée and Phillis, who not only were related, but liked one another with such a close bond of friendship, that they well deserved to be compared to brothers". But after Céladon's suicide, when Lycidas reproaches Astrée for her indifference, he says: "...if he had not *loved* you, or if you did not know of this *friendship*, it would be tolerable..."

66. *Les Affections d'amour de Parthenius Ancien Auteur Grec...* (Lyons, M. Bonhomme, 1555; Bibliothèque Nationale, Paris, Rés. Y^2. 12 22).

Aman, seconde tragédie de Pierre Matthieu... De la grace et bien vueillance des Roys dangereuse à ceux qui en abusent, de leur libéralité mesurée au mérite, non à l'affection (Lyons, B. Rigaud, 1589; British Museum 840. a. [I]).

67. Nicot's *Trésor* begins by defining the verb *"affecter"*, giving five examples:

AFFECTER et désirer d'estre Roy, Affectare Regnum.

Affecter le sang d'autrui et désirer de le tuer, Affectare cuorem alicujus...

Then, within the same article, he gives thirty-five examples of the word *"affection"*:

Affection, Affectus, Studium, Animus, Voluntas.

Affection des-ordonnée, Libido.

Grande affection qu'on a à faire quelque chose, soit bien, soit mal, Studium.

Qui ont leur affection à la guerre, Quibus militia in studio est...

Je connais les affections et fantaisies des amoureux, Novi ego amatium animos.

Mettre son affection à amasser argent, Studere pecuniae.

Mettre son affection à une pucelle, Animum ad virginam adjicere.

Faire quelque chose d'affection, Ambitio se agere, Cupidé.

Accuser par affection, Studio accusare.

Lastly, he defines *"affectueux"* and *"affectueusement"*:

Affectueux, m. acut, C'est affectionné, et ainsi en ont usé les anciens, disant: Il est chevalier affectueux à l'histoire, Deditur historiae, Incubus historiarum lectioni toto animo.

Affectueusement, Intimè, Cupidè, Ambitiosé.

Acheter affectueusement, Cupidè emere.

Faire quelque chose plus affectueusement qu'il ne faut, Ambitiosus aliquid facere.

68. "...beautiful Astrée... did not want ingratitude as payment, but rather reciprocal affection through which she received his friendship and services".

> "...the extreme affection which you could not pretend not to have recognised thousands of times..."

> "The supreme prudence, in love, is to keep one's affection hidden..."

> "She remembered the faithful friendship which she had previously recognised in this shepherd, the extremes of his affection...", etc.

69. *Histoire joyeuse contenant les passions et angoisses d'un martyr amoureux d'une dame...* (Lyons, B. Rigaud, 1557).

> *Roland furieux...qui dit si proprement d'armes d'amours et de ses passions...* (Lyons, S. Sablon, 1544; Lyons, A., 12766.134).

70. Senèque, *Des remèdes contre les perturbations de l'ame et passions du corps...* (Lyons, B. Rigaud, 1558).

> *Aux dames serves de leurs passions*: introductory play in l'*Histoire de Palmerin d'Olive* (Lyons, F. Arnoullet, 1576; Grenoble, E. 30 125).

CHAPTER 3

1. H. Baudrier, *Bibliographie lyonnaise*, Lyons, 1895–1921, 12 octavo volumes.
2. *Le Tuteur d'amour* (1547) is more of a bawdy collection, seeming to mock Platonic love, which was in vogue at the time.

CHAPTER 4

1. It is only mentioned in R. Vaultier, *Le Folklore pendant la guerre de Cent Ans*, Paris, 1965, and particularly in Abbé J. Durand, *Le Folklore de l'Aube*, vol. I, *Les Ages de la vie*, 1962. In these two books, the *créantailles* rite is only mentioned in conjunction with fifteenth and sixteenth century trials in Troyes.
2. The work here is based only on those trials published by F. André, in his *Inventaire sommaire des archives départmentales de l'Aube*, series G. vol. II and III. This is a collection of 225 cases of broken promises of marriage, divided into two series: those from the fifteenth and sixteenth centuries, which for the purpose of this article have been numbered 1^A to 89^A, and those from the period 1665–1700, numbered 1^B to 136^B. In the remainder of this article, the trials will be referred to by their numbers; thus it would be appropriate here to give the specific references for those trials which will later be mentioned: (1^A), vol. II, pp. 266–7, G. 4170, folio 6 verso; (2^A), II, 277, G. 4176, fol. 79 recto; (3^A), II, 290–1, G. 4181, fol. 223...; (5^A), II, 293, G. 4181, fol. 269 v.; (6^A), II, 293, G. 4181, fol. 274 v...; (7^A), II, 293–4, G. 4181, fol. 275 r...; (8^A), III, 102, G.4301, fol. 4 r./v.; (12^A), II, 295, G. 4182, fol. 15 r.; (17^A), II, 304–5, G. 4183, fol. 177 r.; (18^A), II, 305–6, G. 4183, fol. 201 r.; (19^A), II, 306–7, G. 4183, fol. 247...; (21^A), II, 307, G. 4183, fol. 279 v.; (22^A), II, 309, G. 4184, fol. 81 r...; (23^A), II, 454, G. 4216; (27^A), II, 320; G. 4187, fol. 19 v.; (40^A), II, 343, G. 4190, fol. 201; (41^A), II, 344, G. 4190, fol. 266 r...; (42^A), II, 345, G. 4190, fol. 297; (44^A), II, 350, G. 4191, fol. 213 v...; (46^A), II, 365–6, G. 4193, fol. 112 r...; (53^A), II, 374–5, G. 4194, fol. 64–5; (62^A), II, 403–4, G. 4197, fol. 128–9; (63^A), II, 406, G. 4198, fol. 5 r.; (68^A), II, 420, G. 4199, fol. 202 r...; (69^A), II 422-23, G. 4200, fol. 8 v.; (71^A), II, 424–5, G. 4200, fol. 64 r.; (76^A), II, 437–8, G. 4201, fol. 81 r...; (80^A), II, 440–1, G. 4202, fol. 49 v.; (82^A), II, 444, G. 4203, fol. 19 r.; (84^A), II, 448–50, G. 4207, fol. 1–29 and G.4199, fol. 32 r.; (2^B), III, 2, G. 4236, fol. 108 v.; (3^B), III, 2–3, G.

4236, fol. 128; *(4B)*, III, 3, G. 4237, fol. 3 r.; *(5B)*, III, 3, G. 4237, fol. 6–7; *(7B)*, III, 4, G. 4237, fol. 34; *(8B)*, III, 4, G. 4237, fol. 38 v...; *(11B)*, III, 9-10, G. 4239, fol. 5 r...; *(12B)*, III, 12, G. 4239, fol. 49; *(13B)*, III, 13, G. 4239, fol. 73 r...; *(16B)*, III, 15, G. 4240, fol. 45 v...; *(24B)*, III, 18, G. 4241; *(26B)*, III, 19, G. 4241, fol. 15 v.; *(31B)*, III, 21, G. 4242, fol. 8 v.; *(32B)*, III, 22, G. 4242, fol. 36 v.; *(35B)*, III, 26, G. 4243, fol. 9 r.; *(39B)*, III, 28, G. 4243, fol. 34 v.; *(45B)*, III, 32, G. 4244, fol. 24 r.; *(48B)*, III, 33, G. 4244, fol. 41 r.; *(51B)*, III, 35, G. 4245, fol. 5 v.; *(53B)*, III, 36, G. 4245, fol. 14 r.; *(54B)*, III, 37, G. 4245, fol. 15 v.; *(57B)*, III, 38, G. 4245, fol. 28 v.; *(65B)*, III, 40, G. 4246, fol. 8 r...; *(69B)*, III, 41, G. 4246, fol. 20 r.; *(70B)*, III, 42, G. 4246, fol. 22 v.; *(79B)*, III, 45, G. 4247, fol. 12 r.; *(89B)*, III, 47, G. 4247, fol. 32 v.; *(92B)*, III, 49, G. 4248, fol. 13 v.; *(97B)*, III, 56, G. 4250, fol. 3 r.; *(109B)*, III, 65, G. 4252, fol. 1 v...; *(111B)*, III, 65–6, G. 4252, fol. 6; *(114B)*, III, 67, G. 4252, fol. 15 r.; *(118B)*, III, 70, G. 4252, fol. 39 v...; *(127B)*, III, 77, G. 4254, fol. 6 r.; *(128B)*, III, 77–8, G. 4254, fol. 7–8.

3. The *créantailles* rite is mentioned in 28 cases and *fiançailles* in 41 cases. In the remaining 32 cases, only the ideas of "promises", and of marriage "contracted" or "begun" are found.

4. The *promoteur* is the bishop's permanent prosecutor, with responsibility for bringing proceedings against crimes within the jurisdiction of the *officialité*. Although there were three *promoteurs* in the diocese of Troyes, they could not travel around the region in search of crimes: they dealt only with those which were brought to their attention by the victims, *curés* or other informers.

5. The *hoqueton* was a large jacket worn by a peasant or a shepherd over his tunic.

6. Abbé C. Lalore, *Ancienne Discipline du diocèse de Troyes*, Troyes, 1882–1883, 3 vol. vol. II, p. 69, loc. V.

7. J.-B. Molin and P. Mutembe, *Le Rituel du mariage en France du XIIe au XVIe siècle*, Paris, Beauchesne, 1974, pp. 50–1 and 305–6.

8. Trials no. *6A, 7A, 12A, 15A, 19A, 20A, 22A, 38A, 39A, 41A, 47A, 49A, 53A, 54A, 58A, 60A, 61A, 70A, 73A, 82A.*

9. Trials no. *2A, 3A, 4A, 28A, 30A, 33A, 36A, 42A, 51A, 56A, 57A, 59A, 66A, 77A, 87A.*

10. Trials no. *14A, 37A, 40A, 84A.*

11. Trials no. *5A, 34A, 61A, 76A, 80A.*

12. "Livre de famille de Nicolas Dare", in *Collection de documents inédits relatifs à la ville de Troyes et à la Champagne méridionale*, published by the *Société académique de l'Aube*, vol. III, Troyes, 1886, pp. 122–3.

13. In one trial in 1667, a man is accused of living with his "*crantée*" (G. 4238, fol. 7 r.). However this is the only seventeenth century example we found, and it is not part of the series of trials for broken promises of marriage.

14. Trials no. *12B, 45B, 70B, 89B.*

15. Trials no. *31B, 118B.*

16. Trials no. *7B, 8B, 11B, 16B, 31B.*

17. Trials no. *5B, 97B.*

18. File G. 4231 of the *officialité* of Troyes contains a *Traytié de mariage de biens*, made in 1521, and there is no doubt that such contracts were common practice in the fifteenth and sixteenth centuries, both in Champagne and in other regions of France. They were not however considered in trials for broken promises of marriage at that time.

19. Isambert, *Recueil des anciennes lois françaises*, vol. XVI, p. 524.

20. Concerning the paying of the deposit during the wedding ceremony, see Molin and Mutembe, op. cit., pp. 144–51 and 179–86.

21. *Dictionnaire de droit canonique*, vol. I, col. 1050–60.

22. However, two fifteenth century trials undoubtedly refer to deposits without mentioning the word "*arrhes*": Perronne Platot having become *créantée* to Garin Lechat the day before she became *fiancée* to Jean Filet, the latter agreed to give her back her freedom "on condition that she return to him the jewels and objects that he gave her" (*16A*: vol. 2, p. 303, G. 4183, fol. 131 r.); and in 1495 Guillaume Messier demanded

20 *sous tournois* from Guillemette Guerry for damage to a black velvet belt, trimmed with gold and silver, which he had given her "*in favorem matrimonii inter cos alias initi et contracti et nun...dissoluti*" (21^A) [in favour of the marriage which had been begun and contracted and not... dissolved]. But these two references are unusual for this time period.

23. C.-J. Ferrière, *Dictionnaire de droit et de pratique*, 1740, vol. I, article entitled "*Arrhes*".

24. In those few cases in which the official forces an unwilling partner to get married, it is always the young man and always after he has had sexual relations with the young woman. Such sentences were unusual, could be legally contested and probably were contested.

25. Council of Trent, session XXIV, *De reformatione matrimonii*, chap.I.

26. Isambert, op. cit., vol. XVI, p. 520.

27. Matthew 19: 6 and Mark 10: 9.

28. Ferrière, op. cit., article entitled "*Promesses de mariage*".

29. P. Le Ridant, *Code matrimonial*, 1770, vol. II, "*Promesses de mariage*".

30. This is what I suggested, perhaps somewhat imprudently, in *Families in Former Times, Kinship, Household and Sexuality*, translated by Richard Southern, Cambridge, 1979, pp. 169–70.

31. J.-L. Flandrin, *Les Amours paysannes*, pp. 59–75 and 243–6; *Families*, pp. 182–7; and below p. 272.

32. To the evidence of the *Dictionnaire de Trévoux* must be added that of P.-J. Grosley, *Ephémérides*, 1811 edition by Patris Dubreuil, 2 octavo volumes, vol. II, chapter VIII, "*Vocabulaire troyen: Crantailles, promesses solennelles de mariage. Cranter, contracter promesses de mariage*".

33. J. Durand (op. cit., p. 75), after saying that "*créantailles*" meant marriage by promises for the future or promises of marriage, writes: "Marriage by promises for the future is also called: "*les accordailles*"...We also find other names for this stage, such as "*le commencement*","*ils sont promis*" [they are betrothed], "*ils se causent*" [they are talking to each other]. *Nowadays these expressions are not longer current, the most common expression is the word "fiançailles*". The post-Tridentine Church's loss of affection for religious *fiançailles* no doubt encouraged confusion between *créantailles* and *fiançailles*."

CHAPTER 5

1. J.-L. Flandrin, *Les Amours paysannes (XVIe–XIXe siècles)*, Paris, Gallimard, "Archives" collection, 1975, pp. 79–82.

2. J.-L. Flandrin, *Families in Former Times, Kinship, Household and Sexuality*, translated by Richard Southern, Cambridge University Press, 1979, pp. 161–4.

3. F. Furet, *et al.*, *Livre et Société dans la France du XVIIIe siècle*, Paris, Mouton, 1965 (Vol. I) and 1970 (Vol. II).

4. J.-L. Flandrin, "Civilisation and Feelings: A Survey of Book Titles", above, pp. 13–35

5. Ibid., pp. 30–31

6. *Families*, pp. 169–73.

7. Ibid., pp. 145–61.

8. A. Girard, *Le Choix du conjoint*, Paris, PUF, 1974.

9. "*Maraîchinage vendéen*" was a tradition in the Vendée allowing marriageable young men and women to openly "French kiss" and, less openly, to engage in mutual masturbation. See Dr M. Baudoin, *Le Maraîchinage, coutume du pays de Monts (Vendée)*, Paris, 1932, 5th edition; see also *Les Amours paysannes*, pp. 191–200; and "Repression and Change in the Sex Lives of Young People", below, pp. 267–290

10. J.-M. Gouesse, "La formation du couple en basse Normandie", *Le XVIIe siècle*, no. 102–103 (*Le XVIIe Siècle et la Famille*), pp. 45–58.
11. J.-L. Flandrin and B. Le Wita, "Créantailles in Troyes", above, pp. 49–71.
12. Y. Castan, "Pères et fils en Languedoc à l'époque classique", *Le XVIIᵉ Siècle et la Famille*, pp. 31–45.
13. "*Escraignes*" were igloo-shaped buildings in Burgundy and Champagne which were made from lumps of earth or sod. During the winter, young women used to spend their evenings in these "*escraignes*", sewing, chatting, etc. As a result, young men used to frequent these "*escraignes*", in order to court the young women. See B. Le Wita, "Les fiançailles à Troyes du XVᵉ au XVIIᵉ siècle d'après les archives épiscopales de Troyes", type-written Master's dissertation, University of Paris VIII-Vincennes, 1975. See also *Families*, pp. 108–10.
14. M. Hudry, "Relations sexuelles prénuptiales en Tarentaise et dans le Beaufortin d'après les documents ecclésiastiques", *Le Monde alpin et rhodanien, revue régionale d'ethnologie*, no. 1, 1974, pp. 95–100.
15. C. Roy, *Us et Coutumes de l'ancien pays de Montbéliard*, Montbéliard, 1886, pp. 221–228.
16. J. Depauw, "Amour illégitime et société à Nantes au XVIIIᵉ siècle", *Annales ESC*, July/October 1972, p. 1172; C. Fairchilds, "Female Sexual Attitudes and the Rise of Illegitimacy: a Case Study", *Journal of Interdisciplinary History*, VIII, 4, Spring 1978, p. 649.
17. Marie-Claude Phan, *Les amours illégitimes, Histoires de séduction en Languedoc, 1676-1786*, Paris, Editions du CNRS, 1986, 241 pp., pp. 72–74.
18. J.-L. Flandrin, "Late Marriages and Sex Lives", *Annales E.S.C.*, 1972, pp. 1372–1375; and *Les Amours paysannes*, pp. 240–241.
19. Ibid., pp. 238–240.
20. Ibid., pp. 225–231.
21. Ibid.
22. J.-L. Flandrin, "Repression and Change in the Sex Lives of Young People", below, pp. 267–290.

CHAPTER 7

Annales: E.S.C., Nov.–Dec. 1969, pp. 1370–90. Translated by Patricia M. Ranum.

1. Philippe Aries, Historie des populations françaises et de leurs attitudes devant la vie depuis le XVIIIᵉ siècle (Paris, 1948).
2. See the article by Father Riquet in Population, Oct.–Dec. 1949; and Philippe Ariès' reply in Population, July–Sept. 1953. Both are available in English in O. and P. Ranum (eds). Popular Attitudes toward Birth Control in Pre-Industrial France and England (New York, 1972).
3. John I. Noonan, Jr., *Contraception*, a History of its Treatment by the Catholic Theologians and Canonists (Cambridge, Mass. 1966).
4. Among the articles and works by the team at the Institut national d'études démographiques (I.N.E.D.), directed by Louis Henry, see in particular the collective work, chiefly by Hélène Bergues, La prévention des naissances dans la famille (Paris, 1960). It includes a guarded paragraph by Louis Henry on "Relations sexuelles en dehors du mariage," pp. 368–69. Guarded, but ambiguous, since one finds: "This frequency can only be arrived at indirectly through illegitimate conceptions ...; thus anything having to do with prostitution and adultery is eliminated. ..." This implies that other sorts of illicit relations are discernible via the number of illegitimate births.
5. See, for example, Emmanuel Le Roy Ladurie, Les paysans du Languedoc (Paris, 1966). Speaking of the very long period of sexual inhibition "which the young experience before marriage," he explains in note 4 vol. 1, p. 644: "This period of inhibition, much

322   Sex in the Western World

longer and more rigorous than in our contemporary culture, exists as a result of a combination of factors (which the work of Goubert, 1960, and for Languedoc, those of Godechot and Moncassin, 1964, have elucidated): a) the absence or the very minor importance of contraception before 1730 in Languedoc as in the Beauvaisis; b) the very low percentage of premarital conceptions and of illegitimate births in general (0.5% in Languedoc during the entire eighteenth century). If premarital sexual relations were really frequent, they would, as a result of ignorance of contraception, have resulted in a very large number of illegitimate births. That is not the case."

Indeed, in his thesis on Beauvais et le Beauvaisis (Paris, 1960), Pierre Goubert wrote, after having observed that illegitimate births never exceeded 1 percent of the total births in a village, and having said that unmarried mothers went to the city to be delivered: "One trend merits being stressed: the very great respect for the religious law which forbade extramarital conception." This formulation appears to me an excellent one, since it refers to conceptions and not to sexual relations. But one must admit that the unprepared reader risks missing this nuance.

6. Quoted in full by Hélène Bergues, Prévention des naissances, pp. 229–30. Concerning this evidence, see also Noonan, *Contraception*, pp. 401–2.
7. See Bergues, Prévention des naissances, pp. 227–29.
8. See Noonan, *Contraception*, pp. 375–79.
9. See Noonan, *Contraception*. At the beginning of Chap. 9, "Sanctions," Noonan writes: "By stamping contraceptive behaviour as mortal sin, the theologians of the high Middle Ages, in agreement with the penitentials and the Fathers, maintained the most serious and most universal deterrent to contraceptive usage by a conscientious Christian. ... To the extent that the Christian people were informed of the sinful character of the act, and to the extent that they were devoutly seeking their salvation, the branding of contraception as mortal sin must have been the most powerful sanction against its practice" (p. 258). And further on: "The theologians and canonists proclaimed that nonprocreative marital intercourse, including coitus interruptus, was a form of the sin against nature. Peter Cantor, John Gerson, Bernardine, and Antonius assimilated such intercourse to the even uglier category of sodomy. ... In the ranking of sins of lechery, the sin against nature was said by Adulterii malum to be worse than incest. Gratian's ordering was maintained by the standard works of theology. In Thomas' *Summa theologica*, the sin against nature, including the sin in marriage, is the greatest of sexual vices, being worse than fornication, seduction, rape, incest, or sacrilege ..." (pp. 260–61).

> "This kind of ranking contributed to a social attitude: these descriptions functioned as epithets as well as analyses. To the best of their linguistic ability, the medieval scholastics sought to label contraception as an affront to decency, life, and nature. The man who engaged in contraceptive behaviour had not only to ignore the spiritual consequences, but to defy the social ideals of his community" (p. 261).

10. These unnatural acts were oral intercourse (*seminem in ore*) and anal intercourse (*a tergo*) the first of which is encountered in five, and the other in nine of the eighteen penitentials. See Noonan, *Contraception*, pp. 162 and 164).
11. The Saint-Hubert (chap. 57) and the Mersebourg B (chap. 13) are two eighth-century Frankish penitentials. They describe this act as "the spilling of seed in coitus with a woman, as the sons of Judah did to Tamar." (See Noonan, *Contraception*, pp. 161–62).
12. See Migne's Patrologia latina, vol. 99, col. 1971–72:

> "*De fundendo semen. Clericus si semen fuderit non tangendo, septem dies poenitat. Si tangit cum manu, viginti dies. Si diaconus, triginta dies. Si presbyter hebdomada quatuor.*
>
> "*Presbyter si semen fuderit per cogitationem, septem dies poeniteat. Monachus similiter.*"

"Qui voluntarie semen fudit in ecclesia, si clericus est, quatuordecim; si monachus aut diachonus, triginta dies; si presbyter, quadraginta; episcopus, quinquaginta dies poeniteat."

13. Ibid., vol. 99, col. 966. *"coinquinatus es cum uxore tua in quadragesima. Si hoc fecisti, annum unum poenitere debes, aut viginti sex solidos in eleemosynam dare. Si per ebrietatem evenit, quadraginta dies peoniteas."*

14. Ibid., vol. 99, col. 970. *"De fornicatione. ... Adolescens si cum virgine peccaverit, annum poeniteat. Si seme et fortuito casu, levigetur ei peinitentia et tantum usque ad annum plenum poeniteat."*

15. Ibid. *"Si infra triginta annos adolescens fornicationem faciat, tres quadragesimes et legitimas ferias."*

16. Ibid. *"Lacius maculans se cum ancilla Dei, duos annos poeniteat. Si genuerit ex ea filium, annos tres poeniteat. Si sine conjugio est, tres quadragesimas et legitima ferias."* The expression "sully oneself" (*maculans se*) is ambiguous. But if the third case is compared to the first, it appears evident that in the latter it is a question of intercourse. And it is sterile intercourse, as in the second case.

17. See Bergues, Prévention des naissances, p. 209, in which the author comments upon a similar passage from the Cummean II penitential, anterior to the collection edited by Migne. "If a lay person corrupts a virgin devoted to God and loses his reputation and if he has a child of her, let this man do penance for three years. ... If, however, there is no child, but nevertheless he corrupts the virgin, he shall do penance for one year."

18. Synodal statutes of the dioceses of Meaux (1245), Cambrai (1300–1310), Nantes (1387), Alvi (1230, 1553, and 1695), Malines (1570), Besançon (1571), Reims (1585–1621 and 1677), Amiens (1411, 1454, and 1677), Agen (1666–73), Sens (1658); and, from the Somme des Péchés of Benedicti (1584), the list of cases reserved for the archbishop of Lyon and that of those reserved for the bishop of Paris.

19. The word "mollicies" which, in Antiquity, meant passive homosexuality, by the thirteenth century had taken on the meaning of "solitary practices", or masturbation. Before the nubile age, these practices did not involve seminal emissions and were considered to be less grave. Moreover, voluntary ejaculation was not always manual: it could result from "cogitation and delectation", from "locution or conversations with women or men", from "reading immodest books" and "other means", as Benedicti specified in the sixteenth century. Finally, "manual pollution" is not necessarily solitary, and when it is not, the sin is more grave. This is the sole distinction which the bishop of Cambrai makes between autoerotic acts, of mollicies, and "manual pollution."

20. List of cases reserved for the bishop of Amiens in 1677.

21. As in the diocese of Cambrai — if one accepts my interpretation — three synodal statutes fail to mention bestiality among those sins reserved for the bishop: they are those of the dioceses of Malines (1570), Besançon (1571, and Amiens 1411.

22. That of the diocese of Nantes (1387). I call it more strict because it is the only to maintain an old Biblical interdict about conjugal relations during menstruation. In addition, it mentions adultery, incest — both natural and spiritual — and the sins of the flesh *"cum masculis, cum brutis, cum sanctimonialibus."* Its evocation of autoeroticism is instructive: *"de peccato molliciei quod omme adulterum superat."* This detail appears to weaken my thesis. In reality it confirms the fact that this classification is not self-evident, since there is no need to say that much about homosexuality, bestiality, and sacrilege.

23. Bede, in determining the penance imposed for abortion, wrote in his penitential: "It makes a big difference if a poor little woman [*paupercula*] does it on account of the difficulty of feeding or whether a fornicator does it to conceal a crime" (4.12). "The same rule," writes Noonan, "was followed for abortion by Pseudo-Theodore (6.4). The economic reasons which would prompt infanticide or abortion would seem to

operate with equal force to stimulate recourse to contraception." (See Noonan, *Contraception*, p. 160.)

Burchard, in the eleventh century, is the first to assert this: "Have you done what some women are accustomed to do when they fornicate and wish to kill their offspring, act with their maleficia and their herbs so that they kill or cut out the embroy, or, if they have not yet conceived, contrive that they do not conceive? If you have done so, or consented to this or taught it, you must do penance for ten years on legal feriae. But an ancient determination removed such from the Church till the end of their live. For as often as she impeded a conception, so many homicides was a woman guilty of. But it makes a big difference whether she is a poor little woman and acted on account of the difficulty of feeding, or whether she acted to conceal a crime of fornication" (*Decretum* 19, in Migne's Patrologia latina, vol. 140, col. 972, as quoted in Noonan, *Contraception*, p. 160).

24. Since Antiquity, and on into the eighteenth century, contraceptive drugs were generally cited along with abortive measures, poisons, love potions, and all sorts of magic or maleficium. On the other hand, the questions of infanticide, abortion, and contraception by sorcery are often handled together, while contraceptive intercourse is treated with the sins of lechery. Before the thirteenth century, the only examples likening these two sorts of sins to one another is to be found, if I am not mistaken, in these two Frankish penitentials of the eighth century which deal with the sin of Onan.

25. By "Church law" I mean Gratian's *Decretum* (1140) and the *Decretals* begun by St Raymond of Pennafort in 1230. To these can be added the *Sentences* (1154–57) of Peter Lombard, which have the same authority for theologians as the *Decretum* and the *Decretals* for canonists.

26. Here is Noonan's translation of this canon: "He who practices magic or gives sterilizing poisons is a murderer. If someone (*Si aliquis*) to satisfy his lust or in deliberate hatred does something to a man or woman so that no children be born of him or her, or gives them to drink, so that he cannot generate or she conceive, let it be held as homicide" (Noonan, Contraception, p. 168). But none of the great canonist or theologians applies this categorical rule to self-sterilization.

27. The canon "Aliquando" is taken verbatim from the "*Marriage and Concupiscence*" of St Augustine. "Sometimes (*Aliquando*) this lecherous cruelty or cruel lechery reaches a point at which even sterilizing poisons (*sterilitatis venena*) are used, and, if the latter do not work, [they] extinguish and destroy the fetus in the womb in some manner, preferring that their progeny die before being born. Assuredly, if the husband and wife are both like that, they are not married, and if they have been like that since the beginning of their life together, they are not joined in marriage but in seduction. If they are not both like this, I dare say that either the woman is a sort of whore to her husband, or else he is an adulterer with his own wife."

This text was included by Gratian in his decree, "*Si aliquis*" having been superceded. "*Si aliquis*" was taken up once more by St Raymond, who included it in the *Decretals*; he also included the canon "*Si conditiones*," which is a corollary, drawn up through his efforts, of the Augustinian canon. "If conditions (*Si conditiones*) are placed upon the substance of the marriage, for example, if one says to the other, 'I will contract marriage with you if you avoid children,' or 'until I find someone more worthy in honour or in riches,' or 'if you turn to adultery for money' the marriage contract, however privileged it may be, is nullified; although other conditions, base and impossible though they may be, must be held as invalid by reason of the privilege of marriage."

That is to say that the majority of conditions in the marriage must be considered null, for marriage is not conditional. But when these conditions are contrary to one of the basic grounds for the marriage proles, sacramentum and fides, to list them in the order of the canon these conditions are diriment; the marriage is invalid. In particular, to refuse procreation is to refuse marriage.

28. *"Aliquando"* came directly, *"Si conditiones"* indirectly.
29. See the whole of Noonan's *Contraception*, and especially chaps. 3 and 4.
30. St Thomas Aquinas, On the Sentences, 4.33.1.3., quoted by Noonan, *Contraception*, pp. 241–42.
31. St Thomas Aquinas, De Malo, 15.2, obj. 14, analyzed by Noonan, *Contraception*, p. 243.
32. St Thomas Aquinas, De Malo, 15.2, quoted by Noonan, *Contraception*, p. 244.
33. See Noonan, *Contraception*, pp. 244–45.
34. St Thomas Aquinas, De Malo, 3.122, quoted by Noonan, *Contraception*, pp. 244–45.
35. These are, for example, St Raymond (*Summa*, 4.2.8) and Monaldus (*Summa*, fol. 136 r^0) in the twelfth century; St Bernardine of Siena (*Seraphic Sermons*, 19.3) in the fifteenth: as well as the unknown summist used by Chaucer in his *"Parson's Tale"* (authors quoted by Noonan, *Contraception*, p. 250).
36. Noonan (*Contraception*, p. 250) quotes, for example, Alexander of Hales, St Thomas Aquinas, St Bonaventure, William of Rennes, Durand of Saint-Pourçain, Peter de Palude, John Gerson, and St Antonius of Florence.
37. Benedicti, La Somme des Péchez ... (Paris, 1601), bk. 2, chap. 9, "De l'excès des gens mariez" [On the excesses of married persons]. no. 59, Bibliothèque nationale: D. 6502.
38. Noonan (*Contraception*, p. 251) cites, for example, William Auxerre, Alexander of Hales, St Bonaventure, Astesanus, Durand of Saint-Pourçain, St Antonius of Florence, Albert the Great and St Thomas Aquinas liken overly ardent love to "using one's wife as a whore," as Benedicti does here.
39. See my article "Sentiments et civilisations," *Annales: E.S.C.*, Sept.–Oct. 1965, especially pp. 952–57. Concerning the Church's attitude toward love, many interesting things are found in Noonan, *Contraception*, especially pp. 324–25 (but there is a great deal more to be said about the late sixteenth century) and above all pp. 491–504. On the other hand, the author's comments about the Church's attitude toward love in the Middle Ages (pp. 254–57) did not seem very convincing to me.
40. For all theologians there is, indeed, a single, natural position for intercourse. All the interrogations of confessors on this matter begin with the question of statement, "You know the natural position. ..." The thing is so obvious that almost no one ever says why that position is natural, except when they are attacking those which are not. We are faced with a custom whose origin must be sought in prehistoric times; it is connected, I imagine, with the ritual gesture of the plowman, although no text permits me to support this supposition. In any case, it seems clear to me that marital intercourse is a ritual, a fertility rite. Indeed, Thomas Sanchez, more explicit than most other casuists, begins his chapter by an explanation: "We must first of all establish what is the natural manner of intercourse as far as position is concerned. As for the latter, the man must lie on top and the woman on her back beneath. Because this manner is more appropriate for the effusion of the male seed, for its reception into the female vessel and its retention. ..." Sanchez' genius lies in explaining everything promptly. However, when it comes to condemning unnatural positions, the question of pure ritual does not escape him: "It is an abuse of the sacrament of marriage, and it is evident that it is a perversion of the usage and also of the ritual ... and that it is a sacrilege worthy of hell" (*De Sancto matrimonii sacramento [Antwerp, 1607] bk. 9, dispute 16, q. 1*).
41. The position which theologians call "retro" and which Brantôme calls "more canino" had been denounced from the early Middle Ages on as lowering man to the level of the animal. Here it is not a question of intercourse between two partners, but of the honour of the human species. On this subject Sanchez wrote: "... Since nature has ordained this method for animals, the man who develops a taste for it becomes

like them." However, the position *muler super virum* appears more serious, and Sanchez attacks it much more vigorously:

> "4) This method is absolutely contrary to the order of nature since it stands in the way of the man's ejaculation and the retention of the seed within the female vessel. Also, not only the position, but the condition of the persons is important. Indeed, it is natural for the man to act and for the woman to be passive; and if the man is beneath, he becomes submissive by the very fact of this position, and the woman being above is active; and who cannot see how much nature herself abhors this mutation?

> "5) Because in scholastic history (ca. 31 *super Genesium ex Metodio*) it is said that the cause of the Flood was that women, carried away by madness, used men improperly, the latter being beneath and the former above. ... St Paul said to the Romans: 'Their women did change the natural use into that which is against nature,' and he places this sin among the deadly ones."

42. The association of these unusual positions with the condemnation of overly ardent loves is invariable. Though excerpts from theological treatises make this apparent only rarely, manu proofs are to be found. Among the lay writers, for example, Brantôme returns to the subject on several occasions, fascinated as he seems to be by "Aretino's positions": "In addition these husbands, which is worse, teach their wives, in their own bed, a thousand lascivious things, a thousand whorish acts, a thousand tricks, convolutions, new ways, and practice upon them those heinous positions of Aretino; so that from one glowing ember in their body a hundred are engendered, and they are thus turned into whores" (Brantôme, *Dames galantes*, ed. Maurice Rat [Paris, 1960] p. 26). And further on, in a more scholastic manner: "All these forms and postures are odious to God, so that Dr Jerome said, 'Whoever shows himself rather an immoderate lover of his wife than a husband is an adulterer and is sinning.'"

   Of course theologians also refer to this search for excessive pleasure. For example, Peter de Palude in his *On the Sentences* (d. 31, q. 3, art. 2,5[0]) wrote: "Some say ... that the man who knows his wife in an unaccustomed manner, even within the natural vessel, sins mortally, it this is done in a search for increased voluptuousness."

43. Theologians were not unanimous in condemning these unusual positions, and the essence of the discussion was based on their fertile or sterile nature. These positions were called "unnatural" because they are contrary to the ritual of intercourse ordained by nature, because certain ones pervert human nature by modelling man after the animal, because others invert the nature of the male and the female, and finally because they are suspected of being sterile and are therefore contrary to the nature of marriage — unless the inverse is true, that is to say that voluptuous relations are deemed contrary to the nature of marriage and are therefore suspected of being sterile. The direction of this causal relationship is of little importance: what counts is the grouping of these characteristics under the general concept of sin against nature. Moreover, sterile couples were often suspected of having deserved this divine punishment for their lecherous practices. It would be nearly impossible for them to have been deprived of descendants, said the English preacher Bromyard in the fourteenth century, if they had sought the end intended by God: therefore they sought lust or riches in marriage. (See *Summa*. "Matrimonium", 8.10. quoted by Noonan, *Contraception*, pp. 268–69.)

44. The position mulier super virum is even justified in the name of the absorptive nature of the uterus. Such a justification, to tell the truth, is rare.

45. The most frequent case is that of the pregnant woman who was afraid of harming her fruit by having normal relations with her husband. There are also many references to husbands who were too obese to have normal relations.

46. Brantôme, *Dames galantes*, p. 32. The entire discussion of this question, beginning on

p. 25, is very instructive. On several occasions Brantôme refers to the Scriptures, to the Church Fathers, and to the doctors of theology. Perhaps the intention of the discussion — to show that husbands are the chief persons responsible for the dissipation of their wives — weakens the value of his testimony. I do not, however, believe that the entire cause for the author's indignation can be found in this context of a speech for the defence.

47. In an extramarital context, this for example, is what he says: "... He bought from a goldsmith a very beautiful cup in silver gilt, a masterpiece and great speciality which was the best executed, engraved, and hallmarked which one could possibly find, ion which were engraved nicely and subtly several of Aretino's positions showing a man and a woman ... and above ... several showing various manners of cohabiting between beasts" (Brantôme, *Dames galantes*, 27–28). "When this prince entertained courtly ladies and maidens ... his wine stewards never failed ... to offer them a drink from it; ... some remained astonished and did not know what to say; others remained ashamed and colour rose to their cheeks; none of them said to her companions, 'What is engraved on the [cup]? I think those are filthy pictures. I will not drink from it any more. I would have to be very thirsty before taking another drink from it.' ... and therefore, some closed their eyes while drinking, others, more shameless, did not. Those who had heard about the tricks of the trade, both women and maids, began to stifle their laughter; others burst out laughing. ... Some said, 'Those are very lovely grotesques', others, 'What pleasant mummeries'; and others said, 'What pretty pictures.'...

> In short, there were a hundred thousand sorts of jests, and small talk on the subject. ... It was very pleasant banter and something to see and hear; but above all, to my mind, the best was to contemplate these innocent maidens or those who feigned to be so. ... Finally they became so used to [the cup] that they no longer felt any scruples about drinking from it; and others did even better and made use of such visions in proper time and place; and, even more, some debauched themselves in order to try it out: for every clever person wants to try everything.

> Those are the fine results of this beautiful and much talked of goblet. ... In this cup the wine did not laugh at the people, but the people at the wine: for some drank while laughing and others drank while experiencing ecstasy ..." (pp. 27–30).

This account, therefore, has nothing at all in common with the consistently indignant, serious, and moralizing tone which he adopts when speaking of such intercourse in marriage.

48. See Noonan, *Contraception*, passim, but especially p. 46–75.
49. For example, when he writes: "Nevertheless there are some women who say that they conceive better while in monstrous, supernatural, and strange postures than in natural and usual one, especially since they take more pleasure in them and, as the poet says, when they do it *more canino*, which is odious" (Brantôme, *Dames galantes*, p. 31).
50. Here, for example, is what Jacques Dubois, called Sylvius, wrote in his *De mensibus mulierum et hominis generatione* ... (Basel, 1556): "*Coitus inanis. Praeter hos etiam coitus coitui succedens, et coactus alterutrius, vel utriusque concubitus, ut in his qui inviti, et sine amore juguntur, inanis est, ac sterilis: ut voluntarius et jucundus, est foecundus, nisi amor nimis ardens adsit.*"

For a contemporary French translation, see Guillaume Chrestien, Le livre de la génération de l'homme (Paris, 1559), p. 39, which paraphrased reads: In addition, there is also coitus following upon coitus, and coitus in which one person is compelled by the other: and either copulation — like that of those who are bored and are married and united without their will and without love — is vain and sterile, just as that which is voluntary, agreeable, and pleasant is fertile, unless there has been an overly ardent passion.

Is this a matter of a traditional association of pleasure with fertility, or is it the realization by physicians of the day that interpersonal attraction is necessary in marriage? This question deserves further research in other texts.

51. J. Gerson, *Instruction pour les curés* (1575), chap. 6, f. 17.

52. When he justifies this ruling (see *De sancto matrimonii sacramento*, bk. 9, dispute 18, no. 5), Sanchez does not mention sacrilege and on the contrary appears to think that sin is less great when committed with the sinner's own wife than with the wife of another. However, in the chapter devoted to "unnatural positions," he accused these positions of being "an abuse of the sacrament of marriage," a "perversion of the usage and ritual," and of thus being "a sacrilege worthy of hell." (See ibid., bk. 9, d. 16, q. 1). Though Azor, in *Institutionum moralium* (Rome, 1600), vol. 3, bk.3, chap. 20, q. 5, no. 5, does not explicitly refer to sacrilege, he specifies that there is a "special, malicious insult committed upon one's own wife, because she has been taken advantage of, and the wife has the right to a divorce," that is to say, to obtain a physical separation.

53. Brantôme, *Dames galantes*, pp. 38–39.

54. See Bergues. *Prévention des naissances*, p. 143. Commencing on this text from Brantôme, Bergues correctly concludes that within the bourgeoise and the nobility "coitus interruptus remained the most commonly used method and that it was not so rare when the partners were not married." But she fails to pursue the matter further and appears to have forgotten it in the remainder of the book.

55. Noonan mentions extrinsic motives for maintaining traditional Church doctrine in the seventeenth century. (See *Contraception*, pp. 353–58 and 367–72). And we know the place they occupy in the recent encyclical *Humanae vitae*. However, Noonan does not mention Sanchez' text on coitus interruptus during fornication and does not appear to have seen the contrast on this point between marital and extramarital relations.

56. Sanchez believes, in accordance with Galen's theory, that the woman like the man emits seed and that conception is born of a mixture of these two seeds. The fact that one member of the couple emits seed without allowing the other the time to do so would therefore constitute a contraceptive act.

57. There has been some question about the basis of Galen's theory, and about whether the female seed was believed to be expelled at the beginning of intercourse or at the moment of orgasm. If one must choose, several reasons impel me to prefer the second interpretation. Moreover, Sanchez devoted a long and interesting discussion to learning whether — when the man abandons his wife before the moment at which she is supposed to emit her seed — that constitutes a grave sin. This is an interesting track to follow in order to learn about carnal union in different periods, and it should be followed. In the text which I have quoted, when Sanchez wrote "or when the risk of expelling it has become inevitable," it seems to me that he was implicitly drawing a parallel between the beginning of ejaculation in the man and of the orgasm in the woman.

58. In the previous article Sanchez had just stated that one must refuse fornication even under pain of death.

59. He also asserted — and this shows his cleverness in the discussion — that in the event of a grave peril, one could interrupt legitimate intercourse, even if this involved an ejaculation extra vas; for one has a greater duty to one's own life than toward the potential life of a child which might be born.

60. See Sanchez, *De sancto matrimonii sacramento*, bk. 9, dispute 19, q. 7.

61. See André Martin (ed.) *Journal de l'Estole* (Paris, 1960), vol. 3, p. 230, under the date of March 16, 1611. L'Estole and his contemporaries were not scandalized by what

Sanchez says about coitus interruptus, but by the numerous and very explicit pages devoted to sodomy.

62. See the whole of Noonan's *Contraception*, and especially chaps. 3, 4, and 6.

63. Although few historian-demographers explicitly assert this, let us recall that many infer it and that Le Roy Ladurie for his part states this clearly.

64. Many texts, such as Marguerite de Navarre's Heptameron, come from authors favourable to the Reformation. Is this a reason to take exception with them? Though the reformed position is based upon deeper theological foundations, it is also explained by the shortcomings of ecclesiastical celibacy, and the reformers had not trouble using this hostility to celibacy in their propaganda.

65. Pierre Goubert in *Beauvais et le Beauvaisis*, pp. 204-5, indicates that between 1650 and 1679, in the diocese of Beauvais, which included 432 parishes, more than 400 priests were the object of an inquiry or a law suit before the ecclesiastical courts. But breaking ecclesiastical celibacy constituted only one part of these misdemeanours, a part which Goubert calls "considerable" without giving statistics. E. Brouette, on the other hand, gave us a study on the *Excessus et incontinentiae clericorum, dans l'archidiaconé liégeois de Hainaut* (1499–1570), *Revue belge de philologie et d'histoire*, 1956, pp. 1067–72. According to my calculations, between 1499 and 1504 for the entire diocese, each year, about 15 percent of the resident curés were fined for excessus et incontenentiae. The proportion decreases after the middle of the century, but this was a troubled time in which surveillance was perhaps lax.

66. For example, we find the following dialogue in the *Caquets de l'accouchée* written in the reign of Louis XIII: "Who began the quarrel? It was the newly delivered woman's mother, who was sitting next to the bed, at her daughter's right hand, and who replied to the question of how many children her daughter had, and whether this was the first one? — My word, Mademoiselle, it is the seventh, and I am very astonished about it. If I had thought that my daughter would get to work so quickly, I would have let her scratch her privy parts until the age of twenty-four without getting married" (ed. Marion and Flammarion [1890] p. 12). Concerning the marriage of domestic servants, we find in the same text: "'And I' said a servant ... 'I am more to be pitied than you others: for in the past when we had served eight or nine years, and we had saved up a half a belt of silver and a hundred crowns in cash ... we would find a good sergeant to marry, or a good mercer-shopkeeper. And at present, for our money we can get only a coachman or a palfrey, who makes us three or four children without stopping, then, being unable to feed them on their meagre salary, we are forced to go serve as we did before'" (ibid., pp. 14–15).

67. In the fourteenth century the Dominican John Bromyard observed in one of his sermons that when he reproached fornicators for not getting married, some replied that such as they were they could not have a wife; others said that they would marry "if they had a house to which they could take her", others that they would not have enough to support children. *Summa praedicantium* (Nuremberg, 1485) "Lechery," 28, cited by Noonan, *Contraception*, p. 229.

68. I mean that unmarried persons of all ages had to seek sexual satisfaction in adultery and in such "unnatural" practices as homosexuality, bestiality, solitary masturbation, elaborate caresses, etc. Concerning all these practices we have a quantity of judicial, ecclesiastic, literary, medical, and folkloristic documents. I have indicated a few of them in an earlier article (*Annales*: E.S.C., Nov.-Dec. 1972, pp. 1351–78) This illicit and infertile behaviour also included coitus interruptus — undoubtedly used with increasing frequency from the sixteenth century up to the middle of the nineteenth century. It must be given special attention since it — rather than the contraceptive measures passed down from prostitute to prostitute ever since Antiquity — was used by Malthusian French households during the nineteenth century.

69. Even though it appears simple and efficacious, coitus interruptus could not be reinvented by just anyone, in just any milieu, in just any period. In order for the

"Malthusian revolution" to occur in France, an ensemble of favourable circumstances was required, including familiarity with this technique. I am suggesting here that before employing it in marriage, the couples of the second half of the eighteenth century learned the technique from a certain type of illicit relationship — a relationship in which the man is ready to make a sacrifice in order to please the woman. And since it appears that coitus interruptus was used in aristocratic circles before it was employed by the common people, I surmise that servants played an important role in the history of its spread. But this is still merely a hypothesis.

CHAPTER 8

1. J.-L. Flandrin, *Families in Former Times, Kinship, Household and Sexuality*, translated by Richard Southern, Cambridge University Press, 1979, pp. 122–9.
2. Ephesians 5: 22–24: "Wives, be subject to your husbands, as to the Lord. For the husband is the head of the wife as Christ is the head of the church, his body, and is himself its Saviour. As the church is subject to Christ, so let wives also be subject in everything to their husbands."
3. 1 Corinthians 7: 2–4.
4. For example, P. Lombard, *Sententiarum libri quatuor, distinctio XXXII*: "*Sciendum etiam est quia cum in omnibus aliis vir praesit mulier ut caput corpori (est enim caput mulieri, 1 Cor. 11) in solvendo tamen carnis debito pares sunt.*" [It is also necessary to know that in everything else man is superior to woman, as the head is to the body (for he is the head of the woman, 1 Cor. 11), however in rendering the conjugal debt they are equal.]
5. See, for example, the long and involved explanation of a sixteenth century theologian: "They are equal in the aforesaid power, which must not be understood as quantitative equality as in two cubits equals two cubits, for this equality does not mean that man and woman are equal in marriage; neither are they equal in the act itself, since the man is active and the woman passive and thus the man is more noble; nor in the running of the home, for the man governs and the woman is governed, hence the man is called the woman's master, not the woman the man's...neither is the man made for the woman, but the woman for the man. They are however equal according to the equality of proportion, i.e. ...as in double equals double, because the larger double does not have a greater or lesser proportion of its original than the smaller double has of its original, even though one of the doubles is greater in quantity than the other. Thus man and woman are equal as to proportion, for just as, in sexual intercourse and the running of the home, the man owes the woman what is expected of a man, so the woman owes the man what is expected of a woman" (J. Viguerius, *Institutiones theologicae*, Paris, 1580, pp. 640–1, *De redditione debiti matrimonialis*).
6. D. Soto, *In quartum sententiarum commentarii*, Louvain, 1573, d. 32, s. 1, art. 2.
7. Readers younger than myself may correct me on this point if sexual attitudes have changed over the last few decades.
8. T. Sanchez, *De Sancto matrimonii sacramento*, Antwerp, 1607, 3 folio vol., Vol. III, book IX, dispute 2, no. 4.
9. Viguerius, loc. cit.,: "*...vir et mulier non sunt aequales in matrimonio, nec in actu ipsius, quia vir est agens et mulier patiens. Ideo quod est nobilius debetur viro.*" [Man and woman are not equal in marriage or in the marriage act, since man is active and woman passive. That is why the more noble role is credited to the man.] This causal relationship is obviously naïve: the active role was actually only considered more noble in that society to the extent to which it distinguished male from female. In social relationships, on the contrary, those who were able to survive without working were considered more noble than those who rushed about and worked.

10. Sylvestre, *Summa summarum* (Lyons edition, 1593), verb. *DEBITUM*, 6: "*Modus naturalis, quantum ad situm, secundum omnes est ut mulier jaceat in dorso, et vir super ventrem eius incubat, observans ad seminandum vas debitum*". [The natural method, in terms of position, according to all, is that the woman should lie on her back and the man on her stomach, ensuring that he ejaculates into the appropriate vessel.]

11. Sanchez, op. cit., book IX, d. 16, no. 1.

12. Ibid., "*Est enim naturale viro agere, feminae vero pati: vir autem succubans, quantum est ex ipsa situs forma patitur, et femina incubans agit: quam mutationem quantum natura ipsa abhorreat, quis non videat? Quinto, quia in historia scholastica. ca. 31. super Genesim ex Metodio dicitur, diluvii causam fuisse feminas in insaniam versas, abusas fuise viris, illis incumbentibus, his succubis. Et confirmatur. Quia teste Abulense statim referendo, aliqui de hoc modo congresso exponunt locum illum D. Pauli ad Roman. 1. Feminae eorum immutaverunt naturalem usum, in eum qui contra naturam est. Quod inter peccata lethalia Paulus ibi annumerat*". [For it is natural that the man should take the lead and the woman be passive: but the succumbing man, situated and passive in this very same position, and the woman taking the initiative, this is a change which nature abhors, who does not see that? Fifthly, because Methodius says, referring to Chapter 31 of Genesis in his scholastic history that the cause of the Flood was that women were turned insane by the men who abused them, the men on top and the women beneath. And it is confirmed: referring to Abulensis' account, some people speak in this same way of what is said in St Paul's first letter to the Romans — "they have changed the natural use of their women to one which is unnatural". Paul, in this way, puts this in the name of the deadly sins.]

13. Genesis 6: 1–7.

14. Romans 1: 26–27: "For this reason God gave them up to dishonourable passions. Their women exchanged natural relations for unnatural, and the men likewise gave up natural relations with women and were consumed with passion for one another, men committing shameless acts with men and receiving in their own persons the due penalty for their error."

15. Such is the case with rear entry, denounced particularly often during the early Middle Ages. For example, Burchard de Worms wrote: "Have you had intercourse with your wife or with another woman from behind, as dogs do? If you have done so, your penitence will be ten days of bread and water." (*Décret*, book XIX, cap. 5). Sanchez was more explicit when he wrote in the seventeenth century: "Since nature prescribes this method for animals, the man who acquires a taste for it becomes like them" (loc. cit., no. 1, 3rd).

16. For example Brantôme, *Dames galantes*, Ed. Rat, p. 32. See also below, pp. 109–111.

17. A.-C. Ducasse-Kliszowski, *Les Théories de la génération et leur influence sur la morale sexuelle du XVIe au XVIIIe siècle*, master's dissertation, University of Paris VIII, June 1972, 88 typed pages. In the remainder of this article, I borrow freely from this study.

18. C. Galen, *De semine*, book II, chapters I and IV.

19. Aristotle, *Génération des animaux*, Paris, Les Belles Lettres, "Budé" collection, 1961, passim.

20. St Jerome, *Sur Ephésiens*, v. 30; St Augustine, *De Genesis ad litteram*, X, 18, 32.

21. *Les Secrets des hommes et des femmes composez par le Grand Albert*, translated from Latin into French, Paris, undated (sixteenth century), 16mo, 127 pp.

22. "In the opinion of a great number [of writers], women's seed is necessary or at least contributes greatly to reproduction, nature doing nothing without a reason" (A. de Liguori, *Theologia moralis*, book VI, Vol. VI, c. 2, q. 929).

23. For example A. de Liguori: "*Si autem vir jam seminaverit, dubium sit an foemina lethaliter peccet, si se retrahat a seminando?*" [If man had already ejaculated, there exists some doubt: does the woman commit a mortal sin if she fails to ejaculate?] (ibid., q. 918). Or, more explicitly, B. de Fumes: "When one emits his seed, the other not emitting

it, with the intention of preventing reproduction...it is a sin against nature" (*Aurea Armilla*, verb. *LUXURIA*, no. 5).

24. A. Paré, *Oeuvres complètes*, Paris, 1585, Vol. III.
25. Sanchez, op. cit., book IX, disp. 17, no. 7: "*Prima conclusio: Sanum est concilium curetur simul utrumque semen effundi; quare conjugi tardiori ad seminandum, consulendum est ante concubitu ut tactibus venerem excitet, ut vel sic possit in ipso concubitu simul effundere semen...Et ratio est, licet semen muliebris non sit ad generationem necessarium, multum tamen confert ad facilius generandum...*" [First conclusion: it is healthy that both should emit their seed at the same time since they are united; that is why the partner who takes longer to ejaculate must refrain from getting excited by fondling, so as therefore to emit his seed at the same moment in this sexual union. And the reason is that the woman's seed, even though it may not be necessary to actual generation, nevertheless contributes greatly to easier procreation.]
26. Sanchez, op. cit., book IX, d. 45, no. 38.
27. Bossius, *De matrimonii contractu tractatus* (2 volumes, Lyons, 1655–1658), "*De effectibus contractus matrimonii*" no. 55: "*cum frequentius viri quia robustiores, prius seminent...*" [as it is more frequent that men, as they are more robust, are the first to ejaculate], Liguori (loc. cit., q. 919): "*cum frequentius viri, quia calidiores, prius seminent...*" [as it is more frequent that men, as they are lustier, are the first to ejaculate]; etc.
28. Sanchez, loc. cit., d. 17, no. 12.
29. Sanchez, ibid.; and Liguori: "*Si mulieres post talem irritationem tenerentur naturam compescere, essent ipsae jugiter magno periculo mortaliter peccandi, cum frequentius viri, quia calidiores, prius seminent — sed haec ratio non suadet, nam si hoc permitteretur uxoribus, deberet permitti etiam viris, casu quo mulier se retraheret post suam seminationem, et vir maneret irritatus...*" [If, after such excitement, women were bound to repress nature, they would be continually in great danger of committing a mortal sin, since men, being usually lustier, emit their seed first, but this reason is not sufficient, for if women were permitted to do so, their husbands would also have to be permitted to do so, in the case of a woman withdrawing after emitting her seed and the man remaining excited.] (loc. cit. q. 919).
30. On these questions, see J.-L. Flandrin, *L'Eglise et le Contrôle des naissances*, Paris, Flammarion, "Questions d'histoire" collection, no. 23, 1970, 139 pp.

CHAPTER 9

1. H. Van der Berg, *Metabletica, ou la Psychologie historique*, French translation published by Buchet-Chastel, 1961. See A. Besançon's comments in the same issue of *Annales ESC*, p. 237 and following.
2. Some medieval texts, however, seem to exhibit a desire to keep children away from sexual "secrets". Albert the Great's treatise on "women's secrets" is an example of this: "Thus I wished to satisfy your circumspect appetite and courage in writing this little tract, entreating your steadfastness that you be constant and secret in this work and business so as not to allow children *young in age and in morals* to be aware of those things written above..." Ariès recognises that moralists as far back as the Middle Ages were conscious of the innocence of children. This text, moreover, confirms what Ariès tells us of the confusion which occurs in medieval vocabulary between biological childhood and dependence. Medieval commentary on this passage is even more explicit: "The writer is saying here that it is not good for children young in age and in temperament to see this book, because youth and imprudence are naturally quick and inclined to evil rather than good..."

3. R. Mercier, *L'Enfant dans la société du XVIIIᵉ siècle*, doctoral dissertation, 1947, Paris, 1961, octavo (Bibliothèque Nationale: 4° Z 5411).

4. F. de Dainville, *La Naissance de l'humanisme moderne*.

5. Cf. F. de Dainville's articles in the journal *Population*, 1955, pp. 455–88, and 1957, pp. 467–94.

6. Regarding the history of education, R. Hubert's book, *Histoire de la pédagogie* (Paris, 1949, 404 pp.) accepts that, starting in the fifteenth century, it was standard practice for all students in the faculty of arts to be boarders. Regarding the history of the family, E. Pilon's book, *La Vie de famille au XVIIIᵉ siècle* (Paris, 1941, octavo), is informative.

7. Cf., Chapter X, written by P. Ariès in *La Prévention des naissances dans la famille (Travaux et documents de l'Institut national d'études démographiques*, issue no. 35).

8. *Idem.*

9. J. Calvet, *L'Enfant dans la littérature française*, Paris, 1941, 2 volumes 16mo.

CHAPTER 10

1. M. Garden, *Lyon et les Lyonnais au XVIIIᵉ siècle*, Paris, Les Belles Lettres, 1970, pp. 137–8.

2. Benedicti, *Somme des péchés* (quarto edition, Lyons, 1596), book II, chapter IX, no. 63, p. 227.

3. J.T. Noonan, *Contraception: A History of Its Treatment by the Catholic Theologians and Canonists*, Cambridge, Massachusetts, 1965, the book as a whole and chapters II, III and IV in particular.

4. Noonan, op.cit., pp. 81–5, in particular p. 83.

5. J.-L. Flandrin, *L'Eglise et le Contrôle des naissances*, Paris, Flammarion, "Questions d'histoire" collection, 1970, p. 117, document no. 8.

6. Noonan, op. cit., pp. 159–60 and 220–1.

7. P. de Palude, *In Quartum librum sententiarum*, 4, 31, 3, 2. See also Noonan, op. cit., pp. 220–1 concerning the Malthusian intentions of those practising *coitus interruptus*; and pp. 298–9 concerning *amplexus reservatus*.

8. J.-L. Flandrin, "Contraception, marriage and sexual relations in the Christian West", *Annales E.S.C.* November–December 1969 p. 1389, Note 3; see also p. 125 and note 6 p. 346.

9. St Paul, *First Letter to the Corinthians*, 7: 2: "But because of the temptation to immorality, each man should have his own wife and each woman her own husband". And *1 Corinthians* 7: 5: "...then come together again, lest Satan tempt you through lack of self-control".

10. Cf. M. Detienne, *Les Jardins d'Adonis...*, Paris, Gallimard, 1972.

11. Herodotus reports, for example, that Pisistratus "did not want to have children by his new wife and so had intercourse with her not according to custom", cf. Noonan, op. cit., p. 16.

12. Cf. Wrigley, *Population and History*, London, Weidenfeld and Nicholson, p. 126.

13. From 318 onwards, under Constantine's reign, infanticide was considered a crime (cf. *Codex Theodosianus*, 9, 15, 1). It is not until 374, after more than half a century of Christianity, that it was legally considered homicide (ibid., 9, 14, 1). On these points, see Noonan, op. cit., pp. 86–7 and 216–7.

14. Noonan, op. cit., pp. 161–2 and 164–6.

15. Under the heading of "relations against nature", theologians often spoke of inter-course as reprehensible simply because of the position used. This is true in particular of the backwards or *retro* position, referred to in almost all penitentials. The only

sterile positions are anal — *a tergo* — and oral — *seminem in ore*. But when they were discussed, the desire not to have children was never mentioned.

16. What is the meaning of *conceptum* for writers from the early Middle Ages? Compare, for example, two articles which Migne attributes to Theodore:

> "*Necasti voluntarie partus tuos, decem annos poeniteas...Et si vero ante conceptum, unum annum. Si post conceptum, tres annos...*" [Have you intentionally killed your offspring, you must do ten years' penance...If it is before conception, one year. If after conception, three years...] (Migne, *Patrologie latine*, Vol. 99, col. 967)

And *(LXVI) SI QUA MULIER PARTUM SUUM EXCUSSERIT*:

> "*Si qua mulier partum suum ante quadraginta dies in utero sponte perdiderit, annum unum poeniteat. Si vero post quadranginta dies eum occiderit, tres annos poeniteat. Si vero postquam animatus fuerit eum perdiderit, quasi homicida pertineat...*" [66. If a woman disposes of her unborn child: If a woman destroys the child which she carries in her uterus before the fortieth day, she must do penance for one year. If she kills it after the fortieth day, three years. If she destroys it after it is animated, it is like homicide.] (Migne, *Patrologie latine*, Vol. 99, col. 968).

A comparison of these two articles suggests that the child is not really conceived until forty days have passed. And that a certain amount of time must elapse — four months, probably — in order to consider it "animated".

17. Cf. Noonan, op. cit., pp. 159–60.
18. Gregory of Tours, *De virtutibus sancti Martini*, 2nd part, chapter 43, bilingual edition (Latin/French) of the *Société de l'histoire de France*, p. 165.
19. Gregory of Tours, op. cit., 3rd part, chapter 51, p. 257.
20. Gregory of Tours, *De gloria confessorum*, chapter 83, bilingual edition (Latin/French) of the *Société de l'histoire de France*, p. 75.
21. Gregory of Tours, *De virtutibus sancti Martini*, 2nd part, chapter 26, p. 139.
22. Quoted as a commentary by St Jerome on *Isaiah* 64.6 by most theologians from the late Middle Ages, this text is not found in the works of St Jerome edited by Migne. On the other hand, the *Glossa ordinaria* gives it, in that passage, without the writer's name. Probably it was attributed to St Jerome because of his reputation for interpreting the Holy Scriptures and the significance he attached to conjugal continence during menstruation in other texts. For the time being I do not have proof that this passage was written during the early Middle Ages, but I find it difficult to believe that it could have been written before the sixth century or after the twelfth, because of its content.
23. There are several variations in the quotations made by theologians of this passage. But the part which is most important here is always found: "*Ut quia parentes non erubuerunt misceri in conclavi* [or *in conclavi commisceri*] *eorum peccata pateant cunctis et aperte redargantur in parvulis* [or *omnibus et aperitus in parvulis redargantur]*".
24. St Caesarius of Arles, Sermon 292 in Migne, *Patrologie latine*, Vol. 39, col. 2300. This writer returns to this question at even greater length in Sermon 44 of Dom Germain Morin's edition, 1st volume, pp. 187–191.
25. Gregory of Tours, *De Virtutibus sancti Martini*, II, chapter 24. Translation (into French) from the Latin text by Migne, *Patrologie latine*, Vol. 71, col. 951 and 952.
26. In the same way Thietmar of Merseburg (975–1018) reports that a middle-class man who had conceived a child on a feastday lost it just after it had been baptised. Cf. P. Browe, *Beiträge zur Sexualethik des Mittelalters*, Breslau, 1932, octavo, 143pp., p. 48.
27. In Finnian's penitential for example is found, article 47: "If a child dies without having been baptised through the parents' negligence, it is a great crime, for a soul is lost. This crime can be atoned for through penance: a year of fasting on bread and water for the parents; they are not to sleep together in the same bed for the same period". Text translated into French by C. Vogel, *Le Pécheur et la Pénitence au Moyen*

Age, Paris, Editions du Cerf, "Chrétiens de tous les temps" collection, no. 30, 1969, p. 61.

Various similar articles exist, for example in Bede's penitential (II, 40), or in Burchard of Worms' *Decretum* (book XIX, articles 163 and 164), which has been translated into French in C. Vogel, op. cit., p. 76 and 106.

Burchard of Worms' *Decretum*, which provides us with so many indications of the paganizing attitudes in eleventh century Germanic society, suggests that parents had unforeseen reasons for ensuring that their children did not die without being baptised. Thus, in article 180: "Have you done as women have the habit of doing, at the devil's instigation? When a child dies without having been baptised, they take the tiny body and hide it in a secret place. They pierce the child's body with a stake and say that if they did not do so, the child would come back and might seriously injure other people. If yes: 2 years of fasting." (cf. Vogel, op. cit., p. 110)

28. Most penitentials attack infanticide more strongly than abortion after the "animation" of the foetus. For example, Burchard of Worms, book XIX of *Decretum*: "162. Have you caused an abortion...If you have done so before animation: 1 year of fasting; if after animation: 3 years of fasting on the appointed days. 163. Have you intentionally killed your son or daughter after birth? If yes: 12 years of fasting on the appointed days, and continuous penance until the end of your life" (cf. Vogel, op. cit., p. 106).

It does not seem to me that they penalise infanticide before baptism more than the murder of a baptised child.

It is more difficult to compare infanticide with homicide, for the penances for homicide are generally complicated by compensation to the victim's family and the very different types of homicide. But the penances for intentional homicide and parricide in a given penitential seem harsher than those inflicted on the murderer of his own or another's children. See for example Finnian, articles 12, 20 and 23; the lay penitential of St Colomban, articles 27 and 32; Bede's penitential, III, 2 and 12; and book XIX of Burchard of Worms' *Decretum*, articles 1–6 and 163 (cf. Vogel, op. cit., pp. 54–5, 56, 57; 68 and 69; 77 and 78; 81–2 and 106).

29. Gregory of Tours, loc. cit.

30. L. Musset, *Les Peuples scandinaves au Moyen Age*, Paris, PUF, 1951, p. 136.

31. Translated from Latin into French by Vogel, op. cit., p. 108.

32. Ivo of Chartres, *Decretum*, part XV, cap. 159, in Migne, *Patrologie latine*, vol. 161, col. 893.

33. Cf. Noonan, op. cit., in particular pp. 46–8, 131–2, 246–52, 318–9.

34. In writing of the good of procreation in his commentary *On Genesis*, Augustine says that, while it is good to have children, it is not enough to give them life: "the receiving of them lovingly, the nourishing of them humanely, the educating of them religiously" are also important. Cf. Noonan, op. cit., p. 127.

35. Gregory of Tours, *Des miracles de saint Martin*, II, chapter 24, bilingual edition (Latin/French) of the *Société de l'histoire de France*, p. 131, n. 1.

36. Vogel, op. cit., pp. 54–5.

37. This edict was published a great many times between 1557 and the Revolution, with various titles.

38. Indeed Henry II says in the edict's preamble: "As our Predecessors and Progeny the very Christian Kings of France have by virtuous and Catholic acts...shown by their very laudable actions that for right & good reason the said Name of very Christian, has been properly & particularly attributed to them, in which wanting to imitate & follow them, and having by several good & salutary examples displayed our devotion to conserving and keeping this so celestial and excellent title, the principle purposes of which are to initiate the creatures whom God sends to our earth in our Kingdom...to the Sacraments commanded by him & when it pleases Him to call

them back to him, to procure for them the other Sacraments instituted for this, with the last honours of the sepulchre..."

39. Indeed the edict's preamble specifies: "of which being warned & accused before our Judges, excuse themselves, saying they were ashamed to declare their vice & that their Children came out of their womb dead & without any sign of life; such that, in the absence of other proof, the People holding our Courts of Parliament, as well as our Judges, wishing to proceed to the Judgement of criminal proceedings made against such Women fell and entered into diverse opinions, some deciding for execution, others for ordinary questioning, in order to know & hear from their mouths whether in truth the children issued from their wombs were alive or dead; after which questioning borne, for having wanted to confess nothing, prisons are most often opened to them, which has been & is the cause of making them fall again, reoffend and commit such & similar crimes to our very great regret and the scandal of our Subjects..." As to the edict's pronouncement, it ends with these words: "So that this may serve as an example to all and that hereafter there be no doubt nor difficulty".

40. Cf. appendix I, pp. 198–199
41. Quoted by Clément, *La Police sous Louis XIV*, p. 132.
42. In St Columban's penitential, compare article 32 concerning the suffocation of the child to article 20 concerning magic spells (cf. Vogel, op. cit., pp. 69 and 67).
43. In book XIX of Burchard of Worms' *Decretum*, compare article 162 to article 183 (cf. Vogel, op. cit., pp. 106 and 110).
44. "Statuts synodaux du diocèse d'Albi (1230)", *Revue historique du droit français et étranger*, 4th series, vol. VI (1927), p. 437. Synode de Meaux (1245), in Martène, *Thes. nov. anec.*, vol. IV, p. 894.
45. According to Gousset's edition, *Actes de la province de Reims*, vol. I, p. 444.
46. "Statuts synodaux d'Amiens (1411)", published by J.-M. Mioland, in *Actes de l'Eglise d'Amiens*, Amiens, 1848, vol. I, p. 26. According to an anonymous *Confessio generalis* from the beginning of the sixteenth century or the end of the fifteenth (Bibliothèque Nationale, Paris: Réserve, D. 7108), which indicates the "*casus pertinentes episcopus continentur generaliter in his versibus...*" [cases generally reserved for the bishop are contained in these verses]. — *Statuts synodaux du diocèse d'Alby* (1553), kept in the Sainte-Geneviève library under the reference: C. quarto 291. Inv. 291. — The cases reserved for the bishop of Lyons, according to Benedicti, op. cit. (published for the first time in 1584). — J. Chapéaville, *Tractatus de casibus reservatus* (1614), p. 159 — *Statuts synodaux du diocèse de Sens* (1658), p. 79 — "Cas réservés au diocèse de Saint-Omer" (1696), according to Gousset, op. cit., vol. IV, p. 539, article 5.
47. Mioland, op. cit., vol. I, p. 57.
48. Aside from the statutes of Amiens in 1454, see those from Besançon (1571) in Mansi's collection, vol. 36b, pp. 58–9; *Rituel de la province de Reims* from 1677, kept at the Bibliothèque Nationale, Paris, reference: B.1765; and the list of cases reserved for the bishop of Laon in 1683, according to Gousset, op. cit., vol. IV, pp. 433–5.
49. These are to be found at the Bibliothèque Nationale in Paris in:

Le Rituel du diocèse de Strasbourg (1742), p. 134, 8th case;

The list of cases reserved for the bishop of Boulogne in 1734 (according to Gousset, Vol. IV, pp. 734–735), 11th case;

Le Rituel du diocèse de Bayeux (1744), p. 137, 8th case;

Le Rituel du diocèse de Bourges (1746), p. 203, 4th case;

Le Rituel du diocèse de Poitiers (1766), p. 101, 7th case;

Les Statuts synodaux du diocèse de Soissons (1742) (1769 edition), p. 321, 8th case;

Le Rituel du diocèse du Mans (1775), p. 93, 19th case;

Le Rituel du diocèse de Luçon (1768), p. 102, 4th case.

50. In Gousset, op. cit., vol. IV, pp. 494–5.
51. For example, that of Albi in 1695, pp. 95–6 in the statutes; or that of Carcassonne in 1756, pp. 136–41 of *Decreta synodi diocesanae Carpentoractensis*, the 3rd of the "cases which the present bishop reserves for himself and for his successors".
52. *Rituel du diocèse de Langres*, 1789, pp. 221–2.
53. I base this firstly on what Fromageau says of this in his *Dictionnaire des cas de conscience* (Paris, 1733), in the article "*Enfant*", col. 1435: "Civil laws punish those women who abandon their children: they do not distinguish between the mother who suffocates her child at her breast, and one who refuses to help one after its birth: these are considered to be homicide, even though after they have abandoned their children, people might be found to take charge of them and to show charity towards them..."; and secondly on H. Bergues, *La Prévention des naissances dans la famille*, Paris, PUF, 1960, pp. 165–6. This author reports that an imperial decree in 374 condemns the abandonment of children. See also La Poix de Fréminville's *Dictionnaire...* (1769), quoted by H. Bergues, ibid., p. 172.
54. It is probable that this refusal to shed the blood of one's offspring survived in Christian society and explains why straightforward cases of infanticide are so often called suffocation.
55. Lanctantius, speaking of pagans, wrote in the fourth century in his *Divine Institutes*, 5.9.15: "They strangle children born of them, or, *if they are too pious for that*, they abandon them". Cf. Noonan, op. cit., p. 87.
56. Cf. *Mémoire sur les hôpitaux*, by Tenon, quoted by H. Bergues, op. cit., p. 167.
57. Benedicti, op. cit., book II, chapter II, p. 180.
58. Quoted by H. Bergues, op. cit., pp. 166–7.
59. Concerning all these questions, see J. Charpentier, *Le Droit de l'enfance abandonnéeD*, Paris, PUF, 1967, *a work which I only discovered after writing this article. It was in the eighteenth century — thanks to St Vincent de Paul's charitable work and Colbert's populationist policy — that society's attitudes towards the children of sin changed.*
60. Lallemand, *Histoire des enfants abandonnés et délaissés*, Paris, 1885, p. 163. Quoted by H. Bergues, op. cit., p. 171.
61. Abbé Malvaux, *Les Moyens de détruire la mendicité en France en rendant les mendiants utiles à l'Etat, sans les rendre malheureux*, Paris, 1780. Passages quoted by H. Bergues, op. cit., pp. 176 and 177.
62. H. Bergues, op. cit., p. 177.
63. Cf. H. Bergues, op. cit., p. 178.
64. According to Benedicti, in the sixteenth century, the bishop of Lyons reserved for himself the sins of "those who secretly carry their children to hospitals or other public places and abandon them" (cf. pp. 627–8 of the quarto edition of 1601).
    Moreover, the synodal statutes of the diocese of Albi, in 1965, indicate as the 8th of the cases reserved for the bishop: "The exposure and abandonment of Children, putting them to sleep in a bed before the age of one year and one day".
65. Fromageau and Lamet, *Dictionnaire des cas de conscience*, Paris, 1733, 2 folio volumes, vol. I, at the word "*Enfant*", col. 1438.
66. Ibid., col. 1437.
67. Ibid., col. 1435.
68. Cf. H. Bergues, op. cit., p. 166.
69. Quoted by H. Bergues, op. cit., p. 176.
70. Based on statements from 1760, Lallemand claims that there were 4,297 illegitimate children and only 735 legitimate ones out of 5,032 admissions in that year. These figures are much too precise to be convincing: would not all abandoned children have been counted as illegitimate, the others being orphans or poor children and usually older, whose parents it was possible to trace?
71. Benedicti, op. cit., book II, chapter II, no. 19, p. 143 of the 1596 edition.
72. Benedicti, op. cit., book II, chapter IV, no. 19, p. 164.

73. In Gousset, op. cit., vol. I, p. 444: "*Negligentias parentum in igne vel aqua natos perdentiumD*".

74. A. Girard, L. Henry and R. Nistri, "La surmortalité infantile dans le Nord et le Pas-de-Calais", *Population*, no. 2, 1959, pp. 221–32.

75. J. Magaud and L. Henry, "Le rang de naissance dans les phénomènes démographiques", *Population*, no. 5, 1968, pp. 879–920. See p. 893 in particular.

76. Benedicti, op. cit., book II, chapter II, no. 20, p. 143.

77. M. Garden, *Lyon et les Lyonnais au XVIIIᵉ siècle*, Paris, Les Belles Lettres, 1970. The percentages of children from the Hôtel Dieu who died while put out to nurse are given on p. 128. As for the other children, the author writes on p. 134: "Police proceedings at the end of the century show the precariousness of children's fates, and a few examples are enough to show that the fate of a child in Lyons is no better than that of a foundling". For the time being I will accept this assessment, although it seems to me not to have been sufficiently proven. At the bottom of p. 139, M. Garden repeats: "Children of middle-class parents are affected almost as much as the others. However, it would be necessary to collect more specific statistics in order to know whether higher rates for the wet nurse and shorter travelling distances did not decrease mortality in more well-off families".

78. M. Garden, op. cit., p. 137.

79. Ibid.

80. Ibid., p. 132.

81. Ibid., p. 131.

82. Ibid., pp. 137–8.

83. Benedicti, op. cit., book II, chapter II, no. 20: "On this point several mothers offend *who abandon their own offspring*, which even dumb animals do not do...cruel and unnatural mothers as they are, for them it is enough to have brought forth their children from their womb and put them on earth, and then to send them to appalling villages to be fed..."

84. M. Garden, op. cit., p. 121.

85. Benedicti, op. cit., book II, chapter II, no. 20.

86. Fernandes de Moure, *Examen de la théologie morale*, Rouen, 1638, octavo, pp. 692–3.

87. T. Sanchez, *De sancto matrimonii sacramento*, book IX, dist. XXII, no. 14.

88. Gregory of Tours, *De gloria confessorum*, chapter 83: "There was a small child of almost three, still hanging from his mother's breast". Admittedly, at the end of the text, the author adds: "He was not yet quite old enough to walk", which seems strange for a child of almost three. But there may be many ways of explaining this strangeness. And in any case, the fact remains that the author believes that a child of almost three can still be at his mother's breast.

89. H. de la Ferrière and Baguenault de Puchèse, *Lettres de Catherine de Médicis*, see vol. I, p. 62 and following, the letters to Mme de Humières:

    Letter dated 1st June 1552: "...and as for my son Orléans, you will have seen what I wrote to you concerning his wet nurse, but you had not received my letter when you engaged her, and I am very glad that no bad has come of it for I was afraid that the hot blood which was shown by the sores which had appeared on the wet nurse would worsen her milk during the flushes..." The Duke of Orléans at that time was her son Charles-Maximilien, born 27 June 1550, who was therefore almost two.

    Letter dated 10 June 1552: "...As for my son Orléans's wet nurse, to whom he was given for reasons which La Romanerie has explained to me, I consider it a good idea, because he is in good health as a result..."

    Letter dated 13 August 1552: "As for my son Orléans, I would like very much for him to be weaned from her breast when the time is right and the doctor commands it, without waiting to hear from me, for you are better placed to know what he needs than I would know..." Thus one begins to think of weaning at the age of more than two years, when not forced to do so earlier, as is the case here.

Letter dated 22 August 1552: "...I see from the letters that you have written me that my son Orléans has been ill with a cold and a fever, which causes me pain, for I fear that it comes from his wet nurse who may have given him bad milk and thus I beseech you to be careful and to follow Monsieur Burgensis' written instructions..."

From these letters, I conclude that at the age of two years and almost two months, when the correspondence with Mme de Humières ends, the child has not yet been weaned, although they began to talk of weaning when he was about two years old. This confirms what theologians tell us, that is to say that it was believed necessary to breast-feed children until their third year, when possible.

90. Among many other books on this subject, see for example E.H. Erikson, *Childhood and Society*, Penguin Books Ltd., Harmondsworth, 1965. Speaking of the Sioux Indians, the author writes, pp. 129–130: "It is said that the oldest boy was nursed longest and that the average nursing period was three years. Today it is much shorter, although instances of prolonged nursing persist, to the dismay of those whose job it is to foster health and morals". Then he tells the story of a mother who went to school to nurse her eight-year-old boy, to pamper him because he had a cold. He adds: "Among the old Sioux there was no systematic weaning at all."

91. See, for example, the recent article by B. Lacombe and J. Vaugelade, "Fécondité, mortalité infantile et allaitement. Schéma d'analyse", *Population*, no. 2, 1969, pp. 343–8.

92. Pierre Goubert, *Beauvais et le Beauvaisis*, Paris, SEVPEN, 1960, vol. II, p. 41.

93. J. Dupâquier and M. Lachiver, "Sur les débuts de la contraception en France", *Annales ESC* (special issue on *Biologie et Société*), November/December 1969, pp. 1396–8.

94. For example among the Sioux Indians, according to E.H. Erikson, op. cit., p. 129: "The baby's nursing was so important that, in principle at least, not even the father's sexual privileges were allowed to interfere with the mother's libidinal concentration on the nursing. A baby's diarrhoea was said to be the result of a watery condition of the mother's milk brought about by intercourse with the father. The husband was urged to keep away from the wife for the nursing period, which, it is said, lasted from three to five years."

95. Cf. Noonan, op. cit., p. 50.

96. *Monumenta Germaniae Historica. Epistolarum*, vol. II, Pars I: *Gregorii I papae registrum*, book XI, 56a, p. 339. This letter can also be found in Migne's *Patrologie latine* vol. 77, col. 1138 and following.

97. A. Tiraqueau, *De legibus connubialibus*, part XV, no. 139 and 140. See appendix II, pp. 199–200.

98. Benedicti, op. cit., book II, chapter IX, no. 67, p. 166 of the 1601 edition.

99. In the *Summa Rosella* under the word *DEBITUM*, no. 9, one finds: "As for what was said in the canon *Ad eius*...that has been repealed and is a piece of advice rather than a precept". Sanchez and A. Liguori also believe that it is only advice.

100. T. Sanchez, loc. cit.

101. See below, note 119.

102. A. Tiraqueau, op. cit., part XV, no. 40.

103. Gregory the Great, loc. cit.

104. Cf. P. Riché, "Problèmes de démographie historique du haut Moyen Age (Ve-VIIIe siècles)", *Annales de démographie historique*, 1966, p. 44.

105. For example, this is what Dr L. Joubert says in his *Erreurs populaires*, in the second half of the sixteenth century: "... if the wet nurse is married, they do not want her husband to know her in any way: and this for fear that it might affect her milk".

106. M. Garden, op. cit., p. 121: "François Vaché, master butcher, put a child out to nurse with the wife of Giroud, of Saint-Forgeux..."; less than a month after she is given the child, Mme Giroud is pregnant: "Driven by reckless ambition, in no way troubling herself to tell the parents, quite the opposite, she hid her pregnancy as best she could and continued to feed the child with bad milk. Her advanced stage of pregnancy having caused her milk to dry up, she weaned the child at the age of five months, which could not be done without damaging the health of a child who should have continued to have good milk until he reached about one year of age." "The wet nurse keeps the child for another three months, and, when he is returned to his parents, he is in such a pitiful state that the parents must give him to another woman to try to help him regain his health".

And, p. 123, note 87: "This fifth 'spoiled' child had been the victim of a pregnant mother-wet nurse who weaned the infant at six months".

107. T. Sanchez, op. cit., book IX, dist. XXII, no. 15.
108. The clearest analysis of the nature of the infirmity is found in an original passage by St Jerome, in his commentary on *Ezekiel* 18: "At which time, if a man has intercourse with a woman, it is said that the children *acquire the corruption in the seed,* so that they are born leprous and with elephantiasis from such a conception, and *this harmful pus causes the body to degenerate,* by the smallness or largeness of the limbs, *in either sex*. It is *therefore* commanded that men...must know...the times when one should have intercourse with one's wife and the times when one must abstain" (*Patrologie latine,* vol. 25, col. 174). As of the thirteenth century, theologians believe the situation to be thus, without being so explicit: P. de Palude speaks of the "danger of infection", as do St Antoninus of Florence, Sylvester, Dominic Soto, Luis Lopez, Barthélemy de Ledesma, Henriquez, Francisco de Vitoria, etc after him. For his part, the author of the *Summa Rosella* writes: "It is possible to beget children in very poor health, *because of the corruption of the humour*". And from the author of the *Summa Tabiensis:* "This blood is impure blood: that is why, if coitus takes place during menstrual purgation, the foetus is harmed *because he must be nourished by this very impure blood."*
109. Cf. St Thomas for example, *Commentaire sur le IVᵉ livre des Sentences,* dist. 32, art. II, reply to the 2nd question: "It must be said that intercourse with a menstruating woman was prohibited for two reasons: firstly because of the impurity, secondly because of the damage often done to a child by such activity. The first reason was a question of formality, but the second a question of morality...This is why this precept is binding even in the new law, for the second reason if not for the first".
110. Cf. Noonan, op. cit., pp. 283–4.
111. Cf. note 9. But, where St Paul spoke of the purpose of marriage, the theologians of the late Middle Ages speak of the immediate motives for the conjugal act, which seems much more shocking today.
112. Cf. Noonan, op. cit., p. 283, note 7.
113. Basing his work on the study of 20 penitentials, Noonan has underestimated their concern with continence during pregnancy. Of 57 penitentials concerned with conjugal continence, I myself found 33 which considered intercourse with a pregnant wife to be reprehensible. As some of the penitentials devote several different articles to this sin, I am discussing here a total of more than 33 articles.
114. In this debate, Sanchez refers to no theologian earlier than St Antoninus. Yet undoubtedly P. de Palude preceded St Antoninus in indulgent attitudes. However, it would be necessary to establish whether he was not himself preceded by St Thomas, Albert the Great or another thirteenth century theologian.
115. P. de Palude, *Commentaire sur le IVᵉ livre des Sentences,* dist. XXXI, q. 3, article 2, 5th case.
116. Conjugal relations during breast-feeding, which had been denounced by Pline, Galen, Gregory the Great and no doubt many other doctors and sacred writers

during the first six centuries, were no longer discussed between the seventh and twelfth centuries, except for several writers who quote Gregory the Great's phrase, without adding any support of their own. According to Sanchez and Alphonsus Liguori, four authors explicitly authorised these relations in the thirteenth and fourteenth centuries: St Bonaventure, Richard Middleton, Astensis and P. de Palude. From the end of the fourteenth or the beginning of the fifteenth up to the eighteenth century, one can find some theologians who authorise them and other who forbid them quite strictly. Numbered among the former are the Inquisitor Torquemada and the author of the *Summa Rosella* in the fifteenth century, and several seventeenth century writers. Numbered among the latter are the canonists Dominicus and Antonius de Burtio at the end of the fourteenth or at the beginning of the fifteenth century, Alexandre de Nevo at the end of the fifteenth, the jurist Tiraqueau in the sixteenth, Pontius and Bossius in the seventeenth. Between the two extremes, P. de Ledesma, T. Sanchez and Alphonsus Liguori condemn neither the husband who demands the marital debt at such a time, nor the wife who refuses to render it. Most of this information needs to be verified, however, and a systematic study should be undertaken.

117. Peter de Ledesma, *De magno matrimonii sacramento*, q. LXIV, art. 1, 4th difficulty.
118. In his *Commentaire sur le IVᵉ livre des Sentences*, dist. XXXII, q. 1, art. 1, according to Noonan, op. cit., pp. 330–1.
119. Cf. Noonan, op. cit., p. 332.
120. Angelus de Clavasio, *Summa Angelica*, at the word "*debitum*", no. 32.
121. Sylvester da Priero, *Summa Summarum*, at the word "*debitum*", no. 8.
122. St Thomas, *Commentaire sur le IVᵉ livre des Sentences*, dist. XXXIII, art. 2, q. 3.
123. T. Sanchez, op. cit., book IX, dist. XXII, no. 15.
124. All these debates come back to the argument that, if prolonged continence were demanded of couples, marriage would be like a running knot and not a remedy against fornication: because those who chose marriage were not cut out for continence. In the same way, in the debate concerning continence during feastdays and fast days, Richard Middleton wrote in 1272 that the Church "does not intend to put the rope around its children's necks, and that is why — since to prohibit the exaction of the conjugal debt in holy periods would to a certain extent be like putting the rope around their necks, in that the corruption of the flesh arouses concupiscence not only at ordinary times but also during holy times — it does not prohibit the exaction of the debt during holy times, but only advises against it".

We know too that the increase in the number of impediments to marriage — particularly with regard to consanguinity, affinity and spiritual kinship — had created so much matrimonial instability that the Council of the Lateran IV, in 1214, had been roused to action and had done away with a great many of the impediments. Thus, generally speaking, it seems that, between the sixth and the thirteenth century, the Church had tried in various ways to curb sexual activity and that, realising the drawbacks of this policy, it changed to merely channelling sexual activity towards marriage. Undoubtedly it had not yet gone far enough along this road, because in the sixteenth century compulsory celibacy for the clergy was strongly attacked and the Protestant churches abandoned it.

125. Cf. Noonan, op. cit., pp. 279–80.
126. Of the children taken in in Paris, 47% are reported to have died in 1690, 68% in 1751, 92% in 1797 and 68% in 1818. Cf. H. Bergues, op. cit., p. 181. In Lyons, there is a similar regular increase in the mortality rate of children taken in at the Hôtel-Dieu; according to M. Garden: 52.1% die when put out to nurse in 1716–1717; 54% in 1757–1758; and 66.2% in 1771–1772.
127. In the Maison de La Couche in Paris, there were 3,000 foundlings between 1640 and 1649, which increased to 17,000 between 1710 and 1719. The numbers then increased even more quickly to reach one third of births in Paris in 1772. An increase

is also noted in most large towns and cities in France and western Europe. Cf. H. Bergues, op. cit., pp. 170–80.
128. See M.-C. Phan's master's dissertation, *Introduction à l'étude des déclarations de grossesse* (type-written), Vincennes, December 1971 and corresponding article in the *Revue d'Histoire Moderne et Contemporaine*, 1975.
129. Ibid.
130.

	Fertility	Infant Mortality
Sainghin- en-Mélantois	1740–1769: 37.1% 1770–1780: 29.4%	1740–1769: 26.7% 1770–1789: 14.5%
Tamerville	1640–1710: 33.1% 1711–1792: 30.2%	1624–1720: 17.1% 1721–1792: 10.9%
Meulan	1660–1739: 38.2% 1740–1789: 32.8% 1790–1839: 22.2%	1668–1739: 24.4% 1740–1789: 22.6% 1790–1839: 15.5%

Cf. J. Deniel and L. Henry, "Sainghin-en-Mélantois", *Population*, no. 4, 1965. P. Wiel, "Tamerville", *Annales de démographie historique*, 1969. M. Lachiver, *La Population de Meulan du XVIIe au XIXe siècle*, Paris, SEVPEN, 1969.
131. J. Bourgeois-Pichat, "Evolution de la population française depuis le XVIIIe siècle", *PopulationD*, October/December 1951, pp. 635–62; and April/June 1952, pp. 319–29.
132. Curves showing age-specific death rates can be found in Wrigley, *Population and History*, pp. 166–7, but they cover only the period 1845–1955. For the earlier period, see D.V. Glass, "Population and Population Movements in England and Wales, 1700 to 1850", *Population in History*, pp. 211–46. Lastly, concerning the causes for the decline in infant mortality, I used T. McKeown and R.G. Record's article, "Reasons for Decline of Mortality in England and Wales during the Nineteenth Century", *Population Studies*, November 1962, vol. XVI, no. 2, pp. 94–122.

CHAPTER 11

1. For this article, we started by compiling a list of all proverbs relating to children from the collections listed at the end of the chapter. Then, we grouped together those which were similar in form, theme, or in the images used. Based on this work, it is possible to ascertain whether or not proverbs exist, for a given theme, which were collected before or after a given period of time. In the same way it would have been possible to find out in which regions or which social milieux proverbs about a given theme were collected, but for the time being this posed too many problems. In addition, some themes mentioned in these proverbs — for example, the ressemblance between children and their parents or the difference between boys and girls — will not be dealt with here but have been or will be discussed elsewhere. Lastly, this article is only a partial example of the method suggested, in that many ancient or recent collections remain to be examined. Because of this, those of my conclusions which are based on the absence of proverbs before or after a given date remain provisional.
2. Too little has been written to date regarding this point. However, see for example, P. Laslett, *The World we have lost*, London, Methuen and Company, 1965, pp. 69–72.
3. For more detail, see J.-L. Flandrin, *Families in Former Times, Kinship, Household and Sexuality*, translated by Richard Southern, Cambridge University Press, 1979, Chapter 2, "The Household: Size, Structure and Material Life".
4. For a quick overview of the Church's doctrine in this field and the toughening of its

attitude at the end of the nineteenth century, see J.-L. Flandrin, *L'Eglise et le Contrôle des Naissances*, Paris, Flammarion, "Questions d'histoire" collection, no. 23, 1970.

5. Cf. J.-L. Flandrin, "Attitudes towards young children and sexual behaviour", above pp. 141 and 167–169.

6. Regarding the fear of childbirth and its influence on the origins of birth control, see J.-L. Flandrin, *Families*, Chapter 4, pp. 209–12.

7. In M. Garden, *Lyon et les Lyonnais au XVIIIᵉ siècle*, abridged edition "Science Flammarion", 1975, Chapter II.

8. Brantôme, *Les Dames galantes*, Paris, Garnier, pp. 38–9.

9. Montaigne, *Essais*, Book I, Chapter XIV, p. 83 in the Pléaide edition.

10. See, for example, P. Ariès, *Essais sur l'histoire de la mort en Occident*, Paris, Seuil, 1975; or M. Vovelle, *Mourir autrefois*, Paris, Gallimard, "Archives" collection, 1975.

11. This thesis is developed in J.-L. Flandrin, *Families*, Chapter 4, pp. 217–25 and 233.

12. Compare with this the saying: "*Femmes ne sont pas gens*" [Women are not people] (Quittard, 1861). Yet before concluding from this that the status of women was worse than that of children, we would need to know precisely in what situations each saying was used.

13. In this respect, the status of women is very similar to that of children: in general the proverbs express the point of view of men talking to other men about the problem women constitute for men.

14. Such cultural alienation is obviously not peculiar to ancient society nor to childhood alone. But why is it the only one which is never noticed?

15. The same could be said of bastards, serfs, villains, rustics, peasants, women, sodomites, etc. as references to them could also be used as insults.

16. Cf. J.-L. Flandrin, "Attitudes towards young children...", above.

17. Ariès, *Centuries of Childhood*, translated by Robert Baldick, London, Jonathan Cape, 1962.

18. Cf. J.-L. Flandrin, *Families*, Chapter 3, "Domestic Morality", pp. 122–30.

19. I deal with the question of premarital sexual activity in "Late Marriages and Sex Lives" in section three, in the conclusion of *Amours paysannes*, Paris, Gallimard, "Archives" collection, no. 57, 1975 and in Chapter 4 of *Families*. Our knowledge of this field has however recently been improved significantly by Jacques Rossiaud, whose article "*Prostitution, jeunesse et société dans les villes du Sud-Est au XVᵉ siècle*" appeared in *Annales ESC*, March/April 1976.

CHAPTER 12

1. Much research has been done recently concerning the teaching of young working-class women to read and write between the sixteenth and the end of the nineteenth century. See for example François Furet and Jacques Ozouf, *Lire et Écrire: l'alphabétisation des Français de Calvin à Jules Ferry*, Paris, Editions de Minuit, 1977, 2 volumes; and R. Chartier, M.-M. Compère and D. Julia, *L'Education en France du XVIᵉ au XVIIIᵉ siècle*, Paris, Sédès, 1976. Information concerning their love affairs can be found in J.-L. Flandrin, *Les Amours paysannes, XVIᵉ-XVIIIᵉ siècles*, Paris, Gallimard, "Archives" collection, no. 57, 1975; and *Families in Former Times, Kinship, Household and Sexuality*, translated by Richard Southern, Cambridge University Press, 1979.

2. I have mainly used Le Roux de Lincy's collection, *Le Livre des proverbes français*, 2nd edition, Paris, 1859, 2 volumes. Where the author mentions it, I have indicated in which century each proverb was published for the first time; where he does not, I have only indicated that the proverb is old by indicating the author's initials, "LRL". In addition I have used Basque proverbs collected by Oihenart in the seventeenth

century and various collections of patois proverbs from the nineteenth and twentieth centuries.
3. P. Bourdieu, "Célibat et condition paysanne", *Etudes rurales*, April/September 1962, pp. 32–135.

CHAPTER 13

1. Cf. *Annales*, 1969, no. 6, p. 1370–1390; and below pp. 99–116.
2. A. Burguière, "De Malthus à Max Weber: le mariage tardif et l'esprit d'entreprise"; J. Depauw, "Amour illégitime et société à Nantes au XVIIIᵉ siècle", *Annales*, 1972, no. 4/5.
3. Conjugal chastity implies that the partners have sexual relations in order to procreate. But virginal or "perfect" chastity remains superior to conjugal chastity. These are the reservations which can be found in the Church's doctrine. In Christian practice it seems that a certain disrepute weighs heavily on sexuality as a whole. Quite evident during the early Middle Ages, did these "Cathar" tendencies re-emerge in the seventeenth century after being discouraged? P. Chaunu appears to support this (cf. *Annales*, 1972, no. 1, p. 18).
4. Cf. J. Hajnal's article on marriage patterns in western Europe in *Population in History*, London, 1965, 692 pp.
5. "Civilized Sexual Morality and Modern Nervous Illness", translated into English by E.B. Herford and E.C. Mayne in the collection: *The Complete Psychological Works of Sigmund Freud*, Vol. IX, London, the Hogarth Press, 1959, pp. 181–204. The passage quoted is from page 193.
6. In this article, Freud presents three stages of civilisation in the evolution of the sexual instinct: "a first one, in which the sexual instinct may be freely exercised without regard to the aims of reproduction; a second, in which all of the sexual instinct is suppressed except what serves the aims of reproduction; and a third, in which only legitimate reproduction is allowed as a sexual aim." (p. 189) It is self-evident that this is a simplified view of the human mind.
7. For example, the synodal statutes of Cambrai (around 1300–1310) reserve the absolution of men over twenty who have committed the sin of sodomy for the bishop, whereas the penitentiary is authorised to absolve this sin for women of any age and men under the age of twenty (cf. *Annales*, 1969, no. 6, p. 1376).
8. Cf. *Annales*, 1972, no. 1, p. 18.
9. A. Lottin championed this idea in the *Revue d'histoire moderne et contemporaine*, April/June 1970, pp. 293–4. It is also found below article 17 of the second part of the encyclical *Humanae vitae*.
10. See for example, in Cummean's penitential (seventh century), Chapter XI concerning "childish games". There, in fact, the most characteristic act of sodomy is severely punished: "*In terga vero fornicantes, si pueri sunt, duobus anni, si viri tribus annis vel quatuor...*" [For those who fornicate from behind, if they are children, 2 years, if they are men, 3 or 4 years...] But all sorts of sexual games are described which are punished much less severely. For example: "*2. Osculum simpliciter facientes VI superpositionibus; inlecebrosum osculum sine coinquinamento, VIII; si cum coinquinamento sive amplexu, X superpositionibus corrigantur. 3. Post autem annum XX (id est adulti) idem committentes XL diebus separati sunt a mensa et extores ab ecclesia cum pane et aqua vivant. 4. Minimi vero fornicationem imitantes et inritantes se invicem, sed coinquinati non sunt propter immaturitatem aetatis, XX diebus; si vero frequenter, XL. 5. Puer qui sacrificio communicat peccans cum pecode, centum diebus. 6. Pueri autem XX annorum se invicem manibus coinquinantes et confessi fuerint antequam communicant, XX vel XL diebus...8. Supra dicta aetas inter foemora fornicantes, 6 diebus; id iterum faciens,*

annum. 9. Puer parvulus oppressus a majore annum aetatis habens decimum ebdomadam dierum jejunet; si consensit, XX diebus." [2. Those who simply kiss each other will be corrected by 6 superpositions, 8 superpositions for fellatio without ejaculation, or 10 with ejaculation or with embrace. 3. If over 20 years of age, i.e. adults, those who sin in these ways will be excommunicated for 40 days and banished from the Church and they will live on bread and water. 4. Children who imitate fornication and caress each other, but without ejaculating, on the grounds of being too young; 20 days, but if they indulge on a regular basis, 40 days. 5. A child who, having sinned with an animal, goes to communion, 100 days. 6. Young people of 20 years of age who masturbate each other and would have gone to confession before communion, 20 or 40 days....8. Those of the above age who would fornicate between the thighs, 6 days; and those would do it a second time, 1 year. 9. A small child of 10 years, oppressed by an elder, should fast for a week; and if he consented, 20 days.] And when these games take place with a girl: *"17. Puer de saeculo veniens nuper cum aliqua puella fornicari nitens nec coinquinatus, XX diebus; si autem coinquinatus est, C diebus; si vero, ut moris est, suam compleat voluntatem, anno peniteat."* [17. A youth of an intermediate generation who has recently fornicated with any girl, if he did not ejaculate, 20 days; if he did, 100 days; and if, as tends to be the case, he does it fully willingly, he must do penance for 1 year] (Bieler, *The Irish Penitentials*, pp. 126–8).

11. Cf. *Annales*, 1969, no. 6 p. 1376.
12. Gerson, *Confessional...* (Bibliothèque Nationale, Rés. D. 11579), the chapter dealing with the sin of lust.
13. Ibid.
14. Cf. D. Rochemonteix, *Un collège de jésuites au XVIIe siècle: le collège Henri-IV de La Flèche*, vol. II, p. 29. This passage is quoted by G. Snyders, *La Pédagogie en France aux XVIIe et XVIIIe siècles*, p. 40.
15. *L'Ecole paroissiale ou la manière de bien instruire les enfants dans les petits escoles*, Paris 1654. This book had many editions in the seventeenth century and was officialy adopted in many dioceses. Nonetheless today it cannot be found in Paris, and I familiarised myself with it from a photocopy made at the Bordeaux library, which François Furet kindly lent me.
16. Cf. Dr Hesnard, *La Sexologie*, Paris, "Petite Bibliothèque Payot", no. 31, 1959, p. 287: "Surveys in various lands, in particular those reported by H. Ellis, indicate that it is even more widespread in those educational establishments where sexual ignorance reigns together with the terrifying threats against the sin of impurity. At the same time, it is haphazard and more or less short-lived in those milieux tolerant of the natural aspects of sexuality. We have had the opportunity to compare its frequency in various ethnic groups: it is less widespread, sometimes non-existent in working classes and particularly in sexually liberal countries. Thus young Arabs in North Africa consider it unappealing, if not despicable (whereas they engage in allo-erotic games, which are unimportant for them, during which they imitate adults' sexual practices). On the contrary, young Jews in the same regions are attracted by solitary masturbation, which their teachers, for religious reasons, condemn very severely".
17. Ibid., p. 286.
18. Cf. S. Freud, *the Complete Psychological Works of Sigmund Freud*, p. 189.
19. Cf. *Annales*, 1969, no. 6, pp. 1374–5. Strictness towards masturbation varies from one penitential to another and sometimes within the same penitential. But the most common attitude is that of relative indulgence.
20. This point comes across clearly in St Augustine's canon *Adulteri Malum*. It seems to me that all theologians, from Gratian and Peter Lombard onwards, support this point of view. On this subject see J.T. Noonan, *Contraception*, Harvard University Press, 1976, pp. 174, 260, 304.
21. Cf. *Annales*, 1969, no. 6, pp. 1376–7.

22. Guy de Roye, *Le Doctrinal de sapience qui contient tous les estats du monde...*, 1585 French edition (Bibliothèque Nationale, D 50934), pp. 148–50.
23. Op. cit.
24. J. Gerson, *Opera*, 1606 folio edition, t.II (first volume), pp. 309–12, *Tractatus de confessione molliciei*.
25. At the beginning of his treatise, Gerson attributes authorship to "a certain master of theology from Paris who, thanks to abundant experience and careful study, and with God's help solicited by pious zeal, has discovered the things which are hereafter written and which have been very effective for extracting that most abominable of sins which is called *mollities* from the heart of those who are confessing, particularly from young people".
26. Ibid.
27. Cf. Gerson, *Confessional*, chapter about lust.
28. Benedicti, *La Somme des péchés*, quarto edition, Paris, 1601, book II, chapter VIII, pp. 152–160.
29. Although from the thirteenth century at least, theologians use "*mollities*" to designate solitary practices, Benedicti curiously feels the need to justify this interpretation of the use made by St Paul: "It is therefore not without reason that St Paul teaches his Corinthians to hate this filth, when he writes to them: "Do not be deceived; neither the immoral, nor idolaters, nor adulterers, nor homosexuals, nor thieves, nor the greedy, nor drunkards, nor revilers, nor robbers will inherit the kingdom of God". In the Greek, the word used for homosexuals was *mollities*, which to us means those who pollute themselves. It has been used with this meaning equally by the Greek and Latin fathers, just as even last year I learned it from a Greek monk, one of those who are called Caloyers, whom I found in Jerusalem, where he gave me the same interpretation of this word "*mollities*" as our Theologians give us" (ibid.).
30. Ibid.
31. Cf. Noonan, *Contraception*, p. 269.
32. Benedicti, loc. cit.
33. Cf. *L'instruction de Prestres qui contient sommairement tous les cas de conscience*. Written in Latin by the Illustrious and Reverend Cardinal François Tolet, of the Company of Jesus. Translated into French by M.A. Goffar, Doctor of Theology..., Lyons, 1628, quarto, book V, chapter XIII, no. 10 and 11.
34. Cf. Fontaine, *Mémoires pour servir à l'histoire de Port-Royal*, vol. II, p. 486. Passage quoted by G. Snyders, op. cit., p. 45.
35. Cf. Noonan, op. cit., chapter II, section on the Stoic ideal, pp. 46–49. See also J.-L. Flandrin, *L'Eglise et le Contrôle des naissances*, Paris, Flammarion, "Question d'histoire" collection, no. 23, 1970, pp. 24–8.
36. M. Detienne, *Les Jardins d'Adonis: la mythologie des aromates en Grèce*, Paris, Gallimard, "Bibliothèque des histoires" collection, 1972. The author uses the contrast between Adonis and Ceres to stress the contrast between amorous seduction and marriage throughout this book. Among other things, he shows us how society tries to arouse amorous passion at the time of marriage through the use of herbs, but how much, apart from this brief moment, it considers amorous passion to be the antithesis of marriage.
37. L. Thore, "Langage et sexualité", pp. 65–95 in the collection entitled *Sexualité humaine*, Paris, Aubier- Montaigne, "RES" collection, 1970.
38. P. Bourdieu, "Célibat et condition paysanne", in *Etudes rurales*, 1962, no.5/6.
39. "Whether marriage be the family's affair more than the individual's and whether it is realised according to the models strictly defined by tradition, it is enough, in order to explain it, to invoke its economic and social function. But there is also the fact that in society in the past and still today, the segregation of the sexes is marked: from childhood, boys and girls are put on separate benches at school and at cathechism. In the same way, at church, the men gather in the gallery or at the back of the central

bay, whereas the women sit in the aisles or in the nave. The café is a place reserved for men...All cultural training and the whole of the value system tend to develop attitudes of reciprocal exclusion in the members of both sexes and to create a rift which cannot easily be crossed. So that the intervention of the families was in a certain way called for by the system's logic and also that of the 'matchmaker'...The restriction of freedom of choice has its positive side. Direct or indirect intervention by the family and particularly by the mother dispenses with hunting for a wife. One can be oafish, boorish and coarse, without forfeiting any chance of getting married" (ibid., pp. 56–7).

40. Cf. A. Hesnard, *La Sexologie*, p. 289.

41. M. Caumette, *Bénédiction du lit nuptial et Cérémonies contre l'impuissance dans les rituels français des XVIᵉ–XIXᵉ siècles*, History master's dissertation, defended at the University of Paris VIII, December, 1971.

42. A.-C. Kliszowski, *Les Théories de la génération et leur influence sur la morale sexuelle du XVIᵉ au XVIIIᵉ siècle*, master's dissertation at the University of Paris VIII, June 1972.

43. Of the passages quoted by A.-C. Kliszowski, I will cite only the shortest: "*Si autem vir, postquam seminavit, se retrahat ante seminationem uxoris, uxor potest se tactibus excitare donec seminet quia aliter gravem sentiret afflictionem, et illi tactus ordinantur ad completum actum conjugalem qui consistit in utriusque seminatione; et licit semen uxoris non sit necessarium ad generationem, tamen valde utile quia innat ad formandum pulchriorem foetum.*" [If, however, the man, having ejaculated his semen, withdraws before the woman has done likewise, the latter may excite herself manually until such time as she ejaculates, because otherwise she would suffer gravely, and such fondlings have as their aim the completion of the marriage act which comprises the ejaculation of the seed of both partners; and although the seed of the woman may not be necessary for procreation, it is nevertheless useful because it contributes to the formation of a prettier child.] Cf. Bonacina, *Summa theologica*, 1678 edition, *DE MATRIMONIO*, C. 205.

44. Brantôme, *Les Dames galantes*, published by M. Rat, Paris, Garnier, "Selecta" collection, pp. 332–4.

45. Mlle Besson-Leroy, who has been working on sexuality in the Middle Ages for more than a year, under the direction of Georges Duby, appears to already have much to say about the repression of adultery in various urban customs of the twelfth and thirteenth centuries. But I have no knowledge of research of this type being undertaken for modern times, and those who believe in men's chastity in this time period do not quote any.

46. For example the customs of the town of Auch, written up in 1301, prescribe in article LXIII: "In the same way it is the custom that if someone who has or does not have a wife is surprised with a married woman, and *if they are both found naked having removed their clothing*, that they be apprehended in the place when they are found, such a case being proven by two witnesses, each of them will have to pay sixty-five *sous* to the seigneurs, count or archbishop depending on the jurisdiction, *or they will have to run through the town completely naked*, and that depending on the will of those who found them thus, whether they pay the above-mentioned fine or whether they run through the town to the sound of the trumpet" (quoted by P. Lafforgue, in *Histoire de la ville d'Auch*, p. 21). This custom of the naked run or parade through the town is very common and seems to have borrowed much from illegal popular reactions. In the sixteenth century, tribunals generally have the adulterous woman locked away in a convent for a certain amount of time, at the end of which her husband can go to get her if he so wishes. If he does not take her back, she is cloistered away for the rest of her life.

47. As the Third Estate repeats in 1614, in article 54 of its book, a wish which it had already formulated at the Estates in 1576 and 1588: "And because adultery is frequent, because it is only considered a ridiculous act in France...it will be com-

manded that adulterers...sufficiently affected and convicted will be punished by death by execution, without judges being able to commute the sentence for any reason or consideration" (Cf. *Remonstrances faites au Roy par les députés du pays d'Agenois...* published by G. Tholin). Such a passage reveals moreover that, if there is an increase in sexual repression around the seventeenth century, it is not only due to the Catholic Reformation.

48. *Les Caquets de l'accouchée*, Editions Marpon et Flammarion, 1890, p. 12, quoted in *Annales*, 1969, no. 6, p. 1389, note 3.

49. P. Laslett, *The world we have lost*, London, 1965, pp. 141–142.

50. At the moment, I know of only two provinces in France, peripheral ones moreover, where customs similar to that of the county of Leicester, or even stranger, seem to exist: Corsica and the Basque country. Neither one appears to have attracted historian-demographers so far.

   Concerning Corsica, see the reports of missionaries sent to the island by St Vincent de Paul. They note that the peasants rarely "celebrate marriage without having previously lived together" (cf. Mgr. Abelly, *Vie de saint Vincent de Paul*, Paris, 1891, Vol. II, p. 98 sq.).

   Concerning the Basque country, see Orcibal, *J. Duvergier de Hauranne...*, p. 93, notes 1 and 2. According to note 1, in the Basque country they found "the custom of a probationary year during which the engaged couple lived together before marriage under the indulgent eye of the families. Despite the severe measures announced by Bishop Fouquet, in the 1666 statutes, and even, twenty-five years later, the condemnation of his successor d'Olce, this tradition still existed in part in the eighteenth century (cf. Dubarat, *Missel*, p. CCCXII)". P. de Lancre, the witch-hunter, himself confirms that it was usual to take on wives for a trial period of several years before marrying them (cf. J. Bernou, *La Chasse aux sorciers dans le Labour en 1609*, Agen, 1897, p. 112).

51. M.-C. Phan, *Introduction à l'étude des déclarations de grossesse et autres séries documentaires concernant la sexualité illégitime*, master's dissertation defended at University of Paris VIII, in December 1971; and *Les Amours illégitimes à Carcassonne*, Ph. D. thesis, Paris I, 1980.

52. P. Wiel, "Une grosse paroisse du Cotentin aux XVIIe et XVIIIe siècles: Tamerville", *Annales de démographie historique*, 1969, pp. 136–189.

53. All literary descriptions show the young woman pretending to resist and crossing the doorstep by force or seemingly by force. Is it so easy to distinguish such pretended resistance, which in any case is a form of genuine resistance, from the downright refusal which in the end is never serious? If young men know how to play this game, do they not also play it in cases where it would not be wished? And how are we to believe that they only played it with young women who they wanted to marry and who wanted to marry them?

54. Misses Sapin and Sylvoz, *Les Rapports sexuels illégitimes au XVIIIe siècle, à Grenoble, d'après les déclarations de grossesse*, type-written master's dissertation defended at the University of Grenoble in October 1969. This work was conceived and directed by J. Solé.

55. J. Bourgeois-Pichat, "Les facteurs de la fécondité non dirigée", *Population*, no. 3, 1965, pp. 383–424, and in particular pp. 406–8.

56. J. Bourgeois-Pichat is very conscious of the theoretical nature of his table and shows in his article that, in reality, the chances of conception are much lower, even without any form of contraceptive.

57. Since the work of Misses Sapin and Sylvoz, other work concerning illegitimate sexuality has been undertaken at Grenoble, also under the direction of J. Solé.

58. A. Lottin has described certain types of relationships in Lille, but he has barely tried to quantify their frequency and has not studied how they developed. Undoubtedly, the registrations were less detailed than those from Grenoble or Carcassonne. The

situation in Nantes will be considered later. As for the registrations from Carcassonne, as studied in Marie-Claude Phan's recently published book, *Les Amours illégitimes: histoires de séduction en Languedoc, 1676–1786*, Editions du CNRS, 1986, they show practically no rape, and the proportion of single encounters evolves less markedly than in Grenoble. Yet in Carcassonne too, the proportion of steady relationships increases, from 32.5% between 1676 and 1746 to 42.3% between 1747 and 1766 and 56.7% between 1767 and 1786.

59. Op. cit., p. 146.
60. J. Solé, "Passion charnelle et société urbaine d'Ancien Régime: amour vénal, amour libre et amour fou à Grenoble au milieu du règne de Louis XIV", *Annales de la faculté des lettres et sciences humaines de Nice*, no. 9/10, 1969, pp. 211–32.

CHAPTER 14

1. Edward Shorter, *The Making of the Modern Family*, London, Collins, 1976. M. Foucault, *Histoire de la sexualité*, vol. I, *La Volonté de savoir*, Paris, Gallimard, 1976.
2. J. Hajnal, "European Marriage Pattern in Perspective", in D.V. Glass and D.E.C. Eversley (eds), *Population in History*, London, Arnold, 1965, pp. 102–4.
3. J. Benedicti, *La Somme des péchez*, Paris, 1601, book IV, chap. VI, no. 15, p. 504.
4. A. Blanchard, *Examen général sur tous les commandements et sur les péchés de plusieurs estats*, following the *Essay d'exhortation pour les differens estats*, 1713, vol. 2, p. 200, no. 17–18.
5. Benedicti, op. cit., book II, chap. II, no. 42, p. 109.
6. J. Gerson, *Confessional* (sixteenth century edition with unnumbered pages) (Bibliothèque Nationale, Paris, Res. D. 11579), 54th page.
7. "*Oportet filios, ut cum ad annos pubertatis venerint, cogantur aut uxores ducere aut continentiam prosectari(s) ecclesiae; filiae vero eadem aetate aut castitatem aut nuptias elegant volunte paterna*" (quoted by Wasserschleben, in *Die Irische Kanonensammlungen*, p. 239, no. 16).
8. This is shown for example by the following three passages:

> Year 458: "He who is an adolescent, if in an emergency...he has a penance administered, and if afterwards, fearing the pitfalls of juvenile incontinence, he chooses to have intercourse with a wife in order not to commit the crime of fornication, the thing seems to be venial...However, we do not make a rule of this...For in truth nothing is more suitable for he who is doing penance than continuing chastity of mind and body" (Leo I, *Ep. ad Rusticum*, c. 13, in Migne, *Patrologia latina*, vol. 54, 1207).

> Year 506: "Let us not readily give penances to young people either, because of the fragility of their age" (Council of Agde, c. 15, in Mansi, *Sacrorum conciliorum nova et amplissima collectio*, vol. 8, col. 327).

> Year 538: "Let no one risk giving the benediction of penance to young people; assuredly let us not dare to give it to married couples if they are not of adult age and with the consent of the other party" (Council of Orléans, c. 24, in Mansi, vol. 9, col. 17).

9. St Ambroise, *Traité sur l'Evangile de Luc*, I, 43–5.
10. J. Rossiaud, "Prostitution, jeunesse et société dans les villes du Sud-Est au XVᵉ siècle", *Annales ESC*, March/April 1976, pp. 294–6.
11. Ibid., pp. 289–325.
12. They did not have more children than women, which obviously prevents us from calling them "proletarian", in the original Roman meaning of the word.
13. N.Z. Davis, "The Reason of Misrule: Youth Groups and Charivaris in Sixteenth-Cen-

tury France", *Past & Present*, no. 50, 1971. J. Rossiaud, op. cit., and "Fraternités de jeunesse et niveaux de culture dans les villes du Sud-Est à la fin du Moyen Age", *Cahier d'histoire*, 1–2, 1972.

14. J. Vienot, *Vieilles Chansons du pays de Montbéliard*, Montbéliard, 1897, p. 187.
15. Dr. M. Baudouin, *Le Maraîchinage, coutume du pays de Monts (Vendée)*, 5th edition, Paris, 1932. Repeated and discussed in part in J.-L. Flandrin, *Les Amours paysannes (XVIe-XVIIIe siècle)*, Paris, Gallimard, "Archives" collection, 1975, pp. 191–8.
16. Shorter, op. cit., p. 106.
17. Baudouin, op. cit., pp. 132–3; and Dr. Boismoreau, *Coutumes médicales et Superstitions populaires du Bocage vendéen*, Paris, 1911, pp. 45–6.
18. Dr. Pouillet, *L'Onanisme chez la femme*, 2nd edition, Oaris, 1877, 224 pp., pp. 62–3.
19. B. Chaix, *Préoccupations statistiques...des Hautes-Alpes*, 1845, p. 269.
20. A. Hugo, *La France pittoresque*, 1835, vol. I, pp. 291 and 294.
21. Ibid., vol. II, p. 147.
22. Flandrin, *Les Amours paysannes*, pp. 124–6.
23. Ibid, pp. 120–1; and Flandrin, *Families in Former Times, Kinship, Household and Sexuality*, tr. Richard Southern, Cambridge University Press, 1979, pp. 108–9.
24. M. Hudry, "Relations sexuelles prénuptiales en Tarentaise et dans le Beaufortin d'après les documents ecclésiastiques", *Le Monde alpin et rhodanien* (regional journal of ethnology), no. 1, 1974, pp. 95–100.
25. Flandrin, *Les amours paysannes*, p. 183.
26. C. Liberman, *Démographie d'une paroisse basque sous l'Ancien Régime: Urrugne*, master's dissertation, University of Paris VIII-Vincennes, 1976, 118 typed pages. M. Fresel-Losey, *Histoire démographique d'un village du Béarn: Bilhères-d'Ossau, XVIIe–XVIIIe siècle*, Bordeaux, 1969.
27. Flandrin, *Les Amours paysannes*, pp. 123–4; and Hudry, op. cit.
28. Flandrin, *Families*, p. 109.
29. Baudouin, op. cit.
30. K.R.V. Wikman, *Die Einleitung der Ehe: eine Vergleichende ethno-soziologische Untersuchung über die Vorstufe der Ehe in den Sitten des Schwedischen Volkstums*, Abo, 1937; and Shorter, op. cit., pp. 102–7.
31. N. Du Fail, *Contes et Discours d'Eutrapel*, Rennes, 1603, folio 53 verso.
32. C.-F.-P. Masson, *La Nouvelle Astrée*, 2nd edition, 1925, notes on book II, p. 183.
33. According to A. Hugo (op. cit., vol. I, p. 77), there was only one illegitimate child per 62.48 births in the Vendée, i.e. 1.6%, whereas in the last but one *département*, the Ardèche, there was one per 42.11 births, i.e. 2.4%.
34. Concerning the repression of concubinage, see Flandrin, *Families*, pp. 180–4. The following figures indicate its result in the area around Nantes: in the sixteenth century, 50% of the illegitimate children were the result of a long- term liaison, whereas between 1735 and 1750 only 5.5% fell into this category and only 2.6% between 1751 and 1786. This is according to A. Croix's figures in *Nantes et le Pays nantais au XVIe siècle*, Paris, SEVPEN, 1974, p. 96; and according to J. Depauw, "Amour illégitime et société à Nantes au XVIIIe siècle", *Annales ESC*, July/October 1972, p. 1175.
35. A. Bideau, "La population de Thoissey aux XVIIIe et XIXe siècles", *Bulletin du Centre d'histoire économique et sociale de la région lyonnaise*, 1972, no. 2, pp. 23–42. J. Houdaille, "La population de Boulay (Moselle) avant 1850", *Population*, November/December 1967, pp. 1058–84; and "La population de sept villages autour de Boulay aux XVIIIe et XIXe siècles", *Population*, November/December, 1971, pp. 1061–72. F. Desjardin, "Etude démographique du pays d'Arthies aux XVIIe et XVIIIe siècles (1668–1819)", *Bulletin d'information de la Société de démographie historique*, April 1971. C. Pouyez, "Une communauté d'Artois, Isbergues, 1598-1826", Hachette microedition, AUDIR no. 73.944.37.
36. R. Deniel and L. Henry, "La population d'un village du nord de la France, Sainghin–

en–Mélantois, de 1665 à 1851", *Population*, July/August 1965, pp. 503–602. P. Caspard, "Conceptions prénuptiales et développement du capitalisme dans la principauté de Neuchâtel (1678–1820)", *Annales ESC*, July/August, 1974, pp. 989–1008.
37. Flandrin, *Les Amours paysannes*, pp. 238–43; and Shorter, op. cit., chapter four.
38. J.-M. Gouesse, *Documents de l'histoire de Normandie*, Privat, 1972, p. 312; and J. Depauw, op. cit., p. 1173.
39. Ibid.; and P. Caspard, "L'amour et la guerre. Lettres d'un soldat neuchâtelois à sa fiancée, pendant la guerre de Sept Ans", *Musée neuchâtelois*, April/June 1979.
40. Chaix, op. cit., p. 269.
41. A. Hugo, op. cit., vol. I, p. 77.
42. Boismoreau, op. cit., pp. 45–6.
43. E. Van de Walle, *The Female Population of France in the Nineteenth-Century*, Princeton, 1974, pp. 453–5.
44. Depauw, op. cit., pp. 1161–2, and plate I, graphs 1 and 2.
45. Flandrin, *Les Amours paysannes*, pp. 239–41, graphs I and II; and *Families* pp. 184–6.
46. I speak of "Onanism" when I refer not only to masturbation itself, but the pseudo-illness of masturbators as defined in the eighteenth and nineteenth centuries. The quotation marks are very important as Onan's crime was in fact *coitus interruptus* and not masturbation.
47. Flandrin, "Late Marriages and Sex Lives", above, pp. 239–266 and in particular the passage by Tolet, p. 251.
48. J. H. Plumb, "The New World of Children in Eighteenth-Century England", *Past & Present*, no. 67, p. 92.
49. Flandrin, "Late Marriages and Sex Lives", above, pp. 246–253.
50. J.-H. Plumb, loc. cit.
51. Flandrin, "Civilization and Feelings; A Survey of Book Titles", above, pp. 13–35; and "Love and Marriage in the Eighteenth Century", above pp. 73–86.

CHAPTER 15

1. For example, according to an unpublished study by M. Lachiver, which I used in *Families*, Cambridge, 1979, pp. 85 and 119, only 5% of households in Triel-sur-Seine in 1817 employed servants. The 1625 census from Brueil-en-Vexin does not indicate any servants at all (see P. Lions and M. Lachiver, "Dénombrement de la population de Brueil-en-Vexin en 1625", *Annales de démographie historique*, 1967, pp. 521–38.
2. R. Smith, after re-examining the 1377 poll tax, concludes that the proportion of married women and servants at that time was very close to that found in England in the seventeenth and eighteenth centuries. In addition, at the symposium held in Cambridge in July 1976, K. Hopkins noted that many characteristics of the Western family model were already present in ancient Roman society.
3. The illegitimacy ratio is the ratio between the number of illegitimate births and the total number of births. The illegitimacy rate is the ratio between the number of illegitimate births and the number of young women and widows aged between fifteen and forty-four.
4. Colyton, 1581–1640: 2.8%; 1661–1720: 3.0%; 1721–1820: 5.5%.
5. I must point out that I have never systematically studied this question.
6. J. Benedicti, *La Somme des péchez* (numerous editions, dates ranging from late sixteenth to early seventeenth century), book VI, chapter VI, no. 15.
7. The French expression used was "*en gésine*", meaning the time during and after delivery. In social terms, the end of this period was marked by the "*relevailles*", a religious rite in which the woman who had recently given birth went to church to

give thanks. In physiological terms, this period ended when the reproductive organs moved back into place and the menstrual cycle began again.

8. Joubert, *Les Erreurs populaires*, Paris, 1587, book II, chapter I.
9. E. Shorter, "Female Emancipation, Birth-Control and Fertility in European History", *American Historical Review*, no. 78, 1973, 605–40. See also J.-L. Flandrin, *Les Amours paysannes*, Paris, 1975, p. 244.
10. Abbé H.-A. Tessier, "Mémoire sur la Sologne", *Histoire de la Société royale de médecine*, 1776, vol. I, 70.
11. Dr J.-H. Roussillon, *L'Oisan, essai historique et statistique*, paper presented to the Société de statistique de l'Isère on 4 April 1846 (Grenoble, 1847).
12. E. Shorter, *The Making of the Modern Family*, Collins, 1976, pp. 293–4, note 9.

Index

abandonment 153-4, 162-7, 189-91, 196
  see also exposure
abbayes joyeuses 273
abnormal practice
  see solitary practices
abortion 145, 146, 156, 191
  drugs 240
  infanticide 158-9
  potions 148
  sayings 212
  witchcraft 159
Abraham 5
absque coitu 279
abstinence *see* chastity
acceptable love 27
accidents and infant mortality 169-72
active love 80
acts against nature *see* sins against nature
adages *see* sayings
adjectives 44
Adonis 145
adultery 4, 94, 108, 113, 240, 259
  book titles 18, 20
  definition 251
  law/jurisdiction 103, 105, 106
  see *also* extra-marital relations
affairs in sixteenth century 3, 37-45
affection in sayings 228-9
Africa 142, 255
age and marriage 69, 115, 143-4

"ages of life" 130
"*aimer*" (to love) in book titles 29
albergement 276, 277
Albert the Great 118, 122, 181
allegory 28-9
alliances 3
  see also dowry; financial considerations
Ambroise, Saint 270
American Indians 175
amorous conquest and marriage 254-6
amorous passion 109
"*amour*" book titles 25, 26
  defined by lover/loved one 38-43
  frequency of usage 75
amplexus reservatus 125, 142-3, 182, 185-6
ancient adages/proverbs *see* sayings
  ancient liberties of courtship, suppression of 8
ancient social structures 140-80
  development 139
  infanticide and favourable conditions 140-53
  intentional killing of children 153-67
  neglect and lack of concern 167-80
Angélique, Dr 184
anglomania in book titles 76
anti-feminist sayings 222
Aquinas, Saint Thomas 49, 95

fornication and child 187
immoderate love 109
intercourse and procreation 181
lecherous act 103
pleasure within marriage 107
pregnancy 184
Aretino, positions of 110
Ariès, Philippe 129-37, 222, 250
concept of childhood 139, 190, 221
homosexuality 245
immoderate love 109
parental neglect 170-1
sexual repression 267
"unthinkableness" 100
Aristotle 121-2, 257
arranged marriage 84
Arras, Bishop of (1687) 161, 162
Athenagoras 90
attitudes to young children and sexual behaviour 139-98
Augustine, Saint 89, 125, 177, 186, 187
concupiscence 90
continence 4
contraception 107
female pleasure and procreation 122
autoeroticism 105, 106, 246, 251, 253
childhood 247
pre-marriage 256-7
timidity 254, 256
Azor 111, 166

balm application 145
baptism and infanticide 156, 157
Basilides 91, 92
Bassaeus 166
bastards *see* extramarital conception; illegitimate children
Baudouin, Dr 274, 275
Baudrier 16, 37
Bayle 114
beauty in sayings 233
Bekker 286
"*belles-lettres*" 26
Benedicti 189
abandonment 163, 166, 168

breast-feeding and sexual abstention 177
children 141
conception prevention 109
immoderate love 108
marriageable age 269, 303
masturbation 250
smothering and suffocation 170
wet nursing 172, 174
Bergues, Hélène 104
Bernardine, Saint 109
bestiality 102, 106, 113, 147, 246
birth control 115, 140, 146, 168, 193-6
Colyton 299
Malthus 270
birth infanticide 153-8
see also infanticide birth rate 6, 115, 140, 142, 171, 216
births 100
Blanchard, Antoine 269
boarding schools 132
Boccace 259
Bonaventure, Saint 95, 109
book titles
adultery 18, 20
"*aimer*" 29
anglomania 76
"bugger" 21
chivalry 19
coitus 22, 23
divorce 20
emotional phenomena/feelings 29-30, 76
homosexuality 21
love and marriage 27, 74-6
objective wording 24
procreation 21-2
rape 19-20, 21
scientific wording 24-5
sexual context 19, 20, 24, 25, 29
sodomy 21
Bourdieu, Pierre 233, 255, 259
Bourgeois-Pichat, J. 194, 263, 264
Bouvier, Monseigneur 100, 194.
Brantôme 110-11
adultery 112, 113, 114, 115
pleasure and married women 259

Braudel, Fernand 196
breast-feeding 4, 178, 183
   contraception and sexual relations
      6, 177, 186
   marital morality 176-80
   pregnancy 175
Bromyard, John 251
brothels 8, 272, 273, 283
"bugger" in book titles 21
Burchard of Worms 154, 160, 170
Burguière, André 239, 241

Caesarius, Saint of Arles 151
Cajetan 111
Calvet, Jean 135
Cambrai, Bishop of 285
canon law 20, 103
canonical ages for *fiançailles* 68
capital, lack of as birth control 115
carnal love 3
Carpocrates 91, 92
Cartier, A. 16
Cassien, Jules 92
Castan, Yves 83
Caumette, Madame M. 257
cause-and-effect relationship 114
celibacy 18, 115, 241, 280, 298
Central Europe 270
Ceres 145
Champagne 49-50, 70-1
Channey, J. de 40
charitable institutions 166, 189
  see also hospices; institutions
charity and children 190
charity, *see also* public charity
Charles VII 164
Chartreux, Denys le 95
chastity 141, 154, 180-9, 241-3
   education 252-3
   men 246-7
   see also celibacy
Chaucer 109
Chaunu, Pierre 243, 260, 261
child and procreation 129-236
   abandonment 153, 189-91
   burden 5
   charity 190
   demographic changes 189-98
   diseases 174

   distinction with adults 131
   excessive love 5
   harmful attitudes 184-5
   health 189
   intentional killing 153-67
   interest 181-3
   investment/profitability 141,
      208-10
   parental love 148-9
   parental worry 204-8
   power 4-5
   psychology and childhood aware-
      ness 129-30
   responsibility for 5, 180-9
   sexual behaviour 139-98
   soldiers 135
child and sayings
   inferiority 218-19
   sincerity 221
   status 218-23
   upbringing 223-9
childbirth and "impurity" 4
childhood and society 129-37
   characteristics of dress 135-6
   concept 132
   innocence in sayings 220
   medieval art/literature 135
      absence 130-1
chivalry in book titles 19
christian doctrine of marriage 89-97
civil law 20
civilisation and feelings 13-33
clandestine abandonment 165
clandestine marriage 64, 65, 68
Clavasio, Angelus de 184
Clayworth and Cogenhoe 294-5
Clement of Alexandria 91, 92, 93
clerics and illegitimacy 240
coddling 131, 136
Cogenhoe *see Clayworth and Cogenhoe*
cohabitation 8
coitus in book titles 22, 23
coitus interruptus 6, 104, 125, 146,
   158, 240
   absence from Greek/Roman lit-
      erature 145
   extra marital 112, 243
   "migaillage" substitute 283
   origins 188-9

punishment//judicial practice 106, 113
references 143
Colbert 5
colleges 132
Colombanus, Saint 160
Colyton 298-300
conception 107, 168, 182, 263
breast-feeding 180
extra-marital 107
menstruation 180, 184-5
pre-marital 9, 83, 84, 258
concubinage 8, 20, 280
conjugal chastity and good of child 180-9
attitudes harmful to children 184-5
contradictions 185-9
increasing interest 181-3
conjugal chastity, *see also* celibacy; chastity
conjugal debt 94, 187
conjugal duty 124
conjugal morality 101
conjugal relations *see* sexual intercourse
conjugal right 184
consummated marriage 58
continence 154, 178, 185
see also celibacy; chastity contraception 99-116, 133, 148, 188, 244
absence 5, 6
advances 139
coitus interruptus 104
drugs 106-7
extra-marital 104, 106-7, 113, 115
fertility rate 305
ignorance 243-4
infanticide 144-8
intercourse condemnation 111
married couples 106-7
Medieval condemnations 100
methods 145, 298
moral contradictions 188
prostitutes 146
sin against nature 7
steady relationships 265
"unthinkableness" 100

contract, notarised 63
"contrary to nature" 185
see also sins against nature
Corneille, Thomas 77
costume archaism 136
costume, *see also* dress Cotgrave 209
country *see* rural area couples, formation of 49
courtesans 145, 148
see also concubines; prostitutes courtly love 81
courtship 8, 83, 274-9, 282
nocturnal 277, 278
créantailles rite 49-71
absence of priest 54
clandestine aspect 55, 56, 57, 58
conflict with secular *fiançailles* 57
Troyes
disappearance in seventeenth century 60-71
fifteenth to seventeenth centuries 49-71
crimes against nature 104, 119
see also sins against nature
cuckold, definition of 112
cultural background and marriage 80
cultural reasons for infanticide 148-53
cultural reasons for neglect 170
culture, prevailing and folklore 49

Dainville, P. de 131
"*d'amour(s)*" 40-2
Dathaeus, Archpriest of Milan 166
daughter
paternal love, lack of 149-50
sayings
burden 232
fortune goes 232-6
upbringing 235
de futuro marriage 58
debauchery 190, 244, 276
definition 251
deformity 150-1, 152, 153, 163
demographic balance 140
demographic behaviour 1, 99, 139
demographic change 133
child 189-98

child abandonment 189-91
infant mortality and birth control
   193-6
wet nursing 191-2
demographic consequences 241
demographic development in love
   and marriage 85
demographic equilibrium 133
demographic growth rate 299
demographic revolution 132-3, 193
demographic system 170
Depauw, Jacques 239, 241, 265
deposit 61-3
   see also dowry; financial considera-
     tions
depravity 109
desire
   internalisation of 284-8
   young people 270
Detienne, Marcel 255, 257
diachronic research 14
Diana 125
dirtiness in sayings 205
discipline in sayings 225-8
diseases 174
disinheritance and clandestine marriage 65
disordered copulation 105
distancing of words and acts 24-5
diurnal pollution 247
divorce in book titles 20
dowry 50, 294
   see also deposit; financial consid-
     erations
dress, childhood 135-6
drugs 106-7, 240
Dupâquier, J. 175, 194

ecclesiastical celibacy 115
economic advances/progress 1,
   193, 196
economic consequences 241
economic factors
   family size 168
   family unit 294
   infanticide 153
   love and marriage 85
   marriage 81, 255-6
   mortality rate 197

education 80, 129, 131-2, 134, 223-5
effeminacy in childhood dress 136
eighteenth century love and marriage 73-86
Elias, Norbert 267
emission of semen
   disorder 108
emotional gratitude in sayings 207
emotional love 76
emotional phenomena and book titles 29-30
"en amour(s)" 39-40
engagement 261-2, 277
Engels 267
England 76, 132, 292, 294, 295
   censuses 302
   fertility rate 193
   illegitimacy trends 297
   marital fertility 299
   marital love 76
   pre-Industrial 298
   statistics 195
equality of sexes and marital debt
   117-19
eroticization 8, 267, 280, 287
"escraignes" 276, 277
Estoile, de Pierre l' 114
eugenics 154
Europe 153, 175, 292
   Central 270
   sexual maturity 303
Eutrape 127-8
excessive love 5
exposure 162-7
   see also abandonment; infanticide
extended family unit 292, 294
extra-marital conception 107
extra-marital contraception 104,
   106-7, 113, 115
extra-marital relations 103, 107-8,
   178, 258, 260, 297
   behaviour 145
   fertility 100
   nursing mothers 176, 177
   pleasure/sterility 111, 113
   see also adultery

Fail, Noël du 278
Fallopius 285

family life and illicit love 291-306
family 130, 294
  alliance and marriage 3, 73
  allowance 216
  economic changes 294
  extended 292, 294
  fostering 293
  industrialisation effect 292
  intimacy 132
  large 140-2
  modern 132
  multiple 292
  planning 133
  predominance 293
  property inheritance 144
  servants 293
  simple unit 292
  size 168
  social changes 294
fatalism and infanticide 169
Febvre, Lucien 267
feeling references in book titles 76
feelings and civilisation 13-33
Féline, Father 101
female desire 119
  see also women
female masturbation 124, 259
fertility 100, 140, 168-9, 264
  infant mortality rates 195
  marriage 5, 6
  menstruation 304
  sayings 212-13
fertility rate 5, 140, 194, 208-10, 304-5
fertility regulation and marriage age increase 143-4
feudal jurisprudence 50
fiançailles 50, 52, 58, 63
  canonical ages 68
  conflict with secular créantailles rite 57
  origin 53
  presence of priest 54
fifteenth century créantailles rite in Troyes 50-60
financial considerations 58, 59, 140-1, 144
Finnian 156
five ages of life 130, 134

folklore and prevailing culture 49
fornication 115, 240, 244, 260, 285
  and child 147
  see also sexual intercourse
fornicators 251
fornicatory coitus 113
Foucault, Michel 268
foundlings 163, 166, 189, 190
  urban increase 284
  wet nurses 172
  see also abandonment; illegitimate children
France 132, 148, 157, 270, 295
  birth rate 216
  charitable institutions 166
  hospitals 163
  illegitimacy trends 233, 296-7
  infant mortality 169
  marital love 76
  mortality rate 196
  sexual maturity and marriage interval 7
French kissing 274
French proverbs see sayings, French
Freud, Sigmund 8, 241, 242, 246, 250
  sexual repression 267
Fromageau 165

Galen 121, 122, 123
  double seed theory 257
Galeotti, Marzio 22
gang rape 272, 273
Garden, Maurice 140, 172-3, 192
Gascon 212
Gaule, Amadis de 22
genre paintings 133
Gerson, John 142, 270
  contraception condemnation 111
  homosexuality 244
  immoderate love 109
  incest 245
  solitary practices 247-8, 250, 256, 285
gift see ritual gift
Gnosticism 91-3, 115, 141
God 5, 6
God and conception in sayings 215-16
Goffar, M.A. 251

Goubert, Pierre 175
Gratien 181
Greece 154, 163
Gregory the Great, Pope 177, 178, 186
Gregory of Tours 148-52, 155, 174
Grenoble 263, 265
guardians 55

Hajnal, J. 241, 242
handicapped children 154-5
see also deformity
health 189
heir legitimacy 73
Henry II 156, 157, 162, 166
pregnancy registration 190-1
Henry, Louis 298, 303
Héroard 135
Hesnard, Dr 246
Hildebrand, Dietrich von 94
historical criticism 49
history of sexuality 1-9
holy days 151, 181
homosexuality 105, 120, 147, 243, 244
book titles 21
children 245-6
passive 250
"honest woman" 109
hospices 163-5, 190
hospitals 163
Huizinga 267
hygiene 174, 193, 217

illegitimacy 188, 296-7, 301
children 154, 155, 163-4, 166
clerics 240
conception 261, 262
curve 299-301
pregnancies 9, 301
rate 84, 85, 297, 298
ratio 297, 286, 299, 300, 301
illegitimate birth 241, 258, 260, 282
courting freedom 275-6, 278
engagement 261
extramarital sexual relations 100
increase 280
infanticide 156
pregnancy registration 262

repression 247
urban increase 284
illegitimate birth rate 6, 115, 242, 265, 279
France 282, 283
increase 264
illicit act 114
illicit love and family life 291-306
illicit relations 104, 107, 114-15, 260
sexual activity 6, 7
see also adultery; extra-marital relationships
immoderate love 109
impure images 280
impure words 280
incest 103, 105, 106, 158, 240, 251
incontinence see sexual intercourse
Indo-European culture 255
industrial revolution 217
industrialisation effect 280
infant mortality 193-6
accidents through negligence 170
attitudes in sayings 210-17
France 169
premature weaning 175
procreation 167-9
infant mortality rate 140, 171, 172
premature weaning 179
seasonal 174
infant mortality rate and fertility 195
infanticide 107, 140-53, 159, 168, 140
abortion 158-9
baptism 156, 157
birth 153-8
condemnation 180
conditions favourable to 140-53
contraception 144-8
decrease 190
economic reason 153
exposure and abandonment 162-7
handicapped children 154-5
illegitimacy 154, 155, 156, 166, 188
intentional killing of children at birth 153-8
large families 140-2
legal ban 197

legitimate family 156
Malthusian couples 146
maternal/paternal decision 153-4
over-population 142-4
poverty 167
property inheritance 144
psychological and cultural chances 148-53
sexual repression 157
smothering and suffocation 159-62
transfer of responsibility 154
unintentional 159
infantile behaviour in sayings 219
ingratitude of children 210
ingratitude in sayings 207
inheritance 3, 80, 144
innocence of child and sayings 220, 223
intellectual masturbation *see* erotic thoughts
intentional killing of children 153-67
intentional smothering 169
inter crua intercourse 147
inter fermora intercourse 147
internalisation of desire and repression and sexuality 284-8
investment and children 141
Iranaeus 92, 93
Isaac 5
Italy 270
Ivo of Chartes 154, 170

Jansenist moralism 101, 253
Jerome, Saint 142
    adultery 4, 108
    deformity 149-50
    female pleasure and procreation 122
Joubert, Laurent 304
judicial practice 105
Jurieu 114
Justin, Saint 90
juvenile mortality rate 179
juvenile sexuality 257, 270

kissing
    French 274
    shameful 123
Kliszowski, Madame A.C. 257, 259

Lachiver, M. 175, 194
"*l'albergement*" 8
Lallemand 164
"*l'amour*" 42-3
Lancelot 252
Langres, Bishop of (1789) 161, 162
language, synchronic study of 14
large family 140-2
Laslett, Peter 260, 265, 291-306
late marriages and sex lives 239-66
Lawrence, D.H. 25
Layman 166
Le Mans, Bishop of *see* Bouvier, Monseigneur
Ledesma, Peter de 143, 183, 187
legal minority 17
legitimacy 163, 187, 256
Leicester 261
Les Livres de l'année 1961 16
Liguori, Saint Alphonsus 95, 101, 114, 125
literature and children's jargon 136
Lombard, Peter 95, 181
"*Long-term Trends in Bastardy in England*" 296-301
Lopez, Luis 183
Louis XIII 134
Louis XVI 164, 166
love 3, 13-86
    acceptable 27
    active 80
    affairs sixteenth century 3, 37-45
    book title 27, 74-6
    carnal 3
    courtly 81
    emotional 76
    excessive 5
    immoderate 109
    marital 76-4
    maternal 150, 152, 154
    passive 80
    paternal 149-50, 152, 154
    peasant 80-3
    physical 76

platonic 3, 45
profane 4, 27, 29, 30, 45, 73
sacred 4, 73
love and marriage book titles 75-6
  eighteenth century 73-86
    popular practice 80-6
    developments 82-6
    traditional characteristics 80-2
  prevailing culture 74-89
  book title evidence 74-6
    marital love comments 76-8
    marrying for love 78-80
    widening gap 85
love and peasants 80
"lover" 109
lovers and sterile pleasure 110
Lyons silk workers 214

Maître, Martin le 89
"make love" definition 81
Malthus, Thomas, birth control 270
Malthusian acts against nature 147
  families 172, 194
  infant mortality 171-2
  infanticide 146
  practice 245
  revolution 139, 214
  sayings 214
  structures 153
  tendencies 142-3
  tensions 197
Malthusian concern, *coitus interruptus* 143
Malthusian reasoning, demographic revolution 193
Malvaux, Abbé 164, 166
man and wife in marriage bed 117-25
manual pollution 105
"maraîchinage vendéen" 8, 81, 274-5, 277, 279
Marcion of Pontus 91
"mariage d'inclination" 79
marital
  behaviour in procreation 239
  debt 117-19, 182-3, 185
  fertility 283, 298, 299
  love 76-8

see also sexual intercourse marital morality 176-80
Marivaux 254
marriage 99-116
  acceptance 90
  age 69, 115, 143-4, 269-71
  age, increase 143-4, 241, 280, 282, 298-9
  age, minimum 69
  alliances 3
  amorous conquest 254-6
  arranged 84
  birth control 168
  book titles 18, 19, 76
  ceremony 70
  christian doctrine 89-97
  clandestine 64, 65, 68
  consummated 58
  continence 178
  contraception 106-7, 139
  contract 50, 61, 62
    see also marriage promises
  cultural background 80
  de futuro 58
  economic constraints/factors 81, 144, 255-6
  education 80
  family alliances 3, 73
  fertility 5
  financial considerations 73
  infanticide 168
  inheritance 3, 80
  late 239-66, 268
    see also marriage age
  material considerations 73
  notarised contract 52
  parent's consent 65-6
  procreation 110, 121, 145
  promise 51, 60-1, 63-4, 67
  property ownership 271
  social order/prestige 3, 73, 80, 81
  solemnised 50, 65, 67
marriage bed man and wife 117-25
marital debt and equality of sexes 117-19
  role of men and women in sexual intercourse 119-21
  woman's right to pleasure 121-5
marriage of convenience 3

married women and fertility rate
    304-5
marrying for love 78-80
Martin, Saint 149
masturbation 106, 147, 158, 240, 241,
    243, 246
    chastity 247
    female 124, 259
    frequency 248, 251
    general behaviour 249
    increase 9
    males 124
    mutual 274
    penis enlargement 285
    post-coital 124, 125
    prolonged 250, 256
    sin against nature 7
    solitary 8, 286
material
    considerations and marriage 73
    ingratitude in sayings 207-8
    reasons for neglect 170
maternal feeling/love 150, 152, 154,
    190, 192
maternal love 150, 152, 154
maternity in sayings 214
Médici, Catherine de 174
medicine advances 193, 196, 217
medieval art/literature 135
medieval schooling 134
men 7, 8, 125
    active 119, 120
    conflict in urban areas 272
    masturbation 124
    and women and roles in sexual
        intercourse 119-21
menstruation 4, 121, 304
    age 305
    conception 180, 184-5
    continence 185
    fertility 304
    intercourse and deformity 151
    marital debt 185
    puberty 304
    sexual intercourse 181, 186, 187
"migaillage" 275, 276, 283
modern adages *see* sayings, modern
    family concept 132
modesty 119, 235-6

Moheau 5
"mollicies" 105, 106
    see also autoeroticism
mollities 248, 250, 251
Montaigne 131
moral code 144, 253
morality 81, 176-80, 190
mortal sin 108
mortality rate 140, 189, 192-3, 299
    economic reasons 197
    hygiene 197
    juvenile 179
    last born children 175
    Northern France 171
    parental neglect 195, 197
    penultimate child 176
    see also infant mortality rate
mortality in sayings 216-17
mortality, *see also* infant mortality
Moure, Fernandes de 174
multiple family unit 292, 294
municipal brothels 272, 273, 283
Musset, Lucien 153
mutual masturbation 274

Nambikwara 2
"natural fecundity" 100
negative qualifiers 44-5
neglect and lack of concern 167-80
    accidents 169-72
    cultural/material reasons 170
    marital morality and breast-feed-
        ing 176-80
    paid wet nursing 172-4
    premature weaning 174-6
    procreation and infant mortality
        167-9
neurosis 8
nobility 81, 240
nocturnal courting 277, 278
noisiness in sayings 206
non-conjugal relations 111
non-profitability of children 210
Noonan, John T. 7, 89-97
    church and demographic policy
        141
    coitus interruptus 147
    concept of childhood 181

contraception and masturbation 7
immoderate love 109
love and marriage 255
Malthusian speeches 142
sins against nature 102, 103
Northern France and mortality rate 171
notarised contract 59, 61, 63
nursing 174, 185
    see also wet nursing

objective wording in book titles 24
"*obscenitas*" 23
Onanism 103, 285, 286
    see also coitus interruptus; solitary practices
orgasm 121-5
Orient 76
over-population in society 142-4

Palude, Peter de 142-3
amplexus reservatus 182-3, 185
Paré, Ambroise 123
parental authority 81, 84
    difficulties 210
    enslavement in sayings 204
    guilt on deformity 150
    love 148-9
    neglect 170-1, 180, 197
    pressure 55
    responsibilities in sayings 216, 217
    worry 204-8
Paris, Archbishop (1666) 159
parish registers 302-3
passion, amorous 109
passive love 80
Pasteur 174, 193
paternal feelings/love 149-50, 152, 154, 190, 192
paternity in sayings 214
Patin, Guy 159, 160
Paul, Saint 6, 144, 187, 188
    continence 178
    intercourse and procreation 181
    law of nature 93
    natural position 120
    practices against nature 90

sterile acts 102
teachings 197
wife subordination 117, 118
peasants and love 80-3
petting 274-5
Phan, Madame M.-C. 260
Philo of Alexandria 91, 93
physical love 76
physical relations 263
platonic love 3, 45
pleasure 111, 113, 121-5, 145, 239
plural form 38, 39, 40, 44
plural qualifiers 43-5
pollution diurnal 247
    manual 105
    sexual 123, 247, 286
polygamy during nursing 176, 177
population 143
pornographic literature 287
positions of Aretino 110
positions, sexual 119, 120
positive qualifiers 43-4
post-coital masturbation 124, 125
potions 148
    sterilising 158
poverty 166-7
pre-marital cohabitation 8
    conception 9, 84, 258, 260-2
    contradictory observations 83
        rates 262
    concubinage 8
    courtship 83, 274-9
    pregnancies 84, 278, 280-2, 284
    sexuality 257
pregnancy 4, 184
    amplexus reservatus 185
    avoidance 145
    breast-feeding 175
    continence 185
    contradictory observations 83
    decrease 264
    illegitimate 9
    pre-marital 84, 278, 280-2, 284
    sexual intercourse 180, 186
        abstention 90, 181-2
    unnatural positions 185
pregnancy registration 158, 159, 191, 241
    Grenoble 263, 265

illegitimate births 262
rural women 284
social background 260
premature weaning 174-6
prevailing culture and folklore 49
prevailing culture and love and marriage 74-89
Prierio, da Sylvester 184
procreation 129-236
attitude to in sayings 210-17
book titles 21-2
child 129-236
infant mortality 167-9
marriage 110, 239, 121, 145
sexual intercourse 94
Prodicus 92
profane love 4, 27, 29, 30, 45, 73
singular and plural form 37
profitability of child 141, 208-10
prolonged masturbation 250, 256
see also autoeroticism
promises, marriage 63, 63-4
property inheritance 144
property ownership 271
prostitutes 8, 100, 109
abortion 146
bachelors 272
contraception 145, 146, 188, 265
contraceptive potions 148
repression and sexuality 272-4
rural areas 273
proverbs *see* sayings
psychological chances of infanticide
148-53
psychological changes and contraception advances 139
puberty and menstruation 304
public
charity 163
rape 273
purging 23

qualifiers 43-5
qualitative/quantitative study 15
quasi-legitimatization 114
Quitard 222

rape 262, 263, 264
book titles 19-20, 21

gang/public 272, 273
jurisdiction 105, 106
rural areas 273
urban areas 272-4
real love 3
reformation in seventeenth century
131
registering of pregnancies *see* pregnancy registration
relationship, cause-and-effect 114
religious context and singular form
37
religious rites 70
Renouard 42
repression and sexuality 8, 267-88
challenge of statistics 280-4
internalisation of desire 284-8
period of greatest repression 268-
71
pre-marital courtship in country
and banning 274-9
prostitution 272-4
rape in towns in late middle ages
272-4
reproduction 124, 141, 154
book titles 21
sayings against 210-11
sayings in favour of 211-12
see also procreation
reputation and virtue in sayings
234-6
resignation to infanticide 169
Rigaud, B. 40
Riquet, Father 100
ritual gift 51, 52, 55, 70
disappearance 61, 62
humour element 55-6
Roman society 154, 163
Rossiaud, Jacques 271, 273
Rougemont, Denis de 137
Rousseau 131, 220
Roux de Lincy, le 222, 225
Roy Ladurie, Emmanuel le 241
Roye, Guy de 247-8
rural areas
breast-feeding and conception
179
freedom between men and
women 8

illegitimacy 280, 301
illegitimacy rate 85
pre-marital pregnancies 280
prostitutes 273
   rapes 273

sacred love 4, 73
sacrilege, definition of 251
safeguarding in seventeenth century
   131
safety measures and childhood
   awareness 129
Sanchez, Thomas 89-90, 95
   adultery 113, 114, 115
   contraception 143
   intercourse and child 183
   kissing and touching 123-4
   natural position 120
   nursing 174
   pregnancy and intercourse 179,
     187
   premature weaning 177
   unnatural intercourse within mar-
     riage 111
   women's desires 119
Sapin, Miss 263
sayings
   abortion 212
   affection 228-9
   anti-feminist 222
   beauty 233
   child and family, daughter burden
     232-6
   child and family 203-29
     attitudes 203
   child profitability 208-10
   child status 218-23
     dirtiness 205
     discipline 225-8
     infant mortality attitudes 210-
      17
     inferiority 218-19
     ingratitude 207-8
     innocence 220, 223
     noisiness 206
     parental enslavement 204
     parental responsibilities 216
     sincerity 221

source of worry for parents
   204-8
   toilet training lack 205
   upbringing 203, 223-9
   child and family paternity 214
   education 223-5
   emotional gratitude 207
   fertility 212-13
   God and conception 215-16
   grown up children 206-7
   infantile behaviour 219
   Malthusian debate 214
   material ingratitude 207-8
   maternity 214
   modesty 235-6
   mortality 216-17
   reputation and virtue 234-6
   special consideration 219
   sterility 213
   young woman 231-6
Scandinavia 153, 154
   abandonment of malformed ba-
     bies 163
   respecting virginity 279
schooling 130, 132, 134
   see also education scientific word-
     ing in book titles 24-5
Scotland 279
Scriptures, incorrect commentaries
   on 120-1
secular ceremony 70
seduction 281
semen, emission of 108
   non-Sengalese peoples 255
Sens, Archbishop of *see* de Roye, Guy
sensual phenomena and book titles
   29-30
Serbian census 303
servants, movement of 295-6
Sévigné, Madame de 5
sexual
   abstinence *see* chastity
   behaviour
     young children 139-98
     broadening patterns 185
     extramarital/marital 145
   context and book titles 29
   depravity 109, 147
   disorders 113

disorders 113
duties 117
enslavement 119
habits 245
inequality 63
maturity 7, 303, 306
  see also menstruation
relations 89-125
illegitimate children 157
intercourse: see separate entry
pleasure 90, 258, 259
pollution 123, 247, 286
precociousness 306
  see also menstruation
reality 263
relations see sexual intercourse
repression 147, 157, 267, 268
rights of women and men 117
roles 119, 120-1
self-restraint 246
sin see sins against nature
sin in book titles 19, 20
status of women 118
urges and sublimation of 8
sexual intercourse 7, 89-125, 145-6,
    154, 183, 267-8
  book titles 22
  breast-feeding 175, 176, 186
  climax 23-4
  conception and abstinence 182
  conventional 183
  disordered copulation 105
  extra-marital 100, 107-8
  frequency and fertility 168-9, 263
  holy days and abstinence 181
  inter crua 147
  inter fermora 147
  intervals between births 175
  late marriages 239-66
  menstruation 176, 181, 186, 187
  positions 110, 119, 120-1
    Aretino 110
    unnatural 110, 120, 183, 186
    within marriage 119
  pregnancy 90, 180, 186
    and abstinence 181-2
  procreation 94
  roles of partners 119-21
  single people 7, 239-308

steady/continuous 264
sterile 143
taboos 21
unnatural 111
women's seed 123
sexuality
  book titles 24, 25
  history 1-9
  juvenile 257, 270
  medical context 26
  procreation 4
  repression 8, 267-88
  sixteenth century French society
    13
Shorter, Edward 268, 281
  courtship 274, 275, 278
  cultures and sexual desire 270
  fertility rate 305
sleeping without intercourse 279
solitary practices 285
simple family unit 292
simultaneous emission 123
simultaneous orgasm 123
single encounter 263, 264
  see also rape
single people, sex lives of 7, 239-308
singular form 38, 39, 40, 41, 44
singular qualifiers 43-5
sins 108, 154
sins against nature 107, 240, 245,
    248, 254, 285
  ambiguity 105-6
  blanket concept 102
  contraception 7
  masturbation 7
  references 143
  sterility 247
sixteenth century
  créantailles rite in Troyes 50-60
  love affairs 37-45
smothering and suffocation 159-62
  accidental 160-1, 170
  intentional 160-1, 169
  preventative measures 161-2, 191
social background, pregnancy regis-
    tration 260
  changes and family unit 294
  class and marriage 80
  constraints and marriage 81

order, marriage 3
prestige and marriage 73
structures, ancient 140-80
structures and family size 168
taboos 14, 21
society and childhood 129-37
sodomy 113, 244, 248
book titles 21
condemnation 106
definition 251
punishment 102
Solé, Jacques 265
solemnise marriage 65, 67
solitary masturbation 8, 2 8 6
solitary pleasures 8
solitary practices 103-4, 246, 247, 249, 257, 285
lack of capital 115
moral code 253
sons and paternal love 149-50
sorcery 107, 257
see also witchcraft
Soto, Dominic 111, 143, 183
steady relationships and contraception 265
sterilisation 174
sterilising drugs 240
"sterilising poisons" 107
sterilising potions 148, 158
sterility
extra-marital sexual relations 111, 115
intercourse 110, 143, 239
practices 115, 241, 243
sayings 213
Stoic-Christain doctrine 93, 94, 95, 141
sublimation *see* chastity Suenens, Cardinal 84
suffocation and smothering 159-62, 191
see also infanticide suppression 8
Sylvestre 166
Sylvoz, Miss 263

taboos 14, 23, 24
Tarentaise, Archbishop of 278
Tatian 91, 92
Thatine 125

"*The world we have lost*" 293-4
Third World 5, 193-4
Thoré, Luc 255, 257
Tiraqueau 177, 178
Tissot, Dr 286
titling techniques 14-17
Todd, Emmanuel 295
toilet-training in sayings 205
Toledo, Cardinal 251
touching 123, 125
Tournes, J. de 40
town *see* urban area
traditional behaviour 85
traditional demographic behaviour 139
Troyes, Bishop of (1680) 83
Troyes, créantailles rite in 49-71
Tukulors 255
turpitudo 23

uncertified marriage contract 61
unintentional infanticide 159
unnatural acts and the law 103
unnatural intercourse 111, 120
unnatural positions 110, 183, 185, 186
"unthinkableness" and contraception 100
unweaned infants 192
upbringing of children 223-9
urban areas 192, 284
brothels 283
illegitimate birth increase 84, 280
male conflict 272
rape 272

Valentinus 91, 92
Van der Berg, H. 129
Vendée 274, 279
venial sin 108
Viguerisu 119
Villeneuve, Arnauld de 22
violence 17
virginity 243, 279
virtue and reputation in sayings 234-6
voluptuousness 105

weaning 174-6

weddings in sixteenth century 19
Western behaviour and eroticization
    267
Western Europe 7, 132, 241, 255, 270
Western familial pattern 294
Western family characteristics con-
    sidered over time 293-4
Western love 96
Western society 142
wet nursing 172, 174, 178, 179
    birth control 196
    copulation/incontinence 177
    fertility 140
    growth 189
    neglect and lack of concern 172-4
    paid 191-2
    separation and indifference 173
    working classes 192
"whore" 109
    see also prostitutes
Wiel, Philippe 261
Wikman 278, 279
William of Auxerre 94
witchcraft 148, 158, 159, 257
Wolofs 255
woman

comparison with young woman
    231
desires 119
extra marital relations 260
"honest" 8
modesty 119
orgasm 121, 123, 124
passive 119, 120
pleasure and procreation 121-5
sexual duties 117
sexual enslavement 119
sexual rights 117
sexual status 118
subordinance to men 117
women and men and their roles in
    sexual intercourse 119-21
Wrigley 146, 299
Wurtemberg, Duke of 278

Xenophon 145

young children *see* children; infant
young men *see* men
young woman
    in ancient French proverbs 231-6
    and comparison with woman
        231